ENGAGING LARGE CLASSES

ENGAGING LARGE CLASSES

Strategies and Techniques for College Faculty

CHRISTINE A. STANLEY
Texas A&M University

M. ERIN PORTER
University of Texas, Austin

Editors

ANKER PUBLISHING COMPANY, INC.
BOLTON, MASSACHUSETTS

Engaging Large Classes

Strategies and Techniques for College Faculty

ISBN 1-882982-51-7

Composition by Vicki Czech
Cover design by Delaney Design

Anker Publishing Company, Inc.
176 Ballville Road
P.O. Box 249
Bolton, MA 01740-0249

www.ankerpub.com

Table of Contents

About the Editors

Christine A. Stanley is Assistant Professor of Higher Education Administration in the Department of Educational Administration and Human Resource Development, and Associate Director of the Center for Teaching Excellence at Texas A&M University. She has also served as president (2000-2001) and chair of the Diversity Commission (1994-1998) of the Professional and Organizational Development (POD) Network in Higher Education, the North American organization dedicated to faculty, organizational, and instructional development issues in higher education. Prior to joining the faculty at Texas A&M University, she was Associate Director of Faculty and TA Development and Adjunct Assistant Professor of Educational Policy and Leadership at The Ohio State University, where she received the Distinguished Staff Award in 1999. She is the recipient of the Texas A&M University College of Education Development Council's Outstanding New Faculty Award (2000–2001).

A biologist, teacher, consultant, and faculty developer, she has taught courses on college teaching, professional development, and diversity and social justice in higher education. She is a consultant to many colleges and universities on faculty development, and multicultural faculty and TA development initiatives in higher education.

She has contributed numerous articles on faculty development to such publications as *Journal on Excellence in College Teaching*; *Journal of Staff, Program, and Organizational Development*; and *To Improve the Academy: Resources for Faculty, Instructional, and Organizational Development* and has an extensive record of presentations and professional organization service.

M. Erin Porter is Senior Lecturer in the Department of Management Science and Information Systems at The University of Texas, Austin. She teaches undergraduate and graduate courses in business communication in the Red McCombs School of Business and is departmental coordinator for the undergraduate multi-section business communication course. Prior to her current appointment, she was Director of Faculty Programs at the Center for Teaching Effectiveness at the University of Texas, Austin. She has published in *The Journal of Staff, Program, and Organizational Development*; *To Improve the Academy*; and has a chapter in *Practically Speaking: A Sourcebook for Instructional Consultants in Higher Education*. She cowrote *Business Communication*, a textbook published by the American Press. She received the student generated Eyes of Texas Award for fall semester 2001.

She has been a tenured Associate Professor of Speech Communication at Southwest Texas State University where she was director for speech fundamentals and business speech courses at two universities, director of the forensics program, taught graduate and undergraduate classes, and supervised graduate teaching assistants for large sections of introductory classes. She has been an adjunct professor at St. Edward's University and Austin Community College, as well as a consultant in the high-tech industry in Texas.

An educator, faculty developer, business consultant, and communication specialist, she has consulted on issues involving trends in communication skill sets for businesses, teams in the workplace, interpersonal communication skills for business professionals, cross disciplinary teaching projects, and effective teaching methodology in university classrooms. She has authored articles on faculty development and business communication and has an extensive record of presentations, workshops, consulting assignments, and professional organization service.

About the Contributors

J. Douglas Andrews is Professor of Business Communication and Assistant Dean of the Marshall School of Business at the University of Southern California. He has taught and administered both large and small classes at private and public institutions. He has published numerous articles on applying effective communication skills in a wide array of business settings. He has trained executives from many global companies including General Electric, IBM, Korea Telecom, LG Chem, KPMG Peat Marwick, LLP, Texas Instruments, and Price-Waterhouse. He has also worked with professionals at USC, the University of Texas-Austin, Texas Tech University, Northwestern University, CalTech, and the Livermore Laboratory at the University of California-Berkeley. He has conducted several hundred communication seminars and tutored individually more than 100 executives.

Raoul A. Arreola is Professor of Health Science Administration and Director of Educational Evaluation and Development at the University of Tennessee. He has published in the areas of distance education, academic leadership, and faculty evaluation and development systems. He has served as a consultant to over 200 colleges and universities nationally and internationally in designing and operating faculty evaluation systems, faculty development programs, and instructional technology applications to teaching. His book, *Developing a Comprehensive Faculty Evaluation System*, is widely used in colleges and universities in designing faculty evaluation programs.

Derrick Bell has been a law teacher for 32 years and is in his tenth year as a visiting professor at New York University Law School. He is the author of several books, including texts on constitutional law and race and the law. His major teaching contribution has been on efforts to involve students in large classes in what he calls participatory teaching in which, through the use of simulated appellate arguments and the posting of reflections about the subject matter on a course website, students learn by teaching others.

Marialice Bennett is Clinical Associate Professor, Director of the Wellness and Clinical Partners Program, and Pharmacy Director of the University Health Connection at The Ohio State University College of Pharmacy. She teaches courses on the pathophysiology and therapeutics of diabetes, thyroid disease, and dyslipidemias. She also coordinates and plans an annual teaching workshop for pharmacy doctoral students and precept students in pharmacy practice. Her research interests include wellness and prevention, community pharmacy patient care services, and diabetes patient care. She is a fellow in the American Pharmaceutical Association.

Tom Campbell is Lecturer in Management and Leadership at the Red McCombs School of Business at the University of Texas, Austin. He lectures on organizational behavior and leadership issues and has taught in the Business Foundation Program since its inception in 1992. He teaches between 500 and 550 students a semester. He is the recipient of numerous teaching awards, including Most Outstanding Professor in 1993 and 1997, the Harkins Foundation award for Teaching Excellence and the Eyes of Texas Award in 1994. He is a retired, decorated Marine colonel and is the recipient of the Purple Heart. He is the author of several texts, including *The Old Man's Trail.*

Jean Civikly-Powell is Professor Emeritus of Communication and has served as the Director of the Teaching Assistant Resource Center at the University of New Mexico for 18 years and as Interim Director of the newly established Center for the Advancement of Scholarship in Teaching and Learning. She continues to serve as Director of the Faculty Dispute Resolution Program at the University of New Mexico. A Presidential Teaching Fellow, she has taught and team-taught the Introduction to Communication course which enrolls 250 students. She has also coordinated and supervised TAs and undergraduate interns for this course. Her teaching has included courses on mediation, interpersonal communication, classroom teaching skills, and communication for teachers.

Lynda G. Cleveland is Lecturer in the Red McCombs School of Business at the University of Texas, Austin. She teaches foundation of data analysis and information systems to large classes. Her business pursuits in the field of audio-visual production and motivational speaking are recognized nationally and internationally. She is the recipient of numerous state, national, and international awards for her excellence in teaching and skills as a speaker. She has shared the motivational dais with speakers such as Paul Harvey, Art Linkletter, and Dr. Norman Vincent Peale. Her areas of interest and expertise include oral presentation, rhetoric, interpersonal and mass communications, and traumatic brain injury rehabilitation.

Brian P. Coppola is Associate Professor of Chemistry and a faculty associate at the Center for Research on Learning and Teaching at the University of Michigan, Ann Arbor. He teaches and coordinates a 1,000-student structure and reactivity course, which is an organic chemistry program for first-year students that he helped develop in 1989. His instructional strategies for large courses range from improved presentation methods to constructing a menu of supplemental activities to creating student-centered interactions outside the classroom. In 1994, he received the Golden Apple Award for outstanding teaching and in 1998 was selected as part of the first group of Carnegie Scholars affiliated with The Carnegie Foundation for the Advancement of Teaching (Carnegie Academy on the Scholarship for Teaching and Learning) CASTL program. In 1999, he received the Amoco Foundation Award for Excellence in Undergraduate Teaching.

Leta F. Deithloff is a graduate student at the University of Texas, Austin in the Educational Psychology program with special emphasis on learning, cognition, and instruction. Her experience with large classroom includes two years as head teaching assistant for two sections of a management science and information systems course (1,000 students) and a semester of introduction to statistics. Although she currently teaches small writing courses in the rhetoric and composition department, her interests still include monitoring student involvement (as determined by students' attitudes and motivation) in large classrooms, as well as other interests in the field of writing (idea generation, flow as a self-regulated activity, writing apprehension, and writing strategies).

Peter J. Frederick is the Jane and Frederic M. Hadley Chair and Professor of History at Wabash College. He teaches an American survey history course, courses in African American history, Indian history and cultures, and a required course for all sophomores, cultures and traditions, with enrollments ranging from 60 to 225 students. He has written many articles and led many workshops on ways of involving students actively in large lectures. His research, when not focused on 19th century American religious history, involves a practitioner's classroom research on ways of creating holistic (mental, emotional, physical, spiritual) and connective learning in classrooms of any size. He recently received the 2000 Eugene Asher Distinguished Teaching Award from the American Historical Association.

Anne S. Gabbard-Alley is Professor of Speech Communication and Director of the Health Communication Institute at James Madison University. She teaches courses in health communication and is currently teaching a class of 170 students on the processes of human communication. She is the author of several textbooks including *An Interpersonal Approach to Business and Professional Communication*. She is the recipient of several awards, including being twice named the Council for Advancement and Support of Education (CASE) professor of the year by the Department of Communications at James Madison University in 1983 and 1984. Her research and teaching interests include health communication theory, persuasion theory, and rhetorical theory.

Judith Grunert O'Brien is a member of the School of Arts faculty in the College of Visual and Performing Arts and Project Manager at Syracuse University's Center for Instructional Development where she manages the design, development, and evaluation of educational projects, working with faculty across disciplines to improve student learning. Her current research concerns patterns of inquiry and approaches to problem solving in a variety of learning contexts. She is author of the book, *The Course Syllabus: A Learning-Centered Approach*. Her research interests include ways that instructors in higher education can help students become agents of their own education.

Richard P. Halgin is Professor of Psychology in the clinical psychology program at the University of Massachusetts, Amherst and a visiting professor of psychology at Amherst College. He is the co-author of many books, including *Abnormal Psychology: Clinical Perspectives on Psychological Disorders, Third Edition* (McGraw-Hill, 2000) and editor of *Taking Sides: Clashing Views on Controversial Issues in Abnormal Psychology* (Dushkin/McGraw-Hill, 2000). He has published more than 50 articles and book chapters in psychotherapy, clinical supervision, and professional issues in psychology. A board-certified clinical psychologist, he is a recipient of the Distinguished Teaching Award at the University of Massachusetts, Amherst. For more than two decades he has taught courses that attract more than 500 students each semester, and he is often called upon to serve as a consultant to colleagues about pedagogical issues pertaining to the teaching of large classes.

Emily Hoover is the Morse-Alumni Distinguished Teaching Professor of Horticultural Science at the University of Minnesota, Twin Cities. She teaches large undergraduate course sections in horticulture and general biology and supervises classroom and extension teaching experience for graduate students. Her research interests include decision cases for use in science courses and using writing to learn activities in teaching and learning.

John R. Hoyle is Professor of Educational Administration in the Department of Educational Administration and Human Resource Development at Texas A&M University. He has taught science in the public schools, and has been a university faculty member and administrator in five universities including Texas Christian University, Miami University, and Boston University. He serves as a consultant for public schools, universities, corporations, the justice department, and the department of defense (DOD) in England, Greece, Italy, Germany, Turkey, and the government of South Africa. He has taught classes ranging in size from 15 to 250. He is the author or co-author of many textbooks, including *Leadership and Futuring: Making Vision Happen and Interpersonal Sensitivity*. He is the recipient of two awards for distinguished achievement in teaching and in 1999 received the first Living Legend Award at the National Conference of Professors of Educational Administration.

J. Dennis Huston is Professor of English and the Master of Hanszen College at Rice University. He is author of *Shakespeare's Comedies and Plays* and numerous articles on Shakespeare, poetry, and drama. He was named the 1989 U.S. Professor of the Year by the Council for the Advancement and Support of Education (CASE) and the Carnegie Foundation for the Advancement of Teaching. He has taught large discussion-format English classes ranging in size from 60 to 100 students.

Brent L. Iverson is Associate Professor and Distinguished Teaching Professor in the Department of Chemistry and Biochemistry at the University of Texas, Austin. A member of the Institute of Cellular and Molecular Biology and the recipient of several academic, research, and teaching awards, he teaches large course sections of sophomore organic chemistry with enrollments ranging from 120 to 420 students. He also teaches graduate courses in advanced organic synthesis, and physical organic chemistry. He has authored three editions of a study guide for a popular organic chemistry text. His current research interests include the production, characterization, and manipulation of large functional molecules such as novel DNA-binding agents, antibodies, and enzymes.

Doug Jacobson is Associate Professor of Electrical and Computer Engineering at Iowa State University. He developed and teaches an introduction to microcontrollers course for a class of 100 students. He is actively involved in project LEARN, which helps faculty incorporate active learning in the classroom. He has successfully incorporated active learning in all his courses. He is also credited with starting a freshman learning community where 75 first-year computer engineering students live together and take courses together. He engages in teaching and research in information assurance, and his lab is recognized as one of 14 Centers for Academic Excellence. His current funded research is targeted at developing robust countermeasures for a difficult class of network-based security exploits called "denial of service attacks."

Laurie A. Jaeger is Associate Professor of Veterinary Anatomy and Public Health at the College of Veterinary Medicine at Texas A&M University. She teaches large animal gross anatomy, a lecture and laboratory course, to approximately 130 students in the first year of the professional veterinary medicine curriculum. Her research is focused on determining mechanisms of trophoblast differentiation and successful implantation, using domestic animal models. She is a recipient of the Texas A&M University Montague Center for Teaching Excellence Scholar Award in recognition of teaching excellence, a Wiley Distinguished Professorship in Veterinary Medicine, and college- and university-level distinguished teaching awards.

Deborah Kochevar is Associate Professor of Veterinary Physiology & Pharmacology at the College of Veterinary Medicine at Texas A&M University. A diplomate of the American College of Veterinary Clinical Pharmacology, she teaches pharmacology, biochemistry, molecular biology, and introduction to clinical skills to professional students. Her class sizes range from 70 to 130 students. She twice received the Norden Award for Teaching Excellence and is a recipient of college- and university-level faculty distinguished achievement teaching awards. She serves on the American Veterinary Medical Association Council on Education and the Educational Commission for Foreign Veterinary Graduates.

Robert Lundquist is Associate Professor in the Department of Industrial, Welding, and Systems Engineering at The Ohio State University. He teaches engineering economics, required by most undergraduate programs in the college, with a class size of 200 students. He also teaches project management and is part of a team that supervises a capstone design course for industrial engineering students. His current research looks at probabilistic cost-benefit analysis in relation to project selection for government-sponsored research. He is the recipient of a departmental and college of engineering award for excellence in teaching.

James McAuley is Associate Professor of Pharmacy Practice and Neurology at The Ohio State University College of Pharmacy and Medicine. He teaches a number of large courses such as the fundamentals of disease, clinical clerkship, pharmacotherapeutics, and pathophysiology and therapeutics. His research interests broadly encompass the treatment of patients with epilepsy, especially women's issues, neurosteroids, and patient outcomes.

Larry K. Michaelsen is the David Ross Boyd Professor of Management at the University of Oklahoma, a Carnegie scholar, and former editor of the *Journal of Management Education*. He is the recipient of numerous college, university, and national awards for his teaching. One of his pioneering works is the development of team learning, a small-group based instructional process designed for large business classes which has been adapted successfully in over 70 academic disciplines on over 100 campuses in the U.S. and seven foreign countries. Another is the development of an Integrated Business Core (IBC) program that links student learning in three core courses to their experience in creating and operating an actual start-up business whose profits are used to fund a hands-on community project.

Robin Nagle is Director of the Draper Interdisciplinary Master's Program in Humanities and Social Thought at New York University's Graduate School of Arts and Science. An anthropologist, she focuses on consumption and material culture and has written about religion. She is currently conducting ethnographic research with the New York City Department of Sanitation. Her most recent book, *Claiming the Virgin: The Broken Promise of Liberation Theology in Brazil*, was published by Routledge in 1997. She has taught large undergraduate classes in anthropology and in anthropological approaches to the study of religion. Her undergraduate classes, which include introductory anthropology and anthropological approaches to the study of religion, range in size from 60 to 120 students. At the graduate level, she has taught courses about Brazil, religious movements, urban anthropology, garbage, and consumption. She is a teaching consultant and member of the executive committee for EQUAL, the office within NYU that offers help to faculty interested in improving their teaching skills.

Linda B. Nilson is the founding Director of the Office of Teaching Effectiveness and Innovation at Clemson University. Her experience with teaching large classes dates back 25 years. Her first class, occupations and professions at UCLA, had 200 students. She has also taught large classes of introduction to sociology and social stratification, as well as smaller courses in graduate-level sociology, interdisciplinary topics, and college teaching. Now most of her teaching takes the form of faculty development workshops and institutes. Her research focuses on college teaching and student learning. In her book, *Teaching at Its Best: A Research-Based Resource for College Instructors,* she integrates strategies for large classes throughout the text.

Mathew L. Ouellett is Associate Director of the Center for Teaching at the University of Massachusetts, Amherst, and serves as Adjunct Professor of Social Work at Smith College where he teaches a graduate course on the implications of racism on clinical social work practice in the United States. In addition to consulting with individual instructors, departments, and colleges on teaching, his research interests and publications focus on social justice and equity issues in multicultural organizations and faculty development. Most recently, he is author of the faculty development teaching guide, *Disabilities Resources for Teaching Inclusively* (2000). He is President of the New England Faculty Development Consortium and chairs the Diversity Commission of the Professional and Organizational Development Network in Higher Education (2000-2001).

Christopher E. Overtree is Lecturer of psychology at the University of Massachusetts, Amherst. He has taught courses in abnormal psychology and child clinical psychology at the University of Massachusetts, Amherst and Smith College. He has served as a TA for large lecture courses including abnormal psychology and human sexuality and is the author of a procedures manual for a 500-student course. His research and clinical work focuses on child and adolescent psychopathology, adolescent risk behavior, and strategies for effective teaching.

Nancy J. Simpson is Director of the Center for Teaching Excellence and Lecturer in the Department of Mathematics at Texas A&M University. She teaches undergraduate courses in finite mathematics and calculus for life science and business majors. She currently teaches honors students and has taught large sections in mathematics with enrollments of 100 to 125 students. Her professional interests include leading discussions on thinking and problem solving, classroom assessment, and the development of the teaching portfolio.

Mary Deane Sorcinelli is Associate Provost for Faculty Development, Director of the Center for Teaching, and Adjunct Professor in the Division of Educational Policy, Research, and Administration at the University of Massachusetts, Amherst. She is President (2001-2002) of the Professional and Organizational Development Network in Higher Education and a visiting scholar to the American Association for Higher Education (AAHE). She has written and presented nationally and internationally in the areas of academic career development, teaching consultation, and the use of assessment and evaluation information for teaching improvement. She has consulted with hundreds of faculty on teaching large classes and is currently a project director of a William and Flora Hewlett Foundation Grant (2000-2002) to improve large, general education courses through student-centered faculty development.

Michael Smilowitz is Associate Professor in the School of Speech Communication at James Madison University. He teaches courses on public relations, public relation techniques, organizational communication, and communication research. In his 20 years of instructional experience, with class sizes ranging from 20 to 600 students, he has received several awards for teaching excellence, including Ohio University's University Professor recognition. He is the author of numerous published works, especially in the areas of communication and teaching, and consults to both private and public organizations.

James H. Stith is Director of the Physics Resources Center for the American Institute of Physics. A physics education researcher, his primary interests are in program evaluation and teacher preparation and enhancement. A former professor of physics at The Ohio State University and the United States Military Academy, he has designed and implemented TA and faculty development workshops and courses. He has over 30 years of teaching experiences at both the undergraduate and graduate levels and has successfully implemented active learning methods into his courses. He is a former president of the American Association of Physics Teachers, a fellow of the American Association for the Advancement of Science, a fellow of the

American Physical Society, a former president and chartered fellow of the National Society of Black Physicists, and a member of the Ohio Academy of Science.

Michael Theall is Associate Professor and Director of the Center for the Advancement of Teaching and Learning at Youngstown State University. In his 25 years of teaching and administrative experience, he has concentrated on college teaching and learning, instructional design and development, evaluation and assessment, and the instructional applications of technology. He is currently venturing into new curriculum and formats, teaching an online course in an undergraduate, fully online, liberal studies program. His research interests have focused on college teaching and learning and evaluation and student ratings of instruction. He has contributed over 130 publications and presentations to the literature in these fields and led many workshops and seminars on college teaching topics, including teaching large classes. He and co-researcher Jennifer Franklin were recently nominated for the 2001 W. J. McKeachie Career Achievement Award by the American Educational Research Association.

Steven Tomlinson is Lecturer in the Department of Finance at the University of Texas, Austin. He has taught large sections of principles of economics and money and banking courses. The enrollment in these classes ranges from 80 to 350 students. An actor and playwright, he is comfortable with large audiences, and his pedagogical style is based on adapting techniques from theater and interactive performance art to communicate complex principles effectively and to reach students personally. His research interests include writing solo performance pieces about the human side of economics. One such series of monologues is currently being adapted for PBS and is titled, "The Cost of Living."

Donald H. Wulff is Director for the Center for Instructional Development and Research and Assistant Dean of the Graduate School at the University of Washington. He and his colleagues have examined students' perceptions of large classes and published the results in a 1987 Jossey-Bass volume on *Teaching Large Classes Well.* He has conducted research and published widely on issues related to TA preparation. An affiliate graduate faculty member in speech communication, he has taught university undergraduate courses in communication, public speaking, and interviewing, and a graduate course on teaching and learning in higher education.

Topic Location Guide

Using this Topic Location Guide will help you access content information. While we encourage you to read all of the chapters, this guide is a quick reference directory to content of particular interest to you. Part I authors were asked to cover the topic of large classes in a broader scope with very practical suggestions for instructors who are beginning this phase of their career or wish to renew their commitment to excellence. Part II authors provide more specific information on a priority topic or address course concerns within a particular discipline. In addition to being a useful, at-a-glance directory, the guide clearly shows the commonality of issues shared by the contributing authors on teaching large classes in higher education.

The first column on the left of the guide represents the list of chapters in the book. The column headings at the top of the guide represent the pedagogical topics covered in various chapters of the book. Cells with an "X" indicate the topic is covered in that chapter.

Topic Location Guide

	Pre-planning	Objectives	Assignments	Methodologies	Active Learning	Management	Support	Special Topics	Assessment	Student Needs	Rewards	Research
PART ONE												
1 Course Design	X	X	X	X	X		X		X			X
2 Mega Classes	X	X	X	X	X	X	X		X	X	X	
3 Assessing Learning		X	X		X	X	X		X			X
4 Promoting Civility	X			X	X	X		X		X		X
5 Active Learning		X	X	X	X		X					
6 Team Learning	X				X	X	X		X	X		
7 Technology	X			X	X		X	X		X		
8 Teaching for Inclusion		X			X	X	X	X		X		X
9 Working with TAs	X					X	X	X			X	X
10 TA Perspective						X	X	X	X			
11 Administrator's View	X							X	X			
12 Research Review									X			X
PART TWO												
1 Agriculture	X			X	X		X					
2 Business	X	X				X						
3 Business				X		X			X			
4 Pharmacy				X	X		X		X			
5 Veterinary Medicine	X	X		X	X					X		
6 Education	X		X	X			X			X	X	X
7 Engineering	X			X	X				X			
8 Computer Engr.	X			X	X	X						
9 English	X		X	X	X		X		X			
10 Law		X		X	X			X		X	X	
11 Mathematics	X			X	X			X		X		
12 Chemistry	X	X		X	X					X	X	X
13 Pre-med Chemistry	X			X	X		X		X	X	X	
14 Physics	X	X		X					X	X		
15 Psychology	X			X			X		X	X		X
16 Social Science	X	X		X	X	X						X
17 Anthropology				X	X	X	X		X		X	

Preface

Administrators' and senior faculty responses to decreased funding and increased enrollment often overlook teaching development for faculty of large classes. There is an overwhelming need for effective teachers of large classes in higher education. For example, at The University of Texas, Austin with a student enrollment of over 50,000, faculty teach more than 7,000 courses annually, and more than 660 of those classes contained 100 or more students during the school year of 1998-1999. It is the rare instructor who remains undaunted when standing before his or her first class of 100, 200, or even 500 students. Large classes are very prevalent in many universities and are often gateway courses to students' major fields of study.

Many academicians argue that large classes should give students, often experiencing their first year in college, an opportunity to learn from practicing scholars in the field. If these courses provide breadth and depth of course content, then senior and more experienced instructors should teach large classes. This, however, is not the case at many institutions. Historically, large sections are delegated to junior faculty—tenure track assistant professors, lecturers, and in some instances senior graduate teaching associates. These individuals are often inexperienced teachers who many times are fresh out of graduate programs that provide limited exposure to pedagogy.

Engaging Large Classes: Strategies and Techniques for College Faculty offers college and university faculty members and administrators practical, well-established methodologies for teaching large classes. This book features contributing authors who are highly effective large-class teachers, from across the disciplines, who share innovative teaching strategies for teaching large classes. Guided by the insights of experienced faculty development professionals who possess extensive university-level teaching experience, who have large-class teaching backgrounds, and who have worked with instructors enhancing large class instruction, this book not only presents an overview of the research on teaching large classes, but also provides instructors with helpful advice about the mechanics of large-class pedagogy. Contributing authors "walk the walk and talk the talk" and provide suggestions about teaching strategies that work in large classes.

Purposes of this Book

This book provides a discussion forum for instructors teaching large classes. The plethora of knowledge and insights provided by the contributing authors offer practical and proven strategies to personalize the large classroom. The expertise shared establishes guidelines for new and experienced instructors and teachers and provides instructional strategies so as to avoid reinventing the wheel of teaching large classes. This book has the potential to change the viewpoints of academia toward the overwhelming demands of teaching large classes.

Audience

The primary audience for *Engaging Large Classes* is new and experienced faculty who face the challenge of teaching classes with perhaps hundreds of students in fixed-seating, auditorium environments. Anyone who deals with large classes of anonymous students in undergraduate or graduate classes will benefit from the advice and experience of the contributing authors, many of whom have learned that large classes offer greater opportunity than smaller ones. A secondary audience is those involved in professional development and administrators who may need to mentor or counsel faculty.

Overview of the Contents

Following the book's table of contents is the Topic Location Guide that indicates what content issues are covered in each chapter. *Engaging Large Classes* is divided into two parts. Part I includes a brief review of research and also identifies and discusses major issues in the teaching of large classes such as the advantages and disadvantages of large classes; how to engage students in large classes; how to design, plan, manage, and fairly assess large classes; the universality of large-class issues across disciplines, and the continuing challenges of large-class instruction, including classroom management, diversity issues, and working with teaching assistants and undergraduate peer tutors. Authors in this part also share insights into and strategies for using classroom technology, active learning, collaborative learning, and innovative techniques such as academic controversies in the classroom. Part II is organized by discipline: agriculture, business, clinical science, education, engineering, English, law, mathematics, sciences, and social and behavioral sciences. In 17 detailed examples, teachers of large classes from a range of higher education institutions give their perspectives on what strategies and tools promote successful learning in large classes. The final section in Part II is a summary of the key concepts, where we synthesize the key points that have recurred among the chapter and example authors.

All of us who have worked on this book have struggled with the challenges of teaching large classes. We are pleased to be able to offer, in one volume, an array of tested techniques and tools that have worked for us. On a final note, all of us not only have survived teaching large classes, but have learned and had fun along the way. We hope that you will find our experiences relevant, helpful, and at times amusing.

Christine A. Stanley
M. Erin Porter
August, 2001

PART ONE

Key Concepts

1

Course Design for Large Classes: A Learning-Centered Approach

Judith Grunert O'Brien
Syracuse University

In higher education, course design is a process in which specific faculty in certain disciplines and fields craft learning experiences for particular groups of students in distinct institutional settings. In this chapter, I present an approach you may use to design learning experiences that challenge students to assume responsibility for actively shaping their learning and support them as they learn to construct, use, assess, and extend their knowledge. In general terms, when you design learning experiences for classes of any size you attempt to align your perspective on learning with your desired learning outcomes for the students participating in your course, create learning situations in which these outcomes can be practiced and achieved, plan strategies that appropriately and accurately assess your students' accomplishments, and communicate your intentions and expectations to your students.

Context

You are teaching a large undergraduate course at a research university for approximately 250 students who are required to take your course as an introduction to the field. Students meet with you twice a week in large-group sessions and meet once a week in small-group sessions led by your teaching assistants. You have traditionally prepared and delivered lectures, assigned readings, organized discussion sessions, and given multiple choice exams for midterms and finals. You enjoy and take pride in your role as lecturer, and in your ability to interact with students and collaborate with TAs. But you have not been satisfied with the overall level of student achievement, their engagement with course content, or with your ability to monitor student progress. You have decided to redesign your course to promote the level of student engagement and to improve opportunities for ongoing assessment and feedback. You will retain the general structure of the course for the moment, including large lecture sessions, small-group discussion sessions, and multiple choice exams. But you will focus on giving new value to student note-making as part of an active, constructive, recursive practice of writing to learn and will realign other course components to help students learn to use this form of writing to build knowledge, skills, and dispositions of lasting value.

Perspective on Learning

Your approach draws upon perspectives emerging from multidisciplinary research on situated learning and the social construction of knowledge that examine how people enter and develop the ability to participate in particular communities of practice (Resnick, 1987). Guided by these perspectives, you conceive learning in terms of students' increasing ability to participate in the communities of practice to which they belong and design your course to help students learn how to develop the knowledge base, thinking skills, and dispositions they will need to participate in the field.

Situated Learning

Situated learning acknowledges student differences and takes them into account when designing learning experiences. Each student in your course brings a unique set of differences to the learning situation. The students vary in their ability and preparation for academic study, their expectations of a college education, and the nature of their interest in the content area. Students differ in their preferences for talking, listening, writing, and reading as ways to take in, process, and construct meaningful connections with new knowledge. They differ in their needs and desires for structure and support in learning. Since you expect students to take an active role in learning course content and to assume responsibility for their own intellectual development, differences in students' conceptions of what knowledge is and how it is acquired are particularly important (Bereiter & Scardamalia, 1989). Students want to learn, often in limited ways and with mixed motivations (Walvoord & Anderson, 1998), but do not always act in their own best interests. For some students, learning activity is schoolwork, and learning is a consequence of carrying out instructor-initiated activities.

Using the short-term coping skills they have learned, these students set out to complete the activity in a narrow, convergent process in order to achieve a final product, rather than attend to the sense-making for which the activity was designed. When students approach activities in this way, they subvert your goals of learning to build knowledge, skills, and dispositions that will have lasting value (Resnick, 1987).

Learning is a recursive process; new knowledge is built on, and often requires the reconstruction of, prior knowledge. Your course requires students to construct and reconstruct their knowledge and to consider their present knowledge in the light of alternative and future possibilities. You expect students to commit their current effort to long-term goals of understanding and competence (Bereiter & Scardamalia, 1989). You expect students to take responsibility for generating some motivation that will act as an incentive to the quality and intensity of thinking this requires. You expect students to monitor their engagement with course content in order to assess their own learning, and to reflect on and improve their learning process. You also expect students with differing perspectives and degrees of expertise in the content area to contribute to the learning of their peers by acting as questioners, coaches, critics, and editors. Therefore, you design your course to allow for student differences and to prolong periods of exploration, analysis, and you make your expectations for learning explicit and communicate them to your students.

Learning Outcomes

Important learning outcomes are often intuited rather than explicitly stated, making it difficult to distinguish them from the educational experiences in which they are embedded. Articulating these outcomes frees you to explore a variety of approaches that promote the kinds and the depth of learning you desire. It is important to distinguish two approaches to desired learning outcomes. Some may be concrete statements of what students will be expected to learn, specifying what you are willing to accept as evidence of learning. These may be used in circumstances in which tasks must be performed at a fixed standard of competence or when public safety demands that certain tasks be performed only by fully qualified individuals (Hammons & Barnsley, 1992). Others may be open ended, flexible descriptions of a situation or problem out of which various kinds of learning might arise. These would be expectations that delimit the direction of student engagement and assure that standards are met, but would not predefine an endpoint for their learning or try to guarantee a particular interpretation or outcome. More specific objectives emerge as they are appropriate to the individual student in resolving tasks (Streibel, 1995). It is conceivable that both sorts of outcomes may be developed for a single course, unit, or assignment. Distinguishing between them allows you to plan assignments and assessments appropriately.

The purpose of your course is to improve students' ability to use content area knowledge in activities that typically engage experienced practitioners in your field and you frame student learning outcomes in terms of these activities. Experienced practitioners are motivated by their engagement with issues, questions, or problems of the field. They build resource networks, developing rich and evolving arrays of people, materials, strategies, conceptual and technical tools, to facilitate their ongoing learning and inform their participation in the critical, creative, and practical intellectual activity of the field (Pea, 1993). They explore various information sources, evaluate and analyze what they find, making notes and keeping files of ideas. They explore their evolving thinking in ongoing conversation with colleagues and write as a contribution to an ongoing conversation among members of a discipline who may disagree with each other in important ways (Bean, 1996).

Students entering your field are joining a conversation of differing perspectives that requires complex thinking about significant issues. You want students to develop the knowledge base and the conceptual and technical tools they will need to engage these issues. You want them to learn how to build and use their own resource networks (including the perspectives of experts, peers, and their own experiences), and to construct and reconstruct reasoned, well-founded perspectives of content that can inform their ongoing learning. You want them to understand discipline-specific standards that enable them to participate effectively as students entering into the discourse of the field. You want them to learn how to connect their evolving knowledge to key questions, problems, and issues in the discourse; formulate their ideas orally and in writing; and share their developing perspectives with their peers who may have different perspectives. Finally, you want them to learn how to manage the sort of complex learning project that participation in your field requires. These desired outcomes provide you with a basis for planning what is to be accomplished and for assessing student learning.

Learning Experiences

You use note-making, essay writing, and response writing as interrelated components of a recursive practice of writing to learn that will integrate learning and assessment and involve students in sustained intensive engagement with course content and with one another. You want students to understand writing as a way to learn, develop a knowledge base, shape ideas, and develop thinking skills.

You structure your course around the sorts of open-ended issues, questions, problems, and generative themes that engage the members of your field. They serve as an explicit conceptual framework for your lectures in the large group sessions. This framework helps students assimilate and retain information, stimulate curiosity, and provide a source of motivation for student inquiry into ideas and phenomena (Bligh, 2000; Davis 1993; Kurfiss, 1988). It also helps students focus their efforts appropriately in the small-group workshop sessions. These sessions provide students with opportunities for collaboration and criticism, for formulating their thoughts in writing, and for responding thoughtfully and critically to diverse points of view.

Assessment

Assessment is important to learning. You want to use assessment to reinforce what you think is most important and to show students where they should put their efforts. In order to develop some sense of ownership and commitment to the learning process, students must understand discipline-appropriate criteria and standards for monitoring their own performance and judging what constitutes a good outcome. To help students understand, you provide them with clear and thoughtful criteria and standards (in the form of assignment sheets and examples) that they can apply to work-in-progress. These will help students focus their work, monitor their own progress, show them what they have accomplished, and what, with work, they might yet achieve. You expect students to contribute to each others' learning, so you avoid grading in ways (such as grading on the curve) that put students in competition with each other for a limited number of high grades (Davis, 1993). To keep the assessment and grading process manageable, you have TAs grade student writing holistically, giving one overall grade that considers all criteria at once. You have TAs, use a minus/check/plus system: a check-minus indicating unsatisfactory performance, a check indicating work that meets your specifications, a check-plus indicating strongly engaged high quality exploration and thinking (Bean 1996).

Note-making, essay writing, and response writing are intended as an integrated, semester-long project that extends exploration and analysis, creates a climate that encourages revision, and provides a generous amount of attention to developing work. You thread these activities (discussed below) through large-group sessions, small-group sessions, and out-of-class work.

Note-making

Note-making is a course-long assignment that promotes student engagement with course content. You expect students to write and rewrite their notes in order to integrate information from readings, lectures, and other sources in a way that is meaningful to the students. Making good, thoughtfully constructed notes for your course requires that students learn to recognize when they need information, learn to locate and evaluate information, and learn to organize and reorganize information, tailoring it to the needs of their developing perspectives.

Prior to large-group sessions, you expect students to complete assigned readings and make an organized set of notes including any questions raised by readings. Students should add to their notes during lecture sessions. You give students time during and at the end of these sessions in which you expect them to work together in groups of two or three to review, add to, or modify their notes (Johnson, Johnson, & Smith, 1991). They should use these opportunities to review major concepts and significant details, clarify unresolved issues or concerns, and generate questions for discussion or individual inquiry. They should organize their notes around the issues, problems, and questions that frame the course, and work up each portion of their notes as course material develops (Bean, 1996). After class they are to rewrite notes to make them more comprehensive, include new insights, and raise new questions. You expect students to maintain their notes as an electronic file so that they can revise and print updated versions.

You expect students to identify different information as relevant, construct particular understandings or interpretations of course material and resources, and come to different conclusions. Notes should present a plausible and satisfactory interpretation of readings and lectures including facts, key terms, definitions, concepts, etc. They should be organized around problems, issues, and generative themes. There should be evidence that students have explored and analyzed required and recommended resources; that students have pursued some individual inquiry; sought analyzed and integrated information sources relevant to their evolving perspective; explored ideas and selected examples from the literature and from personal experience. While TAs will use these criteria to assess student notes at least twice during the semester, the primary assessment of their notes takes place when students use them to write short essays. Shortcomings in students' essays may point to inadequacies in their present knowledge, to shortcomings in the content or organization of their notes, and to the need for additional information and revision.

Essays and Responses

At intervals (five times during the semester), students use their notes as a resource to write and rewrite brief essays of one page or less. Each essay assignment focuses on an open-ended question, generative theme, problem, or controversial issue raised in lectures, readings, and developed in students' notes. Students write essays to an audience of their peers. The essay assignments are intended to extend exploration and analysis and create a climate that encourages revision. Students write multiple drafts; share work-in-progress; read, discuss, and write responses to each other's essays. This process helps students develop and understand alternative views and contributes to the development of each student's perspective (Bednar, Cunningham, Duffy, & Perry, 1995).

In computer clusters with notes in hand, students write rapid drafts of their essays to get ideas down. They post these initial versions in TA folders and print out copies for review by their peers. They form study groups to read and discuss each other's essays using the assignment sheets you have provided to apply your criteria to work-in-progress. Informed by the discussion, each student in the group responds in writing to another student's essay, identifying strengths and shortcomings in a way that contributes to the development of the author's perspective. Each posts their response to the TA's folder and to the author of the essay within a specified time. Students are expected to rewrite essays out of class, informed by class discussion and peer recommendations, and post the revisions in the TA folders. The final versions should be substantially different from exploratory drafts.

Establish a hierarchy of concerns for essays that will stimulate meaningful revision:

> Assessment of the final versions of essays looks for evidence of high-quality thinking that engages the complexities of the issues and makes it possible to evaluate differing perspectives in terms of the reasoning and evidence that support them.
>
> *Purpose:* clear, consistent purpose or controlling idea throughout
>
> *Development:* well-reasoned, appropriate, and sufficient support for the position
>
> *Organization:* coherent organization with a strong introduction and conclusion; shows a clear sense of audience and purpose
>
> *Overall clarity:* generally free of distracting spelling, typographical, and grammatical errors [papers filled with these will be returned ungraded] (Bean, 1966, pp. 116-117).

Responses to other students' essays are evaluated in terms of the following question: Does the review identify strengths and shortcomings in a way that contributes to the author's perspective?

Provide feedback on final versions in the large-group session using a good response among the check-plus papers as a model (or you write your own, if necessary).

Resources

Develop a well-considered set of resources that guide and deepen understanding of content, and explain to students why you have chosen them. Try to find and order a textbook that elaborates the conceptual framework, and identify other repositories of information (journal articles, indexes, databases, internet resources, films, maps, libraries, museums, etc.) important to the discourse of your field. Since students are to learn to use resources to construct a perspective, do not entirely define the boundaries of what may be relevant. Think in terms of a core body of content that all students are required to know, content that you will make available to support individual student inquiry or projects, and content that might only be of interest to a student who wants to specialize in a particular area (Grunert, 1997).

You see yourself and your lectures as resources among others that your students can learn to use effectively. Use some class time to help students understand what it means to develop a perspective, show how your particular view developed, whether it is typical in your field, with whom you share perspectives, what perspectives you resist, and the strengths and weakness of each as you understand them. Direct students to other perspectives you value that complement, contrast, or conflict with those you present. Challenge students to seek further information or new, even contradictory, points of view that may be relevant.

TAs are an important resource in your course. They facilitate the flow of information and help you to monitor student progress. Because TAs vary in experience, meet with them to assess sample notes and papers so that, with some consistency, they can provide appropriate guidance to work-in-progress and grade final revisions. Ask each TA to provide you with three to five representative essays, to keep notes on successes and pitfalls of each assignment, and on where students have difficulty. This helps you to monitor overall student progress, what they are doing well, and where they need to improve.

TAs lead the small-group workshop sessions. These sessions provide important opportunities for students to clarify confusions and misunderstandings, to gain practice testing their ideas in a public setting, to think through problems, generate questions, and evaluate their own and other's positions. TAs plan lists of questions to guide and focus discussion about the open-ended issues, questions, and problems that frame the course. You help them to differentiate among questions that require different types of thinking. They should pose some questions that are appropriate for assessing students' preparation and comprehension, or for reviewing or summarizing content. They should also pose questions that encourage students to think critically and to analyze and solve problems. To promote discussion and encourage interaction among students, TAs should avoid questions that require only yes or no answers. They should include a few questions that they are not quite sure how to answer, as well as some that ask for hunches, intuitive leaps, and educated guesses (Davis, 1993).

As an alternative, TAs can put students in small groups to generate lists of questions raised by lectures, readings and their own attempts to formulate their thinking in their notes and essays. Each group must reach consensus on one or two key questions they would like the class to discuss. TAs can list these questions and ask the class to prioritize them (Bean, 1996).

Your institution has good technological support and a well developed computing environment that includes networked teaching stations in the large auditorium, networked computer clusters that can be reserved in academic buildings, and clusters in student dorms that help students in their out-of-class work sessions. You want your students to harness this technology to access information and communicate with you, your teaching assistants, and each other, but also to enhance their thinking and sustain their learning in out-of-class work sessions (Brown, 1993). You expect them to use computers to monitor the course website, locate information, write, reorganize and rewrite notes; revise essays, comment on others' essays, post initial and final versions of essays and constructive responses to other students' essays to TA folders on your web site. They may also set up, maintain, and revise their own files; build their own database; share a common database; use such things as spreadsheet, graphic, or statistical software; and build a portfolio.

Take advantage of training opportunities to develop your course web site and to explore the use of course management software. Create links to other sites you value, post an electronic version of your syllabus and handouts that typically take class time. Set up folders for each TA's small-group sessions to collect student work in order to monitor student progress and assess course outcomes at the end of the term. Organize training and ongoing support for your TAs so that they can interact with students online.

To facilitate student interaction with course materials and each other, place electronic versions of standards and criteria for student notes, and for each essay assignment on your web page. Make available examples of student notes that have been evaluated by the criteria to be used to assess current student work. These can clarify your expectations and may inspire students' efforts toward their own work (Wlodkowski & Ginsberg, 1995). Also post annotated examples of inadequate, satisfactory, and excellent essays so students may compare their own essays to these examples.

In Your Syllabus

Use your syllabus as a learning tool to communicate your expectations and intentions to students, allowing them to achieve some personal control over their learning process. Include the following sections:

Instructor Information. Communicate your availability by including basic information about your preferences such as your name, address, phone number, email, office hours, how to arrange for a conference. Include similar information about other important student contacts, such as TAs, technicians, main office staff, and librarians, as appropriate.

Purpose of the Course. Explain that the course was designed to improve students' ability to use content area knowledge in activities that typically engage experienced practitioners in your field and describe how this fits with larger program goals. Try to convey some of your own excitement about the subject, why you value the particular perspective you have developed, and the general and specialized knowledge of content, tools, and practices you have gained through years of your own education and practice in your field.

Learning Perspective. Establish the importance of student responsibility for learning, generating some sustaining motivation, for monitoring their own intellectual development, and contributing to the learning of other students.

Outcomes. Tell students what they will learn, why the particular outcomes are important, how these outcomes are connected to larger program goals, what they will be held accountable for, what opportunities they will have for practice, and under what conditions they will be assessed.

Criteria and Standards for Assessment and Grading. Explain your focus on assessment and grading as tools for learning that keep students informed of their progress so that they can maintain or improve performance. Make your criteria and standards for their work as explicit as you can, and explain how their final grades will be calculated.

Course Description. Provide students with an overview of how the work will proceed. Explain how the assignments and activities will help them to learn in large session lectures, small session workshops, and independent out-of class work sessions.

Resources. Explain the significance of course resources, why lectures, books, readings, and other resources have been chosen, and what their relative importance is to the course or discipline. List all tools and materials that will be needed for the course as well as their location (i.e., the course web site URL, the college bookstore, the reserve room at the library, the computer cluster, etc.).

Course Calendar. Indicate topics or activities planned for each class meeting, assignment due dates, and special occasions or events. Students should be cautioned about the tentative nature of your calendar and clearly understand how revised timetables or plans will be communicated.

Policies. Your syllabus will also inform students about institutional policies regarding attendance, examinations, add/drops, course withdrawals, special learning needs, and academic integrity.

Course Assessment

Try to find out how students experience what is happening as they grapple with the content and process of learning in your course (Angelo & Cross, 1993). At mid-term and again at the end of your course, refer students to the intended course outcomes, and use a simple question to help you to determine whether revisions are required, to reinforce your expectations for students' responsibility in shaping their learning and your interest in their accomplishments:

> Is the way we are conducting class giving you the best chance to learn and demonstrate what you know? (Wlodkowski & Ginsberg, 1995) If so, what is most and least useful to you in this regard? If not, what features of the course might we restructure to make this possible, and how?

You may itemize particular aspects of the course and ask how they contribute to their ability to achieve learning outcomes.

At the end of the term, you will have your syllabus with its explicit statement of intended outcomes, descriptions of assignments, and learning experiences that you designed to help students achieve them. You will have assignment sheets that reflect your criteria and standards for each assignment and test whether students have learned what you wanted from the learning experiences you have designed (Walvoord & Anderson, 1998). You will also have an electronic portfolio of each student's work for the course (a set of notes, two versions of several essays, their written responses to other students' essays, and multiple-choice mid-term and final exams) and student course evaluations. These course embedded materials will allow you to understand where students did and did not do well, and to use that information to make useful improvements in your course.

You may want to reassess several components of your course: Are the outcomes you value sufficiently aligned with program goals and understandable in terms of larger institutional mission and goals? Do your exams and your way of grading assignments and calculating final grades allow you and others to make trustworthy judgments about the quality of student learning? Are directions, standards, and criteria for assignments explicit? Do the activities you have designed and selected help students learn what they need to know to do well on assignments and exams? Is the workload manageable for you, your students, and your TAs?

Continue to build on the course strengths and modify its limits through incremental adjustments to course components, and perhaps to the larger program of which it is a part, to help students build knowledge of lasting value and develop a sense of ownership and commitment to the process.

References

Angelo, T. A., & Cross, K. P. (1993). *Classroom assessment techniques: A handbook for college teachers*. San Francisco, CA: Jossey-Bass.

Bean, J. C. (1996). *Engaging ideas: The professor's guide to integrating writing, critical thinking, and active learning in the classroom*. San Francisco, CA: Jossey-Bass.

Bednar, A. K., Cunningham, D., Duffy, T. M., & Perry, J. D. (1995). Theory into practice: How do we link? In G. J. Anglin (Ed.), *Instructional technology: Past, present, and future* (2nd ed.), (pp. 100-112). Englewood, CA: Libraries Unlimited.

Bereiter, C., & Scardamalia, M. (1989). Intentional learning as a goal of instruction. In L. B. Resnick (Ed.), *Knowing, learning, and instruction: Essays in honor of Robert Glaser* (pp. 361-392). Hillsdale, NJ: Lawrence Erlbaum Associates.

Bligh, D. A. (2000). *What's the use of lectures?* San Francisco, CA: Jossey-Bass.

Brown, A. L., Ash, D., Rutherford, M., Nakagawa, K., Gordon, A., & Campione, J. C. (1993). Distributed expertise in the classroom. In G. Salomon (Ed.), *Distributed cognitions: Psychological and educational considerations* (pp. 188-228). Cambridge, EN: Cambridge University Press.

Brown, J. S., Collins, A., & Duguid, P. (1989). Situated cognition and the culture of learning. *Educational Researcher, 18*, 32-42.

Davis, B. G. (1993). *Tools for teaching*. San Francisco, CA: Jossey-Bass.

Grunert, J. (1997). *The course syllabus: A learning-centered approach.* Bolton, MA: Anker.

Hammons, J. O., & Barnsley J. R. (1992). Everything you need to know about developing a grading plan for your course (well, almost). *Journal on Excellence in College Teaching, 3,* 51-68.

Johnson, D. W., Johnson, R. T., & Smith, K. A. (1991). *Cooperative learning: Increasing college faculty instructional productivity.* Washington, DC: The George Washington University, School of Education and Human Development. (ASHE-ERIC Higher Education Report No. 4).

Kurfiss, J. G. (1988) *Critical thinking: Theory, research, practice and possibilities.* Washington, DC: Association for the Study of Higher Education. (ASHE ERIC Higher Education Report No. 2).

Pea, R. (1993). Practices of distributed intelligence and designs for education. In G. Salomon (Ed.), *Distributed cognitions: Psychological and educational considerations* (pp. 47-87). Cambridge, EN: Cambridge University Press.

Resnick, L. (1987, December). Learning in school and out. *Educational Researcher, 16,* 13-20.

Resnick, L. B. (1989). *Knowing, learning, and instruction: Essays in honor of Robert Glaser.* Hillsdale, NJ: Lawrence Erlbaum Associates.

Streibel, M. J. (1995). Instructional plans and situated learning: The challenge of Suchman's theory of situated action for instructional designers and instructional systems (pp. 145-160). In G. J. Anglin (Ed.), *Instructional technology: Past, present, and future* (2nd ed.). Englewood, CA: Libraries Unlimited.

Walvoord, B. E., & Anderson, V. J. (1998). *Effective Grading: A tool for learning and assessment.* San Francisco, CA: Jossey-Bass.

Wlodkowski, R. J., & Ginsberg, M. B. (1995). *Diversity and motivation: Culturally responsive teaching.* San Francisco, CA: Jossey-Bass.

2

That's Not a Large Class; It's a Small Town: How Do I Manage?

Lynda G. Cleveland
University of Texas, Austin

With today's colleges and universities bulging at the seams, we are seeing more large classes in our universities. Instructors no longer have the freedom of selecting the cream of the crop; nor do we always enjoy a student to teacher ratio of 25 or 30 to 1. This chapter addresses questions for those of you facing the mega-class (400-500). Believe it or not, teaching a mega-class can be a lot of fun and because it *is* a mega-class, it lends itself to some great teaching tools not available in a smaller classroom.

I teach a lower division, three-hour course within the management science and information systems department in the Red McCombs School of Business at the University of Texas, Austin (UT). There are 500+ students in each of two sections during the fall and spring semesters. In order to put this class size in perspective to the overall population of UT (50,000 students), for every 50 students that pass, one of them is in this class!

Focus on the challenges that you face while reading these two most important tips:

1) Accept all questions as valid, especially when you teach large classes.

2) Take advice only from other teachers who teach classes that are similar in size, coursework, and demographics.

If you teach a section of 500 students, advice from another instructor who teaches 200 or 350 is helpful, but not entirely applicable to your situation.

In preparation for teaching a mega-class, your first two duties are really no different than if you were teaching a small seminar. First determine your philosophy for teaching. Secondly, flex your creative muscles.

• **Adopt a philosophy for teaching a large class that is no different than one for a small class.** My personal philosophy is that teaching is a performing art. Our purpose is to instruct, and often when we instruct, entertainment is a by-product. I believe that as we hone our content knowledge and follow the guidelines of instructional systems design (analysis of the learner, the environment, the evaluative objectives, etc.) when preparing our curriculum, it does not matter if we have 50, 500, or 5,000; the audience, essentially the learner, can become engaged.

• **Consider and develop your creative skills.** Do not let your teaching creativity and originality be blocked by perceptual or emotional barriers. Train yourself to be creative. Stretch your imagination. Observe life itself. It is amazing how many teaching ideas you can get by observing people, places, and things. Challenge yourself with games, books, or activities such as brain teasers, puzzles, or word play. Now that you have revisited your teaching philosophy and sharpened your creative skills, let's consider some of the priority questions asked by mega-class teachers.

1) How many and who?
First, how many students and what classifications will be in your class(es)? The interval between 350 and 500 is huge. Secondly, what is the student makeup in your class? My course is designated as a lower-division foundations class. However, it usually consists of not only freshmen and sophomores, but also juniors and seniors. Be prepared! Teaching students with an age range of 16 to 22 is a challenge. Student maturity, workload, and study strategies should be considered in your planning.

Plan ahead.

2) What is the course content?
Content is going to be the core of your preparation. Check with your department and get a course description of what is required. Borrow syllabi from previous semesters if available in your department. Check with anyone who has taught the course which you are about to teach and get a variety of ideas. Review recent syllabi from courses in a similar program with yours.

It will amaze you how effortlessly many creative ideas begin to flow when you have the content blueprint before you.

3) What faculty and support system is available?

The classroom facilities, size of the room, and the support staff will largely determine what you can do in any teaching situation. This is especially true in the mega-class situation. Beyond these constraints, your creativity is your only limiting factor. *Let your imagination soar.*

Before you actually begin to plan your curriculum it is important that you visit the classroom—the physical site—in which you will be teaching. Survey the physical attributes of the facility. Take note of the student seating arrangements; the number of aisles; whether or not the room is raked (elevated) front to back; room lighting; number and view of windows; number of doors; podium location; what audio-visual equipment is available; whether support staff is required for equipment use in the room; location of restrooms, water fountains, drink or candy machines, etc. Once you have a feel for the facility, your preparation is geared to that environment. For example, I teach in a large classroom, called a teaching theater. The first thing I do is to get off of the stage to remove the height distance between the students and myself, I move around the classroom, walk into the center aisle to make a point, and have my teaching assistant run my overheads. The visual aids are coordinated before class, so that when I refer to an overhead, it appears on the screen. I have the freedom to move up and down the aisle or all the way to the back, then turn around and read the overhead as if I were one of the students. Occasionally I even sit next to some unsuspecting student and talk one-on-one. This access makes a huge difference in the attention span of the students.

Prepare any technical support staff prior to class time. A major success factor in teaching the large class is preparation time. Arrange to meet with any media support staff prior to class to discuss timing on your technical needs, such as video or audiotape replays, microphone needs, network links, etc. Your teaching assistants are instrumental in the flow of large classroom presentations; draw them into your creative planning as well as classroom clock management. Your preliminary preparation with support staff not only ensures continuity in presentation, but also encourages their own sense of ownership in your class. Personal investment is always the best for care. Plan and know your facilities.

Success in the mega-class is definitely 10% perspiration and 90% inspiration. Even though your facilities may produce lemons, make lemonade! Visiting the facility early will generate inspiration and detect any lemons that may be lurking.

4) What teaching or learning methods are best?

Remember, the best plan for this class is to plan as you would for a small graduate seminar. Begin with the content that you are interested in teaching and then follow the simple steps of instructional systems design. When you are teaching a large class, begin to step out of the traditional lecture delivery mode. Believe it or not, you *can* do group work with a large class. You *can* engage students in discussion. All the things that you can do in a small classroom, you *can* do in a large classroom with more planning.

For example, it is easier to teach sampling in a class of 500, because you can use your entire class to represent the population. Most importantly, be prepared: Only in the dictionary does success come before work. After all your preparation and planning, take the final step by actually going to class prior to the first day. Sit where your students sit, feel the room, the distance they feel. Practice your entire lecture for the first day, and enlist the assistance of a colleague to critique your first lecture. The weathered adage, "you do not get a second chance to make a first impression" is extremely accurate in the mega-class. Be comfortable with your classroom and yourself.

One approach to mega-classes is to approach learning as if you are teaching a small city, not a class. Get your creative thinking into that gear. I discovered my class had more residents than 400 cities in Texas! My introduction the first day of class begins with the proclamation that we are not a mega-class; rather, we are a small city. Our magical, imaginary city of Cleveland at Texas has a "bank" (incentives for class participation), "insurance and credit card companies" (extra credit opportunities), and jail (penalty for bringing cell phones to class, falling asleep, etc.) to give you a few ideas.

A major project in the city of Cleveland at Texas is the Cleveland Business Fair, a mock trade show. Students are divided into groups (10-12 members each), which become businesses, within the city. Each group must create an imaginary product, then build this business by applying the theories of data analysis and technology being studied. The culmination of each group's work is demonstrated with a written document of approximately 120 pages (group effort in pseudo desktop publishing) containing explanations of the theory applications used in the analysis, design, development, implementation, and evaluation of their product. These imaginary products are premiered in each group's booth presentation at the end-of-semester business fair. In the spring of 2001, 343 community businesses participated with the students as they lent first-hand real world advice to the students. This event has taken on a life all its own, and some students even take the course just to participate in the business fair.

Be creative! How does society use the principles and concepts you teach? Society will offer you many teaching methods that you can use in a large classroom.

5) What are the critical do's and don'ts about making assignments?
Do not be afraid to give written assignments in a large class. Generate an assignment list, then stop and think about your assignments. First, just to get a feel for the grading speed and time required, try the ST (sheet transfer) test. Generate a paper stack—one sheet of paper per student in your class(es). Next, calculate the time it takes for you to lift each sheet of paper from your class stack and place it on another stack. Imagine the time and broken rhythm of paper transfer if you were grading these papers. Simply the physical act of the ST test can serve as a reminder of the time required for grading written assignments in a large class. I would recommend avoiding subjective grading as often as possible.

Think of the physical time and momentum with any activity.

6) What is an effective grading system?
This is a tough one even if you are teaching a small class. Testing in large classes is a challenge; the easiest, quickest grading method is multiple-choice tests. Students' performance skills vary by style of grading opportunity, so be creative. Think outside the box. You diligently followed the elements of instructional design in planning your curriculum; do likewise in planning your grading. Review the levels of achievement you assigned to each learning objective. You created a variety of activities to teach; do likewise in grading. Three examples:

1) **Group work:** teaches group dynamics and evaluative processes. Allow students to evaluate each other. Their evaluation of peers could indicate mastery of the theories taught and generate a grade.

2) **Attendance:** gives credit in some way just for attending a mega-class!

3) **Activity days:** promotes class participation and rewards their participation.

Typically the core of the grade is still generated from multiple-choice tests; but creativity augments the more traditional approach of multiple-guess/choice tests! Include a grade-tracking sheet in each syllabus so that students are responsible for their own achievement level.

Evaluation of student performance is not limited to the multiple-choice test. Be creative.

7) What is the key to testing 1,000 students?
Do it very carefully! The answer to this question is actually a multipart discussion of preparation, formatting, test distribution, timing, and monitoring.

Preparation
One of the keys in a large class is the link between reading material and lecture notes on an exam. Check lecture flow by assigning teaching assistants to take notes and monitor the content during class. When lecturing you may say "that is a good test question," and the TAs jot it down. This allows a direct link of the lecture with the textbook and makes sure to test what is actually discussed in class. The TAs then develop exam questions from their notes to generate the rough draft of the exam. After final revisions, all TAs then check, refine, and actually take the exam, checking for typos, mathematical errors, etc. This testing process is timed to ensure that students have time to complete the exam within the allotted testing time. The major problem is not in the creation of the test for a class this large; rather it is in handling two elements: time and academic dishonesty.

Formatting
The multiple-choice test will serve you best. Generate variations on a theme with multiple-choice questions. Generate multiple forms of the exam by rearranging the answer order, the question order, printing each form on different colored paper. Be sure that your test is prepared well enough in advance so that there are no mistakes. Proofread several times. A typo discovered by one student escalates to an uproar in the mega-class. Likewise, wording that is unclear escalates to a fever pitch during the mega-class exam. Proofread several times. Proofread several times. Proofread several times.

Distribution
The logistics of getting test papers out to 1,000 people needs to be considered carefully—before the exam. Early in a mega-class, carefully

calculate the method that has been successful for other courses with colleagues. New methodology looks great on paper but does not always work under the reality and fire of 500 anxious students! For example, stopping to count out papers and hand them to each row in the traditional way uses up 5 to 6 minutes of your class time. One method that works well is to precount, package, and label materials to be distributed. Brown envelopes containing testing materials are numbered to match row number. When distribution time arrives, the teaching assistants place a brown envelope by each row. When I say "go", the end person opens the envelope and passes the papers along. Almost every row receives the papers within a few seconds of each other. For collecting papers, reverse the order. Remember that the momentum is 500 times more for 500 students than it is for one student. Momentum is the biggest thing to keep in mind as you organize a mega-class.

Timing

Classes taught on a Monday/Wednesday/Friday schedule usually allow only 50 minutes. It is difficult to give a comprehensive exam in that time frame. Choosing an alternative testing time can provide more flexibility for students and instructor. For example, I offer four testing times on a Tuesday night for one and one-half hours. All 1,000 students can choose any testing time between 5:30 p. m. and midnight. Because testing times fall on a non-class day, students are rewarded with an exchange day, a bonus day off from their Monday/ Wednesday/Friday class. Carefully and strategically selected, the idea is well received!

Academic Dishonesty

One teacher could never dream up as many ways to cheat as students in a large classroom. Perhaps my two favorites are the following. A student attempted to convince me he needed to listen to his CD player to cut out all the noise in the classroom. Upon checking his CD, no wonder he wanted to listen—he had burned the answers onto the CD in between song tracks! In another instance, the students were using sign language to signal answers to their peers! Develop a list of rules. Some suggestions to get started:

> *Rule 1:* Earphones, pagers, and cell phones must be on the desk in full view. If one of these electronic wonders rings or vibrates, answer and check-out the caller.

Rule 2: No headgear allowed during testing time.

Rule 3: Equipment such as erasers, calculators, pencils, etc. are not shared.

Rule 4: All student materials should be under the desk and out of view.

Rule 5: Questions from students are limited during the exam.

Rule 6: Proctors are planted as test-takers.

Rule 7: Visits to the bathroom are limited.

Rule 8: Watch for sign language transfer of answers!

Rule 9: Random ID checks are conducted during the test period.

In spite of all your efforts to eliminate cheating, you will probably encounter it at some point. If you discover academic dishonesty, you *must* take a stand and uphold the honor and dignity of your classroom and your university.

When planning an exam, you must think outside of the box to imagine a variety of ways to test mastery of your objectives as well as the many ways students can cheat.

8) Are classroom mechanics easy to control?
The day-to-day mechanics of managing in a large classroom can be a disaster if you fail to plan ahead. Some of the key mechanics are student identification cards, attendance, distribution of materials, extra credit, student complaints, review sessions, and final grades. The key words of warning are, "if it can go wrong, it will." The following ideas are just suggestions to springboard your own ideas.

Student Identification Cards
Expectations are low when it comes to your learning student names in the mega-class. Each student assumes he/she will be simply a number. Student names are a key teaching opportunity...do not pass it up. Make an effort to learn as many names as possible during the course of the semester. The probability of learning all 500 names is slim; however, the students are happy that you are making an effort, and that effort will not go unnoticed. Efforts to learn names will enhance the esprit de corps and the professor/student relationship. Each new res-

ident of the imaginary little city called Cleveland at Texas (where it never rains and no grouchy folks are allowed) is requested to complete an ID card in duplicate. One set remains in the office for TAs to use, and I use the other.

Be prepared: Students can also be very demanding. Occasionally, students will approach you and ask, "Do you know my name? You need to have a few pet phrases such as, "Oh, your name is student," or simply, "Gee, you've got me, I don't have a clue. Help me out." Generally if you tease the student a little bit, someone will give away the name. Everybody likes to be somebody, not just a number.

Attendance
To take or not to take, that is the question. I take it for two reasons: 1) the university encourages it, and 2) the philosophy in the McCombs School of Business is to develop good business habits. Attendance is taken via the class website. Attendance is taken 12 or 13 times a semester and ten are counted toward bonus points. The additional two or three times attendance is taken covers excused absences. The problem with attendance is a hard line that must be drawn. You cannot make an exception. The momentum of hundreds of absence excuses can snowball and become difficult to handle.

Distribution of Materials
My advice is not to hand course materials out during class. Try to create a packet which students may purchase at the beginning of the semester. Do not put materials at the entrances to be picked up as they come in or leave because that creates a bottleneck. Reminder: Distributing anything in the mega-class costs you approximately five minutes of class time.

Giving Extra Credit
Students must learn in kindergarten to ask for extra credit! It is a habit that runs deep. In the mega-class there is no traditional extra credit policy. You need to announce a no extra credit policy on day one. My lone exception is the Cleveland credit card. The Cleveland credit card is numbered to 30, each number worth a tenth of a point. When students see me outside my office and our classroom, they may come introduce themselves and relate something we have discussed in class. If they can give an application example of anything we are discussing in class, then they can earn extra credit points. Generally they receive one-half a point each time I chat with a student. The real extra

credit is the opportunity for me to know them and for them to learn about me. The Cleveland credit card helps them feel important in the mega-class.

Handling Complaints
You will get them, so be prepared! If you get two or three complaints in a small class of 30, then multiply that times 20. The old instructors' maxim is that at any given time about 2% of your class is not going to like you, and you are not going to like them. *Document everything.* Note in your syllabus that it is important for you to be able to review the information each student sends. Keep the notes and all emails. You need not alphabetize it, just keep it organized. The better prepared you are with the information, the better equipped you are to handle complaints. Try not to discuss complaints before, during, or directly after classes. Reserve that task for office hours.

Offering Review Sessions
Review sessions do not work for my course; other instructors use them very effectively. Many students do not study until the last minute thinking, "Doc will reteach the material at the review." The review then becomes a cram session. In our city of Cleveland at Texas, we hold regular discussion groups each week, led by the TAs. This discussion approach definitely works much more effectively for this course.

Calculating/Posting Grades
Know your school policy. Make sure you get a signed release from each student before posting grades. If the student declines to have his/her grade posted he/she may provide a self-addressed stamped envelope for the TAs to mail grades. Do not answer grade questions during class. Time of posting is critical. We post all the grades for each student on our secured web site, and all grades are available 24/7.

If you fail to plan, plan to fail.

9) How much personal time belongs to the students?
Office hours required by your department will form the foundation for outside class time involvement. When you are dealing with the mega-class numbers, there is a feast-or-famine situation during office hours. Office hours tend to be relatively calm except for the times directly before the tests. Also, the time before the end of the semester is hectic. You need to think ahead to limit meeting time per student to

five to ten minutes. Consider even a sign-in sheet to ensure a first come, first served policy. Word spreads that if students wait until the end of the semester, then they might not be able to talk to the professor at all. Students today have email access to professors—a real bonus. Do not publish your home phone number unless you want students to call you. We have an answering machine in the office, and the TAs usually handle calls. Strive to answer every email within 24 hours. The course webmaster has now developed a mail distribution system via our web site that distributes student email to various TAs according to their class responsibilities.

You will be invited to attend many student events, such as sorority/fraternity dinners, stage productions, recitals, and athletic events, just to name a few. Attend such events as you can because they will give you a much better perspective of your students, in a setting away from the classroom. Relating to students outside the classroom improves relationships inside the classroom. The negative side: Some students may accuse you of favoritism. But the positives far outweigh the occasional negative. After all, you are in this profession because you enjoy seeing that moment of discovery light up a student's face.

Imagine that each student wears a huge sign on his/her chest. It reads: "Please make me feel special today."

10) Do teaching assistants really help?
Teaching assistants will be your salvation in the mega-classroom setting…if you plan ahead! Treat them as your team member(s). Seek their counsel on classroom ideas. Allow each teaching assistant to feel ownership of some portion of the activities in class. Ownership breeds loyalty.

There is no "I" in TEAM.

11) Is the class web site beneficial?
One of the true joys of teaching the mega-foundations class is the interaction with students of varying disciplines and ages. Their enthusiasm for applying their ideas and stretching their imaginations to your class is invigorating. The class webmaster, a former student, summarizes the key benefits of harnessing the Internet for the mega-class.

To combat the issues of class dynamics and administration, the professor can turn to the power of the Internet, using this tool to foster open, two-way, symmetrical communication with students and leveraging it to simplify the daunting administrative tasks of managing such large numbers of people.

In this Information Age, our largest concern should not be the information...it is bountiful; rather we should be concerned about the Age of the Information. Use the networked economy and build a website.

12) Can teaching objectives and goals really be met in the mega-classroom?
The answer to this question is unequivocally YES. You will experience the agony of defeat one day and the triumph of victory the next in the mega-classroom. Ideas you have will seem perfect...until you attempt them in class. This roller coaster teaching experience can be one of the most rewarding tasks of your career. Learn from your mistakes, and remember your successes. Always be on the lookout for real world experiences to convert to classroom techniques. Never be afraid to try something different. Learn to laugh at yourself. Always revise and renew to keep your own creative energy flowing. Some days you will surely feel like the "old woman (or man) in the shoe who had so many children..." Most days, you will enjoy the thrill of watching the light of discovery flash and radiate across hundreds of eager faces. Yes, objectives and goals can be reached even in the mega-classroom.

500, That's Not a Large Class, That's a Small Town!

By teaching 1,000 students, you develop a public image. My students fondly dubbed me "The Mayor." You will rarely go anywhere in your community without running into current or former students. Your personal life is now on view. Be aware. You will teach far more by your actions out of the classroom than you realize. Many teachable moments occur outside of the classroom. Enjoy them. Cherish them. Remember them.

You mold the future, you teach.

3

Planning and Assessing Large Classes

Michael Theall
Youngstown State University

Raoul A. Arreola
University of Tennessee Health Science Center

Introduction

Picture a sea of 300 faces on the first day of a new semester. A sea of faces, all of whom you are somehow expected to teach. How can you possibly reach all of them in one short semester? How can you get to know them? And how can you possibly know if they're learning in the ways and to the depth you intend? What teaching methods should you use? What do you do if several students get up and leave in the middle of class? What do you do if nobody shows up for any of the rest of the classes?

Teaching a large class can be a daunting task. But here you are, and it's your job to somehow get the students to learn what you have to teach. This chapter is intended to assist you in this task by 1) providing a perspective on teaching a large class that makes the situation less daunting, and 2) examining methods that may be used to determine if all is going well with both your teaching and student learning.

In exploring these issues, we will summarize various teaching techniques and strategies. Our focus here is to provide information that will help you to prepare to teach a large class and determine if everything is going well. In particular we will examine the contextual environment of large classes and discuss assessment techniques that can help both teachers and students to maximize learning.

The Challenges

Whenever you are dealing with a large group of people in any forum, the laws of probability come into play. Thus, it may be nearly impossible to predict what an individual student will do on any given day, but it is relatively easy to predict what the group will do. For example:

- On any given day in your class a certain percentage of students may be absent due to illness or personal emergency. (This has nothing to do with you so don't take their absence as criticism of you or your teaching.)

- During any class period, the digestive systems of a certain percentage of students will manifest a profound biological imperative that may cause them to get up and leave right in the middle of your presentation. (This has nothing to do with you so don't take their leaving as criticism of you or your teaching.)

- On any given day, given a sufficiently large class, somebody's dog really may have eaten their homework. (Try to remain flexible.)

- A certain percentage of the students will think you can do no wrong, and a similar percentage of students will think you are a pitiful teacher and a pathetic human being. (This is just a result of the great normal curve in all things human, so don't take it personally—unless the percentage of either group rises above 10%.)

- Expect a certain small percentage of students to try to cheat on an exam. Set up testing strategies to minimize this possibility while not putting an undue burden on the rest of the students. For example, create different forms of the exam simply by scrambling the order of the questions or the position of the correct answer, or both.

- When using sophisticated high-tech electronic equipment during your class presentations, remember Murphy's Law (anything that can go wrong will go wrong). (Do not yell at the technicians. You want them as your best friends in a large classroom setting. Instead, always be prepared with an alternate low-tech method as a backup.)

Although these are a few of the more visible issues that may arise in teaching a large class, the important point here is to clarify in your mind which aspects of the teaching/learning environment you can control and which you cannot. A great deal of the fear and frustration of teaching in a large classroom environment results from the natural desire of a good teacher to control the teaching/learning environment so as to ensure a quality educational experience. The more effective teachers in all teaching/learning environments clearly differentiate between those things they can control and those things they cannot, and they prepare accordingly.

Structuring the Large Class Teaching-Learning Experience

The newest forms of delivering instruction use modern telecommunication technology to teach students at a distance and often, large numbers of students are involved. These new forms of instructional delivery pose many of the same problems as are found in teaching large classes. The parallels between the issues facing the teacher in a distance education setting and those facing the teacher in a large classroom setting are obvious, and, as is often the case, the old can inform the new, and the new can inform the old. One parallel, for example, is that teaching a course that uses interactive television may involve many students at several remote sites. Since the students may be spread over a large geographical area, certain procedural arrangements must be made in order to teach effectively in this environment. These include:

1) Ensure that all students can see and hear the teacher.

2) Ensure that the teacher can hear any student who may wish to ask a question.

3) Ensure that students know how to operate microphones or other communication devices and that guidelines or distance etiquette are established.

4) Ensure that the class is connected and disconnected at the appointed time: Careful planning is required.

5) Ensure that all slides and other graphic material are prepared prior to class time and since time is limited, the timing of slides, presentations, videotapes, etc., is carefully scheduled.

6) Ensure security before, during, and after an examination.

Because teaching a large class puts some distance between you and your students, many of the same cautions apply and you will want to be sure to do essentially the same things in support of effective instruction. The following large class list parallels the distance list, and the items are numbered correspondingly.

1) Ensure that students way up in the nosebleed section will be able to hear and see the teacher.

2) Ensure that the teacher can hear any student who may wish to ask a question.

3) Ensure that students know how to be heard and that guidelines for large-class etiquette are established.

4) Ensure that the class starts and stops on time. Careful planning will be required in order to be able to cover everything when it takes everyone so long to get in, get seated, and settle down.

5) Ensure that materials are prepared in advance and that there is time to use them effectively.

6) Ensure the security of the examinations.

But there are unique requirements in every teaching-learning situation, and teaching in a large class environment, like teaching in a distance education format, requires sophisticated skills. Just as many first-time distance education instructors try to use precisely the same techniques and procedures in teaching before the camera as they do in a standard class, many first-time teachers of large classes may try to do the same. Both situations usually lead to unsatisfactory results—both for the students and the teacher.

Unfortunately, large lecture classes are often assigned to the least experienced or most junior of the faculty. In reality, since successfully teaching a large class requires polished professional teaching skills and expertise, special care should be taken to ensure the assigned teacher meets those requirements. Again, drawing on the parallel of distance education, we see that in many institutions, teachers of distance education courses are carefully selected and, in some cases, paid an additional stipend owing to the higher level of expertise required. Just as some distance education faculty feel uncomfortable teaching to a camera in an empty classroom or studio, some faculty feel very uncomfortable facing a large group of students.

Again, interestingly, each teaching format has something to offer the other. In both cases, since it is difficult if not unlikely that the teacher will be able to get to know each student personally, a certain mind set in teaching the class is helpful. In teaching to the camera, the mind set is to put yourself in the position of tutoring a single student who is extremely shy and almost mute. This is accomplished by teaching to the camera as if it were the student and stopping frequently to ask if there are questions.

In the case of the large-class teacher, it is easy to get in the mind set of teaching to a mass of undifferentiated faces rather than teaching to particular students. One can also fall into the trap of teaching to a few particular students, thus adding a psychological distance to the physical distance already separating you from the rest of the students. For example, Parker Palmer (1998) describes a case in which his attention became so focused on three students who weren't participating that he lost sight of the rest of the class and lost their attention as well.

In both the large classroom and distance education cases, structuring your instructional presentations as if they were being delivered as a tutorial to an extremely shy and virtually mute individual serves to facilitate both teaching and learning. Note that this kind of mind set does not mean addressing only one or two students. Rather, it involves interacting with the limitations of the situation in mind. A large class is far removed from a tutorial, but attending to the notion of teaching to each student will help you to keep your instruction relevant, personal, and more effective. There are also things that you can do in advance to make large-class presentations more effective. While the general suggestions below apply to many instructional situations, the key is to incorporate them into the large-class context. For example, the strategy for preparing for a large-class presentation should include the following:

- Develop a set of learning objectives for each class period and consider how they differ from similar objectives for smaller classes and whether they are achievable given the resources, time, and limitations of the large class context.

- Prepare all slides and other graphic materials beforehand and make sure they match and support the learning objective(s) for the day. Ensure that the necessary equipment and back-up mechanisms are in place in case of technical difficulty. In a large class if your projection machinery fails, you will not be able to pass around a graphic for all to see.

- Make sure handouts for a given class period are prepared and distributed or available prior to the class. With these, students will have a better chance of coming to class prepared to learn what you are going to teach that day. This applies to most classes but with large classes, handing out materials during class takes too much time and disrupts other activities. Handouts or other supplementary materials that are available at a convenient location, purchasable at the campus bookstore, or available online, can save time and keep you and your students on task.

- Do not show anything in a slide or transparency that the students don't already have in their handout. Don't make note-taking simply a manual copying exercise, but rather construct your handouts with room for notes next to a slide miniature so students may record their thoughts, questions, and insights. Again, in large classes, if the materials are not self-contained, you will have little time or ability to make on-the-spot corrections or changes, and equally important, you will not be able to go around the room to see if students correctly incorporated the changes.

- Consider how you can incorporate technology into the process of assessment as well as the presentation. If your handouts are available online, why not include questions before class to assess understanding or prompt discussion, and why not provide space for students to note confusion or raise questions about the materials? Resolving such questions before the class means better in-class communication and less time spent making corrections in class.

Obviously there are also issues associated with performing on a stage, the logistics of setting up microphones, projectors, laser pointers, attendance sheets (if necessary), and so on. There are many publications and useful how-to manuals which discuss these and many other issues associated with teaching large classes, and we will not address them all here. Rather, the rest of this chapter focuses on addressing the following questions:

- How can we regularly obtain an accurate perspective on our own performance in teaching a large class?

- How can we regularly obtain valid and reliable indicators of our students' progress?

- What are the ways that we can efficiently gather the information to answer these questions?

Evaluating the Large Class Teaching-Learning Experience

Assumptions

In answering the questions of how we and our students are doing, let us begin with two premises:

- The responsibility for engaging a learning experience will always remain with students.

- The responsibility for creating an instructional experience that has the highest probability of inducing learning lies with the teacher.

Placing the total burden of responsibility for learning on the teacher is neither fair nor realistic. There is considerable research (for example, Keller, 1983; Perry, 1991) that emphasizes expectancy for success and acceptance of responsibility as necessary motivational precursors to the expenditure of the effort required for successful learning. Students must anticipate successful outcomes and be willing to do the work required in order to succeed. These same notions apply to teachers, who must be both confident and comfortable if they are to succeed in large classes. The particular problem here is that large classes are often viewed as difficult, no-win situations in which the best that a teacher can do is to develop and present good lectures. In other words, they present a context in which teacher expectancy for success may be lowered and anxiety increased. Interestingly, research by Marsh (1983) and Centra & Creech (1976), suggests that students are more lenient in their ratings of teachers in very small classes with fewer than 20 students and large classes with over 100 students than they are with classes of 35 to 100. This may (or may not) be the result of reduced expectations about teaching and learning in large classes. We will return to this issue later.

A Starting Point

So, where do we begin? A critical element in effective learning is understanding the realities. Phrased as questions, these are:

- What should you know or be able to do?

- What do you know, and what can you do?

- What don't you know or cannot yet do?

The field of assessment has focused specifically on such questions and provides useful guidelines. Angelo and Cross (1993) have documented a broad array of assessment techniques that allow us to investigate the success of teaching and learning with special emphasis on learning. They say:

> Through frequent observation of students in the process of learning…classroom teachers can learn much about how students learn and, more specifically, how students respond to particular teaching approaches. Classroom assessment helps individual college teachers obtain useful feedback on what, how much, and how well their students are learning…the central purpose of assessment is to empower both teachers and students to improve the quality of learning in the classroom (pp. 3-4).

But there is another set of important questions. These have to do with your performance as a teacher, and they are critical to your success in the classroom, in the profession, and in your career. You want to gather valid, reliable, and useful data about performance, and you want those data to be accurately interpreted and used. Consider the following:

- The general research on student ratings and class size (e.g., Feldman, 1984; Marsh, 1987) shows a small to moderate inverse correlation with overall or specific ratings and some studies (Theall & Franklin, 1991) have found even stronger negative relationships of class size to both ratings and achievement.

- Cashin and Perrin (1978), and Marsh (1987) have reported student prior interest as a significant correlate of ratings.

- Marsh (1987) also reported course level to be significantly corre-lated with ratings, graduate courses receiving higher average rat-ings than lower level courses.

- Required courses receive lower average ratings than do elective courses (Centra & Creech, 1976).

Large classes are most frequently service courses, that is, required, lower-level courses in subjects that students do not necessarily have an affiliation to or an interest in. The problem of size is thus com-pounded by lack of prior interest, lower course level, and required sta-tus. Even a great teacher faces a more difficult instructional task in this situation, and even this teacher may receive lower ratings than usual or lower ratings than a colleague teaching a different kind of course. This chapter does not deal with the intricacies of summative evalua-tion, but there are several useful sources that provide guidelines for the development of effective evaluation systems (for example, Arreola, 2000) and for the appropriate reporting, interpretation, and use of data (for example, Theall & Franklin, 1990). In addition to this text, there are also several useful sources of information about teach-ing improvement and the uses of evaluation data in that context (for example, Brinko & Menges, 1997; Theall & Franklin, 1991).

We must also keep in mind that available resources will affect both teaching and learning. For example, are there discussion sections or laboratories or other opportunities for students to be engaged with the content? Are there human resources (other faculty, graduate assis-tants, academic support staff, library staff) available to support the teacher and the students? Are there technological resources that allow and indeed maximize opportunities for the effective presentation of information, interactions among students and teachers, and the provi-sion of feedback? Without such resources, the teacher's task becomes more difficult. Effective and accurate evaluation requires considera-tion of these issues as well as data from a variety of sources.

Informative Evaluation/Assessment Strategies for Large Classes

Variations on minute papers and brief, end-of-class or out-of-class techniques. A popular assessment technique is the minute paper, developed by a professor at Berkeley and described by Robert Wilson (1986). The process involves asking students two questions: "What is the most significant thing you learned today?" and "What question is uppermost in your mind at the end of this class session?" Students are literally asked to respond in the last minute(s) of class, the short time frame forcing only the most salient information. This process is usable in classes of any size, but the resulting data can be quickly reviewed, and any common questions or issues can be addressed in a subsequent class.

New instructional technologies can supplement this process by allowing quicker response time. For example, a course website or conferencing system would allow a next day response as opposed to one at the next class meeting (which might be as far as a week away). Internet and email systems can also allow more student-teacher or student-student dialogue than is possible in the context of a 90-minute or three-hour class. Given the efficiencies of new technology, it might be possible to use a graduate assistant (GA) more effectively. The GA could assemble and organize the paper or electronic feedback, present a summarization to the teacher, and post an electronic response to the entire class. A major conceptual problem or misunderstanding could thus be corrected before students spend days trying to grasp new material. The GA could also respond to follow-up questions and archive or otherwise store items in a Frequently Asked Questions (FAQ) location at the course website. This compilation would allow both teacher and students to identify those concepts and issues that were most problematic, to see the responses and clarifications, and after only one semester, to have a substantial source of ready information. This source could be used by other teachers in subsequent semesters and eventually support curriculum revisions through its identification of key issues, conceptual problems, and related matters. Course or curricular revisions could be made, or special, additional resources could be assigned to help students avoid common problems.

In-class assessments as part of instructional process and activities. The time-honored method of choice for determining whether students are understanding course content is to ask direct questions. The problem in large classes is that the technique can only involve a few students during any given session... or is it really that restrictive? For example, even something as simple as asking for agreement or disagreement by vote will do three things. First, it will involve everyone. Second, it will get students into the habit of listening more closely to both the question and the answer. Third (and important from an assessment perspective), it will give the teacher a quick picture of the degree of understanding of the whole class. If the initial student response is correct and there is unanimous support, then the teacher has good reason to move on. If the reverse, then more work is clearly needed. If opinion is divided, other techniques can be used. For example, a short-term task might be for the opposing sides to take five minutes to produce three reasons supporting their positions. A short exchange will keep students engaged and with teacher follow-up, the class can explore either the right answer or the equally important conclusion that there is no right answer.

Here is a good example of the effect of content and instructional objectives on a teaching situation. Sometimes only one answer will do; for example in the medicine or engineering fields where the wrong answer can kill someone. A certain set of symptoms that can easily and disastrously be misread must be clearly identified, and a correct diagnosis must be made. There is no room for ambiguity. Students must know basic facts; must consider the symptoms; must evaluate the situation; and must make the one, correct decision, often with very little time to arrive at that decision. The teacher's objective in this case, could be that the student when presented with symptoms A though F, be able, within five minutes, to 1) correctly diagnose the patient's condition, 2) note any anomalies that would suggest complications, 3) prescribe an appropriate course of action, and 4) be aware of contraindicated procedures or medications.

This is a complex and demanding objective, but students would gain from having to defend their decisions within a limited time frame and in posing such a problem to even a large class, the teacher could judge both the accuracy and completeness of the diagnoses and the reasoning underlying them. The question becomes an assessment device that is directly connected to an important objective.

Formative Evaluation: How to Determine if Everything is Going Well

Having discussed both the realities of the environmental context of teaching in a large class, and some strategies and techniques for gathering information on the student learning process, we now move to the larger issue of determining whether all is going well in the course. Although there is abundant literature on summative evaluation of teaching, that is, evaluating teaching for the purpose of making promotion, tenure, merit pay, and other such decisions, our focus here is on formative evaluation; that is, evaluation of the teaching and learning in a large class for the purpose of providing meaningful feedback to the instructor for use in guiding instruction.

Student ratings, Small Group Instructional Diagnosis (SGID), and class documentation. Formative evaluation should be a process that provides the clearest picture of ongoing activity and outcomes. Many formative techniques are informal, and the process is amenable to literally every kind of data collection and methodology. Often, the most useful formative evaluation will combine techniques so as to include quantitative and qualitative data in forms as diverse as questionnaires, interviews, observations, and various media, particularly videotaped class sessions that can be reviewed with the teacher.

In large classes, ratings questionnaires offer particular efficiency and usefulness. Processes for collecting, analyzing, and reporting data are often in place. Large classes provide sufficiently large numbers of responses to allow techniques such as matrix sampling, where different forms of the questionnaire are circulated in order to get feedback on several different issues while still gathering the full set of responses on other issues. And with useful questionnaires and reporting mechanisms, accurate, timely, and understandable data can be returned almost immediately.

But quantitative data can be and should be supplemented by other kinds of information. A common technique that uses what we often call focus group methods was developed by Joseph Clark and Jean Bekey (1979) at the University of Washington. Small Group Instructional Diagnosis (SGID) can take as little as 30 minutes of class time in classes of 30 or less. The full process would take more time with a large class, and consultants often find it very useful to extend the discussion in order to better understand the reasoning underlying expressed opinions. The process involves breaking a class into small groups of four to eight students. Larger classes might use slightly larger groups. One person in each group is selected to be the recorder, and each group is asked to address three questions and arrive at consensus. The questions generally are 1) What do you like about the course? 2) What would you change about the course? and 3) What strategy would you suggest for change? After a short time, the whole class reconvenes and a facilitator (a trained colleague, instructional consultant, graduate assistant, or even trusted student) has each group report its responses to the questions. The facilitator then leads the group through a further effort which combines and sorts the group reports into one, final consensus response. The facilitator then reports the group and class opinions to the teacher. The responses to the three basic questions can be very illuminating, and they have the virtue of identifying critical issues that may be amenable to intervention. Equally important, because the first question asks what is going well, it's almost always possible to begin the teacher feedback session with positive information. Note too that the second question is not "What's wrong?," but rather, "What would you change?" This and the accompanying third question provide constructive criticisms rather than purely judgmental or negative opinions. We have often found that students' suggestions are aimed at improvement, and we have rarely heard simple requests for less or easier work. Teachers respond well to this kind of information and demonstrated concern for learning.

Most often, the results of the Small Group Interaction Diagnosis are shared with the class, and this has two benefits. First it demonstrates that the teacher has listened to student feedback, and second, it demonstrates a willingness to consider alternative approaches that can improve teaching and learning. Even if changes are difficult or impossible, the dialogue and explanation can often defuse problematic situations. In large classes, there is value in returning the feedback in two ways. One way is to discuss the findings with students in class. But in large classes, it is useful to use a second method, namely to use technology to present the findings prior to a class meeting. This would give students a chance to digest the report, and it would also save class time in the discussion of the findings. A private email address/listserv or a secure location on a web site could be used for this purpose, thus providing protection for teacher and students alike.

In all of these activities, it is important to remember that those asked to go public with their work should have the maximum opportunity to succeed. Asking for personally revealing information or assigning excessively difficult problems may result in students' reticence to be involved. The safety factor in group work can reduce anxieties, but the process will work best when it promotes success and positive expectations. For many reasons (for example, diversity, student involvement, fostering the social aspects of learning, exposing students to many and varied ways of thinking), group membership should be flexible. Changing the composition of groups also reduces competition or the sense that one group is superior to another.

Finally, for true triangulation, it is possible to videotape the teacher's class one or more times. This documentation will almost always support the information gathered with the questionnaire and the focus group process, but it has the added advantage of objectivity. The camera is not judgmental: It simply records what happens. While this objectivity has its place, it also has its dangers. On occasion, the teacher will be extremely self-conscious, or the tape will reveal some marginal skills or undesirable habits (for example, lack of organization or an annoying habit such as constantly clearing one's throat while lecturing). While such things can distress the teacher, these are also the kinds of things that can often be addressed in a timely and straightforward manner. Videotape can reveal things that the teacher might not accept on the basis of students' comments. And while it is less common to turn the camera on students, it can be very revealing to tape the class as well. There are two potential benefits. First, the teacher can see patterns of attention or behavior that may be informative, and second, portions of the tape can be shown to the students. In large classes, where inattention, disruption, timeliness, and attendance are often issues, the presentation of the classroom reality from the teacher's perspective can be an eye-opener for students, and it can serve the important purpose of identifying that the formative evaluation is intended to improve both teaching and learning. Students should realize that they are partners in the task, not passive recipients of information who can place the full responsibility for learning on the teacher's shoulders.

Conclusion

Many issues contribute to the concern and anxiety many first-time teachers of large classes experience. Not all teachers will be good at teaching in such an environment, just as not all teachers are effective in a small group or distance education teaching environments. Certain communication and personal interaction issues either contribute to, or inhibit, effective teaching in a large class. However, there are also useful perspectives on the forces in play in large-group settings, as well as effective techniques for dealing with these forces. Our intent in this chapter was two-fold: first, to provide a view of the large classroom environment that would help reduce some of the anxiety teachers feel. We offered a perspective on the forces you can control and those that you can't in the large classroom setting along with some suggestions on dealing with these forces personally. Second, we provided information on techniques and methods for both teaching in a large classroom setting and determining whether all was going well in terms of learning and both teacher and student satisfaction.

Although teaching a large class requires sophisticated instructional, managerial, and assessment techniques, they are no more or less challenging than teaching in any other classroom environment. However, in the large-class setting the effects of a teacher's performance can be significantly magnified either for good or ill. Thus, teaching a large class may not be for everyone. But if the teacher is conversant with the perspectives and techniques presented in this chapter and elsewhere in the book and pursues the development of his or her group process skills, the rewards of teaching in a large class can also be greatly magnified.

References

Angelo, T. A., & Cross, K. P. (1993). *Classroom assessment techniques: A handbook for college teachers* (2nd ed.). San Francisco, CA: Jossey-Bass.

Arreola, R. A. (2000). *Developing a comprehensive faculty evaluation system* (2nd ed.). Bolton, MA: Anker.

Brinko, K. T., & Menges, R. J. (1997). *Practically speaking: A source book for instructional consultants in higher education.* Stillwater, OK: New Forums.

Cashin, W. E., & Perrin, B. M. (1978). *IDEA technical report # 4: Description of IDEA standard form database.* Manhattan, KS: Center for Faculty Evaluation and Development.

Centra, J. A., & Creech, F. R. (1976). *The relationship between student, teachers, and course characteristics and student ratings of teaching effectiveness.* Project Report 76-1. Princeton, NJ: Educational Testing Service.

Clark, D. J., & Bekey, J. (1979). Use of small groups in instructional evaluation. *Insight into Teaching Excellence, 7* (1), 2-5.

Feldman, K. A. (1984). Class size and college students' evaluations of teachers and courses: A closer look. *Research in Higher Education, 21* (1), 45-116.

Feldman, K. A. (1991, April 7). *Grade inflation and student ratings: A closer look.* Paper presented at the 72nd annual meeting of the American Educational Research Association. Chicago, IL.

Keller, J. M. (1983). Motivational design of instruction. In C. M. Riegeluth (Ed.), *Instructional design theories and models: An overview of their current status.* Hillsdale, NJ: Lawrence Erlbaum.

Marsh, H. W. (1983). Multi-dimensional ratings of teaching effectiveness by students from different academic settings and their relation to student/ course/instructor characteristics. *Journal of Educational Psychology, 75,* 150-166.

Marsh, H. W. (1987). Student evaluations of university teaching: Research findings, methodological issues, and directions for future research. *International Journal of Educational Research, 11*, 253-388.

Palmer, P. J. (1998). *The courage to teach: Exploring the inner landscape of a teacher's life.* San Francisco, CA: Jossey Bass.

Perry, R. P. (1991). Perceived control in the college classroom. In J. C. Smart (Ed.), *Higher education: Handbook of theory and research (Vol. 7).* New York, NY: Agathon.

Theall, M., & Franklin, J. (Eds.). (1990). *Student ratings of instruction: Issues for improving practice.* New Directions for Teaching and Learning, No. 43. San Francisco, CA: Jossey-Bass.

Theall, M., & Franklin, J. (Eds.). (1991). *Effective practices for improving teaching.* New Directions for Teaching and Learning, No. 48. San Francisco, CA: Jossey-Bass.

Weimer, M. (Ed.). (1987). *Teaching large classes well.* New Directions for Teaching and Learning, No. 32. San Francisco, CA: Jossey-Bass.

Wilson, R. C. (1986). Improving faculty teaching: Effective use of student evaluations and consultants. *Journal of Higher Education, 57* (2), 196-211.

4

Promoting Civility in Large Classes

Mary Deane Sorcinelli

University of Massachusetts, Amherst

I have been meeting in a bimonthly, cross-disciplinary seminar with ten tenured professors who teach large, lower-division lectures in which class sizes range from 100 to 500 students. Our goal, supported by a grant from the Hewlett Foundation, is to consider how we might improve general education at the university. A key focus is to examine how inquiry-based, active and engaged learning can be infused into large lecture courses in ways that deepen students' abilities in learning. Discussions have been stimulating, exploring such teaching practices as cooperative learning, writing to learn, and classroom-based assessment. Early on in our meetings, however, a desire to share strategies for managing student behavior in the large lecture class surfaced. Promoting classroom civility became the topic of a full seminar meeting and the discussion proved so helpful that the "teaching fellows" are now planning to share their experiences with their colleagues in a campus-wide forum.

Unfortunately, the erosion of classroom decorum appears to be a shared concern among college teachers on many campuses. The last decade has seen an increasing stream of commentary and advice in higher education publications on troublesome behaviors, indecorum, incivility, and misconduct among college students, both in and outside of the classroom (Amada, 1999; Baldwin, 1997; Boice, 1996; Dannells, 1997; Downs, 1992; Kilmer, 1998; Richardson, 1999; Schneider, 1998; Trout, 1998). This chapter looks specifically at issues of civility in the large lecture classroom, where management and discipline problems seem to plague teachers the most (Carbone, 1998, 1999; Carbone & Greenberg, 1998; Sorcinelli, 1994; Weimer, 1987). It first suggests specific ways in which college teachers can promote a classroom community in which mutual respect is expected from day one. No matter how careful teachers are, however, they will still run into some disruptive behaviors in the large classroom. A few recurrent misbehaviors—and ways to work with them—will be discussed as well.

What Constitutes Incivil Behaviors in Large Classes?

Richardson (1999) suggests that classroom incivility is a "slippery concept" because teachers' and students' expectations for classroom decorum are often quite different. For example, what bothers a faculty member with an authoritarian teaching style might not bother a teacher who takes a more laissez-faire approach. In turn, some students might not be fazed by side-bar chatting while other students' learning is impeded by such distractions.

We culled and categorized the kinds of student behaviors in large classes that faculty members in our seminar perceived as most negatively affecting the teaching and learning process. While faculty tolerance stretched across a continuum, we found considerable consensus about student behaviors that faculty regarded as irritating, and the results mirrored other formal and informal surveys (Appleby, 1990; Boice, 1996; Carbone & Greenberg, 1998; Sorcinelli, 1994). Most common were behaviors such as arriving late and leaving early, coming unprepared, acting bored (loud yawns, reading the newspaper, sleeping), side-talking, using cell phones, working on assignments for other classes, causing disruption by packing books and materials before class is over, skipping classes, especially as the semester progressed, and missing deadlines. More serious problems such as cheating, notably plagiarism using the Internet, or challenging authority were much less frequently mentioned but raised considerable angst when they occurred.

Why Do Incivilities Occur?

In an online colloquy in *The Chronicle of Higher Education* (1998) on the issue of civility in the classroom, the finger of blame pointed in a myriad of directions—at students, teachers, administrators, and the larger society. Some argued that in large classes, students may be more willing to engage in rude behavior because class size renders them anonymous and detached from the teacher. Others suggested that students might see little value in large classes, especially required, general education courses. Also, students are separated from each other and teachers by many gaps (age, race, gender, sexual orientation, social class, academic preparation, learning styles, etc.) and bridging those gaps in a large setting is difficult. Some reasoned that because the current generation of students was raised on television, MTV, and video games, it no longer is able to attend to the unidirectional, largely verbal transmission of information often found in large lectures. Finally, faculty members reminded each other that issues outside of class (e.g., a roommate conflict, not getting into a preferred course) might anger and frustrate students, affecting their behavior during class.

Teachers and administrators did not escape fault. Some discussants wondered why more attention is not paid to pedagogical issues in training for an academic career, leaving PhDs without the knowledge and skills to deal with disruptive students. Others asked why teachers themselves devote little attention to learning about instructional practices and pedagogy. Still others called for teachers to examine their own behavior (e.g., over- or under-using authority, expertise, and power) when faced with inappropriate deportment. Some blamed campus administrators for catering to students rather than punishing unacceptable behavior. Even society took a hit for encouraging cultures of consumerism, entitlement, youth orientation, and confrontational oratory, all of which discourage good manners, respect, and civil behavior in the home, school, and community.

Creating a Constructive Large-Class Environment

As instructors, while we may not agree on definition, standards, and reasons for classroom incivility, we can be sure of two things. First, when confronted with behaviors that do not match our basic expectations for classroom behavior, we need to do something. The longer inappropriate behavior continues, the more acceptable it becomes and the more difficult it is to stop it. Second, it is easier to prevent disruptive behaviors than it is to deal with them after the fact. Establishing a positive climate and expectations for large-class learning, for example, can avert many problems.

This section discusses four groups of specific strategies that college teachers can use to guide their efforts in creating a constructive large-class environment: 1) define expectations for student behavior at the outset, 2) decrease anonymity by forming personal relationships with students, 3) encourage active learning, and 4) self-assess your behavior and seek feedback from students and colleagues (Sorcinelli, 1994).

Define Expectations at the Outset

The importance of defining a class at the outset cannot be overstated. The first class meeting offers an ideal opportunity both for welcoming students and for communicating expectations for classroom conventions, such as arriving, leaving, and talking in class. The challenge lies in establishing both a pleasant atmosphere and a code of conduct. One professor on my campus, a microbiologist who routinely teaches a lecture course with 500 students, starts each first class by acknowledging the worries that go with beginning a course in the sciences, by discussing the constraints and the benefits of a large class, and by encouraging students to get to know him (e.g., bringing in topical articles from the local and campus paper, stopping by his desk before or after class). At the same time, he conveys to students the notion that they have certain responsibilities. He explicitly states expectations for behavior, asserting that, especially because the class is large, inattendance, tardiness, and idle chatter can only serve to break down the respect between teacher and students. Another colleague in business law videotapes her first class meeting so that students who are still completing their schedules or waiting in line for a parking sticker will not miss the setting of both tone and conduct.

A clear, informative syllabus can reduce student confusion about appropriate behavior. Teachers should describe, in a positive manner, what they anticipate and would like to see in terms of classroom behavior. Equally important, they should outline, with candor, what they dislike. Put simply, the syllabus should indicate whatever rules are deemed necessary for the course to run smoothly. For example, a professor who teaches introductory sociology adds a classroom behavior contract to his syllabus so that everyone starts out with the same assumptions. It describes rules of classroom conduct for the student (e.g., to cease talking at the bell, to refrain from speaking to seatmates during class, to enter by the front door and sit in the designated front rows when unavoidably arriving late, or having to leave early). It also outlines responsibilities of the instructor (e.g., to be on time for class, to spend at least five minutes after class for individual questions, to put a lecture outline on the overhead daily, to never hold the class for more than 30 seconds after class ends). He explains that the rules have one goal—to make the experience of the course more rewarding and enjoyable for all—fellow students as well as the teacher.

The large-class atmosphere also can be enhanced significantly when the instructor is willing to entertain reasonable suggestions and objections. Giving students some choices for shaping classroom policies within prescribed limits is likely to be appreciated. For example, an instructor might tell students he cannot tolerate side-talking during his lectures, but can live with students drinking a Coke or munching on a candy bar. Other possibilities for choice might include whether to drop the lowest quiz score, how much work to assign over a vacation break, or how many chapters in the text to cover for a given test.

Decrease Anonymity

When a student creates a personal relationship with the teacher as well as peers, civility comes more easily. Large classes present many more challenges than do smaller, more personal classes, however, in reducing anonymity. Lowman (1995) has asserted "the easiest way to begin forming personal relationships with students is to learn their names," (p. 67). A rare teacher can memorize hundreds of names, but there are other ways to make personal contact with students. One way is to administer a background questionnaire on the first day of class. A professor in Germanic languages and literature asks students to share their hometown, what dorm they live in, why they are taking the course, whether they work and how much, and their extracurricular interests or experiences. She tabulates the data and shares it in the next class, announcing that "a fifth of our class is from the Boston area" (the Bostonians cheer), or "will the 12 students in the marching band raise their hands," etc. She uses the questionnaire throughout the term to draw on students' common and unique interests and experiences. A professor in organic chemistry asks her 100 students to fill out background information on an index card and to tape a picture to it. She goes through the cards, repeating each student's name and scanning the face that goes with it. She can identify nearly every student's name within a week. Yet another professor, in information systems, chooses both to lead a computer lab section and spot visit other sections as a way to get to know students outside of lecture and to keep a pulse on how the lectures and labs work together to integrate student learning.

While announced office hours may signal an instructor's accessibility to students, many students are reluctant to use them. A journalism professor encourages personal contact with students by coming to class early. This allows her to work the aisles, chatting informally with students and eliciting their concerns. Similarly, she stays awhile after class to allow students to follow-up with a question or idea that they might have been reticent to bring up in class. Other faculty members find it helpful to schedule their office hours right after class. In that way, students who approach them after class have a chance to accompany the teachers to their offices to continue discussion.

A teacher in classics found that her 475 mostly first-year students were so reluctant to take advantage of office hours that she set up a coffee hour in the student center, reminding students that she would be at a corner table on most mornings at 10:00 a.m. and inviting them to come for coffee and conversation. She discovered students were more likely to arrive in groups of two or three and now encourages small-group visits.

Encourage Active Learning

Studies on active learning suggest that such methods engage students with content in ways that develop positive relationships among students as well as competencies and critical thinking skills—rather than solely the acquisition of knowledge. In large classes, however, students may resist non-lecturing approaches because they are in sharp contrast to the familiar passive listening role to which they have become accustomed. Faculty may fear that the use of active learning strategies will reduce the amount of available lecture time that can be devoted to content coverage (Bonwell, 1996).

Carbone (1998) offers three useful guidelines for getting started. First, be prepared. Decide on the goal of the activity, using an overhead to spell out the assignment (oral directions can lead to confusion). Make sure the task is clear and specific. For example, "Summarize the most important points you heard in today's lecture," or "List as many (fill-in-blank) as you can in the next four minutes." Second, ensure participation by requiring that individual or group assignments are handed in. These may or may not be graded but should require students' names to encourage attendance and participation. Finally, maintain order by limiting time and group size. Most large-lecture teachers that I work with use periods of two to ten minutes for group activities, interspersed with segments of lecture. This format stimulates student thinking, discussion, and learning without requiring large blocks of time. Also, in large lecture halls, even groups of four or five students can prove unwieldy. Having students simply turn to the person next to them and pair up, or twist around to form triads helps keep noise levels down and encourages task completion.

There are a number of active learning strategies that are particularly suited to large classes (Bonwell, 1996; Carbone, 1998; Sorcinelli, 1994). Four effective and low-risk activities include:

Pause procedure. Stop the lecture every 13-18 minutes to allow students to work in pairs to compare and rework their notes for three to five minutes. Ask what questions arose from their review.

Short writes. Punctuating a lecture with short writing assignments is a powerful way to assess the degree to which students understand presented material. Twenty minutes into the lecture, questions might include, "What was the main concept presented in this portion of the lecture?" "Give an example of this principle or concept." "Explain this concept in your own words." "How does this idea relate to your own experience?" Five or ten minutes before the end of lecture, use the "one-minute paper," advocated by Angelo and Cross (1993), and simply ask, "What was the most important thing you learned in this lecture?" or "What questions remain unanswered?" Short writes can be submitted or form the basis for questions or class discussion.

Think-pair-share. About 15-20 minutes into the lecture, put a question or problem up on the overhead. Ask students to think, write, and then talk about the answer with the person next to them. (Writing and then talking about their answers can take five to ten minutes depending on the question's complexity). You may ask several pairs to share their answers with the whole class. You can also collect the writing and grade it simply: check for "okay," check-plus for "great." This technique can reveal how much students are learning from the lecture and lead to a major improvement in student understanding of fundamental concepts.

Formative quizzes. Formative—that is ungraded—quizzes can be used to efficiently determine how students comprehend material. Using the kinds of questions that might be used on your exams, place questions on the overhead, giving students appropriate time to respond. If the question entails multiple choices, students can raise their hands in agreement, as each prompt is featured. (An essay question might be broken into component parts.) This preview can help you determine student understanding and show students problem areas that warrant further study.

Examine Your Behavior and Seek Feedback from Students and Colleagues

Examine your own behavior when faced with inappropriate deportment in the large classroom. Surveys of students' pet peeves about teaching reveal that many are concerned about lecturing behaviors—including poor organization of the lectures; blocking the blackboard; talking too fast, softly, or slowly; poor use of class time (e.g., coming in late and stopping early). Other top complaints include intellectual arrogance—talking down to or showing a lack of respect for students, being unhelpful or not approachable, and employing confusing testing and grading practices (Appleby, 1990; Perlman & McCann, 1998).

Asking students for help in determining what is working and what merits some attention can be incredibly valuable in encouraging communication, establishing a responsive tone, and providing self-correcting feedback. One effective technique is to administer an informal course evaluation early in the semester (many teaching and learning centers will facilitate a midsemester feedback session with your students). Our center's staff ask students either in small groups or individually what they most like about the course and teaching of it, what they would like to see changed or improved, and what would make the course a better learning experience for them. When asked at midterm, we find that most students' responses are substantive and constructive—the technique demonstrates respect for and interest in students' voices and promises to improve their learning experience while the course is in process.

Colleagues can prove a sounding board and offer suggestions on how they approach civility issues in the classroom. For example, we facilitate a process by which early career faculty can visit large lecture classes that are taught by some of our outstanding teachers. After the observations, these senior colleagues join our junior faculty for an informal session in which we talk about what worked, raise questions about large-class problems, and brainstorm solutions. And over the last decade, our teaching and learning center has offered periodic campus-wide workshops on teaching large classes well. Again, we call on seasoned large-lecture teachers to help workshop participants to identify civility problems in large classes and to share best practices.

Some Solutions for Dealing with Misbehavior in the Large Class

Ideally, creating an atmosphere that is conducive to positive, respectful behavior should allow instructors to work smoothly with all students. However, instructors may still run into some students or classes that present problems. Beyond notes in syllabi, instructors need to take a sensible stance on student misbehavior in terms of identifying it, responding to it, and doing so reasonably and consistently. The suggestions offered below address the behaviors that faculty report as most irritating and troublesome. There are several excellent resources to consult when confronted with more serious breaches of classroom conduct; for example, cheating, physical intimidation, harassment, drug or alcohol abuse (Amada, 1999; Dannells, 1997; McKeachie, 1999; Richardson, 1999).

Talking and Inattention

- If students are chatting, make direct eye contact with them so that they know you see them. Sometimes stopping the lecture, looking directly at the students, and resuming the lecture when you have full attention is enough to resolve the problem.

- Physically move to that part of the room, again making eye contact with the students. Often stepping into student space gets the message across.

- Direct a question to the area in which the chatting students are sitting. This focuses attention to that area of the class but avoids confrontations or putting anybody on the spot.

- Call the offending student or students up after class. Students usually appreciate a private reminder rather than public embarrassment. Tell students who talk in class (or read the newspaper, etc.) that their behavior distracts you and the other students, and ask them please to refrain.

- There is peer pressure among students not to confront each other about rude behavior; it is difficult to directly enlist students to reinforce your expectations. An accounting professor uses a subtler tactic. On the first day, she reads excerpts from past student evaluations that make it clear that rude behavior, especially noise during the lecture, irritates students as much as it does the instructor and that students appreciate it when she discourages such behavior.

Arriving Late and Leaving Early

- Establish an understanding with students: You expect them to come to class on time; in return, you will start and finish as scheduled.

- Institute a starting ritual: moving to the podium, dimming the lights, playing music, raising your hand, reading a notable quotation or passage—whatever suits your teaching style.

- Require students to inform you if they need to arrive late or leave early, either verbally or in writing. Some instructors reserve a section in the front or back, near an exit, where such students can sit so that their arrival or departure causes as little disruption as possible.

- Station your TAs along the back of the classroom, and if students arrive or leave early, have them ask students if they are okay, why they are leaving, etc.

- Use the last five minutes of class in ways that circumvent the temptation for students to pack up early. A biology teacher put a multiple choice or short answer question on the overhead projector during the last few minutes of each class. The question gets at the heart of the concluding lecture or previews the next lecture and the students know that they will see some variation of this question on the exam.

- Let students know that there are costs for arriving late or missing class. Don't teach a class twice—make students responsible for getting missed assignments and material.

Inattendance

- Many instructors of large classes leave the question of attendance up to individual students. If you require attendance, be sure to have a system for reliably recording it, such as collecting homework, an in-class assignment, or a quiz at the end of class.

- A psychology professor divides the lecture hall and assigns TAs and their student discussion sections to specific areas. He asks TAs to note empty seats and to follow up on those who are excessively absent.

- A professor in accounting builds into class ten unannounced, short, extra credit writing assignments that essentially reward students for attending class. Roughly once a week, he shows a segment of video, poses an open-ended question on the overhead, etc., and asks students to respond from what they've learned in lecture and through personal experience. To ease the burden of grading, he scans the assignments, evaluates them with a check (or a zero for an absent student), and figures them toward the total grade.

- If a large percentage of students don't come to class, consider the possibility that they do not find sessions useful or that notes on the Internet or sold by companies inadvertently signal that attending class is not important. Make sure not only that the material covered in class is vital to students' mastery of the subject and their performance on tests and papers, but also that students understand the connection.

- On the day you give a test (attendance should be high), ask students to write on a piece of paper the reasons why they are not attending classes regularly.

Deadlines

- Clearly state your policy on missed exams, make-up exams, late homework, writing assignments, written university-sanctioned excuses, etc., in writing and orally at the beginning of the semester. Periodically remind students of such policies in advance of deadlines.

- Make it clear to students that there are logical consequences if they turn in assignments late. If the policy is not to accept late papers, then don't accept them except under the most extraordinary circumstances—and then in private. Always document the rationale for a change in policy should your decision be challenged by a third party.

- Regularly meet deadlines. If you say tests will be graded and returned Friday, then get them back on Friday.

Challenges to Authority

At some point in the large class, most teachers will have to face a student who is resentful, hostile, or challenging. The following are a few suggestions for gaining the cooperation of an oppositional student.

- As a rule of thumb, avoid arguments with students during class. If a student continues to press, table the discussion until later and then continue it with the student privately, in a more neutral setting. Listen carefully, openly, and calmly to the grievance. Sometimes the opportunity to ventilate and express a felt grievance may be more important to a student than is a resolution.

- When talking to a disruptive student, tell the student that you value his or her good contributions, but point out how the behavior that he or she is engaging in negatively affects you when you are teaching. Try to enlist the student's cooperation in setting ground rules for acceptable behavior.

- Don't become defensive and take a confrontation personally. Respond honestly to challenges, explaining—not defending—your instructional objectives and how assignments and exercises contribute to them. Although the purpose of class activities and lectures may be obvious to you, students often need to have these objectives made explicit.

- If the behavior is reoccurring, you may want to write a letter to the student. Describe the behavior, indicate how it disrupts you and other students, restate your expectations for behavior, and outline specific changes you would like to see. Copy the letter to the student's academic advisor or to the dean of students.

- On the rare occasion that a student is alarmingly hostile or threatening, contact the ombudsman's or the dean of student's office. Most campuses have disciplinary procedures that protect faculty as well as students.

Conclusion

For most instructors, teaching the large lecture is one of the most challenging of classroom assignments. Although we have expertise in our content areas, we often have little training for developing positive interpersonal relationships with and managing such large numbers of students. Yet we all want to create a classroom environment of mutual respect, not one rife with adversarial relationships. Paramount to establishing a positive environment in the large class and deterring disruptive behavior is to let students know from the outset what you expect of them and then to hold them to those expectations—intervening directly (e.g., talking privately, setting limits) to deal with inappropriate conduct. Perhaps most importantly, as instructors we need to consider our own behavior as well as that of our students. An honest attempt to understand how our classroom deportment might contribute to a difficult situation may help to reduce incivilities in our classrooms.

References

Amada, G. (1999). *Coping with misconduct in the college classroom: A practical model.* Asheville, NC: College Administration Publications.

Angelo, T.A., & Cross, K. P. (1993). *Classroom assessment techniques* (2nd ed.). San Francisco, CA: Jossey-Bass.

Appleby, D. C. (1990). Faculty and student perceptions of irritating behaviors in the college classroom. *Journal of Staff, Program and Organizational Development,* 8(2), 41-46.

Baldwin, R. G. (1997-98). Academic civility begins in the classroom. *Essays on teaching excellence: Toward the best in the academy, 9* (8). Athens, GA: The Professional and Organizational Development Network in Higher Education.

Boice, B. (1996). Classroom incivilities. *Research in Higher Education, 37* (4), 453-487.

Bonwell, C. C. (1996). Enhancing the lecture: Revitalizing a traditional format. In T. E. Sutherland & C. C. Bonwell (Eds.), *Using active learning in large classes: A range of options for faculty.* New Directions for Teaching and Learning, No. 67. San Francisco, CA: Jossey-Bass.

Carbone, E. (1998). *Teaching large classes: Tools and strategies.* Thousand Oaks, CA: Sage.

Carbone, E. (1999). Students behaving badly in large classes. In Richardson, S. (Ed.), *Promoting civility: A teaching challenge.* New Directions for Teaching and Learning, No. 77. San Francisco, CA: Jossey-Bass.

Carbone E., & Greenberg, J. (1998). Teaching large classes: Unpacking the problem and responding creatively. In M. Kaplan & D. Lieberman (Eds.), *To Improve the Academy: Vol. 17. Resources for faculty, instructional, and organizational development* (pp. 311-326). Stillwater, OK: New Forums Press.

Chronicle of Higher Education. (1998). *Is rudeness on the rise?* Online discussion, 3/23/98. www.chronicle.com/colloquy/98/rude/01.html

Dannells, M. (1997). *From discipline to development: Rethinking student conduct in higher education.* Washington DC: Office of Educational Research and Improvement. (ASHE–ERIC Higher Education Report, Vol. 25, No. 2).

Downs, J. R. (1992). Dealing with hostile and oppositional students. *College Teaching, 40* (3), 106-08.

Kilmer, P. (1998). When a few disruptive students challenge an instructor's plan. *Journalism & Mass Communication Educator, 53* (2), 81-84.

Lowman, J. (1995). *Mastering the techniques of teaching* (2nd ed.). San Francisco, CA: Jossey-Bass.

McKeachie, W. J. (1999). *Teaching tips: A guide for the beginning college teacher* (10th ed.). Lexington, MA: D.C. Heath.

Perlman, B., & McCann, L. I. (1998). Students' pet peeves about teaching. *Teaching of Psychology, 25,* 201-02.

Richardson, S. (Ed.). (1999). *Promoting civility: A teaching challenge.* New Directions for Teaching and Learning, No. 77. San Francisco, CA: Jossey-Bass.

Schneider, A. (1998, March 27). Insubordination and intimidation signal the end of decorum in many classrooms. *Chronicle of Higher Education,* pp. A12-A14.

Sorcinelli, M. D. (1994). Dealing with troublesome behaviors in the classroom. In Prichard, K. W. and R. M. Sawyer (Eds.), *Handbook of college teaching: Theory and applications.* Westport, CT: Greenwood Press.

Trout, P. (1998, July 24). Incivility in the classroom breeds 'education lite'. *Chronicle of Higher Education,* p. A40.

Weimer, M. J. (Ed.). (1987). *Teaching large classes well.* New Directions for Teaching and Learning, No. 32. San Francisco, CA: Jossey-Bass.

5

Engaging Students Actively in Large Lecture Settings

Peter J. Frederick
Wabash College

My friend, Linc Fisch, as creative and wise a person about learning and teaching as I know, once faced the prospect of teaching a college algebra course in a fixed-seating lecture hall of nearly 200 students. Linc resolved to make the course personal and individualized, and to get to know each student by name. He refused to teach from a podium but worked the room with a battery-operated microphone. He asked student spotters to observe and identify for him common difficulties among their classmates. He gave frequent quizzes for students to get feedback on their learning and added a weekly clinic session where students could go to the board and work the problems themselves. All of these were ways of personalizing a large lecture class.

As Linc Fisch's creative efforts suggest, we need not be discouraged by large enrollments in huge auditorium fixed-seat classrooms: We can still use active learning approaches and enhance student learning. This chapter will describe four specific interactive learning and teaching strategies that can be used in large lecture halls: 1) associational brainstorming, 2) evocative visuals and textual passages, 3) debates, and 4) role-playing. The last two strategies, in fact, take advantage of and use the physical features of rows, aisles, and blocks of fixed seats so typical of large lecture halls. Each of the approaches in this chapter is easily integrated with mini-lectures (5–20 minutes). Each is structured to help students practice critical thinking skills of analysis, synthesis, and problem solving, and to develop interpersonal skills such as cooperation, conflict resolution, and empathy. Each strategy involves students in collaborative work and gives students maximum opportunities to talk so that they develop habits of expressing themselves even in large classes. And each strategy engages students both emotionally and cognitively, helping them to become more responsible for their own learning and that of others.

Associational Brainstorming

Brainstorming is ideal for beginning a course or a new unit or for introducing a complex, important concept (for example, romanticism, imperialism, modernization, liberalism, evolution, or uncertainty). Invite the students to call out (or put on cards turned into the front to be recorded) everything they associate with the word or concept. Fill the blackboard or, more likely in large halls, a blank overhead transparency or computer projection screen with the suggestions from students. This is a particularly good technique to use on the first day of a course in order to get a sense of the students' prior experience, attitudes, and knowledge about the content of the course. The result is a kind of pre-test, providing the teacher with a profile of the class. Put the title of the course on the board, transparency, or screen (e.g., General Biology) and ask students to say everything they can think of about that title. Free association; anything goes.

The basic rule of brainstorming is to acknowledge and record every student idea without comment, challenge, or judgment, lest we embarrass or otherwise discourage them from talking in class. The teacher can either record student offerings randomly as they are made or arrange them in categories. Make sure to explain a rationale for the groupings, or, preferably, invite students to determine and name the categories. Whichever approach is used (random or clustering), once a transparency or two have been filled, invite students to analyze the list of offerings, suggesting appropriate categories, themes, patterns, and issues. This exercise, early in the course or a new unit, gives students practice in learning how to classify complex bodies of knowledge and to identify possibly key, overarching themes of a course.

In an introductory psychology course, one can imagine such a brainstorming exercise eliciting categories that describe the essential divisions of the discipline. When I split the two words, "American" and "History," brainstorming each one separately in my survey course on the first day, I regularly get from students the major categories of analysis as well as crucial concepts, themes, and a sense of what they think history is. The mini-lecture that follows picks up on and uses their words, phrases, and comments, thus honoring their prior experience and current attitudes and connecting them more closely to the flow and design of the course.

In brainstorming, pay attention to both cognitive and affective dimensions of learning. After attending a workshop I had led a few years ago, a chemistry professor reported to me that he had used brainstorming on the first day of class, writing "General Chemistry" on the board and inviting words and comments. "Nothing!," he said. "Only silence." He said it again: "Chemistry — what are your thoughts?" Silence. He was ready to kill me. Then he had the intuitive good sense to change the question: "Emotions about Chemistry?" A flood of words, images, and feelings came from the students; he could not, he said, record them fast enough. Had he not let students give voice to these emotions, they were likely to impede learning. Brainstorming is a way of acknowledging students holistically, thus aiding their sense of ownership and motivation.

A brainstorming variation, what I call an interactive lecture, invites students to reflect on the text, novel, laboratory, problem set, artistic stimulation or field trip they had just read or experienced prior to class. Ask them to call out (or record) the concrete visual images that stand out for them from that prior experience. Typically, I would ask them to "close your eyes and visualize a specific scene, or moment that had emotional or intellectual power for you, and that seemed to have enormous importance." For a visual generation, this makes vividly concrete a set of recollections from the book, art object, experiment or problems, and a rich, specific visual backdrop to the discussion, mini-lecture, or small group activity that follows.

As a whole class, or in pairs or small groups where they are sitting, students are invited to analyze the list of visual recollections and identify themes, categories, connections, and patterns. They then note what was missing from the list, or which item they thought was most important. The discussion that followed would then involve appropriate criteria for judgment and value. What makes it most important? That exploration gives students practice in the highest order of thinking: valuing skills.

Evocative Visuals and Textual Passages

Large-lecture settings can be used to help students learn and practice the under-used skill of close reading of texts, written, visual, and quantitative. Using either PowerPoint, traditional slides, or overhead transparencies, put an emotionally evocative painting or photograph (or a video clip) in front of the class, or a powerful text passage, or even a quantitative chart or graph. In each case, select evocative items that will engage students both emotionally and cognitively, passages, visuals, and charts that are likely to elicit multiple interpretations. This will push students to move beyond dualistic modes of thinking to confront and understand the complexity involved in analyzing important, well-chosen text passages, visual images, and quantitative representations of reality.

It is often necessary and wise for the professor to model how he or she would interpret a written, visual, or quantitative text. Sometimes I work through an example first in a mini-lecture. I prefer, however, first to immerse students in the experience themselves. Put the image or words in front of the class, no matter how large, and ask students to begin by brainstorming their analysis. I ask essentially two questions, in this order: first, "What do you see?" or "What's going on here?" and second, "What does it mean to you?" or "What do you think it means?" Record all suggested responses to the second questions and then discuss them. In this way, students immediately practice the skill of close reading and discover that there are many different ways of interpreting the same bit of knowledge, a discovery less likely when professors do most of the interpreting themselves.

In my history courses, I regularly use transparencies to focus a large class in a fixed-seat, sloped lecture hall to engage my students in the interpretation and analysis of primary sources of various kinds. They get to work with bar graphs, paintings, household inventories, artifacts, census data, ship manifests of the sex, age, occupation and homes of passengers, military muster rolls, maps, video clips, personal letters, diary entries, fictional passages, public documents, treaties, and many other sources. Not all students talk, to be sure, unless I ask them to take five minutes and talk about a source in pairs or trios first before inviting the whole class to comment on the item before them. Invariably, numerous differing interpretations emerge. It is obviously crucial to the use of evocative images and texts that there be a common visual stimulus that the entire class focuses on together. It should also be obvious that I have chosen to use this class time for helping students learn the important skills of doing history rather than covering content.

Students with a dualistic view of knowledge as right or wrong and true or false will need, as William Perry (1970) has suggested, support for their discomfort with this messy investigation of what is right and true. Acknowledging that discomfort, even as they are challenged to consider the complexity of knowledge and make decisions about which interpretation(s) they think makes the most sense for them, is important to help the students' learning. By providing both support and challenge, and by honoring the students' personal connection with the learning involved, Perry suggests, as do Mary Belenky and others (1986) in *Women's Ways of Knowing*, is how to move students past dualism to higher levels of complex, connected, and constructed forms of knowing.

Debates

Debates in class are a good way to challenge students to move past their dualism. Debates are also a creative way of taking advantage of the central or even multiple aisles in large lecture halls. Imagine, for example, the following debate topics, which would be preceded by the context-setting and motivational stimulus of a mini-lecture, video, or reading: Burke or Paine on the French Revolution? Karl Marx or Adam Smith on the industrial revolution? Evolution or creationism? Should Nora have left or stayed at the end of *The Doll's House*? Interventionism or isolationism (in any number of foreign policy situations)? Pro-life or pro-choice? W. E. B. Du Bois or Booker T. Washington on the best strategy for African-Americans in 1900? Wave or particle? Mars or Venus? Israelis or Palestinians in Jerusalem? Etcetera.

The professor might alert students ahead of time to come to class prepared to sit on the side of the hall marked by signs which represents their choice on a controversial issue, thus literally putting their bodies behind their convictions. Or, they could be asked to argue the side of an issue assigned to the half of the hall where they happen to be sitting on a given day. Although neither one of two opposing sides of an issue contains the whole truth, it is pedagogically energizing and good practice in forming arguments for students to be compelled to choose and defend one side of a dichotomous question. For example, once students have positioned themselves in the hall, the teacher would ask for, say, "five statements on the hawk side of United States involvement in Vietnam, after which we will hear five statements from the dove side." The process can be repeated, with rebuttals, before concluding by asking for two or three volunteers to make final summary arguments on behalf of their side.

Most questions, however, do not divide into halves, and our good students would never settle for forced dichotomous choices. Fortunately, our large lecture halls often have at least two aisles, thus dividing the hall into thirds or larger sections. This permits the possibility of a third position: those who refuse to choose one side or the other, for whatever reason, sit in the middle. Then they are asked to justify their choice. When I have done a Burke-Paine debate with some 200 students, invariably both sides end up not only disagreeing and rebutting each other, but rather, with special vehemence, attacking those sitting in the middle. Thus, students learn how difficult it is to try to resolve hotly contested, emotional issues or to remain neutral during revolutionary times.

A valuable critical thinking, skill-building variation of the debate is to take advantage of the way aisles divide a lecture hall into thirds. There are often three (at least) different ways of solving a problem in mathematics, or of explaining the outcome of an experiment in chemistry, or of interpreting a passage in a women's literature course or the data in microeconomics, or of explaining a natural phenomenon in physics or inter-group interactions in sociology. There may be (at least) three ways of resolving the decision presented by a case study in social work or public administration. Once presented with the interpretive or explanatory problem, have the students in the three sections of the hall talk to each other in pairs or trios and then invite volunteers to describe their particular explanation of the phenomenon, problem, or passage. Assuming that they will present at least three valid explanations, students would again be exposed to—indeed would themselves come up with—multiple ways of arriving at truth and practice the oral expression of their skills.

Role-Playing

Another way of taking advantage of lecture auditoriums divided into three or more sections is to assign the students sitting in the defined sections with a role in order to participate in an interactive lecture. As you set the stage, ask students to focus on and listen for information about particular roles according to the section where they are sitting. Examples include three different characters in a piece of literature or case study, or three different social class or ethnic groups in an anthropology, history, or sociology course, or even three different enzymes in a biochemistry course. At a certain point during the class period, ask the students to describe and portray the likely behavior of their assigned character, group, or enzyme, or to react in their role to a set of suggested stimuli or provocations.

In the first half of my American history survey course, I connect three sections of our lecture hall to John Adams' observation that the American people were divided into one-third patriots, one-third loyalists, and one-third indifferent during the course of events leading up to the outbreak of the American Revolution. After a mini-lecture providing the context and pattern of action and response among colonists, loyalists, and the British, I present an action by one side and ask the others what they would do or how they would argue in response? Those students' suggested action leads to asking the two other groups what they would then do. And so on. Thus, the lecture proceeds with students playing an active role in it. They listen more carefully because they have a specific purpose and accountable contribution to make.

For those teachers willing to risk losing a little bit of control over their large class in huge auditoriums, there are packaged simulations, games, and role-playing exercises that simulate the messiness of human relations, nature, and history. The packaged ones are not designed for large lecture settings, so I prefer to create my own. Let me explain one, a continuation of the American Revolution, and encourage readers to adapt it to their own context, courses, and learning goals.

After defeating the British, the Americans faced the challenging responsibility of how to rule themselves—and who should rule. I have created a town meeting in Massachusetts (based on the real one) to decide on policy instructions for representatives to a state constitutional convention. As students walk into class, I randomly hand out little slips of paper with well-defined roles for several groups to each student. (In a larger auditorium, TAs could help expedite the process.) The groups include landed patriots, Tory loyalists, lawyers, ministers and other professionals, urban artisans and merchants, freed and enslaved blacks, women (rich and poor), Iroquois, Cherokee, and other eastern Indian groups, and riff-raff (landless, jobless whites who had fought in the revolutionary war and had not been paid or given land as promised). I bring signs for each group and give them 15-20 minutes to meet in their groups to decide on three to five specific recommendations on a list of pertinent issues. I suggest they might want to consider likely allies and opponents and try to form coalitions.

Then we hold the town meeting. I am moderator, and ask groups to report in order of their status in 1779. Certain groups I never call on (blacks, women, Indians, and riff-raff), which creates considerable frustration, for they have dutifully prepared policy recommendations and feel marginalized, as would have been the historical case. More than likely, the riff-raff will act inappropriately, and a certain degree of disorder erupts in the room, requiring a strong gavel by the moderator. In the debriefing that must follow any role-playing exercise, students will realize that such disorder was in fact historically true and was one reason for the move toward a stronger national government embodied in the forming of the U.S. Constitution. Many other historical lessons are also identified in the debriefing, lessons more easily remembered because of the students' emotional involvement in the role-play.

Conclusion

Each of these four teaching-learning approaches is intended to show that large classes in huge, impersonal lecture halls need not be a barrier to the kind of interactive, investigative, intellectually, and emotionally engaged classroom experiences that enhance learning that lasts. Basic to each strategy is the assumption that students learn best when they are able to connect their lives, issues, and prior experiences with the core concepts and learning constructs of the course. As Lee Shulman (1999) has written, "We now understand that. . . . to prompt learning, you've got to begin with the process of going from inside out. The first influence on new learning is not what teachers do pedagogically but the learning that's already inside the learner."

The pedagogy of this chapter is based on Shulman's crucial insight about learning. Each strategy seeks to help students make this inside/outside connection. Brainstorming involves ideas and anxieties already inside the heads (and hearts) of students. So also does connecting the outside stimulus of an evocative visual or textual passage with the inside of a student's active response to and interpretation of it. And finally, debates and role-playing both depend on the relationship between the arguments and emotional experiences of the exchange and the cognitive interpretations and meaning-making that follows during debriefing. These methods of engaged, deep learning, usually thought to be possible only in tutorial or small classes can occur even in large lecture settings.

References

Belenky, M. F., Clinchy, B. M., Goldberger, N. R., & Tarule, J. M. (1986). *Women's ways of knowing: The development of self, voice, and mind.* New York, NY: Basic Books.

Fisch, L. (1996). *The chalk dust collection.* Stillwater, OK: New Forums Press.

Frederick, P. (1986, Spring). The lively lecture: Eight variations. *College Teaching,* 43-50.

Frederick, P. (1987, Winter). Student involvement: Active learning in large classes. In M. G. Weimer (Ed.), *Teaching large classes well.* New Directions for Teaching and Learning, No. 32, pp. 45–56.

Perry, W. (1970). *Forms of intellectual and ethical development in the college years: A scheme.* New York, NY: Holt, Rinehart, and Winston.

Shulman, L. (1999, July/August). Taking learning seriously. *Change,* 11-17.

6

Team Learning in Large Classes

Larry K. Michaelsen
University of Oklahoma

Some 20 years ago, I faced a challenge that had a profound impact on my thinking about teaching. The challenge occurred when, because of enrollment pressures, I was forced to triple the size of my primary course from 40 to 120 students. Based on my experience in smaller classes, I was convinced that group activities and assignments were effective for actively engaging students in learning and applying concepts. As a result, I rejected the advice of my colleagues who recommended making the class lecture-based. Instead, I devised an approach that I now call team learning that is based on using the vast majority of class time for group work.

By the middle of the first semester, it was apparent that the approach was working. In fact, it accomplished two things that I hadn't even anticipated. First, the students themselves perceived the large class setting as being far more beneficial than harmful (see Table 6.1). Second, the approach created several conditions that would enhance learning in any setting.

This chapter has four objectives: 1) to highlight the social and psychological conditions that, in most cases, have a very negative impact on the learning climate in large classes; 2) to discuss why and how team learning offsets and, in some cases, can even reverse the potential negative impact; 3) to highlight a few important keys to implementing team learning that are uniquely important in large classes; and 4) to provide concrete examples that illustrate both why the adjustments are important and how they can be made.

Problems with Large Classes

Large classes typically create two conditions that foster negative student attitudes and inhibit learning: student anonymity and passivity.

Table 6.1 *Can Large Classes Be an Asset?*

Students in five classes (n = 605) in which team learning was used were asked the following question: Which of the following most accurately describes the impact of the large size of the class on what you gained from taking the course?

They answered as follows:

1) It helped more than it hurt.	49%
2) It both helped and hurt (about equal).	18%
3) It didn't make much difference.	24%
4) It hurt more than it helped.	7%
5) It hurt a great deal.	2%

In small classes, instructors generally know the majority of their students by name, and class members regularly interact with the instructor and with each other. But as classes become larger, individual students are lost in a sea of faces, and a smaller and smaller proportion of class members are able to engage in discussions with either the instructor or each other.

Because of the virtual absence of social interaction, students' only active involvement in large classes is limited to their engagement with the material being taught. As a result, most instructors attempt to deal with the problems of large classes by changing their behavior in ways that help keep students' attention focused on the material (e.g., more exciting presentations, increased use of videos and demonstrations, etc.). Unfortunately, few instructors have the creativity and energy required to keep students' attention on the content for any extended period of time. Further, even if the instructor requires (and monitors) attendance to ensure that students are at least exposed to the presentations, he or she has no way to hold students accountable for actively engaging with the material either before or during the class.

By contrast, team learning uses in-class, content-focused group work to change the social fabric of the learning environment. Because most of the class time is used for group work, the interaction patterns resemble a small class even though there may be several hundred students in the same room. Students 1) have many opportunities to interact with each other and the instructor, 2) are explicitly accountable for being prepared for and attending class, and 3) are motivated to do their part in completing the group assignments. In fact, by ensuring that a large number of students are prepared for and attending class, team learning actually turns some of the potentially negative characteristics of large classes into assets.

The Team Learning Approach

The primary features of team learning (Michaelsen & Black, 1994) include 1) permanent and purposefully heterogeneous learning groups; 2) grading based on a combination of individual performance, team performance, and peer evaluation; 3) devoting the vast majority of the class time to small-group activities (necessitating a shift in the role of the instructor from dispenser of information to manager of a learning process) and; 4) a six-step instructional activity sequence, repeated several times per term (see Figure 6.1), that makes it possible to focus the vast majority of class time on helping students develop the ability to use concepts as opposed to simply learning about them (i.e., develop higher level cognitive skills [Bloom, 1956]).

Figure 6.1 *Team Learning Instructional Activity Sequence*

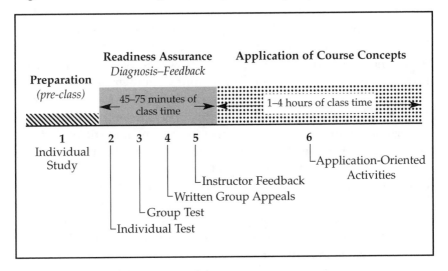

The Readiness Assurance Process

The heart of the team learning model is a six-step instructional activity sequence that is repeated several times per term (see Figure 6.1).

Probably the most unique feature of this sequence is that there are no formal presentations by the instructor until students have studied the material and taken a Readiness Assurance Test (RAT) first as individuals and then as groups—steps two through five in the sequence.

The RATs, each of which takes approximately 1 to $1^1/4$ hours to complete (thus consuming approximately 20% of the class time devoted to each major unit of instruction), enable instructors to accomplish three extremely important things. In large and small classes alike, the Readiness Assurance Process ensures that the vast majority of students will 1) attend class, 2) be individually prepared for the in-class teamwork, and, most importantly for large classes, 3) learn to work effectively with little or no assistance from the instructor.

Two principal factors contribute to the success of RATs. First, they create opportunities and incentives for students to accept responsibility for their own learning instead of creating a dependency on the instructor. Students who complete their assigned homework are rewarded by higher scores on the individual tests and by contributions to the success of their group. Second, if need be, students are exposed to and receive feedback on their understanding of the key concepts at least six different times and in very different ways (see Figure 6.1). In most instances, the students are initially exposed to concepts through assigned readings. The additional exposure during the individual test helps reinforce their memory of what they learned during their individual study (Nungester & Duchastel, 1982). During the group tests, students receive oral input from their peers that often broadens their understanding, and they also benefit from acting in a teaching role (Bargh & Schul, 1980; Slavin & Karweit, 1981). During the appeals, students engage in a focused restudy of particularly troublesome concepts. This process is followed by oral input from the instructor that is specifically aimed at resolving any remaining misunderstandings unearthed by the three previous steps in the process. Subsequently, students are exposed to the concepts again as they try to use them while working on application-oriented activities and exams.

RATs are such an efficient way to expose students to conceptual material that the majority of class time can be spent on group activities and assignments that enable students to see the relevance of the course content. In fact, with team learning, instead of simply covering content, as much as 80% of class time can be devoted to solving problems and/or completing assignments that require students to either apply specific concepts or think through how several concepts relate to each other in meaningful ways (Michaelsen, Black, & Fink, 1996; Michaelsen, Fink, & Knight, 1997).

Team Learning in Large Classes

Based on 20 years experience and working with 1,400 learning groups in a wide range of teaching situations, I am firmly convinced that very few of the requirements for successfully implementing team learning are measurably affected by the size of the class. In fact, the most significant effect of class size is that the instructor's physical presence in smaller classes often masks the negative impact of what is actually ineffective instructional practice. Thus, although some of the lessons we learned during our first few semesters were a bit painful, the large-class setting actually helped refine our understanding of the factors that impact the development of effective learning teams. With over 100 students, several sub-optimal procedures and marginally effective assignments that had worked pretty well in smaller classes created a level of discontent that was impossible to ignore.

Over time, however, I have come to understand two essential keys to successfully using team learning in large classes and two other factors that, if well managed, will measurably facilitate the implementation process. The two essential implementation keys are: 1) adapting to the physical environment (space, noise, etc.), and 2) creating procedures and props to handle the mechanics of running the class (handing out and collecting materials, pacing the groups, providing feedback, etc.). The two facilitating factors are scheduling the classes in longer class periods and getting to know students by name.

Implementation Key 1: Adapting to the Physical Environment

In most cases, classrooms that are large enough to accommodate large classes have fixed, amphitheater-style seating. As a result, adapting to the physical environment generally involves four things. These are 1) providing groups with a space that becomes their home, 2) ensuring that group members are able and willing to arrange themselves so that members have eye contact with each other as they work, 3) providing access to the group space for both students and the instructor, and 4) maintaining control over the noise level during class discussions.

Providing group space. In large-class settings, providing a permanent space for each team is important for three reasons: One is that having students know where they belong helps maintain a semblance of order in what otherwise seems like a chaotic situation relative to students' experience in traditional classes. The second reason for providing a permanent space for the groups is that having a home makes it easier for groups to develop an identity. Members know where they belong and other groups implicitly associate each of the groups with the space they occupy. Finally, having a permanent home provides groups with time to develop procedures for overcoming the limitations (e.g., seating configuration, difficulty seeing and/or hearing, etc.) inherent in the space to which they have been assigned.

Over the years, I have seen colleagues use a wide variety of methods for establishing a home for their newly-formed groups. The most common is creating and posting a seating map or chart showing the groups' assigned locations. Another effective method simply involves announcing that group members should congregate around pre-placed and numbered markers (I've seen everything from cloth flags to helium-filled balloons to large styrofoam cups that were suspended from the ceiling).

Ensuring eye contact. Being able to have eye contact during the group work is critical to the development of effective self-managed teams. In fact, the single most reliable way to monitor the progress in team development is to observe the degree to which members voluntarily position themselves so that they have eye contact with each other. If members fail to notice that a team member is sitting outside the group, they are implicitly sending the message that input from that member is not needed and/or wanted. Further, if the instructor fails to call their attention to the potential problem, then it often becomes a self-fulfilling prophesy that produces resentment from both those who are being ignored and those who are inadvertently doing the ignoring.

Unfortunately, this is not an isolated problem. Students who are naturally outgoing tend to naturally take charge and fail to realize that they are making it difficult for quieter members to provide input to the group. As a result, it is important to help each group develop full participation. This can be done by giving them a space that encourages broad-based member contribution (i.e., as near as possible to having a small round table for the group to work around). Even in undesirable physical settings such as rows in an amphitheater-type classrooms, this can be done by making seat assignments such that members on one row turn around and face the rest of their team seated behind them. Although not ideal, this works fine enough if the group assignments are well-designed.

Providing access. Having access to the teams is important for both the instructor and the students. Access allows the instructor to listen in on team discussions so that he or she has a sense of when the teams need input and what kind to give them. The teams need access so that they can retrieve and hand in the materials that are related to the team assignments.

In many cases, seats are set far enough apart to provide access as the groups work. If not, then I recommend leaving vacant rows and/or seats between groups. With neither built-in access nor the possibility of vacant rows, the best bet is to make students aware of the situation and give the groups some class time to work with each other to solve the problem.

Controlling noise. Surprisingly, a high level of noise can be either good or bad. When students are working on in-class team assignments, a high level of noise is actually helpful. The sound of other groups is a reminder of the importance of staying on task because students know that they will soon be held accountable for having accomplished something. In addition, noise promotes team development because it forces members to literally act like a team (i.e., get physically close together and listen attentively). On the other hand, when a teacher wants total class discussions, even a low level of background noise can be very disruptive. If students can't hear, they can't learn. Thus, to be effective in large classes, instructors must develop ways to move students from a "noise is necessary" mode into a "now it's time to listen" mode.

The key to managing the noise level in large classes is training students to move out of the team discussion mode to a class discussion mode. This generally involves two steps. First, the instructor has to provide a signal (holding up a hand and having class members do the same, whistling, dimming the lights, etc.) to alert students to wind down their team discussions. Second, no matter how long it takes, the instructor must wait until students are quiet before starting to talk. Further, in some large class settings (e.g., large auditoriums) the instructor may need to restate some of the class members' comments and/or use portable microphones that can be passed from team to team.

Implementation Key 2: Managing Classroom Mechanics

Implementing team learning in large classes requires effectively handling four mechanical aspects of running a class. These are distributing and collecting materials, pacing group work, and providing time-ly feedback both on the RATs and on application-focused assignments and exams.

Distributing and collecting materials. Even in very large, lecture-oriented classes, handing out and collecting materials is seldom a problem because the need so seldom arises. In most large classes, the only times that materials are even handed out are on the two or three days on which the instructor gives mid-term and final exams. With team learning, however, each of the RATs and most other class activities require handing out materials and collecting students' work. In smaller classes, the instructor can simply hand out the materials with no noticeable loss of class time. In large classes, however, the same procedure can consume significant amounts of class time and remind students of the negative aspects of being in a large class.

A simple but effective way to solve this problem is to use team folders. Although this requires spending a few minutes before class to put a set of materials in each of the team folders, the payoff is well worth the effort. Except in really big classes (200+), you can hand out the folders to the teams in a few seconds and the teams will be distributing the materials to their members all at the same time. If needed, you can further reduce the class time needed for handling materials by training students to pick up their team folders before class. Then, passing out materials amounts to simply announcing something like, "Would you please pass out the materials in folder B." (Note: In some instances, you might need to use two or more folders on the same day for an activity that uses a sequenced set of materials and/or instructions). In very large classes (200+), you can set up routine procedures for a representative of each group to be the runner for the group folders.

The folders also help with collecting materials from the teams. For example, in the Readiness Assessment Process, I need to collect the individual tests, the group tests, and the appeals from the teams. Sometimes in the application exercises I need to collect materials produced by the groups from each team.

Pacing the group work. Pacing student work is one of the most difficult challenges of any active-learning approach. Team learning partially solves one aspect of the problem but creates another. The learning teams reduce the negative impact of individual variations in students' ability and/or levels of preparation. Although compensating for individual differences does require some class time, the net loss is somewhat offset because both slower and faster students benefit from better-prepared students tutoring their peers (which they are more than willing to do). With team learning, however, the new challenge is finding ways to adjust to the normal variation between teams in their pace of work. And the bigger the class, the bigger the challenge.

A number of strategies can help with the task of proper pacing, all of which are dependent on giving students deadlines for completing their work that are clear and specific but still flexible. The single most useful strategy is starting with a deadline that you think is slightly less than the groups will need, listening-in on the teams (so you can assess how they are progressing) and adjusting on the fly. Another useful strategy involves using the pace of the faster groups to create a deadline for the slower groups by using a five (or some other)-minute rule. For example, I use a five-minute rule that covers both the individual and team RATs. I announce that, "You can start the team test as soon as you have turned in your folder containing the individual answer sheets and, when ___ teams (approximately a third of the teams) have completed their test, the remaining teams have five minutes to finish." Finally, whenever the opportunity arises, I schedule the team assignments at either the beginning of class (to enable slower teams the opportunity to get a head start if they so choose) or at the very end (so that faster teams can leave when they finish their work).

Providing feedback on individual and team work. A crucial key to using team learning effectively in large classes is to provide content-related feedback that is immediate, frequent, and discriminatory, in that it enables learners to clearly distinguish between good and bad choices (Michaelsen, Black, & Fink, 1996; Michaelsen, Fink, & Knight, 1997). This kind of feedback is essential for both learning and team development. Feedback aids learning and retention by both reinforcing concepts that students have mastered and providing input to correct student misunderstandings. In addition, timely feedback on individual and team performance provides both motivation to do well and data that enable team members to learn how to work together effectively.

The RATs offer an ongoing opportunity for immediate and discriminatory feedback in a way that enables cross-team comparisons. The easiest way to provide immediate feedback on the RATs is to use multiple-choice questions with answer sheets that can be scored in class with a portable test-scoring machine. Even if there are several hundred students in the class, instructors can provide timely feedback on the individual tests by scoring them during the team test and immediate feedback on the team tests by having a team representative run their own answer sheet through the test scorer. Providing cross-team comparisons is as simple as recording the team scores on an overhead transparency or on the blackboard. My observation is that this kind of feedback on the RATs has a very powerful and positive effect on the development of the learning teams.

Providing feedback on application-focused assignments and exams. Providing immediate and discriminatory feedback on application-focused assignments in a way that enables cross-team comparisons is a more challenging—but doable—task. Because of the number of teams involved, in large classes the key is creating efficient ways for teams to present the results of their work to each other. One part of the solution to this challenge is for the teacher to find some way for the group to report the results of their work in a simple form, even though the decisions usually involve complex concepts and information. Creating decision-based problems (Michaelsen, et al, 1996; Michaelsen et al., 1997) helps this process greatly. The other part of the solution is to create mechanisms by which the teams can simultaneously report their decisions.

A good example of simple reports of complex team decisions comes from a recently retired colleague who, for a number of years, regularly used team learning in a financial management course of 275-290 students. The assignment was based on a case that would test the students' familiarity with the pros and cons of buying versus renting versus leasing. At the beginning of the next class period, he gave each of his 45 or so teams a legal-sized sheet of paper and a large felt-tip marker. He then announced that they were to act as a financial advisory group and that they had 35 minutes (of a 70-minute class period) to develop a recommendation to buy, rent, or lease a fleet of trucks that were needed to fulfill the terms of a three-year contract. When the time had elapsed, he gave a signal and had the teams hold up their legal-sized sheet of paper on which teams had written a single word—buy, rent, or lease—to reveal their choice to the rest of the class. He then handed out portable microphones to a couple of groups who had taken each of the three positions and conducted a class discussion of the factors that influenced the decision.

By having the teams reach mutually exclusive but directly comparable decisions and represent their work in a simple form, he ensured they were explicitly and immediately accountable for their work. As a result, the teams were both prepared and motivated to challenge each others' decisions, and he had no trouble generating a vigorous class discussion in spite of the many adverse conditions presented by the large class and the awkward physical setting (a very large auditorium with fixed seating).

The importance of having simultaneous team reports is one of the lessons I learned the hard way. For many years, I had successfully used an experiential role-play called the New Truck Dilemma (Maier, Solem, & Maier, 1975), to make the point that employees were more likely to cooperate and have positive attitudes if they are involved in making decisions that affect them. This role-play simulates a situation in which a telephone repair supervisor is allotted a new truck and must decide on how to juggle truck assignments among the members of his or her crew. The effectiveness of the activity is directly related to students' conclusion as to why individual drivers were satisfied or dissatisfied with the truck that they were assigned. The value of the activity is that it sets the stage for students to discover that their emotions can blind them to important insights about managing group decisions. This occurs because their intuitive conclusion that the key issue is the decision itself; i.e., who gets what truck, is seldom consistent across multiple groups. Instead, the process of how the decision is made is more important than the actual decision (i.e., dissatisfaction is far more likely when the supervisor makes the decision than when the drivers actively participate in deciding how the trucks will be allocated among group members). Thus, using the New Truck Dilemma involves students in three separate steps: 1) engaging in the role-play itself, 2) collecting and summarizing the data about what happened in each of the groups, and 3) discussing the implications of the data from the entire set of role-play groups.

The first time I used the New Truck Dilemma in a large class, I planned to follow my normal procedures for running the role play, collecting and summarizing the results and discussing their implications. Thus, I had all of the teams role-play at the same time, then collected and recorded their results one-at-a-time in one of the columns of an overhead transparency (see Figure 6.2 for a simplified version of the one I would typically use for six teams).

Although students were intensely engaged in the role-play itself, the data collection that followed was a near disaster. With 20 teams instead of six, my normal one-at-a-time reporting procedure produced two negative outcomes that, in combination, completely destroyed the value of the entire experience. One was that the repetitive nature of the teams' reports was so boring that students' wouldn't even keep quiet enough for either me or the rest of the class to hear what happened in the other groups. The other problem was that the reporting process took so long that we didn't have time to discuss the implications of what they had reported. I knew something would have to change.

The next time around, I still had all the teams role-play at the same time but changed the way they reported their results. This time, I had

Figure 6.2 *New Truck Assignments to Drivers*

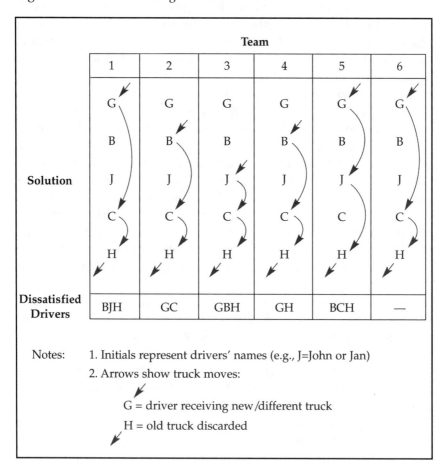

	Team					
	1	2	3	4	5	6
Solution	G B J C H	G B J C H	G B J C H	G B J C H	G B J C H	G B J C H
Dissatisfied Drivers	BJH	GC	GBH	GH	BCH	—

Notes: 1. Initials represent drivers' names (e.g., J=John or Jan)
2. Arrows show truck moves:

G = driver receiving new/different truck

H = old truck discarded

the groups simultaneously record their own results on a strip of newsprint that contained the same data as one of the columns of the chart shown in Figure 6.2 and that was large enough so that each team's decisions could be seen by the entire class. Then I had them bring their results to the front of the room where I taped them to the wall after having grouped them according to which driver had received the new truck. Then, I started the class discussion by asking, "Does anyone have any questions they would like to ask any of the other groups?"

The contrast between the two different ways of having groups report the results of their work was amazing and helped me learn two important lessons about the value of simultaneous reporting. One was that because the teams were all creating their reports at the same time, the simultaneous report-out was so much more efficient that there was plenty of time for whole class discussion. The other lesson was that it actually set the stage for a much richer discussion than was typical in smaller classes. With 20 examples instead of six, there were multiple cases of counter-intuitive results (i.e., examples of groups in which the same people ended up with the same trucks but with very different levels of satisfaction). For example, the sequential order of the results shown in Figure 6.2 hides the fact that two of the groups (1 and 6) reached exactly the same decision (i.e., G got the new truck, G's truck went to C, C's went to H, and H's was discarded), but there were three dissatisfied in group 1 and no dissatisfied drivers in group 6. Second, since the newsprint strips were independent, I could strategically arrange them so that they automatically raised the issues that I wanted to bring out in the discussion (i.e., the way the decision is made is more important than the decision itself). By being able to place these kind of results side-by-side, I could ensure that students focused on exactly the point that I wanted to make without having to say anything at all.

Implementation Facilitator 1: Scheduling Longer Class Periods

Using team learning in 50-minute class periods usually requires making some adjustments. For example, RATs must be either very short or the Readiness Assurance Process has to be spread across more than one class period (i.e., the individual test on the first day and the team test, appeals, and instructor input on the next one). Further, while a lecturer can simply end class when the time runs out and start again at the beginning of the next with very little disruption of the flow of the class, using blocks of time for in-class group work makes timing issues much more important. As a result, longer class periods help in two ways: They allow more efficient use of time and they provide flexibility for designing and managing in-class group assignments.

Efficient use of class time. Short class periods tend to create inefficiency at both ends of most classes. The inefficiency at the beginning stems from the fact that each time a group meets, it takes a few minutes for members to warm up to each other and to their work. With 50-minute class periods, by the time students get comfortable with each other and focused on their assignment, the class is almost over. The inefficiency at the end comes from the fact that instructors are forced to plan their assignments to end with some class time remaining because if there is not enough time to talk at the end, students lose most of the value of an entire class period. Longer class periods reduce both problems simply because there are fewer opportunities for the problems to occur.

Flexibility for designing and managing in-class group assignments. Longer class periods provide flexibility in designing and managing in-class group assignments in two important ways. First, it is easier to take advantage of teaching moments that inevitably occur during the group work or subsequent class discussions. When I teach in longer class periods, I often go to class with materials for several different activities and use the outcomes of each to determine which one(s) I use and/or the order in which I use them. Second, longer class periods provide the opportunity to use difficult and complex assignments to capitalize on the fact that team learning builds groups into effective self-managed learning teams. For example, in teaching about organizations, I often use novels as cases and find that many of students' most remembered learning experiences come from team exams that focused on integrating concepts and that took two or more hours to complete.

Implementation Facilitator 2: Learning Students' Names

The other help in using team learning in large classes is learning students' names. I've found that when I am able to call students by name, it helps in two ways. One is that students respond to me quite differently. For example, they are much more willing to approach me with questions and suggestions and are far more forgiving when I make mistakes. The other is that I have found that when I pay close enough attention to get to know students by name, I am able to do a much better job of reading their reactions and using them to improve my teaching.

Fortunately, compared to large lecture classes, the task of learning students' names is helped by aspects that are inherent in the team learning process. Both the teams and their locations within the class provide cues that aid in the initial memorization process. And unlike giving a lecture to a vast sea of faces, the instructor has the opportunity to get to know students during class as he or she listens in on the teams at work. Most of my colleagues who use team learning in large classes capitalize on both factors by 1) making an initial attempt to memorize students' names from team pictures taped on index cards, and 2) reviewing the names as they circulate from team to team while students work on their group assignments. Although I'm not particularly good at remembering names, I've found that in a class of just over 100 students, it takes me about an hour to memorize the names from the team pictures. Then I have to spend several class periods reviewing the names as I circulate among the groups and call everyone by name.

Conclusion

Team learning can be a very effective way to offset the disadvantages of large classes. However, successfully implementing team learning in any setting requires adherence to the basic key elements of the process. These include:

1) Using permanent and purposefully heterogeneous learning groups

2) Grading based on a combination of individual performance, team performance, and peer evaluation

3) Devoting the vast majority of the class time to small group activities

4) Employing the six-step instructional activity sequence

Successfully implementing team learning in large classes requires particularly careful attention to two additional activities. These are adapting to the physical environment (space, noise, etc.) and creating procedures and props to handle the mechanics of running the class (handing out and collecting materials, pacing the groups, providing feedback, etc.). In addition, scheduling the classes in longer class periods and getting to know students by name will further facilitate the implementation process.

When properly implemented, the team learning approach produces a learning environment that very closely resembles that of small classes. Students are neither anonymous nor passive. The fact the majority of class time is spent on group work ensures that students are accountable for and receive immediate feedback on their work. As a result, most students naturally become actively involved in both the social and intellectual aspects of the class.

In addition, team learning positively changes the role of the instructor by changing the way we interact with both the content we teach and the students in our classes. Since the process motivates students to prepare in advance and attend class, lecturing (what little we do) is far more interesting because we can bypass the basics. In addition, because we spend a lot more time listening and observing, the classroom is a much more social place for us as well. The sea of faces gradually dissolves into individual students with real personalities who are willing and able to assist in the teaching/learning process.

References

Bargh, J. A., & Schul, Y. (1980). On the cognitive benefits of teaching. *Journal of Educational Psychology, 74* (5), 593-604.

Bloom, B. S. (1956). *Taxonomy of educational objectives: The classification of educational goals.* New York, NY: David McKay.

Maier, N. R. F., Solem, A. R., & Maier, A. A. (1975). *The role-play technique: A handbook for management and leadership practice.* Lajolla, CA: University Associates.

Michaelsen, L. K., & Black, R. H. (1994). Building learning teams: The key to harnessing the power of small groups in higher education. In L. K. Michaelsen & R. H. Black (Eds.), *Collaborative learning: A sourcebook for higher education, Vol. 2.* State College, PA: National Center for Teaching, Learning, and Assessment.

Michaelsen, L. K., Black, R. H., & Fink, L. D. (1996). What every faculty developer needs to know about learning groups. In L. Richlin (Ed.), *To improve the academy: Vol. 15 . Resources for faculty, instructional, and organizational development* (pp. 31-58). Stillwater, OK : New Forums Press.

Michaelsen, L. K., Fink, L. D., & Knight, A. (1997). Designing effective group activities: Lessons for classroom teaching and faculty development. In D. DeZure (Ed.), *To Improve the Academy: Vol. 16. Resources for faculty, instructional, and organizational development* (pp. 373-397). Stillwater, OK: New Forums Press.

Nungester, R. J., & Duchastel, P. C. (1982). Testing versus review: Effects on retention. *Journal of Applied Psychology, 74* (1), 18-22.

Slavin, R. E., & Karweit, N. L. (1981). Cognitive and affective outcomes of an intensive student team learning experience. *Journal of Experimental Education, 50* (1), 29-35.

7

Learning in the Dark: Applying of Classroom Technology to Large Lecture Formats

Michael Smilowitz and Anne S. Gabbard-Alley
James Madison University

Whether in the form of the chalkboard, the printed page, or various video formats, classroom instruction has depended on technology to augment learning. Advances in multimedia and other information technologies provide new opportunities to apply technologies in classroom instruction, particularly in the large classroom format.

As with any instructional tool, there are principles and guidelines to using information technology in the large classroom environment. Among these principles is the 3-D—diversity, depth, and demonstration—approach. This chapter illustrates how the use of presentational software, video and film, web-board discussions, electronic writing assignments, and web research techniques promote diversity, depth, and demonstration. It also identifies the resources and skills necessary for implementation and suggests that the development of good multimedia classroom instruction can be easily extended into long-distance educational formats.

The Need for Means of Involving Students

The theatre setting of most large lecture formats promises the entertainment. In reality, the lecture format, theatre seating isolates students from the instructor. Students sit in less-than-comfortable seats, interact only with adjacent people, and strain to maintain attention. Changes in student expectations regarding the presentation of information exacerbate the problems of large lecture formats. Today's college students are born after 1980 and are accustomed to participating in a plethora of stimulating media choices, most of which require little action on their part.

Lecture formats, which comprise 80% of most teaching (Oblinger, 1995), are passive experiences, and unlike the other contexts in which students participate as audience members. Oblinger (1995) notes a substantial lack of interaction in lecture formats, regardless of class size. In classes under 40 students, Oblinger reports that only four or five students interact on a regular basis. The relative percentage of interaction diminishes as class size increases because, as Oblinger notes, the number of students participating in discussion remains only at four or five. The amount of interaction is also small. According to Oblinger, in a 50-minute lecture to 40 students, there may be as little as five minutes of interaction and questions; in larger classes, there is even less.

Alternatives for increasing interaction and participation in large size classes are challenging at best. Most students do not wish to talk to the entire class. Auditorium seating makes group activities logistically difficult. Individual activities are too often ineffective learning experiences as students cannot receive individual guidance, and it is a burden to provide feedback on their individual performance.

Fortunately, advances in information technologies provide viable means for presenting lessons in an interesting and involving way. Direct interaction with instructors can never be replaced by technology, but incorporating more technology into the large lecture format can help involve students in their own learning. As with the use of any instructional tool, following certain principles benefits the application of these new technologies into the large classroom environment. In particular, incorporating technologies that provide for the 3-Ds— diversity, depth, and demonstration—permits instructors to manage some of the burdens imposed by the large lecture format.

Recognizing Diversity with Presentation Software

People learn things differently. Some students are successful with exclusively verbal presentations. Some require other forms of presentation. Some excel at analytical tasks, others with synthetic tasks. In smaller classroom situations, instructors may identify the preferences of particular students for processing and acquiring new information and respond to them individually. The large lecture format does not provide the luxury of accommodating individual students during the lecture. As it is sound pedagogy to expect varied learning styles among students in a large class, diverse materials will increase the number of students able to grasp the concepts.

A second benefit for the diversification of lecture materials is quite simply the interest factor. Most people find it difficult to attend to a lecturer, even one with the most outstanding speaking skills, for a full 50 minutes. Isolated in a large audience setting, students find listening difficult. Pictures and graphs, audio and video clips, all invite audiences to return their attention to the lecturer. And as is true in any instructional setting, including appropriate supporting materials provides the benefits of illustration and clarity.

Benefits of Presentational Software

Presentational software makes the task of diversifying lecture content much simpler. Such programs are simply very convenient ways to prepare slide presentations of text, visual, and audio material. The work for the instructor is to prepare lecture outlines and any illustrative graphs or diagrams, to find suitable visuals for scanning, and to digitize video and audio clips. Once that work is done, preparing a slide presentation is little more than a series of 'copy and paste' operations. Microsoft's PowerPoint is typical of these types of applications and is easy to learn.

Presentation software benefits instruction in several other ways. Mental wandering by students is inevitable. In smaller classes, instructors may notice students drift away and respond accordingly. In large audiences, individual behavior is often unnoticed. But presenting students with the organizational structure of the lecture on a screen allows them to find their place as their minds return to the lecture. The obvious advantages of a large projection screen are worth noting here. Chalkboards are hard to read at best. Carrying large cardboard visual aids to class is always a burden. Well-designed, uncluttered slides are easier to view and are much more interesting.

Complaints about Presentational Software

The biggest complaint from students about the use of presentational software in the classroom occurs when instructors simply type their entire lectures onto slides and then read from the slides. Slides should be used only to display main ideas. The elaboration of the idea is the lecturer's task. Crowding slides with numerous ideas is an undesirable and unnecessary economy. It is much more effective to use more slides with less content on each.

Instructors should be aware of the lighting conditions in the auditoriums where their presentations occur and use color schemes that will project effectively. For example, on a personal computer, using a purple font on a pink background appears to be effective, but will wash out in the classroom, making student viewing difficult. Using a white font with a black or dark blue background, or a black font against a yellow background, works effectively in all classroom contexts.

Many first-time users also try to do too much with all the bells and whistles that come with presentational programs. Having too many video clips, sounds, or photographs, is likely to distract from the lecture's main points. The possibilities for elaborate slide transitions and

Figure 7.1 *Steps for Preparing Lectures with Presentation Software*

1) Begin preparing the lecture as you would prepare any other lecture. But as you do your research, make note of any diagrams, illustrations, or graphs that may be scanned and included in the lecture presentation.

2) Write, gather, and organize the materials of the lecture into four or five subtopics.

3) Presentation software packages typically provide convenient templates to use in building the presentation. Choose a template, and if necessary, modify its color scheme. Black on yellow is generally the most effective combination, especially if the room is not darkened adequately. Be sure to number the slides.

4) Prepare a slide that lists the names of each subtopic to provide an overview of the lecture. Place the name of each subtopic on title bars of all the slides for that subtopic.

5) Prepare the individual slides. Keep the slide content short and simple. Anything more than one briefly stated main point and two or three subpoints will cause students to spend too much of their time copying the slides into their notes. Add into the presentation the graphic or illustrative material and any other supporting materials.

6) Typical software packages allow you to modify the ordering of slides and to easily choose the method of slide transitions.

7) You may choose to post your slide presentation at a website for students to access and print before coming to class. PowerPoint, for example, allows a student to print slides with an adjacent note column.

text animations beckons first-time users into hours upon hours of mastering techniques that do not benefit student learning. Presentation software permits editing of existing slides with the same ease of a word processing program. After the instructor has mastered the basics of presentational software, then it may be worthwhile to experiment with various additions that help to make the issue under consideration more understandable and interesting. The objective should be diversifying the materials of the lecture, not overwhelming students with technological pizzazz.

Providing Depth with Discussion Software

It is a pedagogical axiom that students master concepts as they involve themselves in the application of those concepts. The deeper the involvement, the more certain students will effectively use what they learn in contexts outside the classroom. For many topics, student discussion and writing are valuable processes for exploring issues in depth.

But instructors of large lectures are understandably daunted by the prospect of assigning individual writing projects. There simply is not enough time to review anything more than very brief papers, which at best provide only a cursory treatment of some very narrow topic. Group writing projects reduce the number of papers to be read, but are often difficult to organize in large lecture formats. In large lecture halls, assigning students to groups is time consuming and cumbersome, especially as auditorium seating does not provide a physical setting that facilitates group discussion. Conventional group writing projects also do not generally provide opportunities to evaluate the writing contributions of individual group members.

Computer-mediated communication systems give instructors of large classes the means for achieving the depth provided by group discussion and writing projects found in smaller classes. There are a number of alternatives available for electronic discussions, or virtual groups, and current software options are much simpler to use than the listservs/listprocs procedures of just a few years ago. Most email software packages now provide options for discussion groups. There are also several software programs, such as Groupwise, designed for group discussion and writing projects. Programs such as Webboard and Symposium are easy to operate and provide instructors with full control of group membership and the capacity to track the number and length of individual student contributions. Most software packages allow instructors to form groups via email, monitor the progress of the groups, and evaluate group projects while remaining in their offices.

Figure 7.2 *Using Virtual Groups for Writing Projects*

1) Nearly all campuses have some means for electronic mail. Many have instructional software packages that easily provide for virtual group assignments. Programs such as CourseInfo, Groupwise, Symposium, and Webboard allow for simple point and click group formation, monitoring, and activity recording. A few more steps will be required if such programs are not available, but the campus email system can be used to construct and monitor groups. Registrar offices often times can provide a list of the enrolled students' email addresses, which can be randomly blocked and imported into the program to form the groups. Otherwise, students must email their addresses to the instructor to create the list.

2) Most types of conventional group writing projects are suitable as assignments for computer mediated group interaction. Position papers are particularly useful, especially if the assigned topic is sufficiently controversial to invite a variety of opinions. Students are required to write to each other until they have formed the group position, construct arguments and supporting materials to defend the group's position, and then organize and write the paper—all through electronic discussion.

3) Instructors can expect the following to typically occur. In the early stages of the assignment, group members will check into their groups with much ambiguity over how to conduct the business of the group. As in face-to-face group assignments, a few members will make suggestions for dividing tasks. Since students realize that their participation is much more apparent to the instructor, there is generally a higher frequency of participation by more students than in face-to-face groups. But just as in face-to-face groups, some students make more substantial contributions than others do. Toward the due date, there will be a flurry of activity that makes it very difficult for the instructor to continue monitoring each group's activity. And again as in face-to-face groups, one or two of the more active participants will assume the responsibility of organizing the final draft. As all the contributions are already in electronic format, their task is to cut and paste the individual contributions, provide the final editing, and submit the paper.

4) If the final papers are submitted electronically, instructors can add their comments and then email the paper and final evaluation to each member of the groups. If resources are available, instructors may choose to evaluate each member's contribution and assign individual grades as well.

Instructors can readily choose the kind and type of discussion and writing projects appropriate to their instructional needs. On one end, the assignment might only require that students contribute postings to an electronic discussion group. On the other end, students may be required to use their electronic discussion groups to compose a substantial paper on an assigned or self-selected topic.

Benefits of Electronic Discussion Groups

There are several advantages to using electronic discussion groups in the large classroom. First, the discussions can take place outside the classroom, saving valuable classroom time for other types of instruction. Second, any instructor who has had students work in groups knows the difficulty of students finding a time when all members are free to participate. The asynchronous characteristic of electronic discussion permits students to participate in the discussion when they have the time available. Except for the occasional down times, Internet-based learning environments are accessible 24 hours a day, seven days a week. Third, the use of email discussion groups eliminates space restrictions. Students can gather electronically in groups of any size to discuss topics in real time in chatroom environments or asynchronous time to thread their discussions. And participation in electronic discussions leaves a record that instructors may employ to evaluate the efforts of individual class members.

In addition, instructors can organize electronic discussions to create a learning context that is a virtual intercultural classroom. Through using email discussion groups, students can interact with people from other countries, students in smaller universities can interact with students from larger universities, and students can interact with and obtain information from people from all sections of the country. One of the better sources for international interaction can be found at http://www.iecc.org.

There is evidence to suggest that email discussion groups encourage students to participate in discussion who otherwise might not feel free to speak up in the large classroom. Karayan and Crowe (1997) note that "while class discussion suits those students who are impulsive learners, email discussion groups cater to all students, encouraging those who are impulsive to take time to reflect and insuring that the ideas of reflective students (who take longer to respond) are not lost." The visual anonymity of email discussion groups appears to promote a lack of prejudice on the part of the students (Lewis, Treves, & Shaindlin, 1997). Students, who are uneasy about having their opinions attached to themselves, can change their virtual gender, race, or entire identity if they so choose to ease their entrance into the virtual community. As one student noted "my classmates open up more, and I've found that once you take away color and sex, everyone is similar."

Guidelines for Use of Electronic Discussion Groups

Some guidelines for the effective use of electronic discussions include:

1) Large classes need to be divided into subgroups. Following hundreds of postings is futile. Maximum group size should be six.

2) Set minimum and maximum lengths for postings. Some students will write one sentence which contributes little to the discussion, but count it as part of their required posting, while other students will write at length and sometimes not really contribute much to the discussion.

3) A minimum number of posts for each student per week should be required. However, there should be realistic expectations for students' time to read the postings of others and to write their own postings. One or two postings per week are appropriate for most contexts. And as instructors need to monitor the postings and occasionally find it beneficial to comment within groups, there can a great deal of work if too many postings are required.

4) Although an increasing number of students arrive on campus with considerable computer experience, it is still necessary to make students aware of where they can obtain technical assistance on campus.

Instructors may use electronic communication to require students to complete more formal writing projects such as case analyses, position papers, or any type of writing assignment typically assigned to a smaller class. Assignments such as these provide for the valuable depth of learning made possible by writing projects, but also provide the added benefit of helping students acquire skills for the processes they will encounter in their careers as they complete writing projects with colleagues. Instructors may choose to require that the written project be completed from start to finish with only electronic communication. Instructors may also choose to monitor and comment on the progress of groups as they discuss and divide the topic and begin assembling their materials. As in the case of electronic discussion groups, the asynchronous characteristic of electronic communication often is more convenient for group writing projects. The same guidelines apply, and it is particularly important to set group size at manageable limits.

Demonstration by Computer

The interfacing of computer and projection screen offers instructors of large lectures many opportunities to demonstrate the skills students are asked to acquire. Whether performing computations, creating designs, or editing texts, lecturers can conveniently display the steps they perform as they describe the logic of their own performance.

Incorporating presentation software into lectures is itself a demonstration of skills students will require as they enter careers. As students experience the instructor's choices for the arrangement and support and illustration of ideas, they are learning processes they subsequently use as they later make their own presentations.

One obvious use for demonstration in the large lecture classroom is with assignments that involve the use of the Internet. Students can view events happening in real time via the Internet and can use it to access global information relating to classroom assignments and research projects. A web site that gives excellent examples of how to use the Internet for learning projects is at http://teams.lacoe.edu/. Although this site is directed to K-12 levels, many of the techniques displayed at this site can be redirected to the university level.

This 3-D approach of depth, diversity, and demonstration of applying technology to teaching in the large classroom format engages the student in active learning instead of the traditional passive lecture format. Employing these techniques in large classrooms leads to more student learning than do traditional methods of instruction. Furthermore, the use of technology in the large classroom can lead to greater efficiency for the instructor and the students. Syllabi can be posted online where students can download them and have them available at all times for viewing, or they can be emailed to students via class email lists. Handouts, assignment guidelines, and any other materials that are normally distributed on paper can also be available online, thereby saving copying costs and time spent in distributing the materials in class. Grade reporting can be done with email class lists. If the university has large computer labs, testing can be conducted on the computer.

Designing the Technology Classroom

A number of factors must be considered when designing the technology classroom. The use of technology in the classroom involves much more than simply installing a computer in the classroom. Additional equipment, such as projectors, speakers, document cameras, and video playback devices are necessary. Two important elements that need to be given consideration during the design process are lighting and seating. The light banks of the classroom need to be arranged so that lights in front can be turned off for effective projector use, while maintaining enough lights for note taking. Windows may need to be blocked with curtains. Furniture should be arranged in such a manner that students in all seats can see the projected image clearly. Lecture halls that have fixed seats in semi-circles that preclude effective viewing of images from the seats at the farther edges of the semi-circle need their seating modified.

In addition, there should be sufficient electrical outlets available and sufficient power for all the equipment. There also must be consideration of where to place the projection devices, computer(s), and speakers for optimal use, viewing, and hearing. Furthermore, the security of the equipment needs to be assured.

Obstacles to the Use of Technology

One of the main obstacles to using technology in the large classroom is cost. The initial cost of placing technology systems in a typical university classroom can run from $23,100 to $56,450 depending on the desired comprehensiveness and the type of equipment needed (See Table 7.1). There are also annual costs for equipment service and maintenance, supplies, and support staff. Most equipment will need to be replaced or upgraded every three to five years.

Human factors also need to be taken into consideration. Some faculty will be strongly resistant to using technology in the classroom for various reasons including "it dehumanizes the interaction", "I can't understand the technology", etc. These are meaningful objections and deserve patient responses. It may be necessary to provide faculty with

Table 7.1 *Estimated Costs for a Comprehensive Technology Classroom*

ITEMS	LOW ESTIMATE	HIGH ESTIMATE
Console	$1,500.00	$5,000.00
Computer	$1,500.00	$3,500.00
Monitor	$400.00	$1,200.00
Projector	$6,000.00	$10,000.00
Screen	$250.00	$1,500.00
Speakers w/brackets	$300.00	$2,000.00
RGB Video switcher/DA	$1,000.00	$3,000.00
Amplifier	$300.00	$500.00
VCR	$150.00	$300.00
CD/DVD/laser disc player	$400.00	$1,200.00
Wireless mouse/keyboard	$100.00	$250.00
Document camera	$3,000.00	$6,000.00
Power conditioner/distribution	$200.00	$500.00
Cabling	$1,000.00	$2,000.00
Structural Modifications	$500.00	$3,000.00
Installation Hardware	$1,000.0	$1,500.00
Control system	$2,000.00	$8,000.00
Control system programming	$1,000.00	$2,000.00
Contractor Installation	$2,500.00	$5,000.00
TOTAL	$23,100.00	$56,450.00

Estimates prepared by Olen Burkholder, Media Resources Technical Support Services Manager, James Madison University, Fall 2000.

release time to develop the skills to convert their current instructional materials. Institutions anxious to implement these technologies may wish to determine a reward system to encourage faculty to incorporate technology into their courses. One lecture using various forms of technology can take anywhere from several days to a month to fully develop. Box 7.3 offers some advice for incorporating technology.

Figure 7.3 *Advice for Incorporating Technology into the Large Lecture*

For instructors thinking about using technology to enhance the instructional effectiveness of large lectures, the most important thing to remember is that the software and equipment that will be used is no more difficult than using a word processor. Great strides in software development provide packages with command choices that do about what they say they will do and help keys that often provide ample assistance. Still, it is good to know human help is generally easy to find.

1) Look on your campus for a Teaching, Learning, and Technology Roundtable (TLTR). Established by the American Association of Higher Education, many campuses have organized their own chapters. TLTR groups are comprised of faculty seeking to design and implement successful applications of information technology. Attending their meetings will provide good ideas and introduce people who can assist you.

2) Contact your local computer center, or if available, instructional media center. You will find people prepared and eager to assist you.

3) Look within your own department or college for colleagues to help you. If you recall Tom Sawyer's really important lessons, a cup of coffee is likely to entice a colleague into painting your entire fence!

Conclusion

With some investment of time and money, developments in information technology may be used to permit the large lecture format to provide interactive, participatory learning. And while current technology does not provide alternatives equivalent to the face-to-face interaction of a student and teacher, the exigencies of providing valuable learning experiences in situations with limited budgets are real and must be managed. The careful selection of technology and equipment and the application of sound pedagogy affords the opportunities to provide diversity, depth, and demonstration in the large lecture. The result provides instructors of large lectures with useful tools and skills that they can incorporate into their other courses and in future endeavors.

References

Karayan, S. S., & Crowe, J. A. (1997). Student perceptions of electronic discussion groups. *T.H.E. Journal, 24* (9), 69-71.

Lewis, D. C., Treves, J. A., & Shaindlin, A. B. (1997). Making sense of academic cyberspace: Case study of an electronic classroom. *College Teaching , 45* (3), 96-100.

Moore, M. G., & Thompson, M. M., with Quigley, A. B., Clark, G. C., & Goff, G. G. (1990). The effects of distance learning: A summary of the literature. *Research Monograph No. 2*. University Park, PA: The Pennsylvania State University, American Center for the Study of Distance Education. (ED 330-321).

Oblinger, D. G. (1995). Educational alternatives based on communication, collaboration and computers. IBM Corporation. (Online) http://www.iat.unc.edu/publications/oblinger/oblinger.html.

Russell, T. L. (1999). Web Based Training. (Online) http://cuda.teleeducation.nb.ca/nosignificantdifference/.

8

Teaching for Inclusion

Mathew L. Ouellett
University of Massachusetts, Amherst

Dear Dr. Smith,

As I finished grading Paper # 4 Tuesday night, I came across this rather offensive, ignorant, close-minded paper that I decided not to grade because if I did it would be an "O." I don't feel comfortable grading this paper, and I thought I should give it to you to view. [This student] didn't follow the directions of the assignment at all… I know she didn't get this info from the readings or lecture!

I don't know what I am supposed to tell her in discussion tomorrow as to why I don't have her paper. I was just going to plainly tell her that I didn't feel comfortable grading her paper so I gave it to you to grade and if she has any questions to see you. I want to run this by you first. Will you be in your office tomorrow so I could stop by then and touch base with you?

Thanks,

Ellie

P.S. Now I see why she put a blank cover page over her paper!

This note came to Professor Rose Smith during her course, "Community Health 129: Health Care for All—Myths and Realities." It was written by "Ellie," a teaching assistant and attached to a paper submitted by "Katie," an academically strong first-year student. Katie was 18, white, and female; Ellie was a 25 year-old African-American graduate student

The assignment asked students to write an editorial addressing the health status differences between African-Americans and white Americans and possible solutions. In a passing nod to the lecture content, reading assignments, and discussion section exercises, Katie acknowledged that racism may have played a role in the United States historically, but does not, she insists, prevail today. As proof, Katie cites the Chinese-, African-, Indian-American, and white families she knows socially who have access to health care. She states that lack of access to health care can easily be traced back to being smart enough to know the options and empowered enough to use them. If disparity does exist, the solution is to get an education and a job with health benefits. Likewise, if there is a lack of qualified medical personnel within your community, become a service provider.

Since Katie had not shared that racism does not impact access to health care, the teaching team was surprised by the content and tenor of this paper. How did these dedicated teachers in a course with diversity issues as a core component respond to the emotions, confusion, and doubts generated by this incident?

In this chapter, I explore the strategies used by the teaching team to both understand this complex event and to shape effective and educative responses. By closely examining this scenario, I identify some of the frameworks, teaching strategies, and behaviors useful to instructors who want to teach large classes inclusively.

Background

Changes in the climate and demographics of many college and university campuses have encouraged instructors' explicit attention to the creation of inclusive learning environments. Within this broader social change, instructors are being called upon to teach classes of as many as 500 students. The literature on teaching development (including chapters of this book) offers various resources and strategies for teaching in large-class settings and making these environments multicultural.

Community Health 129 is a popular general education course of approximately 200 students taught at the University of Massachusetts, Amherst. Students from across the disciplines take this entry-level survey course that addresses issues of social and cultural diversity, a focus inherent within the field of public health. Specifically, the course explores health care issues related to Asian-Americans, Native Americans, African-Americans, Latinos, the poor, the elderly, and people living in rural areas. To provide breadth of perspective, the course also examines the organization of health care services in other countries.

Reflective Practice and Teaching Communities

Rose Smith's perspective on teaching is grounded in an appreciation of the holistic nature of the education enterprise. Deeply committed to teaching, she understands how her success and the success of her graduate and undergraduate students are complexly shaped by what each brings to the teaching and learning endeavor. As a professor of public health and health studies, Rose is well respected as a researcher and teacher by colleagues and students alike. She has taught this course many times, regularly receiving excellent student evaluations. In fact, she recently won the University Distinguished Teaching Award.

Rose is committed to mentoring graduate students interested in teaching-related careers. She assembled a team of four graduate teaching assistants, all women in their 20s, studying at the master's level in the School of Public Health and Health Sciences. These TAs facilitated discussion sessions, conducted office hours, and graded writing assignments. Rose regularly met with the TAs to discuss the progress of the course and discussion sections, and to support their teaching development goals.

Additionally, Rose Smith is deeply committed to multicultural issues and to creating inclusive classroom settings. These values helped shape the teaching team: Of the four teaching assistants, three are white and one is African-American. One of the white women is visibly physically disabled.

In the fall of that year, Rose volunteered to participate in the Teaching and Learning in the Diverse Classroom Faculty and TA Development Program (TLDC), a university-wide teaching development opportunity sponsored by the Center for Teaching. She also made arrangements for her teaching assistants to participate in the TLDC.

The TLDC program offers instructors a year-long forum for discussion and support for innovations to incorporate multicultural issues into courses. It is widely believed that significant gains in teaching development come through making public the discussion about good teaching. Often, this happens when instructors participate in learning communities designed to encourage sustained dialogues and support for teaching innovations. This kind of collegial community can be particularly effective when the teaching development goals address such broad and complicated terrain as diversity.

That year, the TLDC program participants came from the School of Public Health and Health Studies but were from different departments and did not know each other well. The group was diverse in terms of racial identity, academic rank, sexual orientation, economic status, and gender. Over the fall semester, the group met regularly to hear guest speakers, discuss readings, and consider teaching development and diversity-related frameworks. As facilitator, I assisted with individual course development projects.

Shortly after Rose received the note and Katie's paper, she talked to me. As she laid out the content of the paper and the accompanying note, I could hear her surprise and anxiety. We discussed the assignment, the clarity of the directions, and previous opportunities for students to receive feedback. We speculated about Katie's intentions and her misunderstanding of the core content of the course. Rose was particularly concerned about Ellie's emotional response to receiving a paper with blatantly racist ideas. Finally, we considered how Rose could tease out Ellie's reactions, her commitment to academic rigor, and her care for Katie's right to express her own values and beliefs.

As we listed questions and identified possible intervention strategies, we decided to bring the issue to the TLDC program for discussion. Prior to the next TLDC meeting, we distributed copies of Katie's paper, Ellie's note, and a note from Rose to the rest of her teaching team regarding the situation.

After a brief overview, Rose and Ellie talked about their complex reactions to Katie's paper and the factors requiring a response. Through group discussion, we came to understand how important it was to identify and articulate the teaching team's feelings and responses as a prerequisite to fashioning an appropriate, balanced response to Katie that would also support Ellie in both her role as a TA and her African-American identity.

We framed our discussion by asking, "What's going on here?" Deliberately refraining from identifying specific strategies or a single interpretation, we brainstormed as many frameworks as possible. As Rose's team worked through the implications of this experience, they became models for how to respond effectively to diversity-related issues. They acknowledged the incident without marginalizing or avoiding it. They also identified and normalized their responses and those of the student involved.

The existing scaffold provided by the TLDC seminar underlay our group discussion. For example, we had previously developed shared definitions of key terms (e.g., *race* and *racism*) and concepts (e.g., defining *diversity* to include race/ethnicity, social class/economic status, gender, religion, sexual orientation, ability, and age). We had the benefit of having reviewed and discussed frameworks for understanding how racial identity development plays out in classroom settings. And we had explored several models of multicultural course development. For example, one model suggests four key arenas of teaching development and diversity: 1) increased teacher self-awareness, 2) awareness of student diversity, 3) teaching methods, and 4) content. Another model, the Universal Instructional Design (UID) model, charges instructors to take a holistic perspective of student needs. This model cautions that traditional value sets (such as the importance of uniformity) can obscure the myriad advantages built into educational settings for majority students and the concurrent disadvantages often faced by students from minority or otherwise disenfranchised groups.

By bringing such perspectives and frameworks to the discussion, we created a teaching and learning opportunity for Rose's team, the student, and the TLDC group. Rose later reported that she learned a great deal more than she expected because she did not handle this incident privately as she might have in the past. In turn, the group concluded that much in this actual case study applied to their own teaching.

Several semesters later, Rose, in reflection, suggested that the regular peer interactions in the seminar had led her to trust that she could bring this issue to the group without being judged negatively. In her view, the group understood the complexity of learning to teach inclusively and the importance of thinking collaboratively about the situation without posing as diversity experts. Finally, Rose learned that important insights on diversity-related issues could come from group members who were graduate students, assistant professors, or non-tenure-track faculty.

This large class experience suggests several implications for teaching and learning in the diverse classroom. They include balancing students' emotional and intellectual growth, defining expertise broadly and taking risks, facilitating effective classroom dynamics, assessing student learning outcomes, and working successfully with graduate teaching assistants.

Balancing Emotional and Intellectual Growth

Chan and Treacy (1996) explore how the objectives and classroom dynamics of multicultural courses such as Rose's invite student resistance, and they caution that teachers should anticipate resistance. Challenges to the material or to the teacher require thoughtful reflection. In some cases, such resistance can be seen as an effort by students to make the issues relevant to their own experiences. Chan and Treacy argue that if learning is to occur, teachers must start where students are developmentally (i.e., intellectually, emotionally, and socially) ready to begin, necessitating an ongoing process of refining exercises and assignments.

Rose and her teaching team solicited work from Katie that, while challenging the material directly, was perhaps the kind of academic engagement with an assignment that they would, in other circumstances, have encouraged and valued. One way to understand Katie's paper is to see that she had the self-confidence to say, "Hold on! I'm unconvinced that I should change my viewpoint!" Paula was clearly daunted that any student could remain so unmoved by the readings, lectures, and discussion sections. It helped to be able to see Katie's resistance as at least partially rooted to the contradictions the assignment posed to her values and beliefs and to viewpoints supported by her family, community, prior education, religious affiliations, and other institutional and cultural pillars of United States society.

In addition, frameworks to interpret students' deeply held beliefs and attitudes about how the world operates could be extremely helpful in constructing effective learning opportunities in large classes. For example, via the lens of one framework—racial identity development—the TLDC participants saw the values and beliefs expressed in Katie's paper as indicative of a level of her racial identity development (Hardiman & Jackson, 1997). Her position can be situated in a level of white identity development, one that explains discrepancies in access to social benefits (such as health care) as individual failure without systemic or institutional roots.

Paramount in helping Katie to absorb new information and broaden her understanding of core content in this course was to help her understand perspectives different from her own. To do this, instructors may first need to help students understand how we are all socialized into constructed beliefs, attitudes, and value systems. In Katie's case, her strongly held belief that US culture offers equal access to health care unilaterally to all citizens may need to be reconsidered in light of the research on the experiences of others. Such efforts to help students make more explicit the values and beliefs that stand behind their views benefits all students and are admittedly difficult to incorporate in large class settings.

Diversity Expertise and Taking Risks

Rose Smith and her teaching assistants had the benefit of disciplinary and personal expertise related to diversity. However, their greatest strengths proved to be the behaviors and strategies available to all instructors.

As committed to teaching excellence as many instructors may be, most do not have the desire or the opportunity to become diversity experts. But even without being a specialist in diversity, it is important to understand one's own objectives for student learning. Examples of learning goals that support diversity-related outcomes include increased student self-awareness; the ability to listen to and understand the perspective of others; the skills to successfully engage in a dialogue with someone who holds perspectives different from one's own; the ability to consider what assumptions about cultural values, beliefs, and attitudes may be embedded in course content.

A year after this experience, Rose continued to consider the event and learn from it. For example, one of the subtle elements that made this encounter so challenging was Rose's unconscious assumption that to be racist was to be uneducated. Therefore, when Katie—an academically bright, likeable, and productive student—believed so deeply in racist stereotypes, she presented a contradiction that took time to identify.

Beyond teacher self-exploration, such as Rose's, yet another benefit comes from expanding the circle of people one turns to for consultation. As demonstrated by the TLDC program, tremendous benefit is derived from establishing relationships with colleagues who can provide insight into situations different from one's own cultural, social, or disciplinary background.

Facilitating Effective Classroom Dynamics

Because of the dynamics of size and anonymity in large-class settings, there may be a strong pressure to stay in charge. Unlike in small classes where a teacher can maintain an ongoing read on individual and group dynamics, large-class settings mitigate against being able to gain such perspective, requiring instructors to expect challenges and surprises.

When a diversity-related incident emerges in a large-class setting, facilitation skills provide instructors the necessary time to respond effectively and respectfully. One way of accommodating the unexpected is through strategies of experiential learning theory and practice, which can make a large class appear smaller through brief writing responses to a focus question, dyad responses, sharing circles, caucus groups, or fishbowl exercises.

Then the task is to engage students in a sustained dialogue broad enough for their thinking to be influenced by the teacher and their peers. It is important to normalize feelings students have, help them identify and articulate what they believe and how they have come to hold such beliefs. Ideally, instructors in such settings act to steady discussion during the expression of strong feelings so that students have the opportunity to express perspectives while being helped to integrate core learning outcome goals. The themes from the students' responses can be used to build more relevant classroom-based discussions.

For example, white students are often afraid of saying the wrong thing in diversity-related situations, leading to a classroom climate permeated by a kind of paralysis as white students become almost completely silent. Students of color may feel hyper-visible and further alienated. By reframing student comments in historical or discipline-specific contexts, teachers can level the perceived risks of active participation.

In the Rose Smith case, Ellie initially felt that Rose should have responded to Katie's paper in the large lecture setting. Ellie's concern was that other students were harboring equally racist ideas but were less naïve about writing them. After the seminar discussion, Rose's team came to see Katie's response as atypical, and the teaching team decided that Rose should meet with Katie individually. This decision also reflected Rose's readiness level to have such a difficult dialogue in front of the entire class.

This decision illustrates the team's capacity for reflective teaching practice, their ability to resist making assumptions about their students' intentions, and their willingness to consult with colleagues about responding to diversity issues. Under other circumstances, the large lecture format may be appropriate for responding to the misunderstandings surfacing in student writing.

Assessment for Student Learning Outcomes

The writing assignment that triggered this incident provided the teaching team an opportunity to hear directly from students about their responses to the core content of the course. Based upon how challenging this incident was, Rose initially considered dropping the entire exercise. However, she ultimately reaffirmed her commitment to the assignment as an assessment tool for measuring students' responses to the challenging information of the course.

One objective of this writing assignment has always been for students to have the opportunity to state and examine their beliefs. But when Rose encountered a student who came to conclusions so different from what she had anticipated, she was thrown off balance. Since deeply held values, beliefs, and attitudes can support or inhibit students' intellectual growth, this exercise had become a way to coach students in the skills necessary for embracing new information by carefully considering perspectives different from their own.

Rose, while deeply committed to encouraging Katie to express her point of view, was galvanized through this experience to clarify and articulate her expectations. This assignment has since become an opportunity to assess whether students have mastered core material and to coach them on how to appropriately take and defend alternative viewpoints in a scholarly manner. Rose has rewritten the instructions for this exercise two more times since that semester, making more explicit her expectations for the assignment. To address academic standards and to maintain the integrity of the course goals, Rose provides her students with directions about how one supports a position by evidence (e.g., inclusion of a bibliography and footnotes) in academic writing.

Katie's paper also led to changes in the timing of this writing assignment. An entire discussion section now provides students an opportunity to express the opinions and beliefs that shape their attitudes on this topic prior to completing the assignment. One of the graduate students who assisted Rose across several semesters noted the important difference these changes have made in what students derive from the assignment. She also reported evidence of the power of peer learning as students heard perspectives that were very different than their own.

Working Successfully With Graduate Teaching Assistants

The emerging demographic changes on many campuses makes multi-culturalism a key teaching development issue in the preparation of graduate students for future teaching-related responsibilities. A more traditional, hierarchical response from Rose would have been to resolve this matter with Katie in private. Aware of the conflicted feelings the team had, Rose decided to handle the response as a team. She recognized this as an opportunity to work closely with her teaching assistants on two levels. The first task was to fashion an appropriate response to Katie's work; the second was to reflect upon this incident as an opportunity to strengthen skills in teaching diversity-related materials in a large lecture setting.

Handled insensitively, this incident could easily have been a teaching disaster. The initial response of the teaching assistant was honest and direct; she thought Katie should fail this assignment. However, Rose was committed to framing a response that balanced her commitment to her graduate students, to confronting racism with education and compassion, and to being fair to students.

The relatively public nature of shaping the response to Katie heightened Rose's commitment to respond assertively out of respect for Ellie. As Rose described it, "clearly this paper was the most explic-itly racist thing I've been handed, but not the first time I've been made uncomfortable." The difference was that in prior incidents, Rose had handled the decisions and interventions alone. By including her grad-uate students and colleagues from the TLDC program, Rose engaged a different strategy. The group discussions became a consultation process that increased everyone's opportunity for support, deeper reflection, and increased self-awareness.

This dialogue across the teaching team and with trusted col-leagues compelled all involved to more clearly articulate and examine the biases and assumptions brought to the teaching situation. For example, the graduate students benefited from hearing the perspec-tive of seasoned professors, and the whites in the group benefited from hearing the perspectives of people of color. Ultimately Katie ben-efited too, as the response from the teaching team was more thought-ful and fair due to this reflective process. Rather than responding reflexively to Katie, the team delved into a deeper understanding of what teaching responses best matched her level of readiness.

Conclusion

Many attributes of teaching effectiveness contribute to successful large class experiences (i.e., disciplinary expertise, course design, organizational infrastructures, active learning strategies, instructional technology, assessment and testing, and working effectively with teaching assistants). And the good news is that many of the behaviors, methods, and resources on teaching large classes provide important foundations upon which instructors can pursue innovations for creating multicultural, inclusive classrooms.

Perhaps the greatest benefit of a scenario-based discussion such as the one offered in this chapter is the opportunity for the reader to actively engage in understanding how the values and beliefs we bring to the teaching endeavor affect how we understand and respond to diversity-related issues. Generally, good teaching consultation advice is deeply dependent on asking each other good questions. Through such dialogue, rich insights can emerge from discussion of the complex variables particular to a specific situation and the diversity of its participants. This scenario serves to illuminate the value of such dialogue for teaching large classes inclusively.

References

Chan, C. S., & Treacy, M. J. (1996). Resistance in multicultural courses. *American Behavioral Scientist, 40* (2), 212-221.

Cox, M. D. (2001). Faculty learning communities: Change agents for transforming institutions into learning organizations. In D. Lieberman & C. Wehlburg (Eds.), *To improve the academy: Vol. 19. Resources for faculty, instructional, and organizational development* (pp. 69-93). Bolton, MA: Anker.

Hardiman, R., & Jackson, B. (1997). Conceptual foundations for social justice courses. In M. Adams, L. Bell, & P. Griffin (Eds.), *Teaching for diversity and social justice: A source book* (pp. 16-29). New York, NY: Routledge.

Marchesani, L., & Adams, M. (1992). Dynamics of diversity in the teaching-learning process: A faculty development model for analysis and action. In M. Adams (Ed.), *Promoting diversity in the college classroom: Innovative responses for the curriculum, faculty, and institutions.* New Directions for Teaching and Learning, No. 52. San Francisco, CA: Jossey-Bass.

Ouellett, M. L., & Sorcinelli, M. D. (1995). Teaching and learning in the diverse classroom: A faculty and TA partnership program. In E. Neal & L. Richlin (Eds.), *To improve the academy: Volume 14. Resources for faculty, instructional, and organizational development* (205-217). Stillwater, OK: New Forums Press.

Ouellett, M. L., & Sorcinelli, M. D. (1998). TA training: Strategies for responding to diversity in the classroom. In M. Marincovich, J. Prostko, & F. Stout (Eds.), *The professional development of graduate teaching assistants* (pp. 105-120). Bolton, MA: Anker.

Schmitz, B., Paul, S. P., & Greenberg, J. D. (1992). Creating multicultural classrooms: An experience-derived faculty development program. In L. L. Border & N. Chism (Eds.), *Teaching for diversity,* (49, 75-87). San Francisco, CA: Jossey-Bass.

Silver, P., Bourke, A., & Strehorm, K. C. (1998). Universal instructional design in higher education: An approach for inclusion. *Equity and Excellence, 31*(2), 47-51.

NB: Special thanks to Paula Stamps, Professor of Community Health Studies, School of Public Health and Health Sciences, University of Massachusetts, Amherst, for her support and feedback in the development of this chapter.

9

Working with Teaching Assistants and Undergraduate Peer Facilitators to Address the Challenges of Teaching Large Classes

Jean Civikly-Powell
University of New Mexico

Donald H. Wulff
University of Washington

A faculty member has just learned that one of her teaching assignments for next semester will be the large introductory course that typically enrolls 300 students. After the panic and anxiety subside, the faculty member is energized to get prepared. Her first outline of goals is to help the students learn the material, to coordinate a teaching team to help with the course logistics, and to structure the class so that content is covered efficiently.

Where does she begin? She quickly realizes that it would be smart to visit this semester's class, and to talk with the faculty member and the TAs who are now working with the course. Her visit and talks reveal several themes. Two positive features are the variety of content addressed and the diversity of students in the class. Of concern, however, is the general frustration about students' perceptions of being in a large course—a prevailing lack of student motivation and energy and the resulting low level of student participation. There is also a sense of futility in trying to address the varied needs of so many students in the large-class setting. With this additional information, the faculty member revises her goals, focusing directly on the students and on ways to create a class climate that promotes more student-student interaction. Her thinking is that having students connect more with each other will decrease the isolation and anonymity often experienced in large classes. She also decides to find ways to change the students' expectations, starting on day one of class, about being in a large class.

Fast forward to next semester, the first day of class: students file in, mostly alone and non-communicative. The teaching team—the faculty member, a teaching assistant, and 16 undergraduate peer facilitators—stands ready in various parts of the room, greeting students as they enter. The undergraduate peer facilitators, who are sometimes called near peers, took the course last semester, earned good grades, and are now getting internship credit for working as small-group leaders. As the class begins, the professor introduces the teaching team and explains that even though this is a large class, a portion of each class period will be devoted to working in small groups, where students can talk, practice, ask questions, and get feedback about the topics studied. By the end of the first class, students have heard about the course requirements, have seen a demonstration of a class concept, and have met the peer facilitator and the students who will be in their small group for the semester. Now, as they file out of class, the energy level is substantially higher, and quite a few students are talking with each other.

Is this fantasy? Most certainly not. But it did take plenty of time and work, and weeks of class still lie ahead. Many of the goals in this class are ones that commonly appear in the accumulating literature on undergraduate education (Smith & MacGregor, 2000), active construction of knowledge; learning by direct experience and inquiry; focused interaction with faculty; active, interactive, and cooperative involvement among students; development of teamwork skills and abilities to communicate with diverse people; and a sense of belonging and community.

With increasing realization that these are important goals, faculty who teach large classes not only welcome but depend on teaching assistants and undergraduate peer facilitators to provide attention to individual students and engage the students more directly with the course content. Although the instructor in the previous example will discover quickly that organizing the many facets of a teaching team for a large class is not easy, she will also recognize there are some helpful ways of approaching the task. Among the important guidelines she might consider are 1) to think broadly about the training of her teaching team, 2) to recognize different developmental stages among the teaching team, 3) to determine an organizational structure for the course, 4) to select and train the teaching team, 5) to communicate her expectations clearly, 6) to evaluate the team's work, and 7) to model teamwork and professional behavior.

Strategies for Coordinating the Work of TAs and Undergraduate Peer Facilitators

Think Broadly about Preparing TAs and Undergraduate Peer Facilitators

A few years ago, a faculty coordinator for a large class could prepare TAs or undergraduate peer facilitators by focusing solely on the course tasks they were assigned. During the last decade, however, through a variety of programs related to preparing future faculty (Gaff, Pruitt-Logan, Weibl, & colleagues, 2000) or to involving undergraduates in student-assisted teaching (Miller, Groccia, & Miller, 2001), our understanding of the role of such experiences in preparing students for their professional lives has greatly expanded. As a result, and as the faculty member in the previous example demonstrates through her goals, it behooves course coordinators to think more broadly about how experiences in the large class might contribute to the preparation of the teaching team for future careers. Whether the careers are in academia or in some area of business or industry, many of the skills that graduate TAs and undergraduate facilitators garner as a result of their association with large classes can be considered preparation beyond their responsibilities in the large class. As Svinicki (1995) has suggested, particularly for TAs,

> The skills which graduate students learn as teaching assistants or in an organized program on teaching will stand them in good stead regardless of their future careers... can even translate directly into the kind of training and development which is becoming such a large part of the private sector... All job candidates will have been trained in the discipline, so graduates will have to demonstrate additional skills to give them the edge over graduates from other comparable programs. Training and experience in teaching may be just the edge they need. (p. 6)

As a large-class coordinator, you can think more broadly about the preparation of TAs and peer facilitators if you do the following:

- Emphasize a broad definition of teaching as "any interactions with undergraduates about the content of the course" and move away from a definition of teaching as "standing up and lecturing". Too often, TAs and peer facilitators working with small groups do not see themselves as teaching and therefore can easily denigrate the importance of their roles. An emphasis on the importance of all teaching roles not only reinforces the importance of these roles for achieving the large-class goals, but also helps TAs and near peers recognize that they are developing a variety of transferable skills.

- Identify some of the key instructional skills such as motivating people, organizing thoughts, synthesizing information, responding to questions, or managing and supervising others, that are transferable to any job setting.

- Recognize that all students, especially the graduate teaching assistants, may not want, or be able, to find careers in academia, especially in the kinds of institutions that offer PhD programs.

- Talk explicitly to students about how to discuss these skills during an employment interview.

Provide Experiences that Recognize Developmental Stages

One way to select and assign roles for teaching assistants or undergraduate peer facilitators is to think developmentally. Particularly for teaching assistants, Sprague and Nyquist (1989, 1991) and Nyquist and Sprague (1998) have studied how TAs develop and how assignments for TAs might address developmental needs. Although the idea of developmental stages is much more complex than originally thought, there are elements of the process which suggest that TAs and near peers can, and should, be given increasing amounts of responsibility in a variety of situations during their training. Here are some ways of thinking developmentally about the preparation of TAs:

- Consider the stage of preparedness when making assignments. In the ideal situation, according to a developmental approach, TAs and undergraduate facilitators with the least experience will have less responsibility for the total range of instructional issues. For example, they may have responsibilities for answering questions when students meet in small groups, grading, tutoring, or meeting students during office hours. Some experienced large-course coordinators suggest that the novices do evaluation that is clear-cut, leaving little room for disagreement. In the middle range of experience, TAs and near peers who have mastered some of the basic skills of grading and one-to-one interaction might be assigned to facilitator roles in sections, studios, or laboratories associated with a large class. For experienced teaching assistants emerging as disciplinary scholars in their own right, there may be opportunities to present occasional lectures or units in the large class.

- Recognize that TAs and undergraduate peer facilitators need varying degrees of structure from you as the supervisor. Most of us would suggest that good supervisors find an appropriate balance of structure and autonomy to meet the level of experience and needs of the teaching team, particularly of the TAs (Meyers, 1995), and give novices increasingly more instructional responsibility and autonomy until they have experienced the range of issues involved in teaching and learning (Duba-Biedermann, 1994; Sprague and Nyquist, 1991). Adler (2000) has stressed the importance of providing close supervision of peer facilitators in the early stages of their work. Many TAs prefer an overall collegial style of supervision, in which course supervisors adopt a friendly, supportive, and flexible manner in dealing with them. However, the more novice TAs typically desire greater amounts of structure and direction from their supervisors (Prieto, 1999).

Decide an Organizational Model for the Course

There are many ways to organize a large class that uses TAs and/or undergraduate peer facilitators (Miller, Groccia, & Miller, 2001). In some of the more common models, the TA performs the following functions:

- Shares lecture and class responsibilities with the faculty member

- Assists the faculty member with class organization, preparation of class materials and classroom setup, office visits, student email, grading and course records

- Organizes and coordinates a cohort of undergraduate peer facilitators during each large-class session

- Teaches discussion break-out sections of the large class that meet at times in addition to the weekly large-class lecture session(s)

- Meet with fixed small groups of students during the large class session to facilitate exercises, discussions, problem solving activities, or small group reports

Decisions about which structural model is most appropriate for a particular course are largely a function of the departmental resources, faculty teaching style preferences, goals for creating a particular classroom experience, and TA/peer facilitator availability. However, if the faculty member is interested in achieving some of the goals currently being espoused in the literature on undergraduate education, careful consideration of the roles of teaching assistants and undergraduate facilitators is a must. The degree to which goals can be achieved will depend on a structure that allows for maximum use of interaction among teaching assistants, near peers, and undergraduate students. The literature is very clear about the potential value of increased interaction with undergraduate students when there are more TAs and peer facilitators available to assist with the instruction (Adler, 2000; Marchetti, 2000).

Select and Train the Teaching Team

No matter which course model is chosen, the selection, training, and supervision of the teaching staff are critical to a positive learning and teaching experience. In an ideal world, the faculty member and possibly one or more TAs would participate in a national, regional, or campus conference/training program on large-class instruction. Additionally, it is helpful if you can do the following:

- Address important criteria when selecting a teaching staff for large-class instruction:

  1) Competency with the course content and direct experience with the course

  2) Ability to work with a multi-level system of instructors and peers

  3) Ability to communicate with a diversity of students in a professional yet welcoming manner

  4) Diversity of the staff (gender, ethnicity, age)

  5) Willingness to participate in training, weekly meetings, and performance feedback discussions

- Organize pre-semester meetings and weekly meetings during the term. Topics for the pre-semester training might describe the course goals for teaching and learning, set expectations about the work of the teaching staff, and detail the specific activities for the first week. The weekly meetings might focus on the specifics of the course content, activities, staff questions, and student progress. The structure of a weekly meeting could include a review of the last week's sessions (what went well, student feedback to the teaching staff, grading matters, questions on both content and process, suggestions), a preview of the upcoming week's class sessions and activities, a practice run of the upcoming discussion topics or exercises, discussion of teaching staff challenges in working with students and class attendance/participation, and possibly individual time for the teaching staff to talk with the faculty member on concerns related to the course. Speaking from experience, we know that it is extremely helpful to have a pre-determined time established for the weekly meetings so that none of the teaching staff will face time conflicts. If deemed appropriate to departmental procedures, the provision of course credit for the weekly meetings can be attractive to the teaching staff and thereby serve as documentation of their leadership work in the course.

- Identify and train teaching staff for the skills they will need for their assigned roles. For example, detail the skills needed for working with groups and individual students, and target specific training to provide those skills.

- Teach the TAs and undergraduate peer facilitators how to evaluate student work. Clearly, it is best to have a grading plan in place prior to the start of the term, to detail that plan in the course syllabus, and to discuss the procedures not only with the teaching team, but also with the students at strategically appropriate times throughout the semester.

Too often, however, the evaluative component is not given sufficient attention when TAs and peer facilitators are involved. If those members will be responsible for any part of the evaluation of undergraduate students, it is important that they be carefully prepared and supervised in their efforts. As Lowman (1987) suggests, "The task of grading papers cannot simply be assigned to TAs and forgotten" (p. 78). Often the teaching staff appreciates sample templates of graded student work that help them formulate their own feedback. They also appreciate discussing ways to provide constructive feedback and seeing examples of exemplary student work which they can use as standards. While results from multiple choice tests do not pose many disagreements, the teaching staff's comments on students' essays or on homework problems might be challenged more often.

Clearly Communicate Expectations for the TAs and Peer Facilitators

The literature suggests repeatedly that in order to reduce potential confusion and conflict, it is important to define the TA-instructor relationship and for supervisors to articulate their expectations for the TAs (Meyers, 1995). Clarifying expectations not only helps to decrease the potential for conflicts among the teaching staff but also addresses the undergraduates' need for consistency between what the professor teaches in the large class and what the teaching staff emphasizes in their interactions with students (Wulff, Nyquist, & Abbott, 1987). It helps if you, as the course supervisor, can communicate your expectations:

- Communicate high expectations for your teaching team. This sends the message that you are serious about the course and student learning. Involve the team in establishing the specific course goals and goals for the team's work and interaction.

- Strive to relieve TA and peer facilitator concerns about full mastery of the course content. The course supervisor can assure the teaching team that they were chosen for their particular expertise and for the perspectives they bring in knowing what questions to ask and ways to think about the course. Assure them that these abilities are more important than complete mastery of the course content.

- Communicate expectations about relationships both between the TA and supervisor, and between the TAs and peer facilitators. Use of undergraduate facilitators requires some rethinking of the more traditional roles of TAs, particularly if the TAs need training skills to assist the peer facilitators in working with undergraduates (Miller, Groccia, & Miller, 2001). In most instances, it is beneficial to identify a clear structure for reporting and responding to difficult issues that sometimes arise. Adler (2000) found that she could resolve some of the teaching team coordination problems if she established "a clear stratification system that located the ATAs (peer facilitators) directly under the benevolent supervision of the TAs" (p. 213).

Evaluate the Ongoing Work of the Teaching Staff

An essential function of the large-course supervisor's role is to set standards and provide feedback about the teaching team's performance. Some excellent resources on the supervision of teaching assistants are available (Nyquist & Wulff, 1992; Civikly & Hidalgo, 1992), along with the literature on mentoring and coaching (Hargrove, 1995, 2000). Too often, feedback, which is so important to the development of the large-course experience, is the part of the training process that gets the short shrift. Researchers have reported that we are still not good at giving enough guidance and feedback to teaching assistants (Duba-Biedermann, 1994). Course supervisors can enhance their mentoring by establishing the expectation that feedback will be included as part of the team's work, and they might consider trying ways to use observation and feedback guidelines suggested by Fowler (1996). We also recommend the following principles to guide course supervisors in incorporating feedback in the training of TAs and peer facilitators:

- Recognize that the teaching staff usually responds better to feedback that emphasizes developing versus performing, and learning versus knowing (Hargrove, 2000).

- Provide feedback! Feedback should be an ongoing part of the discussions during the teaching team's meetings. The course supervisor's feedback is critical to keeping the teaching team apprised of how they are doing in reaching their goals.

- Feedback is a two-way process. At each team meeting, elicit feedback from the TAs and peer facilitators, and brainstorm ways to respond to that information.

- Ask the teaching staff to encourage feedback from the students. The feedback can be from individuals or might be structured weekly as feedback from a designated small group. Again, brainstorm ways for the team to respond to the feedback provided.

Another valuable learning component for the teaching staff is self-feedback that might take the form of periodic self-reflective essays on their development as teachers and facilitators. These essays may be presented as traditional strength and weakness self-assessments or as more innovative examinations of one's teaching passions and vulnerabilities (Palmer, 1998). An additional assignment would ask the teaching staff to identify one self-challenge they each make for the upcoming week or course unit. Other structural forms might include individual contracts on goals with progress reports during the semester, and structured discussions in pairs or small groups of the teaching staff cohort. Any of these processes can provide some of the badly needed time for reflection that scholars emphasize as part of the process of teacher development (Allen, 1991; Nyquist, et al., 1999).

Model Teamwork and Professionalism to the Students

"Instructors are salient role models for TAs and peer facilitators. The attitudes that instructors bring to their courses subtly shape TAs' perceptions of teaching and influence the quality of TA-student interactions" (Boerher & Chevrier, 1991). Students watch the teaching staff do their work and interact with each other. They look to the staff for ways to work with their classmates. As such, it is important to model enthusiasm for teaching and concern for undergraduate students. It is especially important to present a united and authentic image of a teaching team. When it is clear to all instructors, facilitators, and students that the instructional group is working as a team, many of the problems commonly associated with large classes are lessened (Ore, 2000). Here are some ways to model teamwork and professionalism:

- Communicate teamwork to undergraduate students. Let students know on the first day of class that the teaching group functions as a team, including the behind-the-scenes meetings, and then be sure the assistants have the information they need to be consistent with that goal. Carbone (1998) suggests listing the names of each member of the teaching team on the syllabus and involving them directly in the first day's lecture and group activities.

- Provide ways for team cohesion. Most undergraduates are concerned about the coordination between what happens in the large and small groups. Students are adept at hearing one instructor's messages of disagreement with another's approach or response and might use these differences to carve dissension in the large group. Most often such potential for discord can be deflected with the kind of team cohesion that comes from providing informal settings for interaction, such as team meetings. One such way to foster peer support is to provide group training (Nottarianni-Girard, 1999). The teaching staff also needs to commit to directly communicating with one another and to checking in with each other first when they have differences of opinion or hear student complaints. In turn, students need to recognize and should be prepared to expect some diversity of communication and teaching styles among the teaching staff.

Benefits to the Faculty Member

There is no question that teaching large classes and working with the teaching team is complex and time-consuming work. And it would be naive to think that the large-class instructor could occasionally employ a few of these strategies and expect to be a teaching success. The faculty member who begins to think about and address some of the challenges of teaching large classes greatly enhances his/her chances for success.

As the course supervisor, you will be rewarded for attempting to address some of these issues during the planning stages of large-class instruction, and there are a number of very tangible benefits to be gleaned from such foresight and planning. For one thing, as the example at the beginning of the chapter demonstrates, by using a well-organized team you can greatly enhance the amount of student interaction. By incorporating a greater number of specialists in the content, you can achieve some of the goals identified in the current literature in undergraduate education. In addition, a team working together stands a better chance of addressing the diversity of student needs and the many complicated details that arise in the day-to-day logistics of a large course. Similarly, the faculty member who takes time to clarify expectations and keep everyone on the same path at the beginning can decrease the likelihood of conflicts, misunderstandings, and failures down the road. Finally, the time spent in pre-class meetings and in preparation saves time during the actual teaching of the course. Working with a well-organized team, the faculty member can then use the time available to energize and maximize student learning.

References

Adler, P. A. (2000). Employing a team approach in teaching introductory sociology. Personalizing mass education: The assistant teaching assistant (ATA) program. In G. S. Bridges & S. Desmond (Eds.), *Teaching and learning in large classes* (pp. 209-213). Washington, DC: American Sociological Association.

Allen, R. R. (1991). Encouraging reflection in teaching assistants. In J. D. Nyquist, R. D. Abbott, D. H. Wulff, & J. Sprague (Eds.), *Preparing the professoriate of tomorrow to teach* (pp. 313-317). Dubuque, IA: Kendall/Hunt.

Boehrer, J., & Chevrier, M. (1991). Professor and teaching assistant: Making the most of a working relationship. In J. D. Nyquist, R. D. Abbott, D. H. Wulff, & J. Sprague (Eds.), *Preparing the professoriate of tomorrow to teach* (pp. 326-330). Dubuque, IA: Kendall/Hunt.

Carbone, E. (1998). *Teaching large classes: Tools and strategies.* Survival Skills for Scholars Series, Vol. 19. Thousand Oaks, CA: Sage.

Civikly, J. M., & Hidalgo, R. (1992). TA training as professional mentoring. In J. D. Nyquist & D. H. Wulff (Eds.), *Preparing teaching assistants for instructional roles: Supervising TAs in Communication.* Annandale, VA: Speech Communication Association.

Duba-Biedermann, L. (1994). Graduate assistant development: Problems of role ambiguity and faculty supervision. *The Journal of Graduate Teaching Assistant Development, 1* (3), 119-125.

Fowler, B. (1996). Increasing the teaching skills of teaching assistants through feedback from observation of classroom performance. *Journal of Graduate Teaching Assistant Development, 3* (3), 95-103.

Gaff, J. G., Pruitt-Logan, A. S., Weibl, R. A., & participants in the Preparing Future Faculty Program. (2000). *Building the faculty we need: Colleges and universities working together.* Washington, DC: Association of American Colleges and Universities.

Hargrove, R. (1995). *Masterful coaching: Extraordinary results by impacting people and the way they think and work together.* San Francisco, CA: Jossey-Bass/Pfeiffer.

Hargrove, R. (2000). *Masterful coaching deluxe trainer's package.* San Francisco, CA: Jossey-Bass.

Lowman, J. (1987). Giving students feedback. In M. G. Weimer (Ed.), *Teaching large classes well* (pp. 71-83). New Directions for Teaching and Learning, No. 32. San Francisco, CA: Jossey-Bass.

Marchetti, E. (2000). Peer assisted study sessions (PASS). In G. S. Bridges & S. Desmond (Eds.), *Teaching and learning in large classes* (pp. 221-226). Washington, DC: American Sociological Association.

Meyers, S. A. (1995). Enhancing relationships between instructors and teaching assistants. *Journal of Graduate Teaching Assistant Development, 2* (3), 107-112.

Miller, J. E., Groccia, J. E., & Miller, M. S. (Eds.). (2001). *Student-assisted teaching: A guide to faculty-student teamwork*. Bolton, MA: Anker.

Notarianni-Girard, D. (1999). Transfer of training in teaching assistant programs. *Journal of Graduate Teaching Assistant Development, 6* (3), 119-147.

Nyquist, J. D., Manning, L., Wulff, D. H., Austin, A. E., Sprague, J., Fraser, P., Calcagno, C., & Woodford, B. (1999). On the road to becoming a professor: The graduate student experience. *Change, 31* (3), 18-27.

Nyquist, J. D., & Wulff, D. H. (1992). TA training as professional mentoring. In J. D. Nyquist & D. H. Wulff (Eds.), *Preparing teaching assistants for instructional roles: Supervising TAs in Communication*. Annandale, VA: Speech Communication Association.

Nyquist, J, D., & Sprague, J. (1998). Thinking developmentally about TAs. In M.Marincovich, J. Prostko, & F. Stout (Eds.), *The professional development of graduate teaching assistants* (pp. 61-88). Bolton, MA: Anker.

Ore, T. E. (2000). Employing a team approach in teaching introductory sociology. In G. S. Bridges, & S. Desmond (Eds.), *Teaching and learning in large classes* (pp. 241-248). Washington, DC: American Sociological Association.

Palmer, P. (1998). *The courage to teach*. San Francisco, CA: Jossey-Bass.

Prieto, L. R. (1999). Teaching assistants' preferences for supervisory style: Testing a developmental model of GTA supervision. *Journal of Graduate Teaching Assistant Development, 6* (3), 111-118.

Smith, K. A., & MacGregor, J. (2000). Making small group learning and learning communities a widespread reality. In J. MacGregor, J. L. Cooper, K. A. Smith, & P. Robinson (Eds.), *Strategies for energizing large classes: From small groups to learning communities*. New Directions for Teaching and Learning, No. 81. San Francisco, CA: Jossey-Bass.

Sprague, J., & Nyquist, J. D. (1991). A developmental perspective on the TA role. In J. D. Nyquist, R. D. Abbott, D. H. Wulff, and J. Sprague (Eds.), *Preparing the professoriate of tomorrow to teach* (pp. 295-312). Dubuque, IA: Kendall/Hunt.

Sprague, J., & Nyquist, J. D. (1989). TA supervision. In J. D. Nyquist, R. D. Abbott, & D. H. Wulff (Eds.), *Teaching assistant training in the 1990s* (pp. 37-53). New Directions for Teaching and Learning, No. 39. San Francisco, CA: Jossey-Bass.

Svinicki, M. (1995). A dozen reasons why we should prepare graduate students to teach. *Journal of Graduate Teaching Assistant Development, 3* (1), 5-7.

Wulff, D. H., Nyquist, J. D., & Abbott, R. D. (1987). Students' perceptions of large classes. In M. G. Weimer (Ed.), *Teaching large classes well* (pp. 17-30). New Directions for Teaching and Learning, No. 32. San Francisco, CA: Jossey-Bass.

Additional Resources: Helpful Websites

1) http://www.cte.iastate.edu/TIPS/large.html
Dolan, Anne, "Instructors Share Ideas: Large Class Teaching Tips"

2) http://www.id.ucsb.edu/IC/Resources/Teaching/Large.ucsb.html
Shirley Ronkowski, "Teaching Large Classes at UCSB"

3) http://www2.ncsu.edu/unity/lockers/users/f/felder/public/Papers/
Largeclasses.htm
Richard M. Felder, "Beating the Numbers Game: Effective Teaching in Large
Classes"

4) http://darkwing.uoregon.edu/~tep/lizard/clicking.html
Karen Kelsky, "Clicking with Large Classes"

5) http://wolf.its.ilstu.edu/CAT/online/tips/largeclass/massgrading.html
Kathleen McKinney, "Writing in Large Classes: Don't be Overwhelmed with
Grading!"

6) http://www.psu.edu/celt/PST/large.html
Pennsylvania State University, Center for Excellence in Learning and
Teaching, "Teaching Large Class Sections"

10

Maintaining Intimacy: Strategies for the Effective Management of TAs in Innovative Large Classes

Leta F. Deithloff
University of Texas, Austin

The large classroom presents a unique set of challenges to educators and students alike. Often called impersonal and ineffective, this environment "does not allow for the amount of student-teacher interaction necessary for adequate student questioning, feedback, and learning" (McCroskey & Andersen, 2000, p. 1). To optimize learning, the students' needs for recognition and personalized attention must be met without compromising curriculum goals. If professors spend adequate time answering all the questions and concerns students might have in class, little time will be left for pertinent course information. Thus, the problem created by the large class is one of logistics—1,000 students cannot successfully interact with one professor. They can, however, share a meaningful relationship with teaching assistants (TAs).

In the large classroom, TAs can take a more involved role. TAs serve as mentors and professional models (Chirol, 1999) or lecturers and counselors (Mueller, Perlman, McCann, & McFadden, 1997). With increased demands on their time and energy, professors must rely on these advanced capabilities of TAs to maintain balanced lives, but the necessary delegation of classroom responsibilities must be thoughtfully planned to be beneficial. If managed successfully, TAs provide the support that allows professors to meet students' needs and gives them the freedom to experiment in the classroom. However, without a carefully selected team and proper management, working with a team of TAs can be time consuming and challenging.

Therefore, my model for effective TA management, which is based on two years of applied experience, serves two purposes. First, this model provides guidelines for a team-based format of TA management to effectively govern class demands and facilitate professional development for individual members. Second, this model advocates an innovative environment that is not only a possibility for large classes—it is a reality.

A Question of Definition

Before continuing, I must explain what makes the innovative large class different from large classes in general. An innovative class incorporates a variety of teaching methods in addition to lecture in an effort to provide a more interactive, applied learning environment. Any large class comes with complications, making grading, handing out tests, and the facilitation of everyday activities something of an art form. But the innovative class presents a special set of challenges. To be successful, the staff (the professor and TAs) must be more involved and more available to students participating in group work, real world examples, or other activities that may initially seem complex. Despite an increased investment in time and energy, these perceived hardships are worthwhile because they relieve the fear that personal attention and creativity might not be possible in the large-class environment. Teaching large classes can be just as or even more rewarding than teaching a regular size class if the necessary TA support structure is in place.

The Context

The idea for this model came from my two-year employment as head TA for two sections (500 students in each) of one management and information systems course. Part of the business foundations program at the University of Texas, Austin, this course and its instructor offered students the unique opportunity to learn in an environment that treats each individual as an instrumental part of the classroom. Despite a total of 1,000 students, the instructor wanted the class to be as personal and as accessible as possible, which prompted the installation of a team of TAs whose members endorsed this same philosophy. By appointing each student to a TA, establishing group work in the curriculum, and holding smaller review or meet and greet sessions outside of class, I strongly believe we accomplished these goals. Additionally, I am convinced that with the appropriate selection of

TAs and the effective management of the team, professors of other large classes can duplicate this accomplishment.

The Two C's of Effective TA Management

Again, I must preface this discussion with an acknowledgement that general suggestions may not transfer across all classrooms and all learning situations. But while the model itself may not be completely generalizable, the implications inherent within the model contain information about collaboration and communication between faculty members and their staff that would be relevant in any class. Thus the factors collaboration and communication, affectionately labeled the two C's of TA management, serve as the foundation governing all activities both in and out of class. They also represent the basis of the model that bears their name.

Collaboration

To facilitate the active cooperation of all members, this model advocates the development of a team of TAs in which each member serves a particular duty. (Class size determines how many members can be allocated to a team with increased sizes typically producing larger allocations. This particular model is based on four university-appointed graduate students and four undergraduate student assistants working as independent studies for research credit hours under each TA.) Selecting members for this team should be a careful and deliberate process because working in a large-class environment could mean extra hours, so team members should have some identifiable reason for getting involved. Usually this reason relates to the desire for personal development and experience, which large classes certainly provide. With so many jobs to do and not enough people to complete them, large classes guarantee that TAs receive a diverse and advanced education on classroom management/educational practices, which makes them both more comfortable in the classroom and more marketable to future employers. This advantage opens the applicant pool to all disciplines with an emphasis on teaching experience, as long as these potential candidates can demonstrate a familiarity with the course material or can easily learn the information well enough to teach it.

The head TA. Before selecting team members, however, professors must first choose a head TA. The process of selecting this individual is one of the most important decisions a professor will face because the head TA works more closely with the professor than any other member of the team. Together, these two team members form the first group in the collaboration and communication chain of responsibility (see Figure 10.1), indicating that they set the tone for what the rest of the team will follow.

Figure 10.1 *Collaboration and Communication Chain of Responsibility*

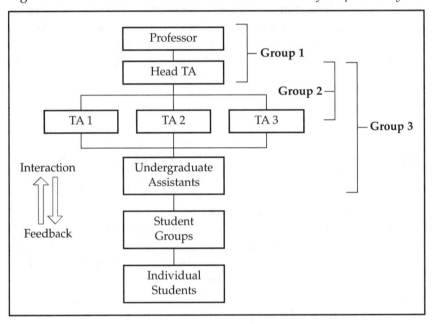

This model indicates the chain of responsibility in terms of typical collaboration and communication. When students have a need, they may access the person with whom they feel the most comfortable. It is important to have this structural flexibility to make students feel important.

To ensure a good working relationship between the members of Group 1, the head TA must share the same teaching philosophy, attitude toward students, and ideas on how class should be structured and conducted. It is not necessary for this individual to have had previous experience in the classroom as long as he or she endorses the professor's principles, has some understanding of what the job entails, and is dedicated to the responsibility it prescribes. If these stipulations are in place, then the professor can trust the head TA to fulfill his or her responsibilities as captain of the other TAs (Group 2 in the chain of responsibility) in a manner that reflects the professor's standards and wishes. Ideally, the head TA should limit the professor's exposure to additional time requirements created by group meetings, a necessary part of collaboration, by directing team meetings and serving as liaison between the professor and the remaining members. But this cannot occur without the professor's faith in the head TA.

The stipulations also guarantee that the head TA will feel comfortable acting or reacting in the professor's absence. With 1,000 students to attend to, professors cannot be all things to each person, so the existence of a head TA with similar beliefs grants professors some flexibility and peace of mind because the head TA can act on behalf of the professor.

Perhaps more importantly, the collaboration between members of Group 1 gives professors someone to brainstorm with about class activities. When dealing with large classes, it is often difficult to anticipate how an activity or a lesson will play out in class. Good intentions can turn into flops in education. Thus, having someone familiar with the class to discuss ideas can be valuable. Asking the question, "What could go wrong?" before attempting the activity can help avoid any potential mishaps. For example, when considering whether or not to use PowerPoint in our classroom, the professor and I talked at length about the pros and cons of this instructional tool. Due to the auditorium-like atmosphere in our room, we eventually decided that the main drawback of turning out the lights to increase visibility for people in the back rows outweighed the perks of using new technology; the classroom would be too dark, making students lethargic and encouraging them to sleep. Without the opportunity to discuss the matter, we might have had to repeat a day of lecture.

The head TA's position is beneficial not only for the professor, but also for the team of TAs (Group 2). As a peer, the head TA relates to the demands of being a graduate student with divided responsibilities between career and school. With large classrooms, the teaching, grading, and advising demands remain constant throughout the semester for professors and their staff, but the stipulations placed on graduate students typically fluctuate between manageable periods and extreme activity. Thus, when team members begin to experience the initial warning signs of crunch time, they feel more comfortable revealing the need for help to an authority figure who can both empathize with their position and temporarily reapportion team responsibilities to cover the member until the difficulty subsides. Without this collaboration between team members, TAs of large classes might become overwhelmed with the workload and experience early burnout.

The team. Constructing effective collaboration depends upon how professors and their head TA both select and prepare team members with the goal of developing a team atmosphere where different personalities can do the job that best suits them based on experience or personal preference. Although all members should have certain common duties (interacting with students or monitoring exams) and should be able to perform each other's jobs in case of absence, a TA team grants members the luxury to perform the duties with which they feel more comfortable. Thus professors and/or TAs should consider the needs and goals of the team and select members who fulfill these certain requirements. For example, TAs who enjoy student interaction could handle lecture, review sessions, lectures to smaller groups on difficult course concepts, question and answer periods (allows students to ask questions of TAs and fellow students about class concerns), and other student-driven activities. Those with creative tendencies could help the professor develop and administer daily class activities that supplement the course material and test individual comprehension. Technical individuals could develop and maintain a class web page in order to make data management more feasible. Those with strong organizational skills could gravitate toward office management and event planning (scheduling supplemental sessions that bring learning to smaller groups of students).

While not every team will have members who exhibit these particular traits, this example serves to illustrate the importance of working with the personalities present in a specific group for the betterment of all involved. By accentuating differences, teams develop a more in-depth picture of the large class that reflects the team's common goals for the course and each individual's unique perspective. Specialized collaboration also allows workers to do aspects of the job they enjoy most, while guaranteeing that at least one person is accountable for each class duty. Thus, individuals equally balance the difficulties of teaching large classes, leaving the team as a whole to enjoy the benefits.

Preparation of team members is another important aspect of collaboration. Group 2 needs to be self-sufficient because professors simply do not have time to supervise both their TAs and their students effectively. Therefore, team members need to understand the demands the classroom will place on them as soon as the semester begins. Part of this preparation involves comprehending that they must be able to adjust under pressure because certain aspects of the large class simply cannot be anticipated. However, knowing how to predict the challenges of this environment is dependent on possessing insight into the nature of those challenges, so TAs should work together to develop possible classroom scenarios (e.g., kinds of student questions, reasons students might seek assistance, potential problems with assignments, etc.). This practice empowers TAs by preparing them for what they can predict and giving them the confidence to handle what they cannot.

Group 2 members should also continually develop their relationships with each other as well as their students. While intellectual skills such as knowledge of the course material and familiarity with discipline-specific, pedagogical principles (Amores, 1999) are essential requirements for team members, these interpersonal rapport skills have begun to take precedence (Lowman & Mathie, 1993) due to the increasing need for student interaction. Large-class TAs will often address the needs of students who depend on them and the personal needs of the fellow team members on whom they depend. Thus TAs should openly discuss the special concerns their students may experience as a result of being a number in a crowd. Some of these concerns deal with a feeling of being lost or unimportant, meaning that TAs should apply basic listening skills. Students have been known to come into office hours with a seemingly banal question about homework and launch into an emotional discussion of how they cannot complete an assignment because their significant other just broke up with them. TAs need to recognize the difference between an attempt to bend classroom policies and a genuine plea for support. While this kind of predicament can occur in any size class, the sheer number of people in a large class make the probability of this particular interaction much more plausible. Therefore, TAs should also identify when students need to seek professional counseling and when they just need someone to listen to them.

Furthermore, TAs striving for collaboration should seek insight into each TA team member's personal perspectives. This knowledge will help members understand how individuals will react in certain situations and what each person needs to perform their job effectively. A team that understands each other works well together because they can anticipate problems before they occur.

Finally, because student concerns usually deal with course-related issues, TAs should share information about every aspect of the course's daily events, including lecture, class activities, and assignments, to anticipate students' needs and questions. This guarantees that when the line of students waiting for a TA after class begins to form, all members can provide similar answers for questions such as, "Can you explain this term to me again because I didn't understand it?" or "What did the professor say about receiving extra credit?" This collaboration also facilitates an individual's professional development by giving team members experience in course planning and management as well as granting them exposure to different teaching styles and techniques. Collaboration of this nature ensures that TAs develop the appropriate blend of classroom experience, education, and empathy for student concerns that advances them beyond typical administrative duties and makes them capable and trustworthy commodities in the large class.

Working with undergraduate assistants. Rather than discussing the many advantages of using student workers in large classrooms or even to show the role these reliable employees fill, this section reveals how TAs should collaborate with undergraduates (Group 3 in the chain of responsibility, Figure 10.1). Essentially, TAs use undergraduate assistants as a source of feedback, since most of these students have either taken the class or are exposed to the opinions of those that do by working with their appointed student groups as consultants on the group project (see Figure 10.1). Through their particular groups, meet and greets, and other events, assistants can often find what the students in the class need and serve as their voice in cases when they are too afraid or unwilling to express their opinions.

Additionally, TAs collaborate with these workers to help delegate certain responsibilities such as handing out papers, answering questions, collecting assignments, and deciphering when a student needs to see the professor or a TA. In some cases, insight from the dual perspective of both a liaison for students and a staff member makes the undergraduate assistant capable of pertinent and influential classroom contributions. For example, one assistant noticed that some students could not finish their practice problems in the allotted time, yet they would not ask for help. When asked what he would do to help the situation, he suggested that we should set up work stations around the class where students could seek help from the staff (TAs and undergraduate assistants) during practice time. We then implemented this suggestion to much success. Undergraduate assistants offer instrumental classroom assistance and a valuable point of reference for TAs in exchange for beneficial experiences in educational practice.

A final word on collaboration. Before moving onto the second C in effective TA management, I should stress that, in addition to its relevancy in this model, collaboration also represents a mind frame. It is a manner for structuring all interactions by using the perspectives of everyone involved in the class to present a more accurate representation of classroom occurrences. For this method to be effective, members of the whole team (the professor and TAs) must be open to and recognize the contribution of each other's ideas. Discussions about class activities between TAs and the professor should be encouraged because they present a more thorough analysis of what works best for the class. However, these discussions should always occur behind closed doors. If students doubt the appearance of a united front, then an element of control has been lost, which could lead to loss of confidence on both sides of the podium.

Communication

Once established, a collaborative team can only remain effective if members continue to communicate with each other, but the effects of communication span outside the boundaries of the team environment into other aspects of the classroom. Thus, the benefits of communication can be expressed through four main correspondence areas: 1) with students, 2) with undergraduate assistants, 3) between TAs, and 4) with the professor.

Communicating with students. The main goal of student interaction, beyond providing answers to questions, seems to be about building rapport with students. My experience demonstrates that students in large classes crave attention, even more than their well-apportioned counterparts. Through interaction, students seem to gain a sense of security and release some anxiety, knowing that someone will always be available to meet their needs. Even the seemingly simple task of responding to email within a 24-hour period projects concern and caring to the students. If this compassion helps students gain confidence and encourages them to ask questions when they do not understand a concept, then the time spent with that student, either in person or online, was well invested. After all, the educational environment should be a supportive one, despite the size of the classroom.

To facilitate student communication, TAs can employ a variety of techniques. The easiest strategy is to use class time to express to the students that the TAs are genuinely interested in and available to them. Through frequent exposure, students will eventually believe that the efforts to convince them are in earnest. TAs can also schedule "meet the TAs" or other sessions outside the classroom to demonstrate their commitment to students. These activities allow the students to feel more comfortable with the staff.

Still another strategy for encouraging communication with students is an online class discussion group. TAs can each volunteer for a certain number of hours per month in which they log on to the class website and answer questions. In this manner, students can address their concerns while remaining anonymous, which takes some pressure off students who might be nervous about approaching a TA.

Another common strategy for handling communication with students is to assign group work as part of the curriculum. The number in the group should vary depending on the assigned project, although smaller groups tend to be more beneficial. As seen in Figure 10.1, student groups provide TAs with one more method of reaching individual students without having to meet with each one individually. TAs can talk to groups of students and personalize their attention without sacrificing valuable personal time. (Undergraduate assistants also share the load by keeping in touch with several small groups.) The advantage to students is that groups provide students in large classes a ready-made support and study system as well as exposure to the viewpoints and habits of other students.

Finally, some students may feel comfortable identifying with only one person in particular. To address this concern, appointing each student to a specific TA can help students overcome their hesitancy to seek help. This simple act also gives students one less obstacle to conquer in times of need because they don't have to think about which TA to approach or wonder if the person is too busy to help them. They will know someone is looking out specifically for them, which can also help with their accountability in terms of class assignments.

With the exception of group work, TAs can taper off these techniques throughout the semester because students are quick to realize that the staff is accessible. If students still fail to seek help despite these varied attempts to reach them, TAs should understand that some students seek large classes because they actually want to be a number in the crowd.

One final note on communicating with students: A discussion on this topic cannot be complete without mentioning the advantages and challenges of email. With today's technology, students can quickly and easily send TAs and professors emails on a variety of subjects. For the most part, this is a helpful tool for the staff of large classrooms because email cuts down on the amount of office hours one must hold to be accessible to all students, and it guarantees that students feel as if their needs are being met. However, when dealing with classes of over 100, the average amount of daily emails a TA will receive begins to increase exponentially. A helpful policy is to set aside a generous portion of a TA's weekly appointment (between ten and 30 hours) just for answering emails. If this allocation, which saves valuable class, does not occur, TAs can begin to feel overwhelmed.

Furthermore, TAs (and professors) need to set boundaries with email. Students often adopt a more brazen attitude on email when dealing with class staff because they are somewhat masked in anonymity. This phenomenon only gets worse when the number of students increases because students feel a TA will never remember them in person. Therefore, TAs need to set and adhere to specific policies for handling communication through emails (e.g., guarantee a 24-hour response, but no response for impolite or demanding requests), and the professor needs to provide complete support for the enforcement of these policies. This unified front protects the employees and establishes a tone of mutual respect between students and staff—a concept often threatened by the large-class environment.

Communicating with undergraduate assistants. Communicating with assistants actually occurs on two levels. Most of the assistants I have worked with were receiving course credit as independent studies in exchange for their help in class. For the first level of communication, which deals with the completion of an assistant's project or assignment, TAs should serve only as resources and allow the professor and the assistant to work out the details. However, in terms of the second level, classroom concerns and occurrences, TAs act as the main source of communication because they are responsible for coordination of assistants during class.

The best method for facilitating communication at this level is to hold biweekly briefing meetings between the members of Group 3

(TAs, assistants, and occasionally the professor). This allows members the chance to relay the events of their particular classroom responsibilities, to report on the activities/issues of their assigned groups, and to discuss any business in need of Group 3's attention. Additionally, each TA should select several assistants (depending on the total number for the semester) to keep in touch with via email or phone throughout the week. This technique ensures that everyone knows his or her job and identifies problems before they occur. If, for example, an undergraduate assistant is sick and has been unable to handle his duties for a week, the TA who discovers this news can notify the rest of the group and temporarily reassign the work until the assistant recovers. Thus, communication serves as a method for keeping on task and for providing support for fellow members so that no one person becomes overwhelmed.

For keeping in touch with the student groups, undergraduate assistants should try emailing and/or meeting with their groups once a week just to make sure the members know what they are supposed to be doing and have everything they need to perform those duties. TAs should handle any communication with students that extends beyond those concerns.

Communicating with TAs. Establishing communication between TAs (the members of Group 2) occurs through weekly meetings. The professor frequently will join these meetings for staff discussions, which address subjects such as which undergraduate assistant should do which job, areas for concern on an upcoming exam, ideas for teaching a difficult concept, and what general questions students seem to be asking. Sessions for TAs often become a forum for discussing personal aspects of the job such as requesting help with certain exam questions, constructing a unified answer for common student questions, and exchanging advice for challenging group situations.

The information exchanged between TAs during these meetings is an instrumental link in the communication chain because it establishes consistency in grading and common procedures for handling student affairs. It also dissuades clever students from circumventing the established system in their quest to find leniency after one TA declines their request. Correspondence prevents these and other kinds of situations in which students attempt to work between TAs, a frequent phenomenon in large classes. Also, effective communication between TAs grants these graduate students the opportunity to continually reinforce each other's training as TAs because they tend to share the successes and failures of their student interactions with each other.

Communicating with the professor. Communication between the professor and the TAs represents the last main area of correspondence. Professors must have an open line of communication with their TAs because, as a staff, these two entities represent a united front. Ultimately, the class belongs to the professor, but during the student rush at the end of each class, this fact does not matter. Students will go to anyone who is available to answer their questions, even if they suspect that person does not know the answer. I once had a student say to me, "I know you don't know the answer to this question because the professor is the only one who knows my situation, but can you give me an answer anyway? I am tired of waiting in line." At that point, the need for some kind of consistent correspondence became painfully clear, and we established a situational report that described daily interactions with students to circumvent any additional surprises.

Additionally, an innovative environment requires that TAs and professors share teaching responsibilities and, therefore, unified standards for conducting class activities. A common practice is to divide the large class into small groups (separate from the groups used for the group project) to work on problems or discuss difficult concepts. For this to occur, TAs, who will be in charge of the groups, must know how the professor would teach these concepts so that consistent and sufficient learning occurs. If the professor has not expressed his or her educational beliefs and policies, then this activity would create more problems than solutions. Ultimately, these innovative activities should nurture intimacy, not undermine learning.

For professors to have an active communication with their TAs, they must first have a strong relationship with their head TA. Meetings between members of Group 1 should occur as often as possible. These meetings can be informative briefings before or after each class. For example, if the professor changes something on the syllabus that involves restructuring a lecture, the head TA might meet with the professor before class to discuss how the change will affect the day's events. The remaining TAs may not need to know this information because their duties may deal with grades or some task unrelated to lecture.

When the items discussed during Group 1's meeting affect the activities of Group 2, then the head TA can relay the information without scheduling a separate meeting with the professor. However, a head TA might want to consider revealing all the details of Group 1's meetings so as not to create any suspicion about what goes on in these meetings. One of the underlying variables that can make or break this model is the amount of trust each member has for the system and his or her place in it. Without this trust, both communication and collaboration will be challenging.

A final word on communication. Collaboration can be a rewarding experience for all involved if team members commit to effective communication development. Without a united concept of how to conduct communicative efforts, members of a team become separate entities operating independently of each other. This type of behavior is harmful to both the team and the students they are meant to serve. Avoiding this complication takes time and energy on the part of the team members, but the rewards from this investment are well worth any sacrifice members must endure. After all, the team either invests the energy initially, or they must double their energy expenditures by first finding and then correcting the misunderstandings that occur when communication fails.

Further Implications

The implications of this model reflect the belief that students are entitled to their basic needs for recognition, despite the size of the class. Intimacy does not have to be a casualty of the large-class environment because students can benefit from effective collaboration with a team of TAs. The results of previous research suggest that students participate more actively in class when collaboration with class representatives is successful because the student experiences increased feelings of accessibility (Gray & Halbert, 1998). In the process, TAs receive the opportunity for professional development and teaching experience most graduate students want (Brown-Wright, Dubick, & Newman, 1997), and professors are able to maintain high teaching standards without sacrificing personal needs. Thus, through collaboration and communication, a working team of TAs can meet the students' needs for intimacy by eliminating the logistical problem presented by the large-class environment.

References

Amores, M. J. (1999). Preparing the graduate TA: An investment in excellence. *Foreign Language Annals, 32* (4), 441-468.

Brown-Wright, D. A., Dubick, R. A., & Newman, I. (1997). Graduate assistant expectation and faculty perception: Implications for mentoring and training. *Journal of College Students Development, 38* (4), 410-415.

Chirol, M. (1999). A touch of class! Creating a handbook on logistics and administrative duties: Advantage for TAs and language program coordinators. *The Canadian Modern Language Review, 56* (2), 355-362.

Gray, T., & Halbert, S. (1998). Team teach with a student: New approach to collaborative teaching. *College Teaching, 46* (4), 150-153.

Lowman, J., & Mathie, V. A. (1993). What should graduate TAs know about teaching? *Teaching of Psychology, 20* (2), 84-88.

McCroskey, J. C., & Andersen, J. F. (2000). The relationship between communication apprehension and academic achievement among college students. Retrieved September 12, 2000 from the World Wide Web: http://www.as.wvu.edu/~jmccrosk/67.htm

Mueller, A., Perlman, B., McCann, L. I., & McFadden, S. H. (1997). A faculty perspective on teaching assistant training. *Teaching of Psychology, 24* (3), 167-171.

11

Teaching the Large Class: An Administrator's Perspective

J. Douglas Andrews
Marshall School of Business,
University of Southern California

Background

I've been a university administrator in one capacity or another for almost 25 years. In those years, I've spent more than a few hours agonizing—as both an administrator and as a teacher—over the issues that surround the teaching of large classes. I strongly suspect most of the areas of concern are similar whether you are responsible for managing the entire process or trying to teach a great class. Simply put, the categories—and the particularities of your environment may call for others—involve scheduling, physical location, classroom environment, smart and appropriate uses of technology, legal issues, and the most important ones: who's doing the teaching and how are they to be supported.

Before I discuss each of these issues, let me recount a personal teaching experience that puts the issue of large class size in perspective. Early in my career, I was asked if I would head up a group charged with creating a good learning experience for some very large classes. Being young and somewhat naïve, I agreed to take on the responsibility. After all, I mused, working with several hundred students at one time would be an interesting challenge. I lost both my youth and my naivete when I realized that this class would include some 4,000 undergraduates!

I recalled, with some bravura, that I had always told my own students that speaking to larger groups was easier than speaking to smaller groups, that in large groups audience expectations usually did not manifest themselves in more than a demand that the speaker be heard and the visuals be seen. Today, handling 4,000 would be simple, hardly more than a mini rock concert with its mind-jarring multimedia walls and deafening sound systems. In this earlier time, however, we were still struggling with opaque projectors, balky overhead projectors, and microphones only a tone deaf drummer could love. I'm pleased to say, in retrospect, that we got the job done. The students learned some things, and I gained a much healthier respect for the process of learning in all its possible permutations.

Perhaps the single greatest lesson I took away from this experience was to be flexible. Consequently, I shy away from checklists and structured plans of action when setting up large classes. Instead, I ask a series of questions that find their genesis in the categories I mentioned back in the first paragraph. I believe you'll find these questions helpful in your quest for a workable plan.

And, oh yes, what do I mean by a large class? From a communication perspective, it's probably any number over 30. In some disciplines it's more than 75. In some disciplines it's probably more than 15; however, I'm not convinced that many of you reading this book teach classes that small. Is there a generic, rather than a quantitative definition? Probably. A large class may be any class where its size requires you to think about the efficacy and efficiency of your traditional teaching style.

Questions For Teachers of Large Classes

How Much Control Do I Have over Scheduling?

This one has a lot of potential answers. You may have direct control over your classrooms, but often the spaces where large classes are conducted are classified as public rooms, and these public rooms are often controlled by a central scheduling body. Sometimes the control is complicated by agreements you may have with the larger institution. In particular, the latest technology is expensive, and you may agree to receiving financial assistance in equipping these large spaces in return for sharing some of the allocated times with other units in your institution.

Where Will This Class Be Offered?

The actual location of the classroom is important. Is it near other classes in the same discipline? Proximity becomes essential when you consider the absolute number of minutes it takes to move a large number of students in and out of a space—and this is without even factoring in exam administration and paper distribution. And since large classes are more often for classes that are available to a broader range of the student body, you have to make sure about building access and the room's proximity to those hardy souls we call in the physical plant who are often called upon to restore utilities or some other process that is critical to the continuation of the class. Many of the large class facilities are not in ideal locations, so you must plan for contingencies that include transporting equipment or handouts great distances and offering troubleshooting from a distance.

What Can Be Said about the Classroom?

A classroom is never just a classroom. What are the conditions of the seating, the walls, the whiteboards (chalkboards), and the floor? How often is the room cleaned? Without scheduled cleaning, some large population classrooms can look like a national political convention was held the previous day. How good are the acoustics? Are there windows? Are there too many windows? How good is the heating and the air conditioning? Not surprisingly, all of these questions come with dollar signs attached to them.

What about Technology?

Not a new question, but the answers are dramatically different. We used to ask if there were sufficient chalk and erasers in the room. Now we wonder if the room has fiber, if it is it Internet-friendly, if the projector has sufficient resolution, what the multimedia limitations are, can the professors use their laptops without any trouble, is there a flexible sound system, and are on-call technicians available if the professor encounters some difficulties? Technology is quite expensive, and your unit may not be able to afford the expense. You may need to consider collaborating with other units or with some central administration. These arrangements certainly make the costs more manageable, but they also create additional scheduling challenges.

Maintenance of technology is also an issue. High-resolution projectors and sound systems are often installed in less-than-easy-to-access locations, meaning that maintenance can be disruptive. You must consider this, especially if you find yourself scheduling the facility seemingly around the clock. In these cases, it becomes particularly important that you visit other sites—both academic and corporate—so you can determine what a reasonable maintenance schedule will look like.

How about the Legal Issues?

The most obvious legal issue is building and room access. I strongly suggest you carefully read the Americans with Disabilities Act and meet with your institution's lawyer. A second issue is student privacy. Public distribution of graded work and grades can be interpreted as violating a student's privacy. Again, you need to consult your campus legal experts, and some discussions with the professors would be very wise.

A third issue is technology related. Many large classes that involve multimedia also involve student performance of one kind or another. While showing student work in class may seem pedagogically sound, these displays may again violate student privacy.

Who Is Actually Doing the Teaching?

As an administrator, you often have no say in this decision. Usually a department makes a choice based on previous teaching performance or on a strong interest expressed by faculty in teaching such a class. Many departments view these large classes as recruiting tools and endeavor to get their best teachers to teach. Some departments, however, often turn to faculty who have expressed a strong interest in teaching. And in some cases the faculty are motivated by the apparent lure of a better schedule or the availability of teaching assistants. While certainly in the minority, these faculty will probably need more help than you had originally allocated.

And compensation can play a disquieting role here. Are you going to pay the professor more to teach a large section, or are you going to consider teaching a large section differently when assigning teaching loads? Both are forms of compensation, but that fact is sometimes lost on the affected professor. And, often, other professors view teaching large sections with help from teaching assistants as a better deal than they are currently receiving. You need to ensure that your direct reports (particularly new department chairs) understand these perceptions and take a proactive stance with other members of their departments.

What Kind of Support Will the Instructor Need?

This question often fails to get the attention it deserves. The management of a mega section can overwhelm even the most skilled professor. Keeping track of attendance, distributing assignments and returning graded work, and informing students of their status in the class can become systemic roadblocks when the laws of large numbers take over some of the course dynamics. All of these bookkeeping processes need to be revisited, and one should always keep and eye and ear tuned to the marketplace where technology is being used to wrestle with these problems—and in increasingly more affordable ways.

Teaching assistants or TAs are another concern. In large classes the professor can have less oversight of these essential persons who are often your eyes and ears with smaller groups of students. What kind of training do they need, and should language issues play a significant role in hiring?

I will only mention counseling. What is the impact of a large class on office hours? Does the presence of teaching assistants mean an additional burden on the faculty in those circumstances where the student wants to talk to him or her about their interactions with TAs?

Finally, after addressing all of these logistical, legal, and technological issues, I can't leave this subject without observing that whether teaching in a large or small setting, the issue is the student experience. Students in large settings can have a great experience. They can still make a personal connection with the subject material despite the obvious limitations on their personal interactions with the faculty.

12

Teaching Large Classes: A Brief Review of the Research

Christine A. Stanley
Texas A&M University

M. Erin Porter
The University of Texas, Austin

Introduction

In February 1980 W.J. McKeachie wrote in *Academe*:

> As budgets tighten, more and more college teachers are going to be involved in dealing with large numbers of students enrolled in a single course. If faculty members protest such increases, there is some suspicion of academic feather bedding. Thus the research evidence on class size is of much current interest. Does an increase in class size lead to a loss of quality of education? (McKeachie, 1980).

These statements and question are as pertinent in teaching large classes at the beginning of the 21st century as they were 20 years ago. University finances are more strained than ever, and to help ease the financial drain of increased enrollments, more faculty members, both novice and experienced, are facing larger numbers of students (Hensley & Oakley, 1998; Zietz & Cochran, 1997).

A review of the research literature on teaching large classes reveals that large classes pose an exciting challenge for some faculty and an enigma for others. For the experienced faculty member, it presents an opportunity to share disciplinary knowledge augmented with innovative instructional techniques to gain students' interest in the subject matter. For the new faculty member, it can be a challenging task to understand and reach audiences of such magnitude. Instructors who teach large classes often lament, "I am teaching these large classes, and I don't know what to do. It is difficult to hold their attention. Everyone is reading the campus newspaper or looking out the window" (Rosenkoetter, 1984; Hensley & Oakley, 1998). Although there are many challenges to teaching large classes, many researchers agree that they are surmountable (Moss & McMillen, 1980; Weimer, 1987; Steffens, 1991; Roberts & Dunn, 1996; Buskist & Wylie, 1998; Freeman, 1998; Hensley & Oakley, 1998).

Definition of a Large Class

"Frequently, large classes are defined operationally by researchers as those that contain 100 or more students" (Chism, 1989, p.1). Faculty viewpoints vary about how size affects their teaching behaviors or student performance. Some faculty think that 50 students is a large class, while others commonly teach 250 to 500 students in one room. Forty students in a writing or foreign language class may well qualify as a large class. Multi-section courses with a common syllabus, tests, and management issues often qualify as large classes. Thus, one definition of a large class does not fit every possible teaching situation (Weimer, 1987).

Without a doubt, challenges of large-class teaching in most disciplines are an emotional issue for faculty, students, and parents. There is a general belief that as classes get larger, students' learning and degree of personal satisfaction decrease. A brief history of large-class research may help temper this prevailing assumption.

Advantages and Disadvantages of Large Classes

Chism listed the following advantages to large classes in her 1989 article written for *Notes on Teaching* at The Ohio State University.

Advantages

Cost. Increased student-teacher ratio in a class lowers instructor costs. Some research indicates that providing teaching assistants, support staff, and services may negate these savings.

Faculty time. Teaching a large class rather than several small classes may allow faculty to manage their time more efficiently. Some faculty would argue that the increased time for management issues counterbalances savings in preparation and contact hours.

Faculty talent. Some faculty appear to be particularly effective with large groups of students per section. Most faculty appear more comfortable and effective with smaller classes.

Resources. One rationale for large-class instruction is that when instruction is planned on a grand scale, faculty can justify expenditures for professional quality audiovisuals, clerical assistance, special guest speakers, specially equipped facilities, or materials, since the course will reach large numbers of students. Reality is often very different, with few or no special resources and inadequate facilities.

Standardization. Departments often depend on large sections to produce sequential order and consistent manner of content presentation for entry-level courses. Mathematics, sciences, and foreign languages, for example, seek this type of sequential progression to ensure that students advance with similar experiences and competencies (Chism, 1989; Wilson & Tauxe, 1986).

Disadvantages

Chism listed the following four disadvantages:

Impersonal nature. Faculty and students alike complain about the impersonal nature of large classes and lack of personal contact and feedback (Aronson, 1987; Bostian, 1983; Chism, 1989; Knapper, 1987). However, Wulff, Nyquist, & Abbott, (1987) found that some students prefer the anonymity of larger classes with less pressure to participate.

Limited range of instructional activities possible. Faculty may feel bound to the lecture format and multiple-choice exams, with few opportunities for interactive student involvement and writing assignments. The contributing authors in this book provide a wide range of tested learning and teaching methodologies that expand the range of instructional activities in large or mega-classes.

Management issues. Large classes do demand more organizational time and management to handle the mechanics involved. At some institutions, faculty may not receive clerical or teaching assistant aid to accomplish the many administrative tasks connected with large classes; i.e., attendance, test design and administration, cheating during exams, office hours, etc.

Reward system. Faculty who teach large classes may be viewed as lower status members in a department and not rewarded fairly for their teaching investment. At some universities, departments offer no extra consideration in course load assignment based on class size (Chism, 1989).

The following review of research shows that long held beliefs about the advantages and disadvantages of large-class teaching may very well be changing as research measurements improve and expand.

Early Research on Class Size

Large-class teaching was one of the first problems approached by higher education researchers. In 1924, early researchers Edmondson and Mulder compared the performance of students enrolled in a 109-student class with students enrolled in a 43-student class in education. Their primary finding was that achievement of the two groups was approximately equal, with a slight overall higher performance of the smaller class on essays and mid-semester tests. At the same time, students in the larger class performed somewhat better on quizzes and the final examination. Students reported a preference for smaller classes (Edmondson & Mulder, 1924). The results of this groundbreaking research encouraged the Committee for Research at the University of Minnesota to complete a classic series of class size studies in psychology, physics, accounting, law, and education. Of 59 experiments, 46 favored large classes for student performance. Cheydleur at the University of Wisconsin, found consistency in the superiority of student performance in small French classes on objective departmental examinations (Cheydleur, 1945). Mueller's, Nachman's, and Opochinsky's, as well as Feldhusen's experiments, also found small classes somewhat superior in student performance, particularly in changes of attitudes toward teaching (Mueller, 1924; Nachman & Opochinsky, 1958; Feldhusen, 1963).

At Miami University, Macomber and Siegel's experiments in 1960 added measures not included in earlier research on large classes. They included conventional achievement tests, but also added measures of critical thinking and problem solving, scales of stereotypic attitudes, tests of student motivation, and tests of student attitudes toward instruction. Significant differences favored smaller classes on measures of change in misconceptions in psychology, problem solving in marketing, and measures of student attitudes in all courses. After two years, knowledge retention in large classes did not prove significantly less than in smaller classes. In eight of the nine classes studied, small differences favored the small class format (Macomber & Siegel, 1960). Since faculty members value content retention, problem solving, and relation of knowledge to relevant attitudes, most early research favored small classes. In addition, in almost all studies, students and faculty clearly stated a preference for small classes (McKeachie, 1980).

Recent Research on Class Size

Over the years, studies on the effects of class size, although conflicting, have "reinforced the idea that large-class instruction is a complicated process that is affected by numerous instructional dimensions" (Wulff, Nyquist, & Abbott, 1987). More recent research reveals that class size is not the major determinant of successful learning or teaching (Gilbert, 1995; Wulff, Nyquist, & Abbott, 1987; Williams, Cook, Quinn, & Jensen, 1985; Feldman, 1984; Marsh, Overall, & Kesler; 1979). Wulff, Nyquist, & Abbott (1987) found no significant differences in student ratings on the following issues:

- Relevance and usefulness of course content in best large class and best small class

- Satisfaction with amount learned in best large class and best small class

Student perceptions of other specific instructional dimensions included a significant discrepancy in the interaction between students and instructor in large classes over small classes. Instructor organization and clarity in large classes can be just as successful in large classes as small classes. Students rated their best large classes higher on organization and the effective use of examples and illustrations than their best small classes. Next to an effective, involved instructor, students in large classes listed an *excellent text book, test reviews, guide sheets, visual aids, and lecture notes* as vital keys to effective learning in large classes (Wulff, Nyquist, & Abbott, 1987). The most recent research in large-class teaching involves incorporating technology, participating in team teaching, and using video conferencing for multiple campus large courses (Roberts & Dunn, 1996; Alimi, Kassal, & Azeez, 1998; Freeman, 1998). Instructors can be encouraged by this information which illustrates that instructional strategies can be adapted to enhance the learning process for students in large classes.

Classic Issues in Large-Class Teaching

Enduring Issues for Faculty and Students in Large Classes

The review of advantages and disadvantages and the history of related research above reveal many of the issues that are classic concerns for faculty: time commitment to large-class teaching; lack of resources, personnel, and facilities; lack of contact and interaction with students; use of the lecture method for all teaching; and lack of rewards and recognition for teaching large classes (Litke, 1995). Faculty often think that student teacher ratings will be lower in large classes than in smaller sections (Harcharick, 1993).

Students listed four professor characteristics that were essential in successful large classes:

1) Instructor competency—experienced or knowledgeable instructor

2) Instructor concern for students—friendly, caring, and available instructor

3) Instructor energy level—enthusiastic and dynamic instructor

4) Instructor speaking ability—easy to understand, interesting, and communicative instructor classes
   (Wulff, Nyquist, & Abbott, 1987)

Student issues listed by Litke in 1995, included instructor style and skill in large sections; use of class time, particularly related to course content and amount of material covered in one semester; interruptions to learning due to physical distractions with large numbers of students; problems establishing a personal relationship with the instructor; and environmental constraints due to defective acoustics or inadequate visual aids. Although recent research presents a more favorable view from students in large classes, student concerns may be lost in the clamor to meet the needs of increasing enrollments at many universities and colleges (Zietz & Cochran, 1997).

Universality of Large-Class Issues Across Academic Disciplines

One very essential part of the academic discussion about teaching in large classes is the universality of teaching concerns, teaching methodologies, and promotion of effective teaching. Articles in the disciplinary areas of psychology, government, sociology, history, education, library science, literature, science education, physics, astronomy, Asian studies, and many others reveal numerous commonalties in the search for excellence in large classes (Hastie, Sanders, & Rowland, 1999; Buskist & Wylie, 1998; Hensley & Oakley, 1998; Galton, 1998a, 1998b; Ghosh, 1999; Martino & Sala, 1996; Corwin, 1996; Harwood, 1996; Christensen, 1994; Day, 1994; Steffens, 1991; Strauss & Fulwiler, 1989, 1990; Berquist, Tiefel, & Waggenspack, 1986; Hamlin & Janssen, 1987; Rosenkotter, 1984; Howes & Watson, 1982; Moss & McMillen, 1980; White, 1974). This text also offers valuable information that can be applied to many courses in different disciplines if we can see the applicability of creative large-class teaching methodology across the university curriculum. Shared knowledge and experience enriches all teachers who look past international or disciplinary boundaries.

Continuing Challenges of Large-Class Instruction

As instructors, we should emphasize the course objectives that determine our approaches to communication skills, cooperative learning (especially small group), critical analysis or problem solving, appropriate use of technology, and variety and relevance, as we move away from the straight lecture format or information download in large classes. These authors, across higher education, provide us with multiple resources to meet the challenges of the large classroom and find great satisfaction in teaching large classes well. The following references provide an additional resource for practitioners.

References

Alimi, M. M., Kassal, B., & Azeez, T. (1998, March). Managing large classes: Team teaching approach. *Forum, 36* (1), 50-53.

Aronson, J. R. (1987). Six keys to effective instruction in large classes: Advice from a practitioner. (pp. 31-38). In M. G. Weimer (Ed.), *Teaching large classes well.* New Directions for Teaching and Learning, No. 32. San Francisco, CA: Jossey-Bass.

Berquist, G., Tiefel, V., & Waggenspack, B. (1986). Coping with the critical essay in a large lecture course. *Communication Education, 35* (4), 396-399.

Bostian, L. R. (1983). Even in classes of 100 to 150, personalization is possible. *Journalism Educator, 38* (2), 8-10.

Buskist, W., & Wylie, D. (1998). A method for enhancing student interest in large introductory classes. *Teaching of Psychology, 25* (3), 203-205.

Cheydleur, F. D. (1945, August). Criteria of effective teaching in basic French courses. *Bulletin of the University of Wisconsin* (Monograph No. 2783). Madison, WI: University of Wisconsin.

Chism, N. V. N. (1989, June). Large enrollment classes: Necessary evil or not necessarily evil? *Notes on Teaching, 5,* (pp.1-8). Occasional papers published by The Center for Teaching Excellence at The Ohio State University: Columbus, OH: The Ohio State University. (ERIC Document Reproduction Service ED 334 875)

Christensen, T. (1994). Large classes and their influence on language teaching. *Journal of Hokusei Junior College, 30,* 121-129.

Corwin, P. (1996, July). Using the community as a classroom for large introductory sociology classes. *Teaching Sociology, 24,* 310-315.

Day, S. (1994). Learning in large sociology classes: Journals and attendance. *Teaching Sociology, 22,* 151-165.

Edmondson, J. B., & Mulder, F. J. (1924). Size of class as a factor in university instruction. *Journal of Educational Research, 9,* 1-12.

Feldhusen, J. R. (1963). The effects of small and large-group instruction on learning of subject matter, attitudes, and interests. *Journal of Psychology, 55,* 357-362.

Feldman, K. A. (1984). Class size and college students' evaluations of teachers and courses: A closer look. *Research in Higher Education, 21* (1), 45-116.

Freeman, M. (1998). Video conferencing: A solution to the multi-campus large classes problem? *British Journal of Educational Technology, 29* (3), 197-210.

Galton, M. (1998a). Class size: A critical moment on the research. *International Journal of Educational Research, 29,* 809-818.

Galton, M. (1998b). Guest editor's introduction: Class size and pupil achievement. *International Journal of Educational Research, 29,* 689-690.

Ghosh, R. (1999). The challenge of teaching large numbers of students in general education laboratory classes involving many graduate student assistants. *Bioscience, 25* (1), 7-11.

Gilbert, S. (1995, Winter). *Quality education: Does class size matter?* CSSHE Professional Profile, 14, pp. 1-6. Association of Universities and Colleges of Canada.

Hamlin, J. & Janssen, S. (1987, January). Active learning in large introductory sociology courses. *Teaching Sociology, 15,* 45-54.

Harcharick, K. (1993, October). *Problems and opportunities in teaching a large class.* Presented at the meeting of the CSU Institute for Teaching and Learning Exchange, San Jose, CA.

Harwood, W. S. (1996, March). The one-minute paper. *Journal of Chemical Education, 73* (3), 229-230.

Hastie, P. A., Sanders, S. W., & Rowland, R. S. (1999). Where good intentions meet hard realities: Teaching large classes in physical education. *Journal of Teaching in Physical Education, 18,* 277-289.

Hensley, T. R., & Oakley, M. (1998). The challenge of the large lecture class: Making it more like a small seminar. *Political Science & Politics, 31* (1), 47-51.

Howes, R., & Watson, J. (1982, January). Demonstrations to wake up large classes. *The Physics Teacher,* 40-41.

Knapper, C. (1987). Large classes and learning (pp. 5-16). In M. G. Weimer (Ed.), *Teaching large classes well.* New Directions for Teaching and Learning, No. 32. San Francisco, CA: Jossey-Bass.

Litke, R. A. (1995, Feb.). *Learning lessons from large classes: Student attitudes toward effective and ineffective methods in large classes.* Paper presented at the Western States Communication Association, Communication and Instruction Interest Group. Portland, Oregon. (ERIC Documents Reproduction Service. ED 384 088)

Macomber, F. G., & Siegel, L. (1957). A study of large-group teaching procedures. *Educational Research, 38,* 220-229.

Macomber, F. G., & Siegel, L. (1960). *Experimental study in instructional procedures.* Final report. Oxford, OH: Miami University Press.

Marsh, H. W., Overall, J. U., & Kesler, S. P. (1979). Class size, students' evaluations, and instructional effectiveness. *American Educational Research Journal, 16* (1), 57-69.

Martino, G., & Sala, F. (1996). *Engaging students in large classes.* A paper presented at the Tenth Annual Conference on Undergraduate Teaching of Psychology. Ellenville, NY. (ERIC Document Reproduction Service. ED 405 033)

McKeachie, W. J. (1980, Feb.). Class size, large classes, and multiple sections. *Academe,* 24-27.

Moore, R. L. (1982). Teaching the big class. *Journalism Educator,* 10-11, 78.

Moss, G. D., & McMillen, D. (1980). A strategy for developing problem solving skills in large undergraduate classes. *Studies in Higher Education, 5* (2), 161-171.

Mueller, A. D. (1924). Class size as a factor in normal school instruction. *Education, 45,* 203-277.

Nachman, M., & Opochinsky, S. (1958). The effects of different teaching methods: A methodological study. *Journal of Educational Psychology, 49,* 245-249.

Roberts, G. A., & Dunn, P. M. (1996). *Electronic classrooms and lecture theatres: Design and use factors in the age of the mass lecture.* Washington, DC: United States Department of Education, Office of Educational Research and Improvement. ERIC Document Reproduction Service. ED 396 743)

Rosenkoetter, J. S. (1984, April). Teaching psychology to large classes: Videotapes, PSI, and lecturing. *Teaching of Psychology, 11* (2), 85-87.

Steffens, H. (1991, May/June). Using informal writing in large history classes: Helping students to find interest and meaning in history. *The Social Studies,* 107-109.

Strauss, M., & Fulwiler, T. (1989, December/1990, January). Writing to learn in large lecture classes. *Journal of College Science Teaching, 19,* (3), 158-163.

Weimer, M. G. (1987). Teaching large classes well. *New Directions for Teaching and Learning, 32,* 1-103.

White, J. B. (1974). How to handle large classes. *Improving College and University Teaching, 22* (4), 262-266.

Williams, D. D., Cook, P. F., Quinn, B., & Jensen, R. P. (1985). University class size: Is smaller better? *Research in Higher Education, 23* (3), 307-317.

Wilson, R. C., & Tauxe, C. (1986). *Faculty views of factors that affect teaching excellence in large lecture classes.* Research on Teaching Improvement and Evaluation, Teaching and Evaluation Services (TIES). Berkeley, CA: University of California, Berkeley. (ERIC Document Reproduction Service. ED 323 902)

Wulff, D., Nyquist, J., & Abbott, R. D. (1987, Winter). Students' perceptions of large classes (pp. 17-31). In M. Weimer (Ed.), *Teaching large classes well.* New Directions for Teaching and Learning, No. 32. San Francisco, CA: Jossey-Bass.

Zietz, J., & Cochran, H. H. (1997, Fall). Containing costs without sacrificing achievement: Some evidence from college-level economics classes. *Journal of Education Finance, 23,* 177-192.

PART TWO

Examples Across the Disciplines

Example 1 _____

What I Wish I Had Known Before I Taught A Large Class

Emily Hoover

University of Minnesota

I enter the auditorium through the doors at the top, look down at center stage, and realize how far down I have to walk. I begin walking down the steps and notice the rows are numbered and start counting as I go... 24, 23, 22, ...until I get to the bottom. I look up at the sea of faces. No one is smiling, there is a little chatting, lots of people staring. I don't make much eye contact. I boot up the computer, arrange my materials, turn down the lights and start talking. I feel pretty detached from the audience, almost like I am in a movie theater. I don't have a clue what the students are doing. Welcome to my very first day of teaching in a large lecture hall.

Does it sound intimidating? My first experience was! Is teaching 150 or 300 students different than teaching 15? Large classes are different than small ones. Organization, preparation, and evaluation are inherently different for large classes than for small (Davis, 1993). I was totally unprepared for how distant the students were and consequently how detached I started to become. I realized after teaching large classes for a few terms that I was treating the students more like an audience in a movie theater rather than a group of learners.

I have learned what some of the major challenges are when teaching a large number of students. I've observed that students are spectators who struggle with apathy, inattention, poor attendance, discomfort with approaching the instructor, failure to prepare for class, and failure to take responsibility in learning when large classes are taught passively. How to break the movie-theater mentality continues to challenge me.

Teaching large classes takes additional thought and preparation but can be exciting and satisfying. I find it challenging to avoid anonymity among students and between students and me. I will discuss the preparations and techniques I use to organize for large classes for active learning using the class Plant Propagation. Since labs are an integral part of the courses I teach, I will also discuss how to integrate lab experiences and lectures.

Large classes often are designed to introduce students to a discipline, and horticulture is no exception. The mix of students in the course includes those students majoring in the subject as well as those fulfilling a general requirement for the university. The course has two 50-minute lectures per week and two 115-minute lab periods per week. Usually there are two teaching assistants involved with the course.

Preparing to Teach a Large Class

One of the biggest differences in teaching a large class versus one with fewer students is the planning and the time that planning requires. I find McKeachie's (1999) book invaluable in helping me plan and organize before the class begins. I have to make decisions about evaluation, assignments, grading, and other integral features of the course early, and changing them once the class begins is difficult. When I teach a class with 20 students, changing assignments is possible if the subject proves interesting or difficult for the group. However, changing assignments during the semester with a class of 100 students is difficult: I liken it to trying to turn a large ship in a small harbor—possible, but not easily done.

Review What You Have Done

When I start to plan for Plant Propagation, I review the previous year. What went well? What really needs to change? What do I want to do differently? How did the assessment tools work? What type of help did I have last semester, and is it the same for the coming semester? I review what happened last year by rereading evaluations, my own self-assessment, and learner outcomes for the course. I organize topics and consider the order of lab activities to reinforce and emphasize material covered in lecture. I also review and develop different lab and lecture exercises by adding onto what we did previously or changing those that did not work well. I assemble the list of plant materials I will use in lab and lecture demonstrations, and share the plant list with the greenhouse staff. Evaluating student progress—what kind of exams, how many, given when—are all issues I that decide on early. After that, I put together the specifics for the course packet and supporting web pages. Davis (1993) gives concrete steps that can be used to organize a large lecture course. Drummond (2000) briefly summarizes practices that constitute excellence in college teaching.

Designing and Administering Exams

Two issues I find that have been really difficult for me when planning for a large class are exams and working with teaching assistants. Exams are more difficult to give in a large class. Usually there are not enough seats in the lecture room to have students sit in every other seat. So is the exam given in lecture or lab? If given in lecture, how many versions of the exam need to be developed? What format will it take? Who will proctor the exam? Who will grade the exam? Who is responsible for recording grades?

The answers to those questions vary for me almost every time I teach. I have settled on, but am still tweaking, most of the answers. This past year, I gave three midterm exams and a final, all during lecture time. I make up two versions of the test, and students sitting next to each other take different exams. I make sure that the exams are copied onto different colored paper so sorting and grading is easier. The exam format I have settled on is short answer, fill-in-the-blank, and problem solving questions. Before the semester starts, I make sure at least one of my teaching assistants is available to help proctor the exams. I try to grade most of the exams myself, but this is only possible because registration is limited to 100 students. Grading the exams myself allows me to find out where the students are having the most difficulty and makes answering questions of how problems were graded easier. To make time for grading, I schedule the entire day after each exam in my calendar for grading.

When questions arise about grading, my policy has been to have students write their reasons for why their answer is correct, and I respond in writing also. After experimenting with many different ways to settle grading disputes, I find this format focuses students on why their answer is or is not correct. This procedure has also given me insight into how each student was thinking when answering the question. I keep the record of all exams in the course, with my teaching assistants often helping me record the grades.

Working with Teaching Assistants

Making sure teaching assistants are connected with the course is crucial. I delegate teaching the lab section, not just assisting, to teaching assistants in Plant Propagation. The teaching assistants have to be able to adjust, through meetings and training, to the open inquiry based lab approach that I use. They also need to be prepared to handle many different circumstances. Let me give an example. We use razor blades in the lab for cutting plant material. Even though we remind students that razor blades are sharp, we have a small number of students who cut themselves, some of them severely. TAs need to evaluate the cut, and if necessary get the student to a medical practitioner. Not your normal TA training!

Teaching assistants are often not notified of which class they are teaching until near the beginning of the semester. They are usually not in on the course planning. I find I need to bring them up to speed on what decisions have been made, and what they need to do in their lab sections at the beginning. I familiarize them with the flow of the course. When I write down why I made certain decisions during planning, and then share this with my TAs, they have an easier time the first few weeks. Prior to the start of the semester we meet and review expectations for students and instructors, content, and organization of the course. Once the term starts, our weekly meetings are used to make sure that all the preparations for the following week are completed, discuss challenges that have occurred, and brainstorm ideas on actively engaging students in discussion about what is happening in the lab. Because the lab does not have a lab preparation person, the teaching team is responsible for ordering much of the material that is needed as well as making up solutions. All of these responsibilities are decided on early, and we develop a timeline for what needs to be done, when, and by whom.

As is evident, logistics of providing and handling material, particularly living plant material, for a large class is difficult. We are always thinking about space: How much will we need, do we have enough for the experiments designed, and are we using the greenhouse efficiently? If we do our planning correctly, then we don't have to move a lot of plant material around. However, mistakes happen. This past semester, we labeled greenhouse benches for each lab. What we did not calculate correctly was the space each lab section was going to take, so lab section one spilled into lab section two's area. By the time lab section five came to put their plants in the greenhouse, there was no space. Needless to say, we moved plant material! We had used pots that were a bit bigger than the ones we had used to estimate the amount of space needed. We learned that four-inch pots are bigger than three-inch pots and thus take up a lot more room!

Before the semester begins, I visit the room where I am going to be teaching. I have had to work at getting a desirable room. As with most universities, our larger lecture rooms have fixed seating, with long rows of chairs that are not easy to navigate. I have to know the limitations of the room ahead of time, and work to figure out how to organize group activities within the space provided. I also make sure I understand how to access the computer projector and other audio-visual equipment. Since I teach the lab section in the greenhouse right before lecture, a six to seven minute walk away, I investigate the different routes from lab to lecture before the semester starts.

First-Day Issues

Now the first day is imminent; how do I keep the movie-theater atmosphere out of my class? I think ahead to the issues that may come up on the first day, and I plan how I will handle them. Some of the issues that continually arise for me on the first day are: registration for the class or changing lab sections; learning students' names; outlining expectations; and getting background information from students. Students also have concerns on the first day: How are grades assigned? What are the "rules"? How accessible is the instructor going to be? Who is sitting near me? I feel that if I am going to have students actively participate during the semester, we have to start on the first day.

Techniques of Teaching

On the first day, I start with an introduction of myself and include a map of how to get from the lecture room to my office and to the greenhouse. Students then introduce themselves to at least four others whom they do not know while I go around the room and introduce myself to as many students as possible. I try to associate faces with names, and continually repeat the names of the previous students as I learn a new name. Obviously, I can't learn 100 names in one lecture period. I have noticed that most students have a preferred seating area in the classroom. As the semester progresses, I introduce myself to different areas of the room until I have a fairly good grasp of most students' names. There are a lot of techniques developed to learn students' names (Pescosolido & Aminzade, 1999), but I find repeating names, concentrating on different parts of the lecture room, and talking with students before class works for me. One other handy technique I use is to always ask a student their name whenever they come up to me to ask a question. Students can hardly believe that I can remember their names. This can change the atmosphere—it is no longer a movie theater.

After the introductions, I have them answer the following questions: What is your major (as of today)? What college are you in? What can I do to help you learn? What are you going to do to help yourself learn? Are you comfortable with science? They turn their responses in and I tabulate them for the following lecture period. I also have them do at least two more active learning exercises pertaining to the subject material on the first day. I have used exercises such as listing all the terms they know associated with plants, or I bring plant material in and have them label all the parts of the plant that they know. Before I close for the day, I have them go back and reintroduce themselves to their classmates.

At the end of class, when the registration questions come forth, I try to deal with the issues immediately or get answers for students that day. I have taken over the assignment of registration numbers, and keep a running tally of how many students are in each lab section. Every university deals with this issue differently but be aware, it will come up!

I have developed lecture notes that students purchase through the bookstore. I have also put them online with password protection, but almost all the students buy them from the bookstore. Students have calculated the cost of printing the pages off the web versus buying copies from the bookstore and have found the cost is less at the bookstore, and much more accessible.

Active participation is important to keep students motivated and learning. But how did I start? I began developing in-class exercises by using classroom assessment techniques developed by Angelo and Cross (1993). I answered the questionnaire on the type of learning I want to go on in my classroom. Then I reviewed the different techniques they describe. An example of one of the techniques that I routinely use is the matrix. Having students working in groups of three, I give them a matrix to fill in. One matrix I have used relates the types of cuttings students have taken in lab with adventitious meristem formation, a topic they are learning about in lecture. I do not usually have my students turn in the assessment, but we always review them during class, and I get a pretty good idea if students are confused. I feel using these techniques emphasizes to students that making connections within a lecture topic or between lecture and lab is important. In addition, I use these techniques to help students think about using them as study skills.

Students want to be involved in their learning, but sometimes they just don't know how. I give students the opportunity to ask additional questions on a topic by placing a box at the back of the room where they can put a question, or they can email questions to me. At the beginning of each class I respond to questions that I receive. When answering questions, I show students how I think through the problem, and ask them to share strategies. I get additional feedback from students by asking them to fill out surveys and midterm evaluations. The key to success of any of these methods, I found, is to respond to class suggestions, comments, and ideas. If I decide not to do something that a number of the class members suggested, I tell them why I am not going to take them up on the suggestion.

I want to return to discussing how to overcome the anonymity that large classes bring to both the students and the instructor. How can I be more than a screen to them and they not more than just spectators? One thing I do as an instructor is learn names. However, other techniques I use no matter the class size: walking among students, having lab sections sit together for certain in class activities, making eye contact and smiling, being available before and after class, pausing for students to think, repeating students' questions and answers. These techniques all share an important quality; students realize the person in front of the classroom is not on screen, and they are expected to participate.

Labs are an integral part of the courses that I teach in horticulture. However, the comment that came up on evaluations over a number of semesters was that there is little linking of material between lecture and lab. The comment is valid in students' eyes, but was a bit frustrating for me. I knew how the lab experiences are supposed to be integrated into lecture, but the connection was not happening for the students. The link was not overt. Now it is. We spend time discussing mitosis (cell division) at the cellular level during lecture. In lab, we put the plants under different conditions to induce cell division. However, we visualize the result in lab by looking at root or shoot growth, not at cells. Making the link overt—cell division occurs at the cellular level, but we visualize the process at the whole plant level—clarified how the concepts were linked.

Towards the end of the semester, bringing closure to the subject becomes important. I go back to the organization of the lab book and the lecture schedule and bring them together. For example, how do the parts of the plant we studied in September tie into the results of the experiments in November? Using the table of contents from the lab book as one side of a matrix and biological processes on the other side of the matrix and filling in, with detail, the aspects that have been demonstrated (and hopefully learned), students begin to fit concepts together.

Teaching large classes well takes patience and planning. I try to treat students in all my classes as learners, not movie patrons. Now, when I walk into a large lecture course for the first time, I smile, I introduce myself, and I welcome a large group of learners to class. The stairway is not so steep any more, and the back row is very accessible.

References

Angelo, T. A., & Cross, K. P. (1993). *Classroom assessment techniques: A handbook for college teachers* (2nd ed.). San Francisco, CA: Jossey-Bass.

Davis B. (1993). *Tools for teaching.* San Francisco, CA: Jossey-Bass.

Drummond, T. (2000). *A brief summary of the best practices in college teaching: Intended to challenge the professional development of all teachers.* http://nsccux.sccd.ctc.edu/~eceprog/bstprac.html.

McKeachie, W. J. (1999). *Teaching tips: Strategies, research, and theory for college and university teachers* (10th ed.) Boston, MA: Houghton Mifflin.

Pescosolido, B. & Aminzade, R. (1999). *The social worlds of higher education: Handbook for teaching in a new century.* Thousand Oaks, CA: Pine Forge Press.

Example 2 _____

A Management Lesson

Steven Tomlinson
University of Texas, Austin

I used to teach economics in the College of Liberal Arts—two sections per semester, 50 or 60 students in each, small classes by Texas standards. Learning names was no problem. Neither was keeping up with each student's personal particulars as they might affect performance in the course. I had a TA to help with grading and recording. I won teaching awards. My job was completely satisfying and almost as effortless as my friends in the business world suspected.

Then I moved to the College of Business. The money was better, the office was nicer, and the sections were bigger. Lots bigger. Like three or four times bigger. No problem, I thought. I've got great performance skills. I know how to work a big house and keep the students engaged. Not just engaged, but spellbound. Seeing no need to make serious revisions, I walked into the large class with essentially the same syllabus I'd used in the smaller sections. I expected to be a big hit.

The disaster that ensued was due only in small part to my lack of familiarity with the new textbook. I should also credit the hyper-competitive culture of business school undergraduates at that time. But when the semester ended and I read through the worst teaching evaluations of my career, it was clear that the real problem was my failure to deal with reality—in this case, the reality of what it takes to get 200 people coordinated and motivated to learn economics, or to do anything for that matter.

The trouble started early in the semester with students' complaints that we were losing their assignments. "I took the quiz, but it's not in the stack." "Where's my midterm?" "The TA must have lost my exam." I'd never had this problem before. In hindsight, I'm appalled at my own naiveté. Why didn't I foresee that stacking the assignments in five piles (A-F, G-K, etc.) along the back wall would lead to a cluttered mess—my liberal arts students knew how to keep piles in order—even if it didn't invite out-and-out dishonesty. And of course, I had no idea whether any individual was telling the truth. How was I supposed to remember who had attended on the day of the test?

Then the requests for special consideration got out of control. Everyone had an extenuating circumstance—interview trip, wedding or funeral, medical emergency—and needed either a make-up exam or dropped quiz or a regrade. As I began supplying exceptions, demand grew. And word about who had been granted what exceptions traveled with greater speed than accuracy. Before long, students who were denied special consideration expected me to explain how their situation differed materially from a well-known case in which I had granted the exception. The final evaluations reflected their frustration—"unfair," "arbitrary," "he has favorites." This was more than I could handle.

On top of all this, the students were coming to class unprepared. Despite my cajoling, my warnings, my scolding, they refused to read the assigned text before the lecture, so that I was reduced to reading it to them. Not literally, you understand, but since the lecture was their first exposure to the material, I was limited to providing definitions and simple explanations. If I tried to do applications, the students crossed their arms and scowled. This body language challenged me to work harder to make the basics even clearer. They had me. They knew I wouldn't proceed until they understood, so they began strategically balking. Then it got ugly. I accused them of obstinacy, and they accused me of poor teaching. I began dreading the class. My stomach hurt before I even got to campus. My identity was tied to my success as a teacher, and I was clearly failing.

During the winter break, I progressed through Kübler-Ross's five stages of grief. My father said, "Look, you're supposed to know something about management. People respond to incentives. It's the manager's job to set up incentives that show the workers what to do and make them want to do it." That's when the irony of the situation struck me—the mismanaged management class.

Now it was a challenge. How do you get 200 people organized and inspired to learn? What could I learn from the management theory I was teaching? How could I make the large-class problem and its solution—part of the lesson? Reflecting on the mistakes of the previous semester, I drafted a three-step plan.

Step One: Name the Truth in the Room

On the first day of the new semester, I asked each student to look around. "This course is more than an economics class, it's a management challenge. Look at you: 200 people—diverse people, representing a variety of interests, a wide range of skills, and a host of competing objectives. How are you going to work together to create a product that has value for each of you? In an important sense, this challenge—coordinating individual actions to achieve a group goal—is what management is all about."

With this introduction, I relieved myself of the need to make this impossible situation work. (I mean if you think about it, this Jiffy Lube approach to education is simply outrageous. And it's outrageous that we just ignore the outrageousness of it and carry on as if packing 200 or 300 anxious and apathetic people in a room with tiny formica-topped, flip-up desks and fluorescent lights made perfect sense.) The students had final responsibility for the success of the class—I was merely their leader—and the success of the class was to be a sign that they had mastered its lessons.

Step Two: Reduce Uncertainty

I established clear and simple rules. That's the leader's first job. The syllabus expanded to 17 pages and read like a legal contract. "No make up assignments for any reason." ("With a pre-approved absence, you may move a mid-term's weight to the final, but I don't recommend it.") "You will have a weekly quiz to verify your progress with the reading. Every student gets four dropped quizzes, with no questions asked, but no more." And so on. Rules about calculators (not allowed) and distracting side conversations (not tolerated) and time limits ("Anyone who continues writing after I call time will have his assignment confiscated and discarded.").

If you've never tried to write an exhaustive set of laws—a rulebook to govern every conceivable situation and anticipate every temptation—you've avoided a transformative experience. The more I wrote, the angrier I got. ("Why should I have to tell these students how to behave? Who has failed these children that they've reached the age of majority without developing basic accountability?" This line of inquiry quickly becomes debilitating.) Then I had the breakthrough. Take them as you find them. If they need a narrow path and a short leash, then provide it. When I had given them too much latitude, they had diverted their energies into unproductive influence activities—they had spent time lobbying and threatening and flattering the professor because under the circumstances this approach had seemed the quickest route to the grade they wanted.

With the rules in place, the students saw clearly that the only way to get the grade was to learn the material and play along with the professor's insistence that they were capable of making mature choices and managing themselves. On the first day of class, I did some role-playing with the students to help them come to terms with the new rules: "Let's say you need to go to a wedding on the day of the midterm. What are you going to do? Suppose you come to my office. What do you say? What do you think I'm going to say? What does the syllabus oblige me to say?" And so on. This strategy worked much better than I anticipated. Almost no one asked for an exception. (From the syllabus: "Don't even think about it. It is disrespectful to ask for an exception—such as scheduling a separate exam date—that could not be extended to all of your classmates given the constraints under which we're operating.") And before long, the influence activities ceased.

I had the students sign a contract at the beginning of the semester: "I accept the rules of this class as reasonable and expect the teacher to enforce them consistently and without bias." On the evaluations at the end of the second semester, the students praised the new syllabus: "At first I was furious to see all of these rules. I felt like he was treating us like children. But it works. I never worried about what was expected of me or how I would be graded." "Tough but fair."

With a small class you can change students' lives with the power of your charisma. In a large class, your charisma can actually work against you. If you and your charisma become the curriculum event, you're more likely to be charged with favoritism and arbitrariness when special situations arise. Large classes present the opportunity to teach students that the rule of law encourages dignity and equality.

Step Three: Delegate Responsibility

Enlist the students' skills in managing administrivia. Heaven knows they're going to be doing plenty of this in the business world. I began by dividing them into ten groups of 20. On the first day of class, each group elected a leader and an alternate. The group leader stood to earn two bonus points on the course average (the currency of this realm) if she or he had perfect attendance on the days of in-class quizzes and exams. (An absence passed the mantle of authority to the alternate.) The group leader recorded assignments turned in, returned graded assignments, and let students in the group check all grades recorded. Any discrepancies in posted grades had to be reported within seven days with a note attached to the misreported assignment.

Any group that showed particular creativity in dealing with paperwork stood to earn one bonus point for each of its members. I delighted in calling class attention to especially effective ways in which students had organized themselves—how they sat, how the group leader handed out papers, and so on. By the end of the semester, I doubt that the extra credit inspired the students nearly as much as the joy of discovering better ways to get things done. They became artists of management. Within the security of the rules, they took creative initiative, a mark of maturity.

A large class is a management problem—or a psychology problem, or a biology problem, or a political science problem, the possibilities are endless—and is therefore an opportunity to teach your students powerful, experiential lessons. Call attention to the situation and engage their curiosity about it. Set clear rules that increase accountability and pre-empt unproductive, opportunistic efforts. Give them a front-line assignment in the war against entropy and chaos. I believe that under the regrettable circumstances of the large class, this approach is the most effective way to change a student's life. Within a couple of semesters, I won another teaching award. This one was different, however, and better than any honor I had previously earned. The award was for effective teaching in large classes, and I knew that the students had given it to me, not because of showmanship or charisma, but because I had cared enough to create an environment that marshaled their energies for achievement.

Example 3 _____

Eleven Very Basic Tips For Teaching Large Business Classes

Tom Campbell
University of Texas, Austin

I have averaged between 500 and 550 students a semester for ten years. The largest classes are 350, or so, and the smallest around 80. In all, I have faced around 11,000 upper division undergraduate students and have developed some self-survival instincts. I believe if you try the following ideas, they will work for you. In my view, they are universal axioms for the large-class environment.

1) Hold Their Attention

When the student fails to learn, the teacher has failed to teach! Or the teacher has failed to put something out there that takes root in a mind. Sun Tzu, the great Chinese philosopher, taught that decadence in leadership was to assess others but not yourself. When students get up and leave the classroom in the midst of your lecture, it's you, not them. Get entertaining. Do something to hold their attention. You must hold their attention to plant the ideas you want them to remember.

2) Use Their Eye

I believe that most of what people learn is from what they see, much less from what they hear, and even less from touch, feel, taste, smell, and the other senses. Always have something on the screen that students can see. I use supplemental readings that the students purchase which are a copy of the teaching points projected on the screen, this gives students a copy of what is on the screen and then they can listen to the amplification/explanation of the particular idea. This strategy cuts the tension level which runs high when hundreds are trying to grasp an idea presented by one person way down at the front of the room.

3) Test What You Teach

Exams must come from the ideas you have tried to plant in class. If they don't, you will be perceived as unfair or worse: You may lose their trust. In my experience, there is nothing more loathsome to a student than teachers who disguise or veil what they expect a student to know. Teachers must be readable to the student, and what is important must be readily recognized.

4) Become a Storyteller

Every bone dry management function that I teach has accompanying stories, cases, and examples. People find it easier to remember and think in the context of stories and examples. I frame exam questions from those stories and examples I use in class.

5) Move

An auditorium classroom has multiple distractions. Never let yourself be imprisoned by a podium. Always move across the front, up the aisles, down a row of seats. This makes students concentrate by following you and watching the screen. A wireless portable microphone is a necessity. If you have specific points to make, be sure they are on your transparencies projected on the screen, and use that as your cue card. If you are unaccustomed to this style of teaching, reserve a classroom and rehearse.

6) Use Yourself Sparingly

Your personal experiences, research, moments of triumph, etc. should be used very carefully. I use "myself" examples of when I fell flat on my face, lost a sure thing, was victimized by fate, or let down by others. It creates a remarkable atmosphere of empathy with struggling students.

7) Utility of the Subject

The subjects of management and leadership have somewhat more pizzazz than, say, vector calculus. You cannot hold students' attention in a large class with irrelevant and unproven theories; the subject must have some real world application.

8) Earn Their Trust

Trust is not a given; it is earned. If you go against the values of the students, they will not trust you. The ultimate value to a student is a grade, so never mess with grades: keep them straightforward and objective. Never use a curve which ensures that half the grades are above or below some arbitrary line. If you do, you have violated idea number eight. You will be perceived as narrow and your effectiveness will plummet.

9) Get Face Time

Every time a student comes to you, take the time to talk to the individual. Get some face time! Sometimes that will be your only contact during a semester, so view it as an opportunity. I take care of all student contact, complaints, and excuses. I accept reasonable excuses for absences. Flexibility and positive personal contact can clear the air and help students see you as someone who is really interested in teaching something rather than hard-nosing students by enforcing iron-clad bureaucratic rules.

10) Avoid Change

Never change anything that you have said you will do. Exams go on the days scheduled, unless the classroom has been consumed by a tornado.

11) K.I.S.S.

Keep it simple stupid! Trying to use complex grading systems based on class participation, group work, written or oral reports, etc. will only cause confusion in large classes and bring the tent down around your ears. I use a simple formula to assign grades: four evenly spaced exams worth 23% each and 8% for attendance. Attendance is computed on completing 17 ungraded attendance quizzes administered over the semester. All exams are ten true/false and 40 multiple-choice questions. Exams are graded and posted by the next class period. It is simple. It is straight forward. It is always accepted by students. They understand where they are in the class, and the incredible tension of a midterm worth 40% and a final worth 60% of a grade is avoided. Tension and fear teach little in a large classroom. KISS!

Example 4 _____

Teaching Large Classes in Pharmacy Practice

James McAuley and Marialice Bennett
The Ohio State University

Introduction

In the pharmacy professional program, students must learn both therapeutic content and a clinical decision-making process to apply the current and future acquired knowledge to the practice of pharmacy and individualized patient care. Lectures can convey large amounts of factual material. Unfortunately, where a gap exists in a large class, lecturing may not result in student learning of the clinical decision-making process. Students can focus on note-taking rather than thinking through the presented material, or they may memorize the notes rather than applying the material in practice. Facts become more important than process, problem solving, and application. Pure lecturing also provides minimal opportunity for the student to develop confidence in applying the material. Active learning in the large classroom helps bridge that gap and is necessary to engage students in the applications to patient care prior to or concomitant with their experiential learning (Hurd, 2000).

In pharmacy education, we teach students based largely on the pharmaceutical care (PC) approach to patient care described by Hepler and Strand in 1990. This nine-step process (Table 4.1) allows students to learn a logical and thorough approach to providing care to their patients.

Introduction and discussion on the approach is conducted in small-group sessions early in our curriculum. Once students are familiar with the process, instructors are able to refer to the approach in teaching specific pharmacotherapy of disease states.

Table 4.1 *Overview of the Nine-Step Pharmaceutical Care (PC) Process*

Step 1 –	Establish relationship with patient
Step 2 –	Gather data (patient- and disease-specific information)
Step 3 –	Identify potential or actual drug-related problems
Step 4 –	Establish desired therapeutic outcomes
Step 5 –	Evaluate all options
Step 6 –	Generate recommendation (important because of need to choose patient-specific medication)
Step 7 –	Design a monitoring plan (when to collect data again?)
Step 8 –	Implement plan
Step 9 –	Follow-up to measure success

Techniques

To assist our students in the large classroom, we have adopted several active learning techniques that have successfully demonstrated the importance of learning process and content during a lecture presentation. These techniques are designed to motivate the students to think during lectures and to see application of the facts to patient care situations.

Think-Pair-Share

Because of many previous attempts to generate discussion in a large classroom after presenting a patient case, we started using active learning techniques after learning about Think-Pair-Share (TPS). TPS is a powerful, yet simple technique that has helped generate much discussion in our classes. After students are given the instructions and the clinical question, they are allowed two minutes to think about the question, pair-up with a close neighbor, and share their thoughts on a response to the clinical question. This partnering is also part of the learning process, working as members of a team. It also allows student-to-student teaching.

Example of Integration of TPS and PC Process

A model that we have found successful is to provide facts on a disease state and then use active learning techniques to work through a patient case. After minimal discussion on establishing the relationship with the patient (PC Step 1), we spend a lot of time in class on gathering pertinent patient data (PC Step 2). Some information concerning an epilepsy patient case is provided to students, both on a handout and on a PowerPoint slide. Students are then instructed to use the TPS method for two minutes to answer the question, "What other information do we need, or do we have it all?" After discussion is generated on what patient data need to be collected and why, we show a slide outlining the instructors' thoughts and compare those with what the students could provide. Using this method allows the students time to be creative, and they are able to come up with more insightful responses than if the question had simply been posed to the large classroom. Sometimes they even come up with ideas that the instructor may not have considered.

As this is a guided case, we now continue from the gathered data. The drug-related problems (PC Step 3) and desired therapeutic options (PC Step 4) are presented to them for this patient. Subsequently, students are instructed to apply the TPS method again to derive (PC Step 5). "What are the therapeutic options to achieve the outcomes for this patient?" After much discussion on what options exist, we move one month into the future on the case and see what happens at the patient's next clinic visit. After I provide more data, students use the TPS method a third time to generate discussion on what the next steps in the treatment plan are for this patient.

After more guided discussion, students are asked to use the TPS method one final time on "Which antiepileptic drug would you choose and why?" This question forces them to make—and support—a decision on treatment recommendations. While the students are working, I write a list of drug choices on the board. After the two-minute time period, they are asked to vote on one of the antiepileptic drug options. Without the active learning exercise, a vote and subsequent discussion is not in-depth, while this method produces significant response. We finish the exercise with what the instructor would do and why. We also summarize the key points of the case. Throughout this exercise, students receive guidance and constant feedback on their thought processes to ensure appropriate choices.

Using TPS as an active learning method to guide the students through a patient case presentation and clinical decision-making is an extremely powerful tool. Other opportunities to use TPS exist in teaching large groups including asking questions like "What can pharmacy students and/or pharmacists do to enhance the pharmaceutical care of patients with epilepsy?" This question results in thoughts and ideas that students and practitioners take into their pharmacy practice environment and implement with very good success.

Mini-Cases

Mini-cases can be used at the beginning of a lecture to peak the students' interests. I have used five mini-cases at the beginning of my lecture on thyroid disease. Each is a scenario a pharmacist could experience while interacting with a patient in a community pharmacy practice setting. Each case poses a problem that will be answered during the lecture. One case poses a controversial situation to pique the students' interest. I allow the students a few minutes to review the mini-cases and write a brief response based on their current knowledge. At the end of the lecture, I have the students use TPS to answer the cases. They all see what they have learned through the course of the presentation.

Mini-cases can also be used as a change of pace throughout a lecture presentation. After discussing how to assess blood sugar patterns to adjust insulin doses, a case using TPS often reinforces and clarifies the process for students. As I walk through a case in class, the students can see my clinical thought process. Then they can immediately apply the new principles to a problem to bridge the gap between content and process.

For more complicated cases, I have used a feedback lecture handout to optimize the learning process. The case is printed on the front of a page, leaving room for the students to document their own problem-solving process. The students work in small groups to problem solve. One group presents the case to the whole class, and the rest of the class has an opportunity to question and add to the case. The key points of the case with support from the literature are on the back side of the page. This technique assures that gaps in the case are covered to prevent holes in the learning and that support for the key points is provided if not covered in the discussion.

Assessment

One-Minute Papers

One-minute papers are an extremely useful and quick assessment tool that helps us gauge what students have learned in one class session so that we can prepare appropriately for the next. In pharmacy, some of our courses are team-taught, especially the pharmacotherapeutics courses. This means that instructors may be given only a few lecture time slots to cover their assigned disease states. In order for us to know whether the students are on track after a learning session, we use the one-minute paper. Just before the class session is complete, we ask students to write down on a slip of paper their responses to the following two questions: 1) What is the most clear about what was taught today? and 2) What is the most unclear about what was taught today? This allows us to look at the responses before the next large-group learning session. If there is a preponderance of the same topic being clear, we know we can spend less time on that during the next class. If there is a strong message of a topic (or topics) being unclear, we know going into the next class that we may have to address that point with another example. Admittedly, there is a tendency for the stronger messages to be unclear than clear. For example, during a recent large-group learning session on teaching the pharmacotherapeutics of epilepsy, a number of students told me that one of the most unclear things about my teaching that day was addressing the issue of epilepsy in pregnancy. With that feedback, I changed the patient case the following session to highlight those aspects. Rather than waiting until the end of the quarter and receiving feedback from formal evaluations when it is too late to make acute changes, this active assessment technique allows a quicker response time and more flexibility to facilitate learning.

As I try various new techniques in the classroom, I find it essential to obtain and evaluate feedback frequently. Using mini-evaluations several times during the quarter not only creates confidence for me but also for the students. A simple questionnaire asking about the depth, speed, and amount of material delivered helps to determine if I am on the same wavelength as the students. Providing feedback to the students on the composite response of the class helps the students know how they stand compared to classmates. The students also realize that you care about your teaching and the learning environment, and they tend to respond more honestly and professionally. Students also provide great ideas on how to improve a case or the learning experience around the case. We have used focus groups at the end of a course to provide direction on how to improve the classroom environment to increase learning.

Challenges

One of the major concerns for devoting classroom time to active learning and process development is the loss of content time in the lecture. One challenge is determining what topics to cover in a course and in what depth. A pharmacy curriculum is expected to produce a generalist practitioner. Postgraduate opportunities are designed to develop areas of specialty such as critical care, neurology, and cardiology. The breadth versus depth debate is not new, and with research discovering new information at a rapid pace, it is increasingly difficult to select which topics are covered and which ones are not.

Actually, the problem of never being able to cover all the material necessary in a therapeutics sequence is the exact reason that teaching a process is so important. For example, the PC process teaches a systematic approach rather than having students memorize facts on a particular disease state and regurgitate for an exam. We estimate that most of the information currently taught will change dramatically within five years after the pharmacy student graduates. If we can teach them a process, they will have the tools to approach the patient and pharmacotherapy of any disease they encounter.

One way to help balance content and process in the learning environment is to expect students to read prior to class and to bring a fair amount of the content with them to use in class. This increases content learning and enhances process learning. Students may need to have some incentive to read prior to class. Material in the readings may be clarified but not repeated. Interactions in the classroom may be built on the reading material, making activities easier and less frustrating if the student is well prepared. A short quiz may also increase student preparedness.

Lectures can be adjusted to enhance content delivery within an active learning environment. A detailed handout may be prepared to communicate areas not covered in a lecture. Connecting to, rather than repeating, material taught in previous courses can also increase classroom efficiency. Pharmacy students learn pharmacology, how drugs act in the body. They also learn therapeutics, how to use drugs to treat patient diseases. Repeating pharmacology in the therapeutics lectures is not necessary; connecting to and building on pharmacology is much more efficient. This leads to the challenge of coordinating order and complementary information on topics among teaching colleagues in concomitant courses.

To tackle the issue of covering many disease states within a ten-week pathophysiology and therapeutics course, (i.e., all of the neuro-logic and psychiatric diseases), we use content experts in our class-rooms to present current course content and to model strong clinical decision-making skills. We ask the local experts to come into the class-room and teach their area of expertise. Having expert practitioners teach the students is a double-sided issue. On the one hand, students learn the most up-to-date information in a particular area from the expert practitioner, but many students, when exposed to an expert, think they can become a specialist overnight. The students do not take the many years of experience in clinical decision-making into account. This is also a problem when asking instructors for good exam ques-tions, because sometimes the instructors fail to take into account the students' lack of clinical decision-making skills. Using active learning techniques to model and bolster clinical decision-making skills help tremendously to bridge this gap between teacher and student in the classroom

Evaluation of learning is a challenge when active learning is intro-duced to the large classroom. If process is taught and application of content is an expectation, evaluations of learning must match the teaching methodology. The traditional multiple-choice exam does not typically evaluate process and clinical decision-making skills. However, students have not had the opportunity in the large class-room to have repetition of activities applying process to content learned. Therefore, the traditional clinical case study examination may be at too high an evaluation level. Thus it is necessary to develop test questions at a middle-ground, where some knowledge of process and a moderate level of application is expected. Another challenge is devel-oping exams for large class sizes that are not too burdensome to grade.

Pearls of Wisdom

As we typically do in summarizing the key concepts of a good patient case, we end this chapter with some pearls.

Proper use of technology can efficiently address content issues. A picture, video, or animated slide can speak a thousand words in a small time frame. For example, describing the clinical presentations of various seizure types is helpful in teaching the pathophysiology and therapeutics of epilepsy, but the use of a video showing patients having the various types of seizures is much more illustrative. Using a web page for a course can enhance communication and follow-up on questions. Web courses in the same topic can be used as back up for clarification of lecture content.

Knowing your students and communicating that you care enhances any learning environment, especially in the large classroom. Requesting and repeating students' names during class can be very powerful. Be available to students before and after class as well as during posted office hours; the informal conversations following a lecture help create comfort zones for students who may not actively participate in class. When possible, faculty presence at school activities also sends a strong message to students about how important your teaching is to you.

Connect with what students are learning in other courses. Openly address conflicts in content and approach in a professional manner showing respect to your colleagues. Review notes from connecting sections and bridge the gaps as much as possible.

Time commitment for most of the techniques we have suggested is small, but the return on investment is huge. Though subjectively we know it works better, we have no objective information that supports the notion that teaching pharmacy students in large classrooms using active learning techniques is better than traditional lecture methods. However, we have personal experience in both approaches and have found that active learning increases the level of student energy and the amount of student participation in the large classroom. We would also attest that active learning is much more fun! We recommend to all that some form of active learning should be part of every classroom, small or large.

References

Hepler, C. D., & Strand, L. M. (1990 March). Opportunities and responsibilities in pharmaceutical care. *American Journal of Hospital Pharmacy, 47* (3), 533-43.

Hurd, P. D. (2000). Active learning. *Journal of Pharmacy Teaching, 7* (3/4), 29-47.

Example 5 _____

Teaching Large Classes in Veterinary Medicine

Laurie A. Jaeger and Deborah Kochevar
Texas A&M University

Teaching large classes in a veterinary school is, in some ways, easier than teaching large undergraduate classes. Similar goals, and often similar student backgrounds, provide the means by which to connect with the class and engage them in the subject at hand. It has been our experience, as veterinarians teaching veterinary anatomy, biochemistry, and pharmacology to first-and second-year professional students, that a relationship can be established with a class that helps transform the large classroom into an enjoyable and effective learning environment. Below, we describe some strategies and behaviors that we have found useful in addressing pre-clinical veterinary students. Most of these approaches are not discipline specific, and should be applicable in most classrooms.

Establish a Good Working Relationship

Get to Know the Students

Establishing a good working relationship with the class as a whole and with individuals within the class improves communication and enhances the learning environment. A first step toward this end is to learn your students' names. The ability to address students by name, both within and outside the classroom, suggests that you care about them as individuals. Learning names is easier if you have contact with students in small groups, such as lab or discussion groups and is facilitated by name tags that the school may require students to wear. You may wish to learn more about your students, such as outside interests and career goals.

Don't forget that establishing a relationship with the class is a two-way street, and many of your students will want to know something about you. Don't be afraid to share information about your background or interests. Finally, if you choose to collect (or provide) personal information, be aware that some students and faculty will not feel comfortable with this exercise. Respecting personal privacy is important, and mechanisms should be in place to allow students to remain relatively anonymous if they wish.

Develop a Professional Bond

If you are a veterinarian, you have some idea of your students' pre-veterinary and animal-related experiences and what they may have seen while working in or observing procedures in a veterinary clinic. If you are not a veterinarian, take the time to learn about those aspects of the profession that have a connection to the material you teach, and use this information in the classroom. One of the easiest and most effective ways to do this is to tap into the expertise of your colleagues in the clinics. You may even consider having a clinician as a guest lecturer, if you can fit it into the schedule. Many veterinary students aspire to clinical practice, and references to clinical veterinary medicine will capture your students' attention as well as help them learn the material in a relevant context. In the least interactive way, one can simply state that a particular bit of information is important because it provides the basis for treating or understanding a specific condition. The classroom is more engaging if one can relate a story or provide opportunities for students to share their experiences.

If you are a member of the profession for which you are training your students, you have another advantage—you were once in your students' shoes. You may find it useful to try and remember which concepts you found to be initially difficult and what experiences eventually led to your understanding of the material, and share this with the class. This approach has many benefits. Your experiences and integration of material may help clarify a concept in a manner that cannot be derived from the textbook; it, again, provides the material with context and relevance. Additionally, by sharing your educational experiences, you acknowledge to your students that you realize some things will take time for them to understand, that you empathize with their situation, and are personally committed to helping them through this phase of their education.

Instill a Sense of Responsibility and Trust

The educational experiences of your students may vary widely, and some may harbor the belief that it is your responsibility to teach them, without acknowledging or even recognizing their responsibility to participate in the process and actively learn the material. This is particularly true in the first year of the professional curriculum. Be clear about your expectations and don't hesitate to explicitly state them, orally and in your course syllabus. Most, if not all, of your students will have been high achievers in their undergraduate years and should be able to handle the requirements of a professional curriculum. Evidence suggests students will usually rise to expectations, so don't be afraid to maintain high standards and hold the students accountable for completion of assignments, required reading, and participation in other classroom activities.

Trust and respect are also key features of a good working relationship with a class. Ideally the students will find you a willing partner in the educational enterprise but will not carry familiarity to an inappropriate level. Likewise, you should let the students know that you value their opinion by asking for feedback and responding to their suggestions appropriately. Student input can be solicited throughout the semester especially after some new or nontraditional activity has been introduced. Some instructors routinely utilize a mid-term evaluation instrument and share the analysis and their planned solutions with the class. You may, for example, tabulate and determine the frequency of individual comments and criticisms and project your findings during the beginning or end of a class period. This activity takes class time that would otherwise be used for covering content; however, it will undoubtedly demonstrate to the students that opinions and perceptions within the class vary; most students will realize that there are limits to what can be changed. While these activities are useful, many instructors prefer to wait until the end of the term for evaluation to avoid distracting the class from mastery of the concepts at hand. Occasionally students are overly enthusiastic about providing input and try to comment continuously on what they like and don't like about the course. These students may be counseled to keep a running list of their remarks and to provide them when the course ends. Although students may tire of writing evaluations at the end of term, you should convince them that their input is important and will be taken seriously. It works well to provide an example of something that was changed in your course as a result of student input in previous semesters. This brings the matter closer to home and should help motivate students to provide constructive input.

Approaches to Learning in a Large Class

Content Coverage

One of the most difficult aspects of teaching in any biomedical field today is the concern over content coverage. The breadth of topics usually stretches well beyond the instructional time allotted. Don't become a slave to coverage. Incorporate evaluation techniques that allow content coverage through homework and reading. This promotes student responsibility for learning and allows you to move beyond factoids and into application of concepts during class time. Some techniques for accomplishing content coverage include graded or pass/fail homework assignments, short end-of-class quizzes, and directed questioning that relies upon information from assigned reading. Well-written objectives also effectively focus students on important concepts whether these are found in the reading or presented in class.

Contextual Learning

Contextual learning may be particularly important in the professional curriculum. Your students are usually focused like a laser beam on the objective of becoming a veterinarian. As previously mentioned, this makes any mention of clinical medicine or practical experience an effective hook for their attention. As a result, case-based learning has become an increasingly popular way to lead students to important pre-clinical concepts and facts. A well-built case introduces useful medical vocabulary, familiarizes the student with the traditional rounds-style presentation of case data, and provides an excellent basis for introduction and application of basic science knowledge.

A typical case-based exercise includes a description of the animal (signalment), chief complaint and history of the present illness, other history including systems review, and physical exam findings. You may want to include diagnostic data with the case set-up (e.g., blood counts, serum chemistry profiles, radiographs); however, we have found that pre-clinical veterinary students are easily overwhelmed. It often works best to limit the case database to history and physical exam and mention diagnostic tests only as part of a future plan. Construction of a problems list based on the history and physical exam is a key summary point in the case presentation. This list should include concise problem statements from the database but should not include differential diagnoses. The problems list is an effective departure point into related topics in the basic sciences (e.g., physiology, anatomy, biochemistry).

A good way to make the transition from the problem list to basic science topics is to ask the students to develop learning issues related to the problems list. For example, one differential diagnosis for a puppy that presents with the problems of pale mucous membranes, lethargy, and absence of routine deworming may be hookworm anemia. Basic science learning issues related to anemia could include characteristics of a red blood cell (histology), protein structure and function of hemoglobin (biochemistry), and the role of hemoglobin-oxygen saturation curves in tissue oxygenation (physiology).

Incorporation of cases and clinically relevant detail generally increases the palatability of basic sciences such as biochemistry, immunology, and physiology; however, if your primary responsibility is, as is ours, to build a basic science foundation for later in-depth clinical training, make sure you don't lose sight of that mission. Many professional students are all too willing to skip over the basic science detail as they delve enthusiastically into diagnosis and treatment.

Implementation

Vary Your Presentation Style

Although large classes don't easily permit roundtable discussions, and most large lecture halls cannot easily be reconfigured, there are ways to make the large lecture hall a more learning friendly environment. For example, don't be afraid to step out from behind the podium, particularly during discussions or when answering questions. Without the barrier created by the podium, one can more directly address students in different areas of the room and can move naturally, as one does in a conversation, toward the student asking a question. We find that this creates a more comfortable environment for us, as well as the students, and helps personalize the instruction to individual students. Remain cognizant of where you are, however, and don't remove yourself so far from the front of the classroom that you end up with your back facing half the class. Also, don't get so engaged with an individual or two that you lose the connection with the remainder of the class. Often students who choose to sit near the front of the lecture hall are more likely to participate in discussion. This is initially very helpful but can present problems if these students monopolize the discussion or begin to ask questions that pertain to very specific but peripheral aspects of a problem. It is up to the instructor to keep the discussion on a level that is of more general interest to the class. Engaging students, especially those who traditionally sit in the back row, or generalizing a more specific question can sometimes shift the focus back to the larger group.

Avoid monotony with your teaching media. Computer programs can be used to create effective and aesthetically appealing slide shows; however, one runs the risk of students merely watching the show and not focusing on the content; the same can happen with projection of traditional 2 x 2 slides. Students often, paradoxically, become disengaged from the material while attempting to write down volumes of information about it. You may find it more effective to illustrate a particular concept using more than one form of media; e.g., show an overhead cartoon or diagram and then project a photographic slide, and conduct some short discussion about the topic. The movement among media keeps the classroom alive and provides various means by which a student can understand a particular concept. If you are fortunate enough to have a classroom with access to the Internet, you may be able to connect to a relevant site during class, such as a web-based program from another veterinary school, an online scientific article, or a commercial site of a biologics or pharmaceutical company. This has the added benefit of illustrating to your students how they can use different resources to answer questions and continue learning throughout their profession careers.

Encourage Participation

If executed in an organized manner, a case-based exercise can be an excellent vehicle to enhance large-class participation and promote active learning. First, you must be willing to devote some class time to case set-up. We provide a projected picture of the patient along with written signalment, history, physical exam, and selected laboratory data. The written case data are available well in advance of class, and

the students are asked to develop two items as a homework assignment. The first is a preliminary problems list based on the case data.
The second item is a list of three learning issues pertinent to the student's understanding of some aspect of the case. On the day the case
is presented in class, students should be prepared to contribute items
to a collective discussion that yields a preliminary and consolidated
problems list and a consensus list of three learning issues. From this
point, consensus learning issues are explored in an in-depth manner
with the focus on basic science concepts. Case discussion may span
several class periods and address multiple traditional topics all within the context of case discussion. The exercise is concluded by class
development of a summary that relates key clinical features of the case
to the basic science concepts discussed.

An essential feature of the case-based approach is the need for an
effective way to encourage student participation. One important feature, student preparation before class, has already been mentioned. A
second key feature is establishment of a nonthreatening way to pose
directed questions. Non-directed questions, in which queries are made
generally to the class, may work but this often elicits either no
response or a garbled chorus of remarks. We have used an alternative
approach to direct questioning in which groups of students, rather
than individuals, are called upon. At the beginning of the semester,
students are divided into groups of three and asked to sit together
during lecture. As case exercises are conducted, groups are asked to
respond to a particular question or pass the question to another group.
Students, especially in the first semester, seem much less intimidated
by this approach and become more responsive as the semester progresses.

Maintain a Sense of Humor

Most of us are not ready for prime-time comedy, nor is this necessarily appropriate in most classrooms. However, all of us can benefit from
maintaining a sense of humor in the classroom. Instructors and students may get a little tense as the semester progresses, exams come
and go, and finals loom in the distance. Despite your inevitable angst
about covering the material, try not to take yourself too seriously. Your
ability to sustain a give-and-take with the students will stabilize the
learning environment and help the students focus on learning rather
than just surviving the semester. Referring again to common veteri-

nary medical experiences (some of them likely humorous), often provides relief in over-filled, high-pressure curricula.

Conclusion

It's the first day of class, and 100-plus eager faces stare down at you
from the intimacy of an amphitheater-style classroom. What are your
options? Hide behind the podium, stick to the notes, and hope that no
one asks a question that you can't answer? No! Embrace the possibilities by getting to know your students, developing their sense of
responsibility and belonging to the veterinary profession, and feeding
their intense desire to learn medicine. The philosophies and methodologies discussed in this chapter have been helpful to us and, we hope,
have enhanced the learning experiences for our students. Not all of
these approaches will be appropriate in every class or will work for
every individual. Keep your goals clear, be honest with yourself and
your students, and try to find teaching strategies that suit you as an
individual. Even small efforts to personalize instruction in large classes will be recognized and (usually) appreciated by your students and
will result in a more effective, as well as more enjoyable, learning
atmosphere.

Example 6 _____

Making Large Classes Small Through Creative Teaching

John R. Hoyle
Texas A&M University

Most of us in higher education have experienced some memorable days as students in large lecture classes. "Chrome Dome" Crenshaw, a legendary professor of educational psychology, is remembered as a very intellectual, but boring lecturer. He believed that he had control of the 210 students enrolled in his educational psychology class. Several years ago during the fall semester, his students became aware that Chrome Dome was frequently late for their 8:00 a.m. class. Each day the sleepy students would fill the 210 seats and begin watching the clock with the hope that the professor would be ten minutes late. One cool October morning, Chrome Dome walked into the lecture hall three minutes early and placed his old Homberg hat on his podium in plain view and went to the bathroom. The students began filling the seats and while yawning, began counting down to ten minutes. Eight minutes, nine minutes, ten minutes, and no Chrome Dome. Two front-row students began the exodus, and the hall was clear in 30 seconds. Students were running and laughing at the thought of pulling a fast one on their professor. Chrome Dome returned to class to observe the backs of his students running for freedom. His anger was followed by choice words about..." ungrateful students who lack the intelligence to appreciate my great knowledge..."

Two days later, Chrome Dome met the students as they entered with his hat in hand and a frown on his face. He raised his soft voice a few octaves and yelled, "Listen here students, the next time you see my hat sitting here, that means I'm here. Don't you dare leave, and if you do, you will receive an F for the day—do you understand!"

"Yes sir," they all dutifully replied.

Two days later, Chrome Dome walked into the lecture hall and looked up to find 210 hats on the desks. Old Chrome Dome stomped his foot and clenched his fists, but then burst into laughter. The hat was on the other head now, so to speak, and he knew that his hat trick had backfired (Hoyle, 1991).

Introduction

Teaching large classes takes a special talent and volumes of attention to the art and science of teaching. Gone are the days that students will tolerate a professor who stands in front of 40 or 400 of them and reads notes taken directly from the textbook authored by the professor. Charles Achilles (1993), Professor of Educational Leadership at Eastern Michigan University, writes about a student who needed more than a professor's textbook to learn. The student's parable begins, "Your book, which I bought, provides me facts... but I need more than facts. I need help in learning. I need to grapple with facts, extend facts. Learning is more than facts" (pp. 427-428). This student is speaking for thousands of others who find themselves trapped in large classes forced to listen to a newly published professor read line-for-line out of the textbook. When this boring show-and-tell-sit-and-get-read-to-from-the-textbook model prevails, students will either drop the course or merely study the text for the next exam. Unless these professors are required to change their teaching styles and strategies, they will merely continue this archaic teaching behavior. As long as large classes are viewed by the administration as cost-saving instructional delivery models, many professors and legions of others will see no need to alter their teaching styles. Who will force them to change? A recent comment by a future teacher about a large class in mathematics and her instructor, reinforced this question. The student said, "Dr. Hoyle, my math teacher told the class that he is not here to teach teachers how to teach math." He said "I am here to teach math, and if you don't like it, drop the class." Another student responded by saying, "You have the wrong teacher. My teacher explains the math concept and gives practical examples to help me learn to teach math." So in the case of these two students it was a merely a matter of luck, rather than careful consideration by the administration and student advisor in helping the student choose the better teacher. In spite of improved instructional technologies and alternative teaching strate-gies for large classes, the majority of large classes are still in one deliv-ery mode: the 50- or 75- minute lecture. In spite of the prominence of this 15th century teaching method, some students are fortunate to have professors who are dynamic lecturers and storytellers. Tales about large classes taught by graduate assistants and inaudible lecturers with foreign accents have grown considerably on many larger campuses. It only takes two or three of these situations to prompt parents to fire off emails or make urgent phone calls to deans and even presidents. These facts or rumors have pressured administrators to urge department heads to assign more senior faculty to the large sections of first- and second-year students.

These large-class issues have not changed much in spite of the increased use of instructional technologies. Professors who view teaching as a one-way intake of knowledge from the master to the student will only camouflage the lecture methods by using PowerPoint, distance learning, or web-based strategies. It is all too true that old 1910 black-and-white photos of business offices and hospital operating rooms are far different than those in 2001, but a quick look into a large university classroom reveals that only the paint on the walls and the attire of the professor and students are different. The world of information technology and pressures from many public schools, industry, medicine, and government have influenced notable improvements in teaching large university classes. But, in spite of millions of public and gift dollars spent to retrofit large classrooms for online learning and research, these delivery improvements are slow to catch on in most universities. The common response from higher education policymakers and administrators about this instructional lag time is lack of funding, faculty resistance to changing their teaching styles, and lack of technical expertise. There remains a gap between the vision/mission statements of many universities that include definitive words that emphasize quality teaching and making large classrooms more learner friendly and real improvements in teaching.

Teaching is never easy, and large classes add to the difficulties. Teaching is time demanding, energy depleting, and emotionally draining. This writer, with a 43-year career in teaching in public schools and in private and public universities in classes with four to 250 students, has encountered many challenges, made many mistakes, and occasionally experienced triumphant moments. In the discipline of education there is little excuse for poor teaching in large classes. Professors in education should be role models for their colleagues in other disciplines. We should show the way by displaying skills in the art and science of teaching strategies, learning processes, curriculum development, student assessment, and creating learning environments for diverse student populations that foster greater motivation for learning. According to Stanley (2000-2001), we must instill in our students the value of diversity in society by making transformations to some of our course content in university classes. This transformation can be difficult for some veteran and beginning instructors. Stanley says, "Typically, many faculty teach the way they were taught. Multicultural teaching affords us an opportunity to broaden our assumptions about teaching and learning" (p. 2).

The remainder of the chapter will include examples of creative strategies for teaching large classes; e.g., problem-based learning, cooperative learning, futuring/visioning activities, debates, and role playing.

Creative Strategies for Teaching Large Classes

Creativity, according to Vance and Deacon (1995), is, "the making of the new and the rearranging of the old in new ways" (p. 42). Thus, creative teaching strategies, for the purpose of this chapter, are primarily examples of rearranging the old in a new way. Each of the suggested strategies has been tried with varying levels of success by this writer in larger undergraduate and graduate classes that range from 35 to 250, in educational psychology, curriculum development and teaching methods, history of western education, and philosophy of education and educational program evaluation. The following steps have proven to be extremely valuable in assisting this writer and others facing 200-plus new faces for the first time or for many years.

Who Are the Students?

For instance, if the reader is teaching a large section of educational psychology, the first and most important way to begin the semester is to ask the students about themselves—their career goals, dreams, and what they hope to gain from the class. I distribute a one-page confidential information sheet that includes the future educator's name, address, email, fax (if available), phone number, and the following three questions:

1) What are your professional career goals?

2) What are your dreams and hopes?

3) What are your expectations for this class to help you toward your career goals and personal dreams?

Collect the information sheets and review them for patterns, norms, and other vital information to assist you in directing the content and instructional materials to student interests and needs. This alone will establish your interest in each student, by taking the time to find out about them as individuals. Before each class, take a few minutes to review the information sheets in order to find connecting points to student interests and needs.

Who Are You, Professor?

Distributing a one-page biographical sketch of your personal background and academic record is a positive way to connect with the students. Information about hobbies, family, etc., show the students that you really care about them as individuals and want to be approachable as a professor and mentor. This effort to build community in a large class in education will help provide an example of collaborative relationships and teamwork vital to the education profession.

What Are Your Expectations?

Prepare a three- or four-page syllabus that includes the following information:

- Purpose of the course

- Statement about the Americans with Disabilities Act (ADA)

- Class schedule that includes dates, topics, readings, papers, test schedule

- Student help-session times

- Web addresses for selected reading assignments and an audio or video copy of each lecture and other class activities for students unable to attend class

- Professor and graduate assistant email, phone numbers

Student Assignments

After a review of the student backgrounds, teaching fields, and personal interests, the professor will generate assignments for all students and strive to tailor individual presentations, papers, and projects to more closely align with the weekly topics and with student interests. This effort will take time, but the return is greater student interest and performance.

The first or second class session could be a lecture using PowerPoint visuals and a video about the importance of educational psychology and teaching. Ormand (1995) recommends that before beginning the lesson on the relationship between educational psychology and teaching, the professor should ask the students to read a short case study about a child with poor academic performance and then ask the students to respond to Ormand's Own Psychology Survey (the OOPS test) (pp. 4-9). After the OOPS test, ask the students to grade their tests and then begin the lecture based on the correct answers, the case study, and research supporting the answers. This activity will energize the students about the course content and its relevance to their lives and future teaching careers. Other student assignments; e.g., cognitive and linguistic development, applying problem-based learning, Piaget's theory and cooperative learning, creating social studies curriculum guide using visioning and futuring are found below.

Student Assessments

A schedule of exams and due dates for student papers and portfolios must be clearly written on the course syllabus and web page and discussed during the first two class meetings. An example of how students are to be evaluated for a final grade is as follows:

Topic/oral presentation	10%
Term paper/portfolio	20%
Problem-based and cooperative learning teams	10%
Vision/futures project	10%
Critiques of research articles	10%
Mid-term exam	20%
Final exam	20%

Professor Image

The professor can create a positive classroom climate by showing enthusiasm for the subject matter and for each student enrolled. Rather than talking about the traditional flunk-out rate based on the bell curve or some other arbitrary and inflexible weeding strategy, the professor should express the hope that every student will make an A or B if they work smart and hard to meet the course requirements. Begin each class with a relevant motivational reading or humorous incident. Students like to laugh. Laughter relieves tension and strengthens the bond between them and the professor. They believe that a warm heart is closely linked to a friendly smile and a good story. Great professors realize touching the heart helps the head respond. Wearing appropriate attire is also a key to student respect. While informal dress codes have caught on in the business/corporate world, professors of education should keep in mind that they are role models and should always present a professional persona.

Class Attendance

Class attendance should be mandatory for both lecture/activity sessions and for small-group, problem-based focus groups and review classes. If the professor announces that there is no role check, it shows lack of interest in teaching the students and the content. Careful attendance records should be kept as evidence to provide more information to evaluate the success level of each student. A seating chart is the best way to simplify checking class attendance.

Teaching Strategies

Variety is the spice of creativity in large classes. Whether the class is 50 minutes or two hours in length, students deserve a variety of teaching strategies to meet different learning styles, and to help keep them focused on the learning objectives for the class period. Problem-based learning, cooperative learning, futuring/visioning, and lecture/discussion are the teaching strategies selected by this writer for consideration of the reader.

Problem-Based Learning

The conceptual framework of problem-based learning (PBL) has become a major teaching strategy of the medical profession as a means to bring meaning and improve the learning curve of medical students. Baska-Vantassel (1998) defines PBL as, "... a student-centered learning approach in which students are expected to assume responsibility for their own learning as they develop skills of higher-order thinking and self-directed learning under the guidance of a teacher in the role of facilitative tutor or coach" (p. 279). Martin, Murphy, and Muth (1993) report that a document by the Harvard Medical School details a curriculum designed to help prepare doctors to cope with the "crises of practice." The Harvard report, "New Pathways to Knowledge" (Nova, 1988), stresses cognitive learning theory:

- Students are taught how to learn rather than required to memorize two years of traditional content.

- Clinical skills are learned early and in conjunction with academic theories.

- The world of client (patient) is emphasized over the world of the university.

- Problem solving tutorials are emphasized over large lecture hall teaching.

- The learning agenda cuts across all disciplines in an integrated fashion.

- The professor's role is to guide, not to determine all content and learning experiences.

- General concepts and principles are emphasized over bits and pieces of information.

- Medical problems and dilemmas are addressed for which no simple solution exists.

- Becoming a doctor is treated as a lifelong process in which problem solving is an essential skill.

Thus, these important PBL teaching and learning issues rely on clinical skills that enable a student to both frame and solve problems of professional practice by exposing them to conditions that resemble the actual practice in a profession (Martin et al., 1993).

Applying PBL in a Large Class of Educational Psychology in the Area of Cognitive and Linguistic Development

Step 1. Begin the topic with a lecture of the current research about cognitive growth and language/linguistic development, presenting the most important stages of development (Cook, Tessier, & Klein, 1996; Ormand, 1995; Woolfolk, 2001). For example, focus on the work of Swiss psychologist Jean Piaget's theory of cognitive development. Highlight the lecture with examples of children at various levels of Piaget's stages of cognitive development.

Step 2. Follow the lecture with a video that reinforces the assigned readings and the lecture.

Step 3. Next, distribute two case studies/profiles of a young child at the pre-operational stage of development and one at the concrete operational stage that students will read and critique before the next class meeting. They should be prepared to answer the following questions:

• At what developmental stage is the child in each case study?

• What are your reasons for placing the child in either the pre-operational or the concrete stages?

• What teaching strategies would probably be the most successful for each child?

Step 4. Before the next class meeting, assign students to PBL teams of seven members and post the names on the web and a bulletin board at the entrance of the class along with a meeting room or location within the large lecture hall. As soon as the groups are organized, ask each group to select a group facilitator. A suggested method for each group is to select the person with the most recent birthday or the one who has the smallest pet.

Step 5. Each group will discuss the three questions listed above, and the group facilitator should be prepared to give a brief report to the entire class. Not all groups should be asked to report because of the time constraints.

Cooperative Learning

Another proven and creative teaching strategy is known as cooperative learning. It is defined as an "arrangement in which students work in mixed-ability groups and are rewarded on the basis of their work" (Woolfolk, 2001, p. 593). For continuity for the reader, the writer uses the Piaget theory of cognitive development for the content to be taught and learned in the cooperative-learning example.

Step 1. For the next class session, give a brief overview of how to use the cooperative-learning process and then ask the students to rejoin their PBL groups. Ask the groups to select a new facilitator on some fun criteria; i.e., the person living the greatest distance from the classroom.

Step 2. The facilitator will reteach the basics of Piaget's theory and direct the discussion.

Step 3. The facilitator will administer a one-page exam from Ormand's text on the essential elements in each stage of the theory and matching items on teaching strategies for children/youth in each developmental stage.

Step 4. As soon as the group members have completed the answers, the facilitator will give the correct answers to each question.

Step 5. After the self assessments, the facilitator will ask each member about his score and which, if any, item needs to be discussed and retaught.

Step 6. All group members will then return to their assigned seats, and the professor will ask if anyone had any problems with the test.

Step 7. After the professor clears up any concerns, he/she will administer a similar test, and the scores will be recorded as part of the students' course grades.

Classroom Observations

Students will observe one student in pre-school through sixth grade and record the student's cognitive development level. The future teacher will look for developmental signs of the child moving from the pre-operational stage to the concrete operational stage or the formal operational stage. This three- to four-page report is added to the students' end-of-course portfolio.

Visioning and Futuring

One of the more recent additions to teaching strategies for large classes in education is visioning and futuring (Hoyle, 1995). Visioning/futuring as a teaching method has been successfully used in several fields; e.g., landscape architecture, information technologies, visual arts, urban planning, engineering, business, education, and health. While the concept of imagining and attempting to predict the future can be traced to the Oracle of Delphi in ancient Greece in 500 B.C., it has moved from mythology to the art and science of futuring/visioning. Futurists in education concentrate on changing demographics; learning technologies; and other local, state, national, and global trends in family structures, language, religions, value systems, politics, and educational delivery systems. For large classes, visioning/futuring is being successfully used to create interest about course content and to heighten student self motivation about creating their own futures. The following methodologies could be applied in any large education class; I have used it in a course in the humanities and social studies for future elementary or middle school teachers (Kracht & Nolan, 1999).

Step 1. After the professor has used a variety of teaching strategies to assure that the class has a good grasp of the field of social studies and the key content strands that make up the field of study; e.g., geography, demographics, social foundations, etc., he/she is ready to begin using futuring/visioning.

Step 2. The professor organizes the class into visioning teams of eight by assigning names to each team; e.g., Fortune Tellers, Soothsayers, Visionaries, Palm Readers, Wild Guessers, Princess Leahs, Sky Walkers, High Priest Yodas, Futurists, Oracles, Crystal Ballers, etc.

Step 3. The professor will either conduct or invite another person to conduct a visioning session for the entire class. The class will be instructed to relax and envision being in a cabin before a warm fire looking out of a picture window at snow-covered mountains and watching the snow fall. The leader will then ask each student to relax and clear their minds of any distractions and look 20 years into the future. What are the cities like? What is the same, and what has changed? What are people talking about? What are people wearing? What kinds of foods are they eating? How long do they live? How diverse are the communities? What types of transportation do you see? How are schools teaching children ages four to ten about the world around them and about cultural and language differences? After about ten minutes of silent visioning, ask each future teacher in the class to record as many ideas as possible for the vision teams' cities of the future.

Step 4. Charge each vision team to create a curriculum guide for teaching K-6 students to create the ideal city for 50,000 to 100,000 people who live 20 years in the future. The vision teams will decide the age and grade for which the curriculum is targeted; i.e., K-2; 3-4, or 5-6.

Step 5. I provide a reading list of journal articles, news items, and book chapters available on reserve or on the Internet to each team with information about city planning; e.g., food production, medical health system, parks and recreation, education, government, religion, water supply and sewage treatment, police protection, education systems, transportation, and communication, diversity, etc. (World Future Society, 2000-2001).

Step 6. The vision teams will be given three class sessions over a three-week period to complete their curriculum guides to teach K-6 grade students about creating the ideal city of the future. The curriculum guide will be a group portfolio with a name of the team member and his/her contribution to the team activity.

Step 7. The professor will evaluate each vision team's curriculum portfolio and provide feedback to team members as to the organization, age appropriateness of the unit, feasibility of the ideas, team work, creativity, and the depth and interdisciplinary blending of the social studies (strands) content areas.

Step 8. After evaluating the work of each vision team, the professor and a group of students selected randomly will meet with the professor and help select four of the curriculum portfolios to be presented orally to the entire class.

Step 9. The professor will present small awards—Star Trek or Star Wars stickers, clear marble-crystal balls, or other small tokens to remind them of their out-of-the-box thinking about teaching social studies to future generations.

Debates, Games, and Role Playing

The use of debates on controversial topics; i.e., school vouchers, behavioral versus cognitive and constructivist views of learning, teaching moral education, and religion in the schools works well in groups of ten or in the large-classroom setting. Individuals can either volunteer or be selected as members of the pro or con teams. I have found that debate engenders high interest and promotes better test performance on controversial issues than traditional lecture/discussion formats. Role playing can be very effective in capturing the interest of large history or philosophy of education classes. I have used a brief skit with a student playing the role of Mary McLeod Bethune (1875-1955), the founder of Bethune-Cookman College and a national leader and advisor to President Franklin D. Roosevelt. Another student could play the life of Horace Mann (1796-1859) and his leadership to provide well-trained teachers in well-equipped classrooms. Finally, the entire class would gain inspiration from a student playing the role of Maria Montessori (1870-1952), who was the first female physician in Italy and a leader in providing education for the mentally handicapped. She believed that all children needed to learn in well-planned classrooms and that all children can learn with practical familiar teaching materials (Sadker & Sadker, 1991).

Conclusions

Teaching large classes can be exciting for both students and the instructor; however, it does take a special desire, talent, and considerable attention to the art and science of teaching. Instructors who make the effort to teach each of the 200 or more students one-at-a-time will look forward to the challenges of each class day. By making the large class appear to be small and intimate, the professor uses research findings and models best practices in classroom instruction. This careful planning and concern for the future of each student builds a climate of trust and helps to create the desire to become a successful educator. Striving to learn as much about each student in the large class and using positive language to encourage each student to become an outstanding educator are keys to making the students look forward to attending the often-dreaded large education class. By introducing a variety of teaching strategies; e.g., problem-based learning, cooperative learning, futuring/visioning, and other methods, the students will be better engaged in the course content and observe proven teaching methods.

References

Achilles, C. (1993). If all I needed were facts, I'd just buy your book. *People in Education, 1*(4), 424-435.

Baska-Vantassel, J. (1998). Problem-based learning in teaching educational administration courses. In R. Muth & M. Martin (Eds.), *Toward the year 2000: Leadership for quality schools.* The sixth yearbook of the National Council of Professors of Educational Administration. Lancaster, PA: Technomic.

Cook, R., Tessier, A., & Klein, D. (1996). *Adapting early childhood curriculum for children in inclusive settings* (4th ed.). Englewood Cliffs, NJ: Merrill-Prentice Hall.

Hoyle, J. (1991). *Good bull: Thirty years of Aggie escapades.* Bryan, TX: Insite Press.

Hoyle, J. (1995). *Leadership and futuring: Making visions happen.* Thousand Oaks, CA: Corwin Press.

Kracht, J., & Nolan, S. (1999). *Texas social studies framework.* Austin, TX: Texas Education Agency.

Martin, M., Murphy, M., & Muth, R. (1993). Problem-based learning: A new approach to preparing school leaders. In J. Hoyle & D. Estes (Eds.), *NCPEA: In a new voice.* The first yearbook of the National Council of Professors of Educational Administration. Lancaster, PA: Technomics.

Nova (1988). *Can we make a better doctor?* (video). Boston, MA: WGBH.

Ormand, J. (1995). *Education psychology: Principles and applications.* Englewood Cliffs, NJ: Merrill-Prentice Hall.

Sadker, M., & Sadker, D. (1991). *Teachers, schools, and society* (2nd ed.). New York, NY: McGraw-Hill.

Stanley, C. (2000-2001). Teaching excellence: Toward the best in the academy. *Professional and Organizational Development Network in Higher Education, 12* (2).

Vance, M., & Deacon, D. (1995). *Think out of the box.* Franklin Lake, NJ: Career Press.

Woolfolk, A. (2001). *Education psychology.* Boston, MA: Allyn & Bacon.

World Future Society (2000-2001). *The Futurist Journal.* Bethesda, MD.

Example 7 _____

A Learning-Focused Approach to a Large-Section Engineering Course

Robert Lundquist

The Ohio State University

Twenty years ago, when I first started teaching at Ohio State, I had several years when my average section size was fewer than 20 students. When I first started teaching, more than 60 students in a class was rather intimidating. A few years later I had my first, and only, section of more than 200, and it was actually not bad. Now I average about 180 students per quarter in my large course, and it feels just fine. What did I learn about teaching in that time that made a section of that size work for me? The most important lesson was that being a successful teacher for a large class requires the same skills and attitudes as in a small class. The real trick was convincing myself that the proven techniques of good teaching (see, for example, McKeachie's *Teaching Tips,* 1999) could be used in my situation. In other words, I decided that section size couldn't be used as an excuse for reliance on lecturing as a primary tool, an impersonal approach to students, inaccessibility, simplified assignments and examinations, etc. Good teaching takes more of my time but it would in a small class too.

My course is engineering economics. This course has an industrial and systems engineering number, but I have always told my students that I am not an industrial engineer (all of my degrees and experience are in mining engineering) and the course is not an industrial engineering course. It is an engineering course, period! The material is, indeed, equally important to all engineers. Actually, engineering economics is something of a misnomer. The material is closer to finance than economics and would be more accurately called finance for engineering projects, but I know I am about 70 years too late to influence this universal appellation.

I have taught this course for three quarters every year and four quarters most years (about 50 times) since the fall of 1986. When I took over the course, it was required only for industrial and systems engineering and agricultural engineering majors and had been taught by TAs for several years. Only a few other engineering students took it as a technical elective, so it was serving about 200 junior- and senior-level engineering students per year with section sizes averaging 50 or so. Like many engineering courses, this course was information dense. I felt the need, as do many of my colleagues, to cover as many topics, in detail, as I possibly could in a three-quarter-credit course, so I used the lecture format exclusively. I believe I was quite good at it. As the reputation of the course improved, it was used as a technical elective by increasing numbers of students. Section sizes grew to about 80 students.

I have always believed that anything I taught could be improved. At first this focused on the content of the courses I taught, which were at that time in mining engineering. I was fond of saying that any time I didn't learn more than my students in each course I taught I was probably going stale and should teach something else. Gradually the emphasis turned from the content itself to finding better ways to teach it. To me this meant better explanations of each topic in a lecture: clearer examples and stronger analogies. This was the approach I brought to the engineering economics course as well. To me, good teaching meant good lecturing.

In the early 1990s, two things happened which completely changed my view of teaching. The first was a change in the College of Engineering curriculum which required that all undergraduate majors include engineering economic content. Most programs decided that the easiest way to satisfy the requirement was to have their students take my course. Enrollment ballooned to about 650 students per year with section sizes of up to 200 students during the academic year and about 80 in the summer. I had always felt that any section of more than 40 or 50 students was large and that it really made no difference beyond that, but I quickly learned that this was incorrect. The second occurrence came in the form of a knock on my office door in early 1993. A graduate student from adult education, Michael Colburn, had come to ask if he could use my course for his research. His initial premise was that the principles of adult learning theory (ALT) (Brookfield, 1988) could be combined with the ideas of total quality management (TQM) to improve the design of an engineering course. At the time I knew next to nothing about ALT, but I was incorporating TQM into the material of another course and was intrigued immediately by the idea of applying it in education. In a weak (or fortunate) moment, I agreed to participate.

We created a team of four faculty members from my department, all of whom had taught engineering economics at one time, and the graduate student, who was an engineering consultant and had taught engineering courses as an adjunct. We started with a series of directed readings in ALT and TQM, followed by two all-day workshops to discuss the readings and decide how they would apply to course design. This produced what we called the five new paradigms.

Developing New Paradigms

Explicitly Recognize and Respond to the Needs of Customers

The problem here was to define who were the customers. Clearly students can be thought of as the primary customers, but they are also the workers. Other customers (more properly called stakeholders) include the faculty of courses in the students' own major which rely on engineering economic knowledge, future employers and their customers, and, since The Ohio State University is state supported and a land grant institution, the people of the state of Ohio. Focus groups with employers showed that we were including more material than was needed and that the real emphasis should be on the basic understanding of how money works and how it influences project selection and day-to-day engineering work.

Distinguish Testing From Grading

Adult learning theory makes it clear that the purpose of testing is to provide feedback to the learner. The purpose of grading is to provide certification. The general confusion which results from this makes grading an absolute barrier to learning. Most of my students have been conditioned by the educational system in which they have labored for the past 15 or 16 years to believe that grades are more important that learning. As a result, retention is poor, and many of my colleagues begin each course with an extensive review of the previous material needed for understanding the new material presented. Total quality management, and virtually all of engineering practice, tells us that there should be only two grades for any problem, examination, assignment, or course. I call these grades "do it right" and "do it over."

There is no partial credit in practice. An engineering analysis which is 95% correct is simply wrong and must be fixed. No employer would consider paying 95% of base salary to an employee who was right only 95% of the time. Certification, then, should be held to a high standard. As in adult education, the teacher must determine what is essential for the student to know and then certify competency only when it is certain that the student actually knows it.

Use Team Approaches Both in Course Design and in Learning Activities

As I have described above, the redesign of my course was guided from the beginning by a team. Early on we made a group of undergraduate students a part of that team. Using students to help in designing courses, as we did in this instance, primarily satisfies the first paradigm by listening to the needs of the students as customers. Team approaches are common in both ALT and TQM applications in practice. We believe that students learn better when learning from each other. Teams are also ubiquitous in industry. This paradigm has proved difficult to implement in my course but it has been successfully applied to my project management course and to most other undergraduate courses in my department.

Incorporate Activity-Reflection Cycles in Learning

This paradigm immediately suggests the use of active learning in the classroom and is an essential element of most adult education. I have found some parts of active learning to be difficult to implement. Classrooms which can accommodate large sections typically have tables or auditorium chairs fixed firmly to the floor so that breaking into discussion groups is impossible. Engineering students are not accustomed to communicating with peers in the classroom. They believe that all professors' questions are rhetorical and do not readily respond. I have succeeded in making my lectures more active by having the students work problems at several points during a lecture.

Change The Primary Role of Faculty from Lecturer to Facilitator of Learning

The brilliant lecture is not the most important contribution of the faculty member to the learning process. Since most of the learning, and especially the retained learning, takes place outside the classroom, it is much more important for faculty to put major effort into course design and management.

While the paradigms would apply to any course, their implementation in a specific course was subject to institutional constraints. With my course, the most important of these constraints was size. The then chair of our department was a member of the team, and he made it clear that no additional resources could be made available to reduce my load. If this was to be a large-section course, our objective was to make it the best large-section course possible. Both the constraint and our response continue to govern my decisions.

Implementing the New Paradigms

After the new paradigms were agreed upon, there was much discussion about how to implement them, both in the long-term design of all our courses and specifically in my course to provide a controlled experiment for Michael Colburn's dissertation. Since it was apparent that no controlled experiment could test all of the paradigms, we decided that for the latter we would focus on the testing/grading paradigm. Specifically, we were interested in testing the notion that learning would improve if students were given the opportunity to retake portions of their examinations to improve their scores.

After the increase in section size, which followed the college curriculum changes, I had tried teaching the course in two smaller sections. I had concluded, after two tries, that the small classroom advantage in sections of 80-90 as opposed to 160-180 was not enough to offset the time and logistical disadvantages, and I had already given up on it. It was easy, however, to set up our experiment with two sections. The treatment section, meeting at 8:30 a. m., was allowed to retake up to one half of each of three examinations with scores replacing the original ones problem by problem. The control section, meeting at 3:30 p. m., was not given retakes. At the end of the quarter, the students were given a common final. While the difference was not large, the final examination grades of the treatment section were better by a statistically significant amount. Since I had noted in previous quarters that the afternoon section was more alert and responsive and did better on exams than the early morning section, I suspect that the effect of the experimental treatment was greater than measured.

I was now free to implement other changes in the course based on what I had learned. Most of the significant changes were made after the fall course, but more are made each quarter as a result of a philosophy of continuous quality improvement. I often say that the most important thing we learned from W. Edwards Deming is that we will never get it right! It would, of course, be more accurate to say that we'll never get it perfectly right. What Deming actually said, in explaining his point five (improve constantly and forever the system of production and service) was that every process could be improved, even if it had been improved before.

The first step was to split the assessment process into two independent parts: core competency, which is based on the examinations, and learning projects, which includes all work done outside the classroom. A perfect competency score can earn the student up to a B in the course and no more. To add one full letter grade (as from B- to A-) to the competency grade, the student must complete 150 points worth of learning projects. This is offered in increments of 50 points to improve the course grade by one mark (as from B to B+.) There is no interchange of points between competency and learning projects.

Despite the belief that everything should be graded on a do it right or do it over basis, it is not practical to give infinite retakes on the exams. The need to give a letter grade at the end of the quarter, the tendency of students to procrastinate, and the logistics of administering the retakes have required that I limit them, as in the original experiment, to half of each exam. The retake problems are similar to the problems on the original examination, and the grade on the retake always replaces the grade for that problem. This is to prevent a nothing-to-lose approach to studying for the retake. Most students recognize and appreciate that this is their opportunity to learn material that they had not understood at the time of the original exam. Many report putting exams aside and never returning to study those problems that they missed. There is really no reason for us to demand that they be able to answer specific questions covering an (arbitrary) subset of the course at a particular time on a particular day. We should, instead, decide in advance which concepts are most important and then certify the student's competency whenever these concepts are mastered.

In the first quarter I used this grading system, I declared that I would no longer be willing to certify competence at the D level. I believe that if I am to give a passing grade in a required course so that students need not repeat it, I should be certain that they really understand, at some minimum level, the concepts of the course. Students to whom we give D's don't meet this criterion. Over the next few years I gradually increased the standard to eliminate the entire C range as well. The result has been only a small increase in the number of students failing the class. My impression is that those who would have gotten D's now fail more frequently but that those who might have gotten C's by just getting by in a conventional system recognize that they need to put more effort into passing and learn more in the process. Currently about three-fourths of the class gets what I believe to be well-earned A's and A-'s and about 3–4% fail.

Obviously the preceding will alarm those who believe in the bell curve. I am sometimes accused by colleagues of being too easy because my grades are too high. On the contrary, my standards are among the highest of anyone in my college. Currently it takes an 80% average on the exams just to pass the course with B- competency. An 85% average can raise the competency to B. To offer an incentive to exceed this level, students with a 90% average on three midterms and no single midterm grade lower than 85% are also excused from the final.

Maintaining Standards

I hold these standards high for several reasons. First, I believe in what one of my early engineering economics students dubbed "reality-based education." The material of the course is important to nearly all the students taking it. It may be the only course in the engineering curriculum that we can guarantee will be used in the future by everyone. Second, the material is not very difficult for most students. I need to assure, then, that I certify a student's competency in the subject by asking questions on examinations that I expect every student to be able to answer. If I could allow more retakes to force the students to repeat until they got it right, I would do so. For this reason, I argue that the 80% average to pass the course is really a compromise downward from the desired 100%. Finally, there is considerable evidence to show that high standards, fairly applied, are a strong predictor of students' satisfaction with teaching.

Actually, curve grading makes no sense at all. If everyone learns what they should, all should get A's. If no one does, all should get E's. Professors who use the bell curve are really confessing that they are incapable of teaching what is needed to some given number of individuals in his class. The mistakes in the other direction are equally onerous. The next time you cross a bridge, consider that it was probably (hopefully) designed by an engineer who got an A in structural design. In many cases, this was achieved by curving a grade of 60% or so to an A in a class where 40% may have been passing. Does this mean that only 60% of the bridge was designed correctly? Thank heavens the student who got the passing D didn't do the design. Actually this indictment of the curve, in addition to being overly simplistic, is rather mild. I refer you to Milton, Pollio, and Eison (1986) for a more thorough treatment.

As you can see, I don't really believe in letter grades. Given the practicalities, however, I believe I have gone about as far as I can in unilaterally eliminating both the grade and its undesirable consequences on learning.

Using Learning Projects

Learning projects are mostly what we used to call homework with three major differences. First, I allow students to select from a large menu of choices how they will get their learning project points. Some of these will be described below. The only requirement is to do two of the four spreadsheets, which the students and I have agreed are an essential part of the class. Second, all but the quizzes are graded on a strict do it right or do it over basis with no partial credit. Students are allowed to correct mistakes and resubmit as many times as it takes to get it right. After a date given for each project, success is worth only half the specified points, and at the end of the quarter, required spreadsheets are resubmitted for no points. Third, there is no interchange of points between learning projects and the competency grade.

Spreadsheets are the primary tools used for engineering economic analysis in practice and thus an essential part of the course. My experience and most of my students tell me that the best way to learn spreadsheets is to use them. Lectures are not effective. The concepts are also difficult to test on paper. Students consistently recommend that I require completion of two spreadsheet assignments to pass the course. Spreadsheets are submitted as attachments to email to addresses assigned to the course and accessible only to my graders. This makes it easier to grade and provide feedback since the underlying formulae are available. Since printed submissions often contained ten or more pages, this use of email has saved countless trees. It also speeds up the response and allows the student more chances to complete the assignment correctly.

Other learning projects include sets of homework problems from the textbook, eight in-class quizzes, (the only project for which partial credit is given and the only one that takes place in the classroom) a report on an interview with a practitioner of engineering economic analysis, and a report on a book of the student's choice. This last is intended to encourage lifelong learning, as is another project which involves keeping a journal focused on how the student learns best.

Since the first quarter in which I restructured the course, I have given learning project credit for a quality improvement advisory group. This volunteer group has ranged from as few as four to as many as 18 students. They function as a self-directed process improvement team, similar to teams that most of them will be involved with in industry after graduation. It provides a rare opportunity for them to work with students outside their own discipline since few pre-major courses involve teamwork. It has provided me with a lot of useable ideas, particularly in the areas of course management and the learning projects. When I started, I naively assumed that it would give me a few ideas for awhile and then its usefulness would fade. This, of course, ignores the continuous improvement maxim of Deming. Even after more than 20 times, I still get useable ideas from this group every quarter. Likewise, the students continue to report each quarter that the experience has been valuable to them.

Another learning project gives the students points for coming to my office, either alone or in groups of up to three, to simply get acquainted with me. This is perhaps the best thing I have done, but it is also the largest investment of my time. I schedule these meetings in half-hour blocks, but they average between 15 and 20 minutes. Generally about two-thirds of the class take advantage of this opportunity. The only requirement is that the student bring at least two questions to ask me. Often they ask about ten times that many. I also have a list of questions I ask the students. The benefits of this are many. It is my primary way of learning names so that by the middle of the quarter I can call on at least some students without pointing at them. It is one of the many ways I can get feedback on my teaching and course organization. For many students I am the first faculty member with whom they have a real, personal contact. It has also become a recruiting tool for my department. Often I am the first person to talk to the students about industrial engineering, usually in response to their questions, and this has led to a number of them choosing or switching to ISE.

Conclusions

Most of what I have described would be applicable to classes of any size. Insofar as this is a book addressing the teaching of large-section courses, one might wonder how specific my experience is to teaching large sections in engineering. Part of my answer would be that good teaching is good teaching without regard to section size. Class size cannot be used as an excuse for impersonal relationships with students, lectureholism, or a canned approach to lecturing. Some effort is required to avoid these pitfalls, but the rewards are great.

The most important learning takes place outside the classroom. A unique system of testing and grading is one way to facilitate this learning. First, by forcing students to go back over the material they have missed on examinations to achieve a high standard on a retake examination, their attention is focused on material that they might simply pass over in a conventional system. Second, an emphasis on work outside the classroom, combined with some degree of control, encourages time spent on activities which promote retention.

No course design is perfect, and none should be stagnant. Students can be active participants in continuous improvement of courses and can benefit both themselves and future students as a result.

References

Brookfield, S. D.(1988). *Understanding and facilitating adult learning.* San Francisco, CA: Jossey-Bass.

McKeachie, W. J. (1999). *Teaching tips: Strategies, research, and theory for college and university teachers.* Boston, MA: Houghton Mifflin.

Milton, O., Pollio, H., & Eison, J. (1986). *Making sense of college grades.* San Francisco, CA: Jossey-Bass.

Example 8 ————————————————

Getting Students in a Technical Class Involved in the Classroom

Doug Jacobson
Iowa State University

I teach courses ranging in size from 24-100 students. I will focus here on the methods I have used to promote interaction among both students and instructor in a sophomore microcontroller programming class in Computer Engineering (CprE 211) with over 100 students.

Setting the Tone in a Large Class

Day One

I start using interactive techniques on the first day of class, with exercises that create a fun and safe environment for the students. Apprising your students of your intentions and motivations is critical to making these activities work. On the first day, I write "Learning is Social" on the board before class. When I start the class, I refer to the statement on the board and discuss my belief that learning takes place when students interact with each other and with the faculty. I tell them this will be the driving theme for the class. I have found a noticeable difference in the way the class reacts to interactive exercises when they are told up front that it is a firm belief you have.

The first period of CprE 211 is spent building community among the students. They engage in an interactive activity within the first ten minutes of the first day. Students work in groups of four to six to answer questions based on this theme: What is an electrical or computer engineer? They answer the following questions as a group and write their answers on 25 x 30-inch Post-it notes, placed on the wall in a gallery fashion to encourage discussion.

- What team skills are needed?

- What technical skills are needed?

- What type of personality does a computer (CprE) or electrical (EE) engineer have?

- What job duties or functions does a CprE or EE have?

This exercise is designed to get students thinking about the course and the discipline, and it introduces them to the philosophy of working in groups. I explain to them that teamwork is essential to their success in the course.

Another good first-day exercise is developing class ground rules. I put the students in groups of four to six to develop at least one ground rule for the class. I then have groups report back the rules. Depending on the number and nature of the rules, you may need to reduce or modify them. I have found that students typically come up with a core of rules that are consistent with what I would use. The most common ground rules are: come to class on time, respect others, and do not talk while the instructor is talking. I provide copies of the rules the following class period. This helps students feel ownership of both the class and their education.

We close the first day by doing a one-minute paper (Angelo & Cross, 1993). The students are asked a question that can be answered in about one minute, and they turn the answer in on their way out the door. The first day I ask them what their favorite class was and why. It takes me about ten minutes to skim through the papers. Doing these activities on the first day helps set the expectation for the rest of the semester and helps build a safe environment for the students in class.

Day Two

The next time the class meets, we work on getting to know each other. One exercise that works well and gets the students excited is a scavenger hunt. I provide the students with a sheet of paper with five to ten questions. The students need to find another student who can answer the question "yes", and have that person sign the sheet. The questions are simple personal questions: " Find a person who was born in Iowa," "Find a person who likes to ski," etc. This gets the students walking around talking to each other. Since a student can only sign once on a sheet, the students each need to talk to about ten to 20 other students. After about 15 minutes, I ask the students to stop and sit down. I then ask how many items they found. For example if there were ten questions, I would start by asking how many had five, then seven, nine, and finally all ten.

One question I often get from other faculty members is how I get students to buy into an interactive classroom. First, I let the students know that I am committed to interactive learning, and second, I let them know exactly what I am doing and why. When I first started using formal interactive methods, they were not always received well by the students. Once I started explaining why we do these activities, the students accepted them and were more than willing to participate.

In the past, I have used nametags for each student. The nametags do help students feel more comfortable in class and promote interaction. The downside of nametags is the overhead associated with creation, distribution, and management. In a large class I require nametags for the first few weeks and then make them optional. Another way to get students to know each other is through the use of a Venn diagram (see Figure 8.1). The students are in groups of four with each group subdivided into pairs. Each pair finds things they have in common and things they do not. They write the things they have in common in the intersection of the two circles; things they do not have in common are written into the circles. Once they are finished, the two pairs get together and jointly develop a list of things they all have in common. The exercise works well if you have the class working in groups either outside of class or during class. For accountability, I ask groups with three or more things in common to raise their hands. I then count up by one until I reached the limit where no more groups have their hands raised. I often have groups with seven to ten things in common.

Figure 8.1 *Venn Diagram*

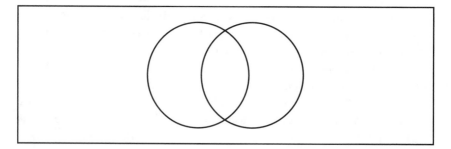

While these activities take precious class time, I have found that they set the tone for the entire semester and create a safe environment where students want to learn and have fun at the same time.

Tricks to Get a Large Class to Talk and Work Together

Often one of the most difficult parts of having a large class is getting the students to work together in groups during class. Over the years I have found several techniques that seem to work well in both large and small classes. I have found it critical that a student feels that what they are doing is important and that the faculty member shows an interest. This section will outline a few methods that are easy to do, yet work very well.

Accountability

One of the most difficult tasks for groups in a large class is keeping students focused on the job at hand. The simple solution is to make them accountable for what they do. I have several methods I use to make students accountable. One method is to use worksheets for in-class group activities. On each worksheet, I leave space for students to put their names on the sheet. The worksheet serves as a method of accountability when they turn in the sheet at the end of class.

Another method of accountability is to call on groups when the exercise is finished. If you divide the answers into small parts, you can call on several groups for each exercise. If you ask groups based on some pattern in the room (like one group from each row) you can spread the accountability throughout the room. I often use both methods together; they will work on the worksheets, and I call on groups to provide the answers once the exercise is finished. I also ask them to turn in the sheet at the end of class. This allows the students to get immediate feedback on the answers and removes the burden of formal grading of the worksheets.

Another method of accountability also serves as a method of informal assessment. During the time the students are working on the worksheets, I walk around the room connecting with as many groups as possible. This helps keep them on task and provides them with a chance to ask questions. I have discovered that the best questions come while I'm wandering around the room, and I have also found that I can quickly assess the level of understanding on a topic by just listening to the groups interact. I have used the feedback to stop exercises that are not working or to give the students more time when I discover they are learning the material.

Feedback

The final trick that I use is the one-minute paper or "muddiest point" (Angelo & Cross, 1993). I have already described one use of the one-minute paper; the muddiest point works the same way, except you ask the students to put down one thing that was not clear to them or one thing that became clear today. With both of these techniques it is essential that you read the papers and act on them. I will often start the next class period by making comments on one or two of the muddiest points; I have even altered the entire class period if a large number of students have the same muddiest point. I typically do not have the students put their names on the muddiest point papers.

By having students turn in their work and by responding to it, they know you care. I do not grade the worksheets or the one-minute papers; I do however give points for turning in the work. In my class, about 5% of the grade comes from in-class participation.

The Most Rewarding Classroom Experiences

This section describes three classroom experiences or techniques that I have found the most rewarding in terms of student learning and student interaction: academic controversy, problem-solving groups, and teaching interactive skills.

Academic Controversy

The academic controversy is, which with a large class takes 40-50 minutes, used to get students energized and thinking, I divided the class into groups of four. Each group of four is divided into two pairs (side A and side B). To help facilitate the group selection, I use two different colors of paper with the dilemma and preliminary instructions written on it; side A is one color, and side B is another. The students are told to divide into groups of four based on the color of the paper. The class is presented with a controversial dilemma that has no clear-cut answer. The students are asked to privately come to an opinion about the dilemma. The two pairs within the group are each assigned a different side of the dilemma and are given a few minutes to brainstorm how to make their case. Then all of the side A pairs in class talk to each other in groups of no more than two or three. The side B pairs do the same with other side B pairs. They must get out of their seats and walk around the room to find other students with the same color paper. The goal is to come up with new arguments to support their side.

After a few minutes, the pairs come back together and work for a couple of minutes more to refine their arguments. Each side makes their case without comment. Three minutes are allowed for any member of the group to ask clarifying questions. After the questions, the two sides switch and must prepare to argue the opposite side of the dilemma; the member who did not present the case the first time presents the new case. Once both sides have presented their arguments, the group of four is asked to come to a consensus position on the dilemma. There are several ways to handle the results of this activity. First, ask which groups agreed with side A and which with side B. Then ask how many students changed their opinion from the one they had when the class started. You can often get a good discussion going about the exercise itself, how it felt to argue both sides, how a consensus was achieved. I often talk about the issue itself and use this technique to introduce ethical concerns in the course and make the dilemma relevant to the course material. An example dilemma I have used is the following:

Controversy example. You are a software engineer at a small start-up company developing code for an embedded microcontroller. The product that contains your group's software is key to the company's survival. The ship date has been set, and there's a big press conference scheduled to demonstrate the product. Unfortunately, after your group's software was integrated into the product, you discover a bug that could disable the device. It's not likely the bug will appear, but it's definitely possible. You know that the first software update for the product is not scheduled until three months after the product has started shipping, and that the boss will not approve an interim fix. I forgot to mention... the product controls patient life support systems in hospital intensive care units.

Side A will support the shipping of the product, and side B will start out opposed.

Controversy example. Another controversy I have used is less technical in nature, and deals with email and harassment.

You are a network administrator for a large corporation. Your company has a strict policy that protects the privacy of personal email and files. During one of your routine monitoring sessions, you notice a large amount of traffic going to an email server. Your curiosity gets the better of you, and you start looking around in the computer system. While searching through files you find several email messages that you open and read. The email messages are from the boss's son to his girlfriend (both are employees of the company) and are threatening in nature. The son threatens to hurt his girlfriend, and each message is more threatening than last. What do you do? Do you turn in the son, or do you forget what you have seen? By the way, the last network administrator was fired for reading other employees email.

I have also served as guest speaker many times in the department's course on ethics and professionalism. The enrollment in the class is between 100 and 150, depending on the semester. I use the academic controversy exercise in this class to help teach ethics. This exercise is always well received. This exercise can be very powerful for the students and can really get them to think about social and ethical issues in a technical course.

I'm often asked what makes a good controversy. I try to find issues that students can relate to without being too controversial or emotional. They must not have a clear-cut answer so that they generate different views and opinions. I like to link the controversy to something they have a chance of experiencing. The email dilemma is one I have first-hand knowledge of, which can add to the discussion after the exercise is over. I find the post-exercise discussion to be one of the most rewarding parts of the academic controversy. The students are more than willing to discuss the dilemma.

Problem-Solving Groups

Another powerful tool I use is problem-solving groups composed of two to four students who work on long problems in class in exercises that typically take 20 to 30 minutes. The key to making the problem-solving groups work is the selection of the problem they work on; the best problems have multiples of increasing difficulty. I have managed to create problems where the last one or two parts require material or knowledge students may not have yet. If you have set up a safe environment in class, these new knowledge problems become great teaching moments. The students are begging you for the material; they really want to learn.

The mechanics of the problem-solving groups have been indirectly outlined in the previous section. Worksheets are critical, as is student accountability. During this exercise, I wander around the room, gauging students' level of understanding and judging the length of time they need to complete the problem. I have found that this exercise works best after about ten minutes of lecture. A typical 50-minute class will be divided as follows:

Opening lecture	10 minutes
Problem-solving group	25 minutes
Follow-up on lecture	10 minutes
Closing (one-minute paper, etc.)	5 minutes

I try to have at least one problem-solving group exercise a week, however the material must lend itself to a 50-minute period. The best types of problems are ones that can be done in a short amount of time with minimal resources. I like to have about four short problems of increasing difficulty. The first problem is a minor modification of the problem I just completed in the lecture. I discovered it is important that students can work the first couple of problems as a class, which gives them confidence to work the more difficult problems. The fourth problem cannot be solved using the method I discussed in class so I need to watch the class to make sure they do not get too frustrated. After the students have spent some time working on the problem, I stop the class and have them report back their answers. When we get to the last problem, I give a short lecture on the new method and provide the solution to the problem. If I have time, I will have students work on another problem or two based on the new knowledge.

Teaching Interactive Skills

The third activity I use in class involves teaching interactive skills in class. I typically teach interactive skills the day before the first exam. First I divide the students into groups of four and give each member a different piece of paper. One piece tells the student that he or she is the leader, and another piece designates the recorder who will write down the group's answer. The other two students get a note telling them to not be part of the group and to talk about anything else but the problem. I put a problem on the board and tell them this is an example problem for the test and they have five minutes to work it as a group. The exercise never lasts five minutes. One of two things happens: either they figure it out and the group starts laughing, or their leader and recorder get frustrated. In either case, I stop the exercise after a couple of minutes and we talk about what happened and about staying on task. We then work the problem in the groups and continue on with the review. An activity like this or the academic controversy adds excitement to the class, helps motivate student involvement, and provides a great learning experience.

There are many more types of activities that can promote student involvement work in a large-class environment. The key elements to each of these exercises are group interaction, accountability, and student acceptance.

Conclusions

Due to the lack of a control group, it is difficult to quantify improvements in learning due to the use of cooperative learning methods in class. I do, however, have some evidence that the students have an increase in learning coupled with a strong positive attitude about the course. For example, the CprE 308 course uses material taught in the CprE 211 course. The faculty member who teaches 308 has started to notice an increase in the abilities of the students in the areas covered by 211 since active learning was introduced. I have also noticed higher test scores from the middle range students and a better understanding of the material. I believe that student-centered learning has made a difference in the way the students work in class and in the level of learning that takes place. The attendance rate is higher when class consists of interactive activities. Another positive effect of this method of teaching is an increase in student participation in class. The students ask more questions and engage in dialogue as a result of building the safe environment. The feedback I get from class surveys and questionnaires indicates students prefer an interactive class.

Several key concepts are critical to having a successful interactive classroom experience.

- **Create a safe classroom**
  A safe classroom is critical to getting students to talk in class because many students have been trained to think the classroom is a place to listen and not be heard.

- **Clear expectations**
Let students know what you expect and that you firmly believe in an interactive classroom. When students get a view of your beliefs it makes them more willing to work with you.

- **Student accountability**
This is the most important and often overlooked aspect of interactive classrooms; students want to be held accountable. When they are held accountable, they know you care about their learning and will try harder to work with you. They will start to take ownership in their learning.

- **Keep the students informed**
Take the mystery out of what and why you are doing an activity. If students are going to take ownership of their learning they need to be empowered with the knowledge needed to understand learning.

- **Keep them talking**
Learning takes place when students talk to and teach each other. It has been said that it takes 17 repetitions to put an idea into long-term memory. When the instructor is the only one talking, that is just once, but if the students are talking, there can be numerous repetitions in one exercise. Plus, as we all know, teaching something is the best way to learn it.

- **Content versus learning objectives**
One issue that I have not brought up is that of content versus interactivity. I have had many colleagues tell me that they do not have time in the classroom to do these interactive activities. The best thing I ever did for my class was to develop learning objectives (Pregent, 1994). Learning objectives helped me focus the course and eliminate the things I used to cover because I thought they were fun to teach, not because they met the course objectives.

- **Have fun**
I think the most important thing is to have fun in the classroom; as teachers we have been given a unique opportunity to help shape the future leaders of the world. If you and the students are having fun in the classroom, they will want to learn, and the odds are they will become lifelong learners.

Using interactive methods in my large classes has brought fun and excitement in to the classroom and at the same time has improved student learning. We should treat the classroom experience as a journey that you and your students take together. You are the guide in their learning experience and as a guide you will help them over the tough spots and will react to their needs. Education is best when done together.

References

Angelo, T. A., & Cross, K. P. (1993). *Classroom assessment techniques* (2nd ed.). San Francisco, CA: Jossey-Bass.

Johnson, D. W., Johnson, R. T, & Smith., K. A. (1991). *Active learning: Cooperation in the college classroom.* Edina, MN: Interactive Book Company.

Pregent, R. (1994). *Charting your course: How to prepare to teach more effectively.* Madison, WI: Magna.

Example 9 _____

Managing Discussion in Large Classes

J. Dennis Huston
Rice University

For well over a decade I taught large English classes at Rice University. At least they were large by Rice's standard—between 60 and 100 students each. That I taught them in discussion format made them large classes of their kind for any university; very few undergraduate discussion courses, I suspect, exceed enrollments of 30 students. Mine, however, often do. I teach all of my classes this way because for me the joy of teaching comes from interaction with my students, from the discoveries that we make together. I love teaching, and what I love about it is not only the subject matter—that goes without saying—but also the process itself: the combination of fear and anticipation I feel before every class as I prepare for it, the adrenaline rush I often get in the classroom as we all improvise our way toward understanding, and the buzz I feel afterward when things have gone well (for the purposes of this chapter I will overlook the depression I feel when they do not).

Teaching a large discussion class is not really very different from teaching a small one: It is much more time-consuming and involves much more work, but the pedagogical principles in both cases are the same. The trick to making large discussion courses work is really no trick at all; it is just doing with a lot more people the same thing one does in a seminar. The successful teacher of a large discussion class still must know the names of all her students; must listen carefully to their answers; and must use their answers to build the arguments she wishes to make that day, even if those answers disrupt the planned order of things. In a large class the teacher must also make everything bigger: she must use a louder voice, larger gestures, and more energy because she has to fill a bigger space. And she must move the action around the room more and faster so that one portion of the class does not feel left out while another portion gets all the attention. But these adjustments are variations upon the techniques of any good seminar teacher, who does the same thing in not quite so big a way.

I know of a very successful large chemistry class, of nearly 300 students, taught in a modified discussion form. To encourage the active involvement of his students, the teacher of this course, my colleague, John Hutchinson, not only answers questions in class but also employs strategies that force students to participate actively in the learning process. He poses a problem to them and then has the students talk about that problem with two or three other students around them. Then the groups of students poll their answers and discuss them in class.

Another colleague of mine, Alan Grob, does a similar thing with his Shakespeare class. He asks a question about a problematic moment in the play they are discussing; for example, when, in *Twelfth Night*, does Olivia fall in love with Cesario? He has them write brief arguments supporting their answers to this question, and then he asks students to read their answers. The differences in the students' answers serve as a focus for further discussion.

Sharing the Enterprise

In large discussion classes, I try to meld my educational philosophy with my pedagogical methodology. For me teaching is essentially a human and humanizing activity that brings my students and me together in a shared enterprise of learning, where we all profit from working together, from learning both about and from one another. In the process, we build a community of people who accomplish more together than any of us could accomplish separately. And even though that community dissolves at the end of the semester, its memory may abide for many of us. A class that works, that fosters genuine intellectual excitement and inquiry in an atmosphere of trust, is a class whose effects reach beyond its scheduled time and place to touch—and occasionally change—lives. And that is what I hope every class I teach will do: change lives, by changing the way my students and I think and feel about ourselves, the people around us, and what we value. I realize, of course, that classes rarely do such things. But that fact does not keep me from wanting to do them: I try to prepare and teach every class as if it could have this kind of effect on the student—and on me.

To have such an effect, however, a class needs extraordinary commitment from its students, a fact I emphasize on the first day when I try to explain my methodology, my style, my aims, and my expectations for the course. Although many of my colleagues think of the first class as focused on bookkeeping activities—handing out a syllabus, talking briefly about the text or texts, and making the first assignment—I think of it as hugely important because it gives me time to explain why I teach by discussion, even in a course of 100 students. The opening class thus becomes in part an apologia for my whole educational philosophy.

I feel I need to offer such an apologia because what I do in class is so different from what most of my students are used to. On the whole, Rice students (and, I suspect, most of their peers in other universities) have been conditioned by their previous educational experience to be passive receivers—consumers—of information. They have got where they are by being good students which often means that they have been rewarded for absorbing and regurgitating information. Such an activity is a necessary part of any learning experience, but it should not be the primary or only skill required of "good" students. Such students should also be able to think for themselves, to trust their own perceptions and feelings, to formulate questions of importance, and to recognize patterns the teacher overlooks.

Many of my students, however, have almost never been asked to do these kinds of things, and almost none of these students has ever been asked to do them in a class, in the presence of other students. Rice students have almost no experience thinking on their feet. Even some of my very best students would, if I would let them, remain forever silent in class. But I will not let them, which is what I explain to them on that first day. Because they have been conditioned to play it safe as students, to listen and absorb without actively participating in class discussion, I have to use radical methods to break down this kind of conditioning: I will thus force them to participate in class discussions, I tell them, by calling on them randomly, without prior warning. The questions I will ask them may be general or particular, open-ended or precisely focused, comparative or context-specific. Sometimes they may even be questions whose answers I myself do not know because the most interesting questions are often of that kind. I ask such questions, I explain, not because I want to make them feel uncomfortable— though I understand that many of them will feel this way, at least at first—but because I think they have an obligation as educated people to articulate their ideas, to submit them to the judgment of others, and defend them against the challenge posed by conflicting ideas.

Explaining the Aims and Expectations

In the process of explaining this methodology, I necessarily must talk also of aims and expectations. Many teachers, I know, choose to include this information in their syllabi, and I include some of it there, but I prefer to talk about it at length in the first class. That way I know for certain that my students understand what I expect of them and why. They also can tell from my tone and from the amount of time and energy I devote to my aims and expectations for the course how important they are to me and should be to them: I count partly, then, on the fact that this first class is different from any they have sat in before, as I intend the classes that follow to be different also, though not quite in the same way as this one. I also explain that this is the only time I plan to lecture in the course, that I am laying down ground rules, not yet practicing what I preach. That world of mutual adventure and discovery lies all before us, in the classes that follow.

When I talk about my aims and expectations I focus on the aims first, in order to justify the expectations. These aims for my students always include the following:

1) Developing their ability to think more imaginatively, independently, and carefully about the texts they encounter, texts that include not only the reading in the course but also the life they lead outside it

2) Broadening and deepening their knowledge of literature

3) Learning to trust their own critical instincts and feelings, even when they conflict with other students' or my reading of the text

4) Developing their capacity to articulate and defend their ideas in oral discussion and encounters

5) Sharpening their writing skills

6) Seeing class preparations and discussion as at once work and fun (since most of the students I teach tend to think of work and play as bifurcated rather than related activities)

The Role of Journals

To achieve such ends, I explain to my students, they must meet certain expectations I have of them. They must do the reading assignment for every class before the class meets, since they cannot effectively discuss an assignment they have not read. In addition, they must attend class regularly because effective discussion depends upon active participation, which, of course, depends upon students' being there. And finally, I ask all of my students to keep reading journals, notebooks in which they free write for approximately ten minutes after they have completed the reading assignment.

In these journals, whose form I borrow from Peter Elbow (1973), I want students to ask—and provide possible answers to—questions raised by the text: What strikes them as surprising, inconsistent, difficult, troubling in the reading assignment? Why? Where have they encountered anything like this before? How does the reading relate to something in their own experience? Did some moment or passage in the text seem to them particularly significant? Why? I also ask students to write their entries fast so that they will not become bogged down in the usual matters in composition: order, logic, precise phrasing. Instead, I want them to go where their imaginations and the very act of writing take them; I want their journal writing to be, if possible, an exercise that frees their imaginative and creative energies. I also tell my students that I will read their journals, responding to their ideas with marginal notes, but that I will not grade them. I want them to write primarily for their own satisfaction, not mine.

Because I do not grade the journals, students sometimes have difficulty keeping them up to date. Conditioned to work for good grades, Rice students sometimes cannot bring themselves to work for no grade at all. I therefore collect journals without warning (usually about ten at a time, so that I can return them by the next class), which means that students must bring them to class every day. And I warn students that if they do not keep their journals up to date, they will have to drop the course; I may not grade them, but I take them very seriously indeed.

I think journals may be the single most effective way to prepare students for class discussion. To write a journal entry, the student must first have thought with some care about the reading assignment: They cannot just skim it quickly, reading words but not really thinking about what the words say. If students are to write intelligently about a text, they must make real intellectual contact with it; they must encounter and perhaps even do battle with it. Only then can they write intelligently and meaningfully about their experience of the text. Students who have written journal entries have at least thought about the assignment with some care. They know what troubles them in it, or what seems to them surprising or important, or what ties this reading assignment to something else they have read in this course or another. As a result, they can talk in class in an informed and intelligent way about the assignment. Having struggled with the text on their own, they often want to share their perceptions.

The worth of journals, however, does not stop with improving class discussion. They have other important effects as well. Often journals provide students with ideas that they can develop into papers. One of my students spent a whole week of journal entries developing, qualifying, and elaborating upon ideas that eventually grew into her first paper for the course. Sometimes, too, journals provide a medium for conversation: Students may raise questions in the journals that they do not raise in class, either because the questions are too personal or because class discussion focuses on different concerns. The journal thus provides me with an opportunity to answer questions, either in marginal notes or in conference, that I would not otherwise know existed. And because students sometimes reveal things about themselves in journals that they would not reveal in class, one or two students a semester may indicate in their journal entries signs of real emotional or academic problems, which gives me an opportunity to talk to them about getting help with these problems. In addition, because some students write more natural-sounding, more humanly voiced prose in their journals than in their essays, journals occasionally provide critical evidence of writing skills I would not otherwise know a student possesses. Having been taught to write essays in sterile, awkward, turgid prose, these students feel empowered when they discover that the prose they write for themselves is also the prose they should write for others. And finally, journals are useful because for some students they become an end in themselves. When I remarked recently in the margin of a student's journal that she was under no obligation to write as much as she was writing, she replied in her next entry: "I write these entries for myself, not for you."

Getting to Know the Students

The final thing I do on the first day of class is to begin to gather information about my students. I pass out 4x6 index cards and ask the students to print their names (and the pronunciation of their names), their year, their major, their hometown, their school telephone number, and their email address. In addition, I ask them to write briefly about what they did last summer, about their principal extracurricular activities at Rice (or in high school if they are freshmen), and about what they imagine they will be doing in 15 years. These cards, which often prove an invaluable resource, serve many purposes. They give me basic information about the students, which helps me to learn their names, and sometimes, to understand reasons why some of them have trouble in the course (lack of experience with the discipline, weak high school education, intense focus on other activities or subjects). To contact such students, who often stop coming regularly to class, I need only refer to the phone numbers on their cards.

In addition to this basic information, the cards also tell me important things about a student's experience outside both the classroom and Rice, information that I can sometimes use during class discussions. If, for instance, I want to draw a parallel or an analogy between something in the assignment and sports, or theater, or movies, or politics, or music, I can call on a student who I know has the knowledge of this particular field. In addition, the cards often tell me something about my students' hopes and dreams, which again proves useful when I want to ask content-specific questions. The cards, then, help me to know my students better. And knowing them better enables me to teach them more effectively. For this reason, I review the cards nearly every day during the first two weeks of class and with some regularity during the rest of the semester. Even when I begin to know the students pretty well from their class performance, journals, and papers, I often discover something important about them from rereading their cards.

The cards also help me to learn students' names because I add information to them in the first weeks of the semester. After I first call on a student to speak in class, I write notes about his appearance on his cards—after class—to help me put names with faces. Some faculty members I know have an even more efficient way of learning names in a large class. On the first day they divide the students into groups of ten, having them make name-tents, and then take Polaroid pictures of each group. The method one selects for learning names does not really matter; what matters is what works, for perhaps nothing helps build a sense of community and trust in a classroom more than learning names. In the most basic way, the teacher thus shows her concern for her students: she cares about them; she knows who they are. A teacher who does not learn names in a discussion class—even a large one—sends a signal that undermines the whole discussion process because it implies that she does not care enough about the students (and, by implication, about their ideas) to learn the most basic thing about them. Learning names, then, is an absolutely crucial part of a teacher's responsibility in a discussion class; not to do so is a breach of trust.

The Importance of Classroom Space

I realize that I have said nothing about the classroom space itself, which often profoundly affects the course: A good room definitely helps promote good discussion, and a bad one is a constant problem to be overcome. Thus, I always make my preferences known early to the person in the university responsible for classroom assignments, because most universities have very few good rooms for large discussion classes; there may, in fact, be none. For me, the ideal room for a large discussion course is a big rectangle, more deep than wide, which enables me to see almost all of the students at once. That way, the students in one part of the room do not feel left out of the discussions when I am talking to a student in another part. The room should also contain moveable chair-desks (so that students do not feel nailed down to the floor), arranged to provide one or two aisles that give me access to the back of the room. That way I can get in the faces of the students who often try to hide back there. Sometimes, too, I may find an empty chair next to them when I can sit and create moments of real physical and emotional closeness, moments that help me to emphasize ideas or exchanges of particular importance. The worst kind of room for a large discussion class is the large lecture hall with raised stage and auditorium seats secured to the floor. Such a room countermands in almost every way what I am trying to do in the class because it separates me from, and raises me above, the students—as if I am the true word, and they were there, lined up and nailed down, to receive it. One *can* make discussion classes work in such a room—by sometimes climbing down from the stage, sometimes bringing students up onto it for group work, and sometimes walking along the sides and to the back of the room in order to force a new perspective on the students. But such a room always works against the best interests of the students and teacher; it is a problem to be overcome, not a space that promotes communication and community.

Beginning the Discussion

I think of the second day of class as the real beginning of the course. In it we engage in class discussion for the first time and to it I bring a number of pedagogical objectives. I want the class to be fun and exciting. I want to get a lot of people talking. I want to make something positive out of as many students' answers as I can so that others feel inclined to participate. I do this by writing some of their own words on the board, which enables them to see their ideas valued. Another thing I do in this class is to make sure that students are listening to one another, not just to me. So I may ask one student to elaborate upon an idea suggested by another. During this class, too, I want to help the students move toward at least one really surprising interpretive insight: I want them to feel the excitement of discovering something together that they had not noticed on their own. And finally, I want to dig deeply into at least one student's answer—when it's a good one—following it up with other questions, designed to make the student elaborate upon and qualify his original answer. In this way I can suggest that discussion in the class does not always stop with one answer, that good answers obligate students to think more deeply about their own ideas. I want the first discussion class to set the tone for the class as a whole: I want it to be full of intellectual energy and surprise, involving as many people as possible in an enterprise they feel is interesting and exciting. And I want students to feel that time in this class rushes by because there is so much to say and because everyone is having a good time.

Our first discussion may not affect many students in this way, but I try to make as many of them as I can feel my enthusiasm for what we are doing. I concentrate hard on putting students' names with their faces. And whenever possible, I make references to ideas students have raised earlier in the discussion. I also watch faces very carefully as I teach because they tell me a lot. What students seem most or least interested? Early in the hour, I usually look for faces showing enthusiasm to build my confidence, but as the hour progresses, and I have a better sense of where the discussion is going, I pick out students who look tired or bored, and call on them, trying to draw them into the discussion. I cannot stress too much the importance of really looking at faces during class because they often provide the best evidence of how the discussion is going, not only by signaling enthusiasm or boredom, but also by indicating when students do not understand a concept or argument: It is not hard to tell from students' faces when they are confused. In one of the best essays ever written about teaching, Roland Christensen (1991) talks about the crucial importance of reading students' physical responses—not only their faces but also their body language and their behavior: What does a student's way of slouching in his chair or waving his hand or suddenly growing silent suggest about his response to this subject or this discussion? If we watch our students carefully as we teach, they will show us what is working and what is not. In addition, a student answering a question will often send subtextual signals about what she is thinking or feeling. She may stop talking, for instance, but her face or eyes may indicate that she is not yet really finished. If the teacher then waits a few moments longer, the student may say something really interesting.

Listening to Students

All of which brings me to what may be the single most important skill a good teacher of discussion classes must possess: the ability to *listen* to students' answers, to hear what the students are really saying, not what the teacher expects them to say. For years I have observed graduate teaching assistants in the classroom, and their most common difficulty is really hearing the students' answers to their questions. The teaching assistants have often spent hours preparing a text and designing questions to get at its crucial themes and problems. But they too often know exactly what answer they want to each of their questions, and if they do not get this answer, they feel flustered. Instead of running with the students' ideas, improvising with the material they have been given, they dismiss the student's answer as "interesting" and then ask again the same question they have just asked, hoping the next student who speaks will give them the answer they are looking for. It does not take students long to realize that what they are being asked to do is not to discuss, not to think their own ideas, but to read the teacher's mind. And they quickly lose interest in answering questions.

Sometimes a teacher looking for a particular idea may think she hears it in a student's answer, may misinterpret what the student says because of what she expects him to say. This mistake I constantly watch for in my classes because my excitement about the interpretation we are constructing together makes me anticipate answers. I may start to develop an idea that I think has been voiced by a student and suddenly see that student's face clouded with confusion. Then I have to backtrack and listen again to what the student has actually said. Listening—really listening—to what students say is crucial to building a successful discussion.

Improvising

Along with listening goes another skill essential to building good discussion in the classroom: improvisation. Lively, interactive discussion develops only when the teacher effectively manages the discussion process by helping students to see beyond the immediate implications of their ideas, to ask questions they did not themselves think to ask, to connect their ideas to those of other students, and to note similarities and differences between different parts of this text or between this text and others. To improvise successfully, the teacher must be prepared to build on ideas as they come from the students, not as he has conceived of them outside of class. In a class built on discussion, organization, which is often the linchpin of a successful lecture, has very little importance. To be sure, the teacher must periodically summarize the important ideas that grow out of the discussion—looking back at where the class has been in order to anticipate where they are going. But the class may get where it is going in a circuitous, disorganized way, often wandering off the beaten path to travel down blind alleys or follow winding detours because the student choose to go that way. Or, suddenly excited by a glimpse of their destination, the students may jump whole sections of the journey and conclude it precipitously. Then the teacher, with the end already attained, must help the students backtrack over the missed parts. When the discussion develops naturally, it often does not move forward in a very organized way, but the students do not care; they are too busy making discoveries and building arguments to be bothered by a little disorganization. If as teachers we lecture to students, we need to organize our arguments clearly so that the students can follow them, but if, instead, we build classes on discussion with students, their minds structure and organize the arguments as they develop them. When students actively participate in and shape what they learn, they do not need the same kind of organizational help that they require when they are merely passive receivers of information.

Monitoring the Process

Although the teacher of a discussion class does not have to concern herself much with organization, she has to think constantly about process. The success of the class depends on controlling both the subject matter and the process of discussion itself. The teacher must constantly monitor and control the dynamics of the group: What does the energy of the class feel like today? Who has prepared the assignment particularly well? Is this material that most of them find interesting or boring? How well have students understood the reading? How many of them want to participate? Are one or two students carrying the discussion? If so, how can I draw others in? Today who is talking less than usual? Do I need to call on one of my best and most articulate students to give the class a lift? Or is this the kind of subject that might enable one of the quieter, less assertive students to shine? Can I stir them up with some kind of really surprising question? If so, can I think of one? Am I focusing attention too much in one part of the room or on too few students? Am I pushing an interpretation too hard in one direction? Should I come at this topic from a different angle? How? These are the kinds of questions I ask myself during class while I am simultaneously asking questions of students, summarizing what they say, elaborating on their ideas, and pushing them to think more carefully about the text and the discussion. As Christensen (1991) has argued, the successful teacher of a discussion is always doing at least two things at once—managing both the process of discussion and the subject being discussed.

Preparing for the Discussion

To handle this kind of challenge, one must spend substantial preparation time thinking not only about the subject matter but also how to make that subject matter available to a particular group of students. As I prepare for class, I first go over the material assigned, trying to identify the ideas and passages that seem most important, both for me and for these students. What themes, problems, issues, and questions do these people in this class find most interesting? What important ones are they likely to overlook? Because I tend to see things in clusters and groups rather than in ordered structures, it is relatively easy for me to improvise in class: Student answers tend to bring up information from one cluster or another, and then students and I begin to build upon these clusters, often crossing from one cluster to another. As I prepare questions designed to provoke discussion, I tend to think only of opening gambits for each cluster of ideas, trusting that other questions will occur to me once we have begun talking about those ideas. I do, however, spend a good deal of time thinking about these gambits. Do I want to open with a shocking question, designed to surprise the students into really imaginative thinking? Or should I choose instead a much more predictable kind of beginning: How is this work like ____? What in this work did you find most confusing, important, or notable? Should I perhaps open the discussion in a low-key way by simply asking what issues the students want to talk about, what questions they want answered? Should I focus on a particular moment in the text or use it as a way of discussing crucial themes or problems? Should I begin with a context-specific question that has important subcontextual ramifications? Sometimes, even after careful preparation, I cannot make up my mind which of these kinds of questions to ask or what cluster of ideas to explore first. Then I simply trust my instincts: When I arrive in class, I select the one that feels right at the moment. Like an actor, carefully rehearsed, I may feel I have prepared thoroughly enough to live my part moment to moment.

As I prepare, I often think, too, about whom I plan to call on, particularly at the beginning of the class. Who has personal experience that qualifies him to talk in an informed way about these ideas? Who has written perceptively in his journal about the issues we will be discussing? Who has not talked much recently in class? Who in the past has shown real interest in some of the problems I mean to address? Who seemed hostile to, or defensive about, these kinds of themes the last time we discussed them? How can I make positive use of that student's hostility or defensiveness? By asking myself such questions as I prepare for class, I sometimes can anticipate the shape that the class discussion will take and who the major players will be. But more often such preparation serves as a source of information to draw on as I improvise my way through a discussion.

When I begin, what questions I ask and whom I call on are often decisions I make on the spur of the moment. Those decisions feel instinctive, and in a way they are, because I improvise them as I go, firing them off of the sparks generated by students' ideas. Behind those instinctive responses, however, there is a great deal of careful preparation and attention to detail, particularly human detail. Teaching an effective discussion class is for me a deeply human and humanizing activity, a process built both on community and on communication, in which all of us work together—questioning, listening, examining, qualifying, challenging, explaining and elaborating—to build something more imaginative, more interesting, more satisfying, and ultimately more enduring than any of us could build alone.

References

Christensen, C. R., Garvin, D. A., & Sweet, A. (Eds.). (1991). *Education for judgment: The artistry of discussion leadership.* Boston, MA: Harvard Business School Press.

Elbow, P. (1973). *Writing without teachers.* New York, NY: Oxford University Press.

Example 10 _____

Defying the Norms: Teaching Large Law School Classes in Accordance with Good Pedagogy

Derrick Bell
New York University

Education must begin with the solution of the teacher-student contradiction, by reconciling the poles of the contradiction so that both are simultaneously teachers and students.

—Paulo Freire

Barriers to Effective Teaching in Large Law School Classes

The ideal in effective teaching, as expressed by Paulo Freire, is very hard to achieve in large classes. With good reason, we celebrate those rare teachers able to combine the skills of the actor and comedian to gain and hold the attention and transmit subject matter to auditorium-size classes. Even those students, though, are listeners, and not necessarily learners. Active participation in the learning process is particularly difficult in large-class settings, and involving students in teaching, the most efficient form or learning, is almost impossible.

The challenge is greater in law schools where, particularly in the first year, law classes of 100 to 150 students or more are quite common. Traditional teaching in these settings, almost of necessity, ignores the norms of good pedagogy. Courses cover a tremendous amount of material, generally through lecture or a combination of lecture and discussion. Thankfully, the teaching process through intimidation portrayed in the film, "The Paper Chase," is no longer popular. Even so, variations of the so-called Socratic method in which the teacher knows the answer he or she wants and the student feels on the hook trying desperately not to look stupid remains more the rule than the exception. It is a passive process that discourages dialog and innovative thinking.

Fortunately, some who teach in law schools are fine teachers, but—with few exceptions—they were hired and promoted based on their potential for scholarly writing and publication. When hiring committees, as a chairperson of one major law school committee reported, seek applicants with intellectual power. This quality is sought among the top graduates of the major law schools who edited their law reviews and gained judicial clerkships with prestigious judges on top appellate courts. No actual law practice experience is required, and the applicant with too much of it is deemed suspect. After all, if the applicants really want a scholarly career, many hiring committees reason, why would they waste time in practice? While they would never concede as much, law schools seek the individual who turned down an offer from Harvard or Yale to join their faculty. Given the highly regarded potential for what is called "theoretical scholarship," the ability to teach well is simply assumed no matter how often in the past that assumption proves in error.

Students who receive little feedback either in class or from other sources during the course, often have no way of knowing how they are doing until the final exam, which is graded on the student's ability to communicate in writing, quite the opposite of the classroom where oral skills are called for. Final exams are often graded on a curve that is intended to provide grade consistency across sections of the same course but can further distort actual student attainment and the grades students receive.

I mention these factors, and there are many more, to illustrate the major challenge facing law school teachers of large classes who wish to depart from the law school classroom norm. The administration is seldom supportive of unorthodox teaching styles if it slows research and writing—particularly for the young teachers seeking promotion and tenure. Faculty colleagues, who may be impressed, do not want to take on the greatly increased workload. Even students are often resistive to a new approach, which requires that they forego the usual practice of cramming a week or so before the final exam in favor of much more work, and involvement during the course. In my 32 years of teaching, I have found that any departure from the usual procedure—a lecture and discussion followed by a final exam—does require more work for the teacher as well as the student. Even so, course structures designed to teach a large class with the techniques of a small seminar can be both effective and rewarding.

Participatory Teaching

The design of my course is the antithesis of the traditional inculcation of passivity as the norm so common in legal education. In my experience—and as my students frequently have told me—they do vastly more work and learn more from an engaged teaching methodology, one which requires that they perform very much like the lawyers they will soon become. The demands on individual students mimic, in many ways, the world of practice, and require that they assume substantial personal responsibility for their professional education. Law students gracefully rise to the challenge and meet it with a competence that might surprise some educators.

My text, *Constitutional Conflicts* (Bell, 1997), is a substantial departure from the norm in Constitutional casebooks. It supports participatory learning by doing simulations, mimicking the kind of process that an attorney researching an unfamiliar area of law might use to investigate prior decisions. In practice, lawyers are called to research and to write; to comprehend legal arguments; to guess at the probable effect of and interaction between judicial, statutory, legal, and policy arguments in court; to argue, persuade, and debate; to work cooperatively with colleagues; and for some, to judge those arguments and decide cases and issues of law. Once their research skills are in place, most students are aware that they have the capacity to learn, relatively quickly, whatever they need or want to know regarding any legal question.

For many students, this task-oriented process brings back some of the involvement-based excitement of first-year moot court where students brief and argue a hypothetical case, usually under the supervision of older students. Students entering the classroom on the first day of l Law believe the course will be unique. They feel a strong sense of anticipation. This course is likely to be, they have been told, the high point of their legal education. After all, they have been reading about Supreme Court decisions in the media for as long as they can remember. Now, they will study and wrestle with these cases that define the legal conceptual foundations of our nation. Usually, some of a law school's best teachers offer the Con law courses. As traditionally taught, though, students' anticipation can be substantially diminished as the classroom takes on the form of their other classes, relying on passive lecture and discussion led by the teacher, the expert, he or she with whom you dare not differ too heatedly. In this environment, only the most resolute of law students see the possibility of testing today's unresolved dilemmas on the battlefield of Constitutional law as a project in which they themselves could engage.

My course procedure does not assume that the teacher is all knowing and thus should occupy center stage in the classroom. Rather, by decoupling several traditional aspects of legal instruction, it frees the student to learn to analyze and perform independently. The instability and malleability of Constitutional law doctrine renders certainty a myth and *stare decisis* a fiction. The teacher can guide students through the precedential confusion, but primarily must impart, through experience, the knowledge that each student is competent to do so. I find that this guidance is most effective as the students seek to find their own way through the thicket of conflicting rules and multi-opinion decisions. While students must grasp the concepts key to the making of a Constitutional argument, it is quite clear that because Supreme Court decisions defy even the most skilled efforts to explain or harmonize as neutral, or objective, interpretations of the Constitutional text—in itself a dubious exercise—the important point, the one each student should retain long after the case names fade from memory, is to understand that rather than a revered relic bequeathed by the founding fathers, to be kept under glass and occasionally dusted, the Constitution is a living document, one locus of battle over the shape of our society, where differing prescriptive and proscriptive visions compete, over what is, what should be, and what will be the governing legal principles in areas of controversy and difference.

Under my participatory approach, students spend long hours haggling over the facts in cases they are writing and practicing the arguments that they must present before their peers. The quality of case presentation varies, but my classes are far more exciting when students are involved in this way than when I stand before them and try to convey the "word" through lecture. In fact, students are far more ready to listen when I inject my views after they have often heatedly discussed their understandings of what the cases mean. Certainly, whether they adopt or reject my views, they are deeply engaged. They have experienced the Constitution as a living document, one with contested meaning, greatly influenced by historical context, a vehicle capable of conveying and sustaining a moral vision; and susceptible as well to interpretations that frustrate the hopes and expectations of those who, lacking power and wealth, look to the law for recognition, for protection, for simple justice.

Student interest and learning is enhanced if they are actively engaged in the learning and teaching process. An analogy to driving a car, or riding a bicycle, may not be exact, but as with skills requiring coordination of many faculties, understanding, much less advocacy of legal issues, is facilitated greatly by practice. Learning of this character tends to stay with students, if not in all its details, at least in general format.

Student understanding of the precedents and, more importantly, the economic and political pressures that underlie the ebb and flow of legal doctrine increase when they use these precedents to support arguments they are making as advocates in front of their peers, or when, as justices, they seek to find flaws in those arguments. While the cases they argue and decide are hypothetical, they provide effective training for those who will become advocates tomorrow.

Students often discover that they are drawn to teaching while they are in law school, but few at that time experience the responsibility for conveying the substance and debates pertaining to a given topic to other students. Some are drawn to scholarly debate, embark on careers which contribute to the intellectual life of the profession, and go on to teach. As my students are required to argue a contested question of law in a manner sufficiently persuasive to sway their peers, they master areas of Constitutional law in much the same way as does a teacher: well enough to clearly explain the concept to other students. This early experience of the demands of teaching is helpful both to students who already know they may want to teach, and to those who would make excellent teachers but have not yet considered teaching as a career option. The value of the process is not limited, however, to those specific few who will enter teaching.

Course Components

Here, in summary, is the procedure I use to transform a large class into hypo teams, small groups of three to four students who each teach one portion of the subject matter to the class through briefing and presentation on an advocacy basis of a hypothetical case. My Constitutional law course meets 28 times in three-hour sessions over the span of 14 weeks. There is no final exam. Students are graded on their presentations to the class, the quality of the essays (op-eds) posted on a course web page, presence and participation in class discussions, and the innovative features of a new hypothetical problem that each hypo team writes for use in the next course.

Class Assistance

While I can and have taught this course without assistance, its quality is much improved by the presence of six teaching assistants (TAs) chosen from among the most able and involved students in the previous offering of the course. These students receive either course credits or hourly pay from my research allowance. For the last few years, I have also had a full-time "Derrick Bell Fellow," usually a former student or graduate student who is paid by the law school and who supervises the teaching fellows, monitors the posting of papers, and often makes brief presentations to the class on special features of legal doctrine.

The Course Web Page

In addition to my text, *Constitutional Conflicts*, that contains summaries of the subject matter, the law school's Internet site contains a course web page designed by the school's computer center. It contains hundreds of edited cases of the kind usually incorporated in law school casebooks. There are also sections where hypo teams can post their briefs and bench memos. And, most important, there are sections where students can post their comments about each of the hypothetical cases in essay form that we call op-eds.

Hypo Teams

I prepare a class schedule or docket based on student selections of the cases on which they wish to serve as either an advocate or a chief justice. Students review all the hypothetical cases—a process with the added benefit of requiring that students peruse the text at the beginning of the course. Except for the first class given over to course organization and overview of the law, each class session features a presentation by the designated hypo team. Each team consists of two advocates who represent the opposing parties in the hypothetical case, and one chief justice who presents a summary of the applicable law and leads the class questioning of the advocates.

Each advocate briefs and argues one case. While styled briefs, they are really points and authorities, three-to-five-page outlines of the arguments and the authorities that support those arguments.

Chief justices prepare a six-to-ten-page bench memo, containing background reading from law reviews, social science, and other material dealing more specifically with the case than the general reading in the text. The purpose is to deepen our understanding of the issues contained in the hypo and provide summaries of what commentators have said about them.

The teaching assistants, each of whom is assigned to three or four hypo teams, provide help as needed and ensure that the briefs and bench memos are posted on the web page in time for the class to read and perhaps print them out for class. They also supervise the presentation of the argument.

Hypo presentations. Arguments last approximately one hour. Each advocate has five to ten minutes to summarize his or her position in a conversational style; i.e., not read. The advocates then take questions from the class serving as the court. Advocates will participate and provide their expertise during the conference following the argument leading up to the class vote. Chief justices will each preside over one case argument and will initiate the court's discussion by directing one question to each pair of advocates. At the conclusion of discussion, they tally and record the vote.

Op-ed essays. Following the argument, each member of the court (with advocates and chief justices exempted unless they feel strongly motivated) may prepare and file in a designated place on my web page under the heading "Op-Eds & Responses" a one- to two-page op-ed-style essay explaining the precedent, policy, and other factors that went into his or her vote. These should be comments on the applicable law and policies involved in the case rather than judicial opinions. In the following class, we will spend the first hour or so reviewing the postings from the previous class.

These op-eds are an important part of the course learning process. Thoughtful and carefully crafted (resembling an op-ed piece in a newspaper rather than a legal opinion), students are expected to post them within a few days after the class ends. Posting on the web page rather than handing in hard copy makes each student's views available to everyone. Under time pressures, students may turn in less than great work when they expect only the teacher will read it, but writing for their peers, no student wants to look stupid or out-of-touch.

Friends and roommates tell me that my students spend many hours composing their op-eds, usually after engaging them in lengthy discussions about the subject matter. Those students without access to the school's network at home, post their op-eds and other papers using the library computers.

Like the op-ed pieces published in many newspapers, I advise that op-eds should have the following characteristics:

1) Length: short, usually from 800 to 1000 words.

2) Point of view: usually one major point with support and consideration and rejection of contrary views.

3) Hard hitting: This is no place for "on the one hand," or "on the other hand." Students are expected to take and argue a position. It may not be on the case outcome, but rather a critique of the law that makes a meaningful outcome feasible, unlikely, even impossible.

4) Perspective. What unique or different view can you bring to the subject, based on personal experience, insight, and skill?

5) Well written: publishable op-ed pieces take time, even for the professionals. Op-ed writers I know can spend 10 to 15 hours or more on a single op-ed piece. I don't expect, but quite often get, that kind of commitment from my students. The test—Is this a piece I would not mind having published in a newspaper or magazine?

Students are asked to file no more than ten to 12 op-eds, including op-ed-length responses to those filed by other students. These must be posted throughout the term rather than all in the last few weeks of the course. Students may also post additional comments of relevance to the course in the Global Comment space on the web page designed for such entries. Brief responses to op-eds posted by others are encouraged and may—if sufficiently substantive, count toward the ten to 12 required op-eds.

Grades: Measuring performance in a nontraditional course with traditional measures is the most difficult and frustrating aspect of my participatory teaching method. I warn students on the first day that because of the grade curve, I will not be able to give every student as good a grade as he or she deserves. Even so, some students are also disappointed that all their hard work does not result in the grade they think they earned. I make every effort to grade the course in accordance with the school's suggested grade curve. I look for consistently thoughtful and insightful contributions to class discussions and op-eds, including the introduction of relevant outside materials that enhance understanding of the subject matter. At the end of the term, the TAs and I review the files containing all the work each student has completed during the course. I then write a memo to each student regarding performance and assign a final grade. It is a tremendous amount of work, but students deserve more than an unexplained letter grade on a transcript, and the memos provide a goodly amount of substantive material for lengthy letters of recommendation.

Mid-term evaluation. This course has evolved over the last dozen years and has benefited from student input. Suggestions are always welcome, but in recent years, I have provided a mid-semester evaluation in which each student is asked to respond anonymously to three questions: 1) What are the things we do in the course that are most helpful in meeting your learning needs? 2) What could be changed to make the course more useful to you? and 3) Please add any other comments you wish to make. My teaching fellow and I read all the evaluations and prepare and distribute to each student a summary that serves as a basis for an hour-long discussion. The evaluation process enables me to clear up misunderstandings and clarify course goals. There is always at least one good suggestion that I incorporate into that or future courses.

The final exam. As reported above, I no longer end the course with a final exam. The work done during the term is sufficient to provide students with the course information they should have and is more than adequate for determining a final grade. I want to share the approach I used, though, because it fit well into my participatory teaching method. In addition to their other responsibilities, each hypo team prepared a final exam question based on the legal doctrine in their hypo presentation. I reviewed and edited the 30 or so questions and had them reproduced and distributed to each student. When the course web page was instituted, the questions were posted there. On exam day, each student learned which one of the 30 questions he or she was to answer in a fashion reflecting understanding of the applicable law and how the legal issues should be resolved. I asked students to be innovative in their approach to their problems. Theoretically, any student could prepare 30 answers in advance and turn in the one that he or she was assigned to write on final exam day. I told students that such preparation was encouraged rather than barred. They were aware, of course, that the final exam would count for perhaps only one-fifth of their final grade.

Students were given one hour to write their answers. I then collected them and, with the help of the TAs, distributed the answers to the hypo teams that wrote the questions. These students then gathered in their groups across the classroom or in the library, read and discussed the answers, wrote comments pointing out errors or misconstructions, and complements where they were deserved. They also suggested a grade. I reviewed all the answers, but almost always agreed with the assessments by the grading students. When the students' exam answers were returned to them, they likely contained more feedback than they had ever received in their other courses.

The practice of students grading other students is seldom done at the law school level. Competition for good grades, it is assumed, will overpower honesty and integrity. That has not been my experience. Student circles discuss in serious detail the relative merits of the answers they are grading. Their comments are usually right on target and far more detailed than students usually receive from even the most conscientious teacher. In my overall grading, I usually comment on the comments, but I seldom have to correct statements that are either wrong or wrong-headed. They are also a bit astounded to find that they cannot bring themselves to recommend an undeserved "A" for an exam paper: They prepared the question, have an idea of what would comprise an excellent response, and differentiate between better and worse with sudden understanding that grading, while no science, is also not entirely random.

For most students, alas not all, grades become a secondary consideration to the benefits they gain from learning Constitutional law on a participatory basis. It is said of a great teacher that "he taught as a learner, led as a follower, and so set the feet of many in the way of life." That is quite a model. It moves me to close with the admission that more important than teaching structure or technique or writing style or jurisprudential philosophy, is the effort of all successful teachers who succeed in communicating not only subject but self.

We all know that the memorable teachers in our lives hold that status even though we do not recall a single thing they taught us. Rather, we remember them as enviable individuals who spurred us to learn on our own, both the subject matter and ourselves. In the law school curriculum, there are few courses that are better suited than Constitutional law as vehicles for the accomplishment of this transference.

Conclusion

The process I use in the classroom is a model rather than a rigid formula. It can be altered to fit class size and student and teacher inclination. The key is to replace a basically passive procedure, consisting of assigned reading and lecture listening, with one requiring active involvement, similar to the multiple aspects of practice, teaching, and judicial functions. For all the pressures of the legal curriculum, students give every indication of welcoming responsibility, opportunity, and challenge. For myself, I find that I learn from my students' fresh encounters with the Constitution as we look at new questions and question old answers. Potentially, such a procedure allows us to approach the Paulo Freire ideal: that students become teachers and teachers become learners.

A Final Word

My participatory learning method was put to a severe test when a few years ago, midway through the semester, I was hospitalized for three weeks with a severe case of viral pneumonia. I missed the final ten class sessions. In my absence, the class continued with the teaching fellow that year. Deborah Creane, serving in an oversight role, kept the arguments on track and supervised the flow of briefs, op-eds, and final exam questions. The students seemed to take a great deal of pride in continuing on in my absence. Two NYU faculty members, Professors Larry Sager and Bert Neuborne, made guest appearances in a few classes but, as I would have done, injected comments and questions rather than lecture. It was not an absence I planned, but it was very gratifying proof that, given an adequate structure, students can teach one another.

Actually, this should not be a surprise. Law schools look to their law reviews and other student publications as a major exemplar of their intellectual strength. It is taken for granted that these publications will be run by students who solicit or write the manuscripts, perform both substantive and technical editing, and oversee production and distribution tasks, all with little or no faculty input or supervision. And students who serve on law reviews virtually always count their labors as among their most rewarding law school experiences. The challenge for teachers is to emulate in the classroom the law review experience so that all students, rather than a selected few, can gain the many benefits of participatory learning. While it is true that legal scholars and more than a few teachers in law depart from the traditional in legal writing and teaching, we do so precisely because we share your view that law students need a thorough grounding in the law—as it is. Many of our students are committed to careers in public service or law reform. They must both learn contemporary doctrine and gain skill in using that knowledge to structure arguments and write briefs that effectively challenge the many injustices that much of the world and the law would prefer to ignore.

Reference

Bell, D. (1997). *Constitutional conflicts*. Cincinnati, OH: Anderson.

Example 11 _____

Mathematics and the Large Class: Meeting and Mastering the Challenge

Nancy J. Simpson
Texas A&M University

Introduction

In many large universities, students taking introductory mathematics classes find themselves in classes of 100 or more. Few teachers of mathematics would claim to prefer teaching these large classes, and most would agree that a more effective job could be done in smaller sections. Nevertheless, for many students, large mathematics classes are a fact of life, and the faculty who teach these classes work hard to put into practice what they know to be principles of good mathematics teaching in any size class—and the challenges are many. In preparation for this chapter, I interviewed ten faculty, from two public universities, each of whom has a reputation for successfully teaching large mathematics classes. I asked them to describe the most significant challenges posed by the large mathematics class. They cited the wide range of student preparation, ability, and confidence, the sense of anonymity felt by students in large classes, the tendency of students in large classes to be passive, and the ease with which students having difficulty can hide. One professor described sitting in the back of a colleague's large mathematics class and being alarmed by how far away the blackboard seemed. When asked about effective teaching strategies, much of what these teachers told me could be described as efforts to shrink that distance—the distance between students and the "mathematics on the blackboard."

Some of the faculty interviewed had been teaching for over 25 years; others were relative newcomers to college teaching. As expected, the strategies described reflected their individual differences in philosophy and background. Yet, in every case, the approaches to teaching described as most effective reflect principles supported by research on the learning of mathematics. The specific methods reported by these teachers fall into three basic categories: strategies to keep students actively engaged during class; strategies to facilitate the development of problem-solving skills; and strategies to address affective characteristics of motivation, confidence, and anxiety. Strategies for each category are described in greater detail in the following sections. All of these suggested approaches come from the work of one or more teachers who have used them successfully. While the primary objective of this chapter is to provide practical, usable strategies for faculty teaching large mathematics classes, a brief summary of applicable research is included to supply a necessary foundation.

Active Engagement

Questions about how people learn mathematics have been approached from primarily two perspectives: behaviorist and cognitive. One contribution of the behaviorist theory of learning to mathematics education is the recognition that practice is essential. For many of us, this statement may conjure up memories of long dreary hours doing multiple pages of long division problems. This is not the only kind of practice. Stephen Willoughby, in *Mathematics Education for a Changing World* (1990), a monograph that discusses the major recommendations of the National Council of Teachers of Mathematics and ways to implement them, notes that "practice need not be unpleasant." Cognitive learning theory does not disagree that practice is important, but emphasizes the importance of meaningful practice. While the role of the teacher in the behaviorist's view is that of arranging the environment to elicit the desired response (e.g., graded homework to encourage students to do it), the cognitivist sees the teacher's primary role as that of structuring the content of the learning activity (e.g., extensive experience with carefully sequenced examples to help students uncover a concept [Merriam & Cafarella, 1991; Silver, 1987; Svinicki, 1991]). Closely related to cognitive learning theory is the constructivist perspective of mathematics education. This perspective says, essentially, that mathematics is actively constructed rather than passively absorbed. Every teacher of mathematics with whom I have spoken emphasized the importance of the work that students themselves do. But how does a one keep a class of 100 actively involved? And how does one require homework of 100 students without being buried under an avalanche of papers to grade?

Strategies to Encourage Active Engagement and Thoughtful Practice both in and out of Class

Active practice. Tell your class, early and often, "Math is not a spectator sport." Reinforce this message with classroom practice. Give your students notes with lots of white space. Include essential terms, theorems, and problem statements and expect students to fill in the white space with definitions and the problems that are worked in class.

Time to practice. When working on a particular type of problem (e.g., related-rates problems or linear programming problems), give students time to work an example problem in class. Ask them to compare their work with the person sitting next to them. You can use this time to move around the room, listening to the discussions and making note of common questions or errors in thinking. After a reasonable amount of time, display your own solution and give students time to check their work and ask questions. This process is more likely to result in good student questions than the familiar, "Are there any questions?" A variation of this strategy would be to distribute a few blank transparencies around the room and ask several pairs or teams to put their work on the transparency. You can then put this work up for all to see, and call attention to correct approaches as well as common mistakes.

Warm-ups. Apply a principle used with physical activity to the intellectual activity of the classroom by putting a problem on the overhead to be worked as a warm-up as students are entering class. This can serve to remind them of concepts discussed during the previous class session and/or to prepare them for the day's topic. Ask for volunteers to put their solutions on the board and spend a few minutes discussing these solutions.

Group work. Put a multiple choice question on the overhead. This should be a question that tests understanding of a particular concept. Ask students to vote for the correct response. From the vote, you can determine whether or not more discussion of the concept is needed.

Practice and review. Assign a few carefully chosen practice problems to be turned in for a homework grade, or to be used as the basis for an in-class quiz. To keep students from simply doing the problems mindlessly, ask them to answer questions such as these: "We did several examples in class. Which example is problem #22 like? Explain." "In order to work this problem, which of the following concepts (or definitions or theorems) will I need to use? Explain." "Define variables that will help you to solve this problem. Describe what your first step will be."

Interaction. Use an interactive lecture style. When you ask questions, pause long enough for students to think about the question and suggest an answer. Give examples that will help students predict definitions or theorems. For example, one instructor describes putting just the conditions of the Intermediate Value Theorem on the board and then stepping back and asking, "What do you think we can we conclude?" Another instructor describes giving students several problems in which the derivative at a point is found numerically, by evaluating the slope using smaller and smaller intervals around the point in question. She then asks students to carefully describe the process for finding the derivative at a point, puts their words on an overhead transparency and compares it to the formal definition of the derivative.

Dr. Ludy T. Benjamin, Professor of Psychology at Texas A&M University, defines active learning to be "hands-on sometimes, minds-on always." For this category of strategies for active engagement, all of what the teachers interviewed told me could be summed up in this definition. Instructors of large mathematics classes have to work harder to keep their students in a "minds-on" mode, but it is possible, and it is essential for successful mathematics teaching. And with all of these possible teaching strategies, it is important to remember what one teacher stated: A critical factor in maintaining student attention is a logical presentation of concepts.

Mathematical Problem-Solving Skill

When asked about strategies for developing mathematical problem-solving skill, much of what teachers describe falls under the heading of metacognition, or thinking about our own mental processes (Willemsen, 1995). As it relates to mathematical problem solving, metacognition has two components: knowledge about cognition and regulation of cognition. Schoenfeld (1987b) and Lester (1985) have observed that a critical difference between expert and novice problem solvers is that experts spend much more time planning, while novices tend to impulsively plunge into the execution stage. Schoenfeld (1987b) also noted that novice problem solvers tend to pursue their approach come hell or high water, while experts check their progress at regular intervals. McCleod (1985) states that students need to be aware of the metacognitive decisions they make while solving problems: "bringing these decisions out of the unconscious into the realm of conscious planning seems to be an important part of problem-solving instruction" (p. 271). To this end, Schoenfeld (1987b) suggests four classroom techniques which will serve to focus on metacognition, three of which would be useable in large classes: 1) teacher modeling of problem-solving processes, 2) whole class problem-solving sessions with teacher as moderator and scribe as well as metacognitive regulator and checker, and 3) small-group problem-solving with teacher as coach. Most of the strategies described by the teachers interviewed fell into one of these three categories.

Strategies for Developing Students' Problem-Solving Skills

Let students see. Let students see you work through problems on the board or on a blank overhead transparency. When students see a completely worked problem neatly typed on an overhead transparency, they erroneously assume that every solution should pop out of their heads, fully formed and clearly communicated. This can undermine the development of a habit of perseverance in problem solving.

Ask questions. Ask aloud the questions you ask yourself throughout the problem-solving process. "How should I start?" "What do I know?" "What is this problem asking me to do?" "What are the possible approaches?" "How am I doing?" "What am I forgetting?" "Does this answer make sense?" Be explicit about why you are doing this. ("I'm asking these questions because these are the questions I want you to develop the habit of asking.") Give students time to think through these questions with you. In large classes, you have to be careful that you are having this conversation with the entire class and avoid the trap of interacting only with those in the first few rows.

Model strategies. Model specific strategies for students. After reading a word problem, one instructor says "Wow—that's a lot of words. I might be tempted to say 'I don't have a clue where to begin.' Instead, let's break it up into pieces." Other instructors describe doing many examples and helping students look for patterns: "How is this problem like the one we did a few minutes ago?" "What do you notice that makes you think this problem is describing a binomial experiment?" Another instructor describes making a big point of keeping the destination in sight (e.g., the identity matrix when doing Gauss-Jordan elimination).

Give credit for analysis. If you value and want to encourage self-regulatory strategies, give credit for evidence of this on exams and other assignments. Show students that a wrong answer is worth more if it is accompanied by "I know this answer does not make sense, because... " than if it is simply circled as the final answer.

Use email. Use email questions as an opportunity to help students with their problem-solving strategies. When students ask a question via email, ask them to articulate their thinking up to the point where they get stuck. This will often give you examples you can use in subsequent semesters.

Provide focus. Give students many problems to practice, and provide focus for their practice. "In these problems, do not do anything more than describe how you would define variables and why." "Draw a picture that represents the information in these problems."

Use small groups. Use small-group problem-solving in class. Have students take turns thinking out loud while others monitor the process.

A critical need in mathematics courses is to help students move beyond the attitudes and practices that come from viewing a course as a stand-alone hurdle rather than a building block for additional learning. Emphasizing the mastery of problem-solving skills over the memorization of rules and formulas promotes the necessary level of engagement even in the large-class setting, and provides students a foundation for learning that will serve them well in math courses and beyond.

Motivation, Anxiety and Confidence

There are many affective issues connected to the teaching of mathematics that cognitive research is beginning to address. Among these issues are motivation and anxiety. Making students aware of affective variables is probably as important as making them aware of their use of metacognitive strategies. As McLeod (1985) points out, "teaching students about heuristics helps them become more aware of the cognitive strategies that they may want to use in solving problems. Teaching students about the affective variables that may be influencing them can make them more aware of limitations that they have imposed (usually unconsciously) on their choice of problem-solving strategies" (p. 271). One model of motivation proposes that motivation to perform a task is a function of the student's expectancy for success and the value the student places on the task (Brophy, 1987; Pintrich,

1987). The value component of this model includes both an inner desire to perform the task because of a drive to master it, or because of a love of challenge, and the perception that the task is useful or important. The expectancy for success component of this model includes students' beliefs regarding the relationship between effort and success. Several studies indicate that success alone is not enough to increase motivation; success must be accompanied by the student's perception that his/her effort (rather than forces over which there are no control) was responsible for the success (Wittrock, 1986). Willemsen (1995) describes two reasons that an "I can do it" attitude is crucial for student success in quantitative courses. First, a belief in one's ability allows attention to be directed to the material rather than to thoughts of "I'll never be able to do this." Second, such a belief increases willingness to persist in the face of difficulty or frustration. The challenge to the mathematics instructor, then, is to help students develop an expectation that they are capable and to communicate the importance of the concepts and skills being learned. In large classes, this can be more difficult because, as one faculty member pointed out, "It is so easy for the problems (i.e., students who are struggling) to hide." It is equally easy for students of high ability to hide, and not be challenged to fulfill their potential. Use of the strategies described below will serve to diminish the anonymity and increase confidence and motivation in all students.

Strategies for Increasing Student Confidence and Motivation

Eliminate negativity. Be very direct about the importance of eliminating negative beliefs about oneself. One instructor announces early and repeats as often as necessary, "In this class, we do not practice bad math-speak" (e.g., "I've never been good at math" or "I hate word problems" or "I'm not a math person"). Another instructor refuses to allow the expression "I'm totally lost," and instead says "Tell me what you do know," pointing out that knowing something means that one is not totally lost.

Be direct. Be direct about the nature of mathematics in general and college mathematics in particular. If you have students who were very successful high school students, warn them against thinking that they do not need to work hard because they already know the material.

Know your students. Make efforts to get to know your students early. On the first day of class, ask students to send you an email describing the math courses they have taken, their hopes and expectations for this course, and any other information that will help you get to know them. (One instructor reported that she asks students to send her a joke in this initial email—something that helps to break the ice in her large class.) While it is generally not possible to respond personally to every student, one teacher pulls the messages that communicate worry or fear about the course and makes a special effort to send a reassuring reply.

Communicate. Write notes on the quizzes of students who perform poorly on first quizzes, asking them to come to your office. Ask them to tell you why they think they messed up. Use the opportunity to discuss learning strategies (e.g., practice working problems without your notes or solution manual, give yourself a timed practice quiz) and to reinforce the message that they can do it.

Be encouraging. Write notes on the quizzes of those who perform exceptionally well on first assignments and quizzes, inviting them to come to your office. Use the opportunity to discuss the possibilities of a mathematics major and to encourage the student to continue to develop his/her mathematical ability.

Be personable. All of the teachers interviewed described efforts to communicate to their students that they were more than willing to help, that their office hours were posted with the expectation that they would be used. Many go to class early just to chat with students. All make a concerted effort to learn names.

Consider some form of retesting opportunity. If a student does poorly on a first exam and feels there is no way he/she can earn better than a C or D, there will be less motivation to continue to work hard. (Maintaining a C takes less effort than working for a B.) Two forms of retesting were described by the teachers interviewed. One instructor asks students to write down the problems for which they would like an opportunity to retest, along with a description of what they did incorrectly. They are then given the opportunity (during office hours) to write answers to different questions that test similar concepts/skills and to regain up to half the points lost. This process clearly requires considerably more work on the part of the instructor but pays off in terms of student motivation and learning. A second approach is to give a quiz consisting of the most commonly missed problems from the exam during the class period after the exams are returned.

The fact that teachers have potential to powerfully influence their students' motivation and confidence is illustrated in a story recalled by one professor. During the first year of his 30-year teaching career, he was teaching a large class of second semester calculus students and had announced to them the opportunity to take part in a mathematics competition. One of his students had made a 100 on every exam, and the professor noted that this student had not signed up for the competition. The professor announced to his class, with conviction, "the winner of the competition is in this room if only he or she will sign up." Subsequently, 11 of his students signed up, and all three winners were among those eleven students. Never underestimate the power of your own belief in your students' ability!

Conclusion

In my conversations with the mathematics faculty interviewed for this project, I asked the question "What does ineffective large-class mathematics instruction look like?" Almost to a person, the responses reflected some variation of "the teacher knows and loves math but seems disconnected from his/her students and unaware of their level of understanding." While it would be difficult, if not impossible, to do a good job of teaching mathematics without a love of the discipline, it is equally difficult to do a good job of teaching mathematics without an awareness and enjoyment of the students in one's class. The dynamics of large sections make it unlikely that students will interfere with a professor who continues to lecture after having lost student attention and comprehension. This can quickly become a downward spiral since, when "Are there any questions?" is met with glazed looks and silence, the path of least resistance for the instructor is to continue with new material. And so we return to the challenge expressed in the opening of this chapter. Those who teach mathematics well—whether to one or to one hundred—continually seek to shrink the distance between their own love and understanding of their discipline and their students' appreciation and understanding of mathematics. The faculty members interviewed for this chapter were generous with their offering of strategies that have helped them to meet this challenge, and it is my hope that the ideas communicated here will prove useful to others.

References

Brophy, J. (1987). Synthesis of research on strategies for motivating students to learn. *Educational Leadership, 45* (2), 40–48.

Lester, F. K. (1985). Methodological considerations in research on mathematical problem-solving instruction. In E. A. Silver (Ed.), *Teaching and learning mathematical problem solving: Multiple research perspectives* (pp. 41–70). Hillsdale, NJ: Erlbaum.

McLeod, D. (1985). Affective issues in research on teaching mathematical problem solving. In E.A. Silver (Ed.), *Teaching and learning mathematical problem solving: Multiple research perspectives* (pp. 266–280). Hillsdale, NJ: Erlbaum.

Merriam, S. B., & Caffarella, R. S. (1991). *Learning in adulthood.* San Francisco, CA: Jossey-Bass.

Pintrich, P. R. (1987, April). *Motivated learning strategies in the college classroom.* Paper presented at the annual meeting of the American Educational Research Association Convention, Washington, DC.

Schoenfeld, A. H. (Ed). (1987a). Cognitive science and mathematics education: an overview. In *Cognitive science and mathematics education* (pp. 189–216). Hillsdale, NJ: Erlbaum.

Schoenfeld, A. H. (Ed). (1987b). What's all the fuss about metacognition? In *Cognitive science and mathematics education* (pp.1–32). Hillsdale, NJ: Erlbaum.

Silver, E. A. (1987). Foundations of cognitive theory and research for mathematical problem-solving. In A. H. Schoenfeld (Ed.), *Cognitive science and mathematics education* (pp. 33-60). Hillsdale, NJ: Erlbaum.

Svinicki, M. (1991). Practical implications of cognitive theories. In R. J. Menges & M. D. Svinicki (Eds.), *College teaching: From theory to practice* (pp. 27–37). San Francisco, CA: Jossey-Bass.

Willemsen, E. W. (1995) So what is the problem? Difficulties at the gate. In R. J. Menges (Ed.), *Fostering student success in quantitative gateway courses* (pp. 15–22). San Francisco, CA: Jossey-Bass.

Willoughby, S. (1990). *Mathematics education for a changing world.* Alexandria, VA: Association for Supervision and Curriculum Development.

Wittrock, M. C. (Ed.). (1986). Students' thought processes. In *Handbook of research on teaching* (pp. 297–314). New York, NY: Macmillan.

Example 12 ————————————————

Strength in Numbers: Making the Large Chemistry Lecture Class Work

Brian P. Coppola
University of Michigan

Why create another collection that assiduously reviews the literature on teaching large classes and provides yet more examples from actual classroom practice? What can anyone say about the large college course that has not been said a hundred times already? Within the usual assumptions about this topic, the answer may be very little, I expect. (Wait! Do not close the book. I am not giving up on the idea that there is something new to say.) For instance, if any reader of this volume enters any key word, phrase, or technique mentioned here into www.google.com (or pick your own favorite search engine), the result would be a high number of hits, all supporting the virtues of whatever idea was searched. The literature on large classes is there for the taking. All of the subject domains are represented. Highly credible educational research has been carried out, and many of the recommendations are highly aligned. So what is the deal? What are we missing that we need to revisit this topic so often?

What assumptions can be examined in order to bring different insights to this topic? I would like to answer in two ways. First, I will begin this chapter with a brief framework for answering the question about large classes and describe some examples from my practice to illustrate the ideas. This is the traditional strategy; namely, I will share examples in a way that I hope others will be able to learn from. Yet a large lecture class is not disembodied from its context, and my instructional setting and its parameters are as idiosyncratic as they would be for anyone else. So I also mean to address the problem of instructional design and implementation from a systemic perspective. In my second answer, I will describe a future faculty development program designed to break higher education out of the decades-old cycle of rediscovery and reinvention that now occurs with each new generation of faculty.

As a matter of setting a context, the large course that I am involved with is a two-term introductory chemistry course called Structure and Reactivity. In 1989, my colleagues and I instituted a large-scale curricular change to introductory chemistry instruction at the University of Michigan (Ege, Coppola, & Lawton, 1997; Coppola, Ege, & Lawton, 1997). The Structure and Reactivity courses use organic chemistry to introduce students to the fundamental concepts of chemistry instead of using the physical chemistry approach traditional to general chemistry courses. In the fall term, there are approximately 1,000 students who elect the first term of Structure and Reactivity, 55% of whom are first-term, first-year students. There are three large lecture sections taught by three different faculty members, one of whom is the course coordinator. Student groups of 18-24 meet for recitation sections, and these same groups comprise the laboratory sections.

We give common examinations that are assembled by the three faculty instructors. The examples used on the exams are generally drawn from the primary literature (Coppola, 2001a). We do not use low-level questions (multiple choice, matching, definition, or ranking the order) in favor of problems where students must draw chemical structures and provide explanations for unfamiliar phenomena. We assign grades on a historically determined absolute scale. Finally, we also provide a number of different opportunities for students from the large, impersonal lecture setting to form small peer-led study groups that are led by undergraduates experienced in the course (Coppola, 1995). Beginning in 1994, we used this model of peer-led instruction as the basis for the honors option, called Structured Study Groups (Coppola, Daniels, & Pontrello, 2001).

The Framing Article

From among hundreds of articles written about large-course instruction, I have selected just one to frame the first part of my discussion. In 1987, Wulff, Nyquist, and Abbott suggested three dimensions about teaching that are particularly useful for thinking about large courses.

Teaching Is a Complex Process

First, they remind us that teaching is a complex process and effective teaching more so. And increasing the scale of teaching and learning from one-on-one to one-on-500 further increases the complexity by expanding the number of choices and decisions that need to be made.

Good Teaching Follows from Understanding

Second, Wulff, Nyquist, and Abbott say that good teaching follows from understanding. Although they do not use the term, they mean pedagogical content knowledge (PCK) (Gess-Newsome & Lederman, 1999). PCK acknowledges that content and process are not on opposites ends of a linear spectrum, but rather interact with each other (Ege, Coppola, & Lawton, 1997). A forthcoming reformulation of Bloom's taxonomy is predicated on this idea (Pintrich, 2001). Understanding, as encouraged by Wulff et al., includes both subject matter knowledge (one's expertise in the content) and its intersection with the range of pedagogical choices that one might make in deciding what would constitute effective instruction (student learning). PCK is that set of skills, or understanding, by which an instructor can use disciplinary expertise and pedagogical knowledge in order to decide how to deploy a classroom methodology that is linked to the desired instructional outcome. There are many variables that need to be taken into account in order to make effective PCK-based decisions, including balancing conflicting criteria in what are surely instructional dilemmas. For example, effective use of the large lecture classroom pits the economy of scale against the benefits of personal interaction. In their survey work with students, Wulff, Nyquist, and Abbott say the benefits from the large-class setting are 1) the presence of lots of other students with many different perspectives, 2) a low-pressure environment, 3) a sense of independence, and 4) a variety of attendance options. On the down side, the students report 1) lessened individual responsibility, 2) the impersonal nature of the instructional setting, and 3) noise and distraction. These are choppy waters for an instructor to navigate.

How Students Perceive Instruction

Third, Wulff et al. encourage instructors to understand how students perceive the instruction they receive. I add to this the idea that instruction always involves human subjects, not just when we are funded to do pedagogical experiments, and that our subjects (our students) deserve a kind of informed consent when they enter our classes. The unstated corollary is that students, like anyone, will create attribution for why something is being done to them. If you are explicit with your instructional goals and your plan to attain them, this can frame the way students see the course. If you do not let them in on your thinking, they will still have an opinion or explanation for why you are doing what you are doing, but it might not match your reasons at all. This third point, then, recommends that we do a better job at giving out the rules of the game we are playing and be sensitive to the messages that are being received in addition to those being sent.

A Plurality of Goals

A plurality of instructional needs and objectives creates a familiar tension in formal education between training students in the technical content of the disciplines and more overarching liberal arts values. Large courses also tend to be service courses, meaning that most of the students are there in order to fulfill some sort of requirement imposed by their academic program or professional objective (such as medical school). In our program, we have found value in creating a taxonomy of goals in order to remember that there are many things we are trying to accomplish in our teaching, and that these goals can sometimes be in conflict. At the liberal arts level, we want students to leave our courses better able to 1) recognize recurring elements and common themes, 2) see relationships between things that may seem different, 3) combine familiar elements into new forms, 4) arrange their thoughts in logical order so as to write and speak clearly and economically, 5) tolerate ambiguity, 6) become accustomed to a relatively unstructured and unsupervised research and discovery process and feel comfortable with nonconformity, and 7) learn about the kind of creativity that leads to visionary solutions (Ege, Coppola, & Lawton, 1997). Such values describe *general intellectual goals* for education. *Professional intellectual goals* are the overarching values for a more specific literacy at the disciplinary level (e.g., chemistry, biology, or science). Instructors need to attend explicitly to the connection between the *professional* and *general intellectual* objectives, namely, to answer how learning science is connected to a liberal education. Lastly, individual courses are embedded within the richness of *professional technical* goals: the factual subject matter that typically comprises a written syllabus or table of contents. Technological progress in the disciplines and the detailed articulation of the *professional technical* subject matter should be exploited in order to make clear connections between the facts and the overarching lessons. Instructors need to think explicitly about how learning triple integrals, solving a problem in chemical synthesis, and translating Goethe are not only representative of *professional intellectual* objectives, but also addresses *general intellectual* ones. This connection, which is often simply left up to the student without even a direction to do so, is the greatest step towards making learning relevant for students, namely, to let them know why they are there.

Teaching and Learning Strategies in the Classroom

A critical aspect of my teaching philosophy for large classes is that not all strategies are equally important for all students. My students are required to do one thing: take my examinations. I prefer to offer a menu of different learning options to my students in order for them to succeed at this task. This does not mean that the infrastructure of the course is not tightly managed; when it is, it does not guarantee success, but when it is not, then there is inevitably trouble.

Five principles have guided my thinking. A detailed discussion of classroom activities organized by these categories is published (Coppola, 1995).

Give out the Implicit Rules

Every discipline creates linguistic and symbolic representations for concepts in order to facilitate communication. In professional associations, we share critical assumptions about representations and rules of operation used by our disciplines, including how these are connected to one other. Beginning learners in any area strive to build a picture based on necessarily incomplete information, and their understanding lacks the sophistication that allows experts to make judgments based on the information which is only implied and not at all apparent in the surface features of any word, symbol, or action. Like the fundamental lessons in semiotics provided by the surrealist painter Magritte, "H-O-H" is not water, but only its representation (Hoffmann & Coppola, 1996).

Socratic Instruction

Anything that turns a passive listener into an active participant is a good thing. Unlike others who advocate dismantling the lecture classroom, I claim that what you do with your class time is the key. Certainly, a lecture to a group of novice learners cannot be like a professional seminar because the audience lacks all of the prior knowledge, shared assumptions, and understandings. On the other hand, it may not be necessary to demand individual accountability on the part of every student when a question is asked, as is the benefit in small-group work, but rather the opportunity to respond out loud to questions along with hundreds of others. I regularly teach in a 400-seat lecture hall. I do not need to hear every answer as I count to ten after asking a question, but instead I want all of my students to understand that I want them thinking in their seats about the hour's topics, and that I intend for all of them to participate. Some instructors make the error of acknowledging only the expected response from the noisy clamor, affirming the efforts of those who "got it right" without considering how and why other attentive learners could come to the "wrong" answer. Exploring the range of possible solutions allows me to demonstrate the kind of reasoning skills I want the students to emulate. I ask open-ended questions nearly every time I judge that I am making an informed decision, which makes the questions very brief, concrete, and focused rather than broadly philosophical. The opportunities to ask questions arise spontaneously, so they might occur three times in one minute, or after a ten-minute monologue, but the effect is a kind of conversation between the class and me. Training a classroom of first-year students how to have this conversation is a PCK-based strategy that must be mastered.

Creating Alternative Metaphors for Learning

When instructors say "study, learn, and do problems," we do not account for the variety of ways studying, learning, and doing problems might be interpreted by our students. I might memorize and recite lists of items as one way to learn if I judge that to be an appropriate strategy. But as an expert learner, I have developed a toolbox of techniques, and I readily create new tools as I need them, refining and discarding them according to the tenets of self-regulation. What do we mean when we say "do problems?" How can I express the difference to students who beat on every problem they face with the same wooden club, and who might just as soon look at one of my sophisticated, refined tools, pick it up, and start to hammer away with it? One strategy, perhaps the most powerful, is through metaphor because, when done effectively, it anchors understanding in prior knowledge in its comparison.

Make Examinations Reflect Your Goals

A set of examinations outlines the expectations of a course much better than a syllabus. If these goals also include higher order learning and thinking skills, then care must be taken in order to actively pre-clude unwanted skills. In other words, if I do not want memorization and recitation to be successful, then I must 1) design tasks that do not reinforce these skills, and 2) include explicit instruction for alternative strategies.

Education Is Not a Neutral Activity

Mentoring is not an activity that can be turned on and off at will. Faculty members are role models for intellectual citizenship through all of their words and actions when they take on the public trust of education. Faculty members influence directly how the next generation of intellectuals will behave. One of my colleagues, Ralph Williams, uses the wonderful phrase "full human presence" to describe the combined professional and personal obligations of a faculty member to the responsibilities of guiding the development of students (Coppola, 2001b). "Full human presence" represents an ideal. It charges us to be honest and fully realized people in our interactions with those whom we mentor and educate. Ultimately, "full human presence" may be a particularly poignant idea in mentoring and educating undergraduate science students because the research literature indicates such a strong dis-identification of young people from the scientists they see (Seymour & Hewitt, 1997).

The Skill, the Will, and the Thrill

It is not enough to want to do something; one must also know how to do it (McKeachie, 1994). The question of professional development frames the second half of my discussion about large classes. Commitment to good teaching, regardless of its venue, is like any other activity: It requires more than the decision to do so in order for it to happen; it requires the knowledge, and in particular, pedagogical content knowledge (PCK). Scott Paris, a psychologist at the University of Michigan, has nicely capsulated two distinct interactions, namely the "skill" and the "will" for what is called strategic learning, and I think these apply quite well to faculty members in their teaching (Paris, Lipson, & Wixson, 1983; Paris & Cross, 1983). These ideas about teaching and learning as change are generically useful. In addition to the intellectual (skill) and behavioral (will) dimensions, one of Paris' colleagues has also suggested that reward (thrill) should be included, too (Paris, 1997).

Educational psychologists have used *skill*, *will*, and *thrill* to remind educators that motivational issues and learning skills play a significant role in student success; I suggest these work equally well when the student is a faculty member learning to be a more effective instructor. Many instructors are motivated to do well (that is, they have the will), and reward structures are a common topic in conversations about institutional structure. I now turn to the root question behind the development of PCK: Where does the skill come from? The traditional answer is inadequate: attend workshops on campus and read chapters in books such as this one! The answer, to me, follows from recognizing that effective teaching is at least as demanding as carrying out effective research. Where and when can a faculty member learn and practice the diversity of pedagogical strategies and how to align them with instructional goals, assessments (Heady, Coppola, & Titterington, 2001), all the while drawing from the core strength of the PhD training? The same place and time, I contend, where they learn to design, implement, assess, and document their research skills: during their formal education.

Developing the Scholarship of Teaching and Learning: Chemical Sciences at the Interface of Education

New faculty members face incredible challenges when they begin their careers. Joining the professoriate means taking on a set of responsibilities and obligations for which the new PhD is basically unprepared.

For over a decade, the Carnegie Foundation for the Advancement of Teaching has advocated a broader understanding of scholarship and its relationship to faculty work. In *Scholarship Reconsidered* (Boyer, 1990), the Foundation's then-president, Ernest L. Boyer, reminds us that scholarship is a mode of thought and a way of practice that can be applied to all aspects of faculty work. Boyer (1990) put it this way:

> We believe the time has come to move beyond the tired old 'teaching versus research' debate and give the familiar and honorable term *scholarship* a broader, more capacious meaning, one that brings legitimacy to the full scope of academic work… Specifically, we conclude that the work of the professoriate might be thought of as having four separate, yet overlapping, functions. These are 1) the scholarship of discovery,

2) the scholarship of integration, 3) the scholarship of application, 4) and the scholarship of teaching (p.14).

Boyer implies that research, teaching, and service can be done in more or less scholarly ways. The scholarship of discovery (research) has been continually refined in order to minimize non-scholarly work. Over the long term, this has been a core feature of intellectual progress in the scholarship of discovery. Unfortunately, this type of winnowing has never been applied to teaching or service. Instead, teaching and service have not benefited from scholarly development because they have been deliberately moved outside the realm of scholarship.

Inasmuch as *Scholarship Reconsidered* provides a broadened answer to "What is Scholarship?," its follow-up, *Scholarship Assessed*, answers the next implicit question, "What tools do we use to distinguish the more scholarly from the less scholarly?" (Glassick, Huber, & Maeroff, 1997). In the strength of its persuasive argument, *Scholarship Assessed* also provokes a new question, and that is, "How does scholarship arise?" If research is not the exclusive domain of scholarship, then understanding how we develop our research scholarship becomes a model for how we develop scholarship in general. Scholarship arises through a deliberately constructed infrastructure of professional development in which mentoring relationships play a large role. Through formal and informal work, undergraduates are identified for their scholarly potential and, in the majority of institutions today, provided with opportunities for increasing autonomy and responsibility through independent study and research. These same principles apply to graduate students, with some variation in the balance between formal course requirements, tasks such as proposals and seminars, and research. Research has become the focus of scholarship, and scholarship's infrastructure has become synonymous with the development of research skills. This development continues through the post-doctoral level and provides a momentum for a faculty member's professional career.

What would it look like to broaden the infrastructure of professional development to include the broadened notion of scholarship? In my work, I have been creating the pieces of the infrastructure that are devoted to the scholarship of teaching, beginning at the undergraduate level and extending to the faculty level. CSIE: Chemical Sciences at the Interface of Education (http://www.umich.edu/~csie) is a project devoted to creating and documenting exemplars within the professional development infrastructure that supports the scholarship of teaching in chemistry. We are exploring undergraduate curriculum design that allows students to have a mentored experience in examining their potential for teaching. Junior and senior students can move into more independent work in design, implementation, and assessment. In the graduate program, first-year chemistry PhD students can take their cognate courses in education science or educational psychology and then work with experienced faculty in designing, implementing, and assessing curriculum ideas in our department. As in the department's research program, graduate students are playing a significant role in the teaching program. In their third and fourth years, these students participate in weeklong mentored teaching internships at nearby institutions that are quite unlike our own. This solution to the problem of improving teaching, including managing the intellectual problem of the large lecture course, is to take the intrinsic strengths of our existing program of scholarly development in research and broaden it to include all aspects of future faculty development. The current faculty get to work with informed, enthusiastic undergraduate and graduate students, and the next generation of faculty gets an education quite unlike their predecessors.

The CSIE argument underlies some recent recommendations for improving precollege education. Seymour Sarason (1998) points out that blaming teachers for the inadequacies of education is blaming "the well-meaning victims of an educational system that they did not design" (p. 12). Ken Wilson and Constance Barsky (1998), in the same issue, propose that only by studying and understanding the success of continuous change in our existing sociotechnological systems will we be able to bring lasting reform to education. They conclude that education is the system most in need of learning from applied research and development. Until we provide mentoring for a broadened notion of scholarship, we will not break free from repeating cycles of reinventing reform in each generation. What we call curriculum reform is more often than not faculty re-education because the informed professional development of faculty for instruction is lacking. Larry Cuban (1990) asserts that the process of reform is itself unexamined:

> ... waves [of reform] occur on the surface [of formal education] and, in some instances, programs, like the skeletons of long-dead sea animals, get deposited on the coral reef of schooling... [yet reform itself goes crit-

ically unexamined]... I end with a plea for rationality... If we do not heed the plea, we will continue to mindlessly speculate, and as Gide observed: Everything has been said before, but since nobody listens, we have to keep going back and begin again (pp. 12–13).

References

Boyer, E. L. (1990). *Scholarship reconsidered: Priorities of the professoriate.* Princeton, NJ: Carnegie Foundation for the Advancement of Teaching.

Coppola, B. P. (1995). Progress in practice: Using concepts from motivational and self-regulated learning research to improve chemistry instruction (pp. 87-96). In P. R. Pintrich (Ed.), *Understanding self-regulated learning.* New Directions for Teaching and Learning, No. 63. San Francisco, CA: Jossey-Bass.

Coppola, B. P. (2001a). Literature-based examinations and grading them: Well worth the effort (pp. 84-86). In E. D. Siebert & W. J. McIntosh (Eds.), *College pathways to the science education standards.* Arlington, VA: NSTA Press.

Coppola, B. P. (2001b). Full human presence. In A. G. Reinarz, & E. R. White (Eds.), *Beyond teaching to mentoring.* (pp. 57-73). New Directions for Teaching and Learning, No. 83. San Francisco, CA: Jossey-Bass.

Coppola, B. P., Daniels, D. S., & Pontrello, J. K. (2001). Using structured study groups to create chemistry honors sections. In J. Miller, J. E. Groccia, & M. Miller (Eds.), *Student assisted teaching and learning* (pp. 116-122). Bolton, MA: Anker.

Coppola, B. P., Ege, S. N., & Lawton, R. G. (1997). The University of Michigan undergraduate chemistry curriculum. 2. Instructional strategies and assessment, *Journal of Chemical Education, 74,* 84-94.

Cuban, L. (1990). Reforming again, again, and again. *Educational Researcher, 19,* 3-13.

Ege, S. N., Coppola, B. P., & Lawton, R. G. (1997). The University of Michigan undergraduate chemistry curriculum 1. Philosophy, curriculum, and the nature of change. *Journal of Chemical Education, 74,* 74-83.

Gess-Newsome, J., & Lederman, N. G. (Eds.). (1999). *Examining pedagogical content knowledge.* Dordrecht, The Netherlands: Kluwer.

Glassick, C. E., Huber, M T., & Maeroff, G. I. (1997). *Scholarship assessed: Evaluation of the professoriate.* San Francisco, CA: Jossey-Bass.

Heady, J. E., Coppola, B. P., & Titterington, L. C. (2001). Assessment standards. In E. D. Siebert & W. J. McIntosh (Eds.), *College pathways to the science education standards.* (pp. 57-63). Arlington, VA: NSTA Press.

Hoffmann, R., & Coppola, B. P. (1996). Some heretical thoughts on what our students are telling us. *Journal of College Science Teaching, 25,* 390-394.

McKeachie, W. J. (Ed.). (1994). *Teaching tips: A guide for the beginning college teacher* (9th Ed.) Lexington, MA: D. C. Heath.

Paris, S. G. (1997). Private communication to the author.

Paris, S. G., & Cross, D. R. (1983). Ordinary learning: Pragmatic connections among children's beliefs, motives and actions. In J. Bisanz, G. Bisanz, & R. Kail (Eds.), *Learning in children,* (pp. 137-169). New York, NY: Springer-Verlag.

Paris, S. G., Lipson, M. Y., & Wixson, K. (1983). Becoming a strategic reader. *Contemporary Educational Psychology, 8,* 293-316.

Pintrich, P. R. (2001). University of Michigan, private communication.

Sarason, S. (1998). Some features of a flawed educational system. *Daedalus, 127* (4), 1-12.

Seymour, E., & Hewitt, N. M. (1997). *Talking about leaving: Why undergraduates leave the sciences.* Boulder, CO: Westview Press.

Wilson, K., & Barsky, C. (1998). Applied research and development: Support for continuing improvement in education. *Daedalus, 127* (4), 233-258.

Wulff, D. H., Nyquist, J. D., & Abbott, R. D. (1987). Students' perceptions of large classes (pp. 17-30). In M. G. Weimer (Ed.), *Teaching large classes well.* New Directions for Teaching and Learning, No. 32. San Francisco, CA: Jossey-Bass.

Example 13 _____

What My Students Have Taught Me

Brent L. Iverson

University of Texas, Austin

Over the course of a career, I have found that the best way to ensure an effective, improving teaching style in large classes is to establish a strong and constant feedback connection to the students. They will know before you when a problem has arisen, and they will also generally have a refreshing number of constructive suggestions. This chapter provides brief descriptions of several lessons I have learned from my students, predominantly premedical students, in classes of organic chemistry ranging in size from 150-420 students. While many of the lessons apply to classes of any size, they are especially critical to successfully teaching a large class.

Lesson 1
Recall The Mirror Effect

The most important lesson I have learned from students is that a class's attitudes are a direct reflection of the attitudes projected by the instructor, much like a mirror reflects both the good and bad features of an object placed in front of it. This is the single most important tool an instructor can use to create a thriving learning environment, particularly in large lecture halls.

Project Enthusiasm

An effective instructor must project sincere enthusiasm for the subject matter. Once the students perceive that an instructor simply cannot wait for class because he or she is bursting with excitement, the students will respond in kind. Even struggling or skeptical students will give grudging benefit of the doubt when presented with an enthusiastic lecture. If you think back upon the most influential teachers in your own education, chances are they showed great enthusiasm.

So how do you remain enthusiastic for the 20th time through a course?

1) Constantly strive to remember what it was like to hear about your subject for the first time, and remember why you were convinced to make a career out of teaching it. Point out to the class those things that you found fascinating. Tell stories about how you felt when you originally learned the material. Were some topics hard for you? If so, why?

2) Ask students in office hours or after class what they think is the most interesting subject matter in the class. You will then know what to amplify or enhance the next time around.

3) Imagine you had to explain to your relatives around the holiday dinner table why the subject matter in your class is so interesting. If this is hard to answer, look for new class material to give you more ammunition! You will be an award-winning teacher when you can convince your teenage nieces and nephews that you have the coolest job of any of their relatives.

Respect Your Students

College students often have considerable growing up to do, but always treat them with respect. Remember, struggling students need you the most, and it is on these students that you will ultimately have the most profound influence. If you can reach them and turn things around, even a little, you will have made a permanent positive difference. Treating students with respect and professionalism at all times during and outside of class will also foster their respectful treatment of you. Projecting a judgmental attitude full of contempt, disappointment, or arrogance will only breed their contempt and resentment of you. If you feel resentment or anger coming from a class, examine your own attitudes and course policies.

One of the most important ways to project respect for students in a lecture hall of 300+ students is to praise and encourage all questions during lecture. It takes courage for a student to ask a question in a large class, especially if it is a question on basic material. If, instead of projecting disappointment, you praise such a question while giving an enthusiastic answer, other struggling students get a message that you respect them enough to help them no matter how far behind they are.

Lesson 2
Go Out Of Your Way To Encourage Questions

The fear factor prevents many students from asking questions in a large class. The larger the class, the more students fear asking what might be—in your eyes—inappropriate questions in front of their peers. But student questions during a lecture provide essential, real-time feedback on how a lecture is being received. A trick I use to encourage questions is to have a bag of candy at the podium, and give each student a piece of candy for asking a question, no matter the level of the question. Besides praising the students for asking the question, a nice piece of candy provides a small, but highly prized, incentive that can often make the difference. More than anything else, showing up to class with a bag full of candy makes it clear you *expect* questions. Of course, the students get no candy for raising their hand and asking "Can I have a piece of candy?" It usually takes the sharper classes about two lectures before someone tries that one!

Lesson 3
If An Entire Class Performs Poorly On A Quiz Or Exam, Take The Blame

If an individual student performs poorly on an exam, it may be his or her fault. If an entire class performs below your expectations, chances are you have not reached them as well as you think. The most effective single thing I have done in a large class is to temporarily ignore the course syllabus and go over important material a second time while explaining that I understand I did not cover it effectively the first time. This second effort, provided with a large dose of humility on my part, inspired the students like nothing else. When students understand that you care deeply about their learning, not simply covering material, they are more motivated. In fact, if students tell you they want to perform well to avoid disappointing you the second time around, you will know that you have provided inspiration.

When you feel it is appropriate to review material, ask students in office hours or after class how they suggest you present it the second time—and use their suggestions. Tell the class you are presenting material based on a student's suggestion; you will be amazed at the response. The students will be convinced that you care most about their learning, that you are trying your hardest so they should try their hardest, and most of all, you take their ideas very seriously.

Lesson 4
Tell Students How To Study

Especially for very difficult or highly technical classes, students may not know how best to study. They may not have any personal experience with many of the topics (who has seen a molecule or electron, after all?), and they may have wildly disparate backgrounds. As instructors, we are aware of which study methods work best in our individual disciplines, but new college students probably aren't, so it pays to tell them. For example, I spend an entire lecture describing in detail how to outline lecture notes and assigned readings, how to catalog formulas or other special types of material, and how the outlines and catalogs provide very efficient time management for test preparation.

The value of telling students how they might study is two-fold. First, it will help students perform better in your class, as well as in other classes. I have often been told by former students that my how-to-study lecture improved their overall grade point average in college. Second, the students will be further convinced that you care very much that they learn the material and that you are trying hard to help them.

Lesson 5
Provide A Written Set Of Take-Home Messages for Each Lecture

Students will spend a finite amount of time learning new course material. Students often have difficulty sorting out important points from trivial details. Providing students with a written list of the important points, presented in concise single sentences, gives them a record of what they need to take away from each lecture. This information will prove invaluable to them as they prepare for exams and the final. It is a great way to ensure that they are studying what you want them to be studying, namely the important material.

Lesson 6
Make Sure The Exams Emphasize The Important Material

A trust must be developed between the instructor and students with regard to evaluation methods. If an instructor provides written take-home messages to stress important material, that same important material must also be stressed on exams, quizzes, and other graded assignments. It is fine for students to leave an exam thinking it was difficult, but not to be surprised at the content. Otherwise, students are likely to lose motivation and take on a counterproductive, fatalistic approach to the course. If I put new material on an exam, I label it as such; e.g., calling it an "apply what you know question." In this way, students do not feel that they failed to pick up on important material.

Some could view my attitude on exam coverage as being overly catering to students. However, I see my approach as a way to make sure the students are studying the important material and to motivate them with the knowledge that their test scores will indeed be proportional to their overall effort in the course. This is especially important for large classes, since the anonymous feeling of sitting in a large lecture can quickly translate into a feeling of hopeless isolation.

Lesson 7
Bring Their Everyday Experiences Into The Classroom

Students are very conscious of whether a class is relevant to them. One way to engage students effectively is to bring real-life examples into as many lectures as possible. For example, in my organic chemistry class we discuss "molecules of the day", in which the concepts of the lecture are illustrated with a molecule they are familiar with such as the pollutant dioxin, the active ingredients in sunscreen, or new pharmaceuticals. Students often tell me this is the most interesting part of the course because it means something to them and gives them academic topics to discuss during social interactions. College students feel pressure to demonstrate their intelligence for family and friends, so giving them good material they can use in these situations provides extra motivation to study for your class. Do not underestimate the importance of this latter point when it comes to a student's overall impression of, and effort in, your course.

Lesson 8
Bring Some Of Your Own Personality And Experiences Into The Classroom

Students will respond positively, and you will build rapport with them, if you bring elements of your own personality or experiences into the classroom. For example, after finishing a chapter in the text, I show a few of the underwater slides I have taken while scuba diving. I also encourage students to think about their health, and I actively advertise local 5K and 10K races in my class. If you play an instrument, bring it to class and play a few notes to wake them up or emphasize important material. There is nothing like a trumpet fanfare to startle students into noticing that something important is about to happen in class! Each semester, I encourage the students to bring canned food—which is donated to a local homeless shelter—to the last review session. Although not a requirement to get into the review session, there is always close to 100% compliance by the students and we collect several hundred pounds of food. The idea here is to bring more than just subject matter to the class, reinforcing the notion that college is a place to learn about the world—not just the academic world—in a number of ways. Importantly, the students will begin to think of you as person, not a talking head.

Lesson 9
Always Warn Students When You Are Covering Material That Has Historically Been Difficult

Every course has material that confounds even many of the most serious students. What may seem straightforward during a lecture can become confusing when confronted by individual students during exam preparation. By keeping track of such material, an instructor can warn subsequent students that a given topic is generally difficult and should be treated with care and extra effort. Such a warning is valuable for at least two reasons. First, it alerts students so that they can prepare accordingly for exams. Second, it reassures the struggling students that the material is indeed difficult, and they are not the only ones to have difficulty.

Lesson 10
Use Technology To Enhance Lectures

Today's students learn more visually than previous generations, a fact that can be exploited by using technology during lectures. In fact, these students are well-conditioned to absorb a great deal of visual information in a short period of time. Going live to an interesting web site during lecture, or using computer animation to show in 30 seconds what would take several minutes to describe otherwise, will enhance the lecture experience for students. Molecular sciences are particularly well-suited to a technology approach, since molecules can be visualized in three dimensions using computer graphics and calculations, providing rapid illustrations for concepts that are not possible to explain effectively using only the two-dimensional blackboard. Each discipline has specific aspects that lend themselves to technology presentation, and the instructor should identify these aspects and prepare or obtain the necessary technology materials.

A good rule of thumb is that five to ten minutes of technology presentation per 50-minute lecture is about the right amount to keep the students alert and interested when watching animations or other technology lecture enhancements. Today's students have been raised with MTV and rapidly moving video clips, not 50-minute, slowly moving documentary videos. A quick hitting, make your point and move on, five-minute computer animation/video will galvanize the attention of the entire class. Warning: Do not use technology for technology's sake. Computer animations or streaming video clips that are too long, move too slowly, or are not really appropriate will only drag down an otherwise good lecture.

A major concern about using technology in classrooms for the first time is that there might be some trouble getting the equipment to operate during precious class time. This concern can be addressed head-on in at least two ways. First, the instructor should become familiar with as much of the classroom technology as possible before the semester starts. What may be less obvious is that if something does go wrong during lecture, the very first thing to do is ask if anyone in the room can help. In large classes, there are usually many students who are technology experts, and they are eager to help. The student(s) can get to work on the problem while the instructor moves on with the lecture or starts asking for general questions. In six years of using computer technology daily in my own lectures, I have never had a crippling problem that students or I could not quickly rectify. The bottom line is that computer and projection technologies are extremely reliable these days; don't avoid using technology.

Lesson 11
Create A Sophisticated Class Web Site And Keep Adding To It Each Semester

Occasionally, technology may present material more quickly than students can absorb and record it. For example, this is usually the students' largest complaint when an instructor uses a PowerPoint presentation for entire lectures. Also, presenting an animated, three-dimensional, full color computer rendering of an object may be the most efficient way to depict the object during a lecture, but how do the students record the information? The way to prevent such problems is to have a class web site that is updated daily. Place images or short animations on the site that convey the essence of your class technology presentation so the students can study the material whenever they need it. I find having a calendar on the class web site is useful, so students can simply click on the date of the lecture to get to the appropriate lecture material, complete with written explanation if necessary.

A good course web site allows the instructor/student communication that is not constrained by time or place. However, constructing such a web site requires tremendous time and expertise. In my experience, it takes about one week to learn the software required to author an effective web site from scratch, and about two to three hours per lecture to add the material to the site. No doubt about it, this is a major commitment, and the exact amount of time can vary considerably depending on an individual instructor's situation. Nevertheless, I have found the investment worthwhile because of the tremendous educational benefits to students. Powerful course web sites can be created in a cumulative fashion, building a basic site throughout the first semester, and then adding enhancements each time through. After several semesters, quite a sophisticated body of work can be incorporated into the web site.

Useful course web site features include a frequently asked questions (FAQs) section, old exams or problem sets, auxiliary problem sets, links to other related web sites, an archive of all the written take-home messages from each lecture (Lesson 5 above), and, of course, the technology lecture materials from every lecture. This is just the beginning. When one considers the value of hyperlinks to archived databases of all kinds such as sounds, movies, photographs, documents, another university's course web site, etc., the potential educational power boggles the mind. On top of that, many textbooks not come with an associated web site that you and your students can use.

If you do not have the time or expertise to personally start a web site, you might ask your present, or better yet, former students, if they want to create a course web site for you. You will probably get a tremendous response, having to pick and choose among several interested students. The students will also likely already know how to create a great web site. The approach of using students to create and maintain course web sites has been used to tremendous advantage on campuses around the country.

Lesson 12
Keep Class Spontaneous And Exciting By Periodically Doing The Unexpected

One of the clearest memories I have about one of my own college classes is when a brilliant biochemistry professor once asked my class if any of us had a lipid molecule handy, since he had forgotten his. Before we had time to ponder what was happening, two plastic molecular models came flying through the air from the middle of the class toward the professor. He nonchalantly caught the models and proceeded to use them as visual lecture aids for the remainder of the lecture. Such a ploy, obviously orchestrated ahead of time, added a great deal of spontaneity and pizzazz to the lecture that I remember to this day. I often use the flying lecture aid trick in class, asking if anyone has a particular improbable item and then having the item immediately come flying at me from somewhere in the class. Of course, I take the obvious safety precautions. Nevertheless, the net result is a much more alert atmosphere in the auditorium for the rest of the class period. Other unexpected happenings during a lecture, such as having teaching assistants dress up and act out skits that illustrate selected concepts, make indelible impressions regarding important material. (A note of caution: Be sensitive to TAs, and do not make them feel that such activity is mandatory in any way.) The best part is that the students know you are having fun while trying to reach them, and they will reflect this positive attitude as they approach learning the material on their own. No one said lectures couldn't have spontaneity, fun, and excitement in them, did they?

Lesson 13
Don't Let Them Just Sit There

Students in large lecture classes assume they are anonymous and that their lack of attention or participation will not be noticed. Unfortunately, they are correct to some extent. The best way to keep all students engaged in a large lecture is to constantly ask them thought-provoking questions over material you just covered and to have them vote on which possible answer is correct. This will always be met with only one or two votes out of several hundred students. The rest will simply look at you blankly. Do not accept this: Repeat the question and demand another vote. Alternate between asking for a show of hands and a voice vote. You can even try having them stand to acknowledge the correct answer. Keep this up until everyone votes. They will get better and better during the semester once they know you are serious. This tactic, used up to three or four times per lecture, accomplishes several things. First, it reengages students who may have temporarily lost focus. Second, it gives you instant feedback on the students' understanding of the material. Third, it helps students realize if they don't understand the material or have not been paying close attention. Finally, if the entire class gets the question correct, you have an opportunity to praise them.

Lesson 14
Don't Stay Behind A Podium

When trying to keep the attention of a large class, the simplest trick of all can also be one of the most effective. Don't stay behind a podium, but wander into the seats when you speak. Moving among the audience will capture their attention and make them feel less anonymous. Also, when a student asks a question, move as close to them as possible when you give the answer. On my own campus, I have noticed that moving among the students during class is common among award winning instructors.

Summary

Large classes provide wonderful and unique opportunities for teaching and learning. It takes effort, but establishing communication with students during office hours or other times during the semester will provide the constant feedback needed to keep a large lecture course (and teaching career) on the right track. Let's face it: The vast majority of students in college have spent more time in some type of classroom than they have devoted to any other single activity besides sleeping. (I will avoid the obvious similarities in the way some students approach these two activities.) Students are, therefore, experts when it comes to what makes great teaching, and they are always willing to share useful insights on teaching if you are willing to listen. The best way to cultivate a productive relationship with students is to convince them, even the struggling students, that your primary concern is their learning. In addition, by treating the subject matter with enthusiasm and the students with respect, you will be able to enjoy a class that mirrors these essential attitudes in return. Almost by definition, the best classes involve a lot of teaching and learning. The most important lesson of all is that the instructor is at his or her best when doing a substantial amount of both.

Example 14 _____

Large-Class Instruction: Having a Private Conversation in a Crowded Room

James H. Stith
American Institute of Physics

There is general consensus within the academic community that one-on-one instruction is the optimal way to help students understand and appreciate the subject matter. Hence, the academic reputation of many institutions is built on the ability to offer all instruction in small classes. At many large institutions however, economic concerns lead to instruction in large classes, often of 300 or more students. In this environment, it is difficult for the faculty member to get to know students well and become familiar with the special needs of each student. This chapter describes some steps taken by innovative faculty to overcome the aforementioned limitations and describes techniques used to effectively address student needs in large classroom settings.

Some good resources that go well beyond the scope of this chapter include *Teaching Tips* (McKeachie, 1994), a must read for all faculty; *Science Teaching Reconsidered* (National Research Council, 1997), a practical guide to teaching for "college teachers who want to explore new ways to enhance student learning;" and *How People Learn* (Bransford, Brown, & Cocking, 1999), an excellent primer that gives the non-expert a base for understanding how students learn and how instruction may be tailored to maximize student learning.

Teaching Tips

Teaching large classes requires some serious compromises, but it is possible to create an environment in which students can become actively involved in the learning process. It is important to remember that though the instructor may tell a student something, however slowly and clearly, it does not follow that the student will learn it. Furthermore, students don't gain much by having the instructor repeat what is in the course text. The goal should always be to convince students that education is a partnership between student and teacher. It is not possible to cover everything that is important in the hour that is allocated for the class. Hence, to maximize learning, faculty should build the expectation that students come to class prepared and that the instructor will build upon this preparation.

The First Day

The first day of class is probably the most important, especially for large classes. Use it to introduce yourself as well as the course to the student. Don't be afraid to let them know something about you, and allow them to share something about themselves as well. I often write a paragraph about myself that I share with the students and ask them to do the same. Ask them to tell you why they are taking the course and what they expect to gain from it. While many will see this as a trivial exercise, many students will think seriously about the request and give you some valuable hints that will allow you to tailor your instruction to their particular needs. Try to get your students to see you as a person, rather than just as their instructor for the course.

Student Expectations

From the beginning, let students know your expectations for their course performance. By experience, students have learned to expect a certain level of anonymity in large classes and often use it as a rationale for not preparing. Let them know that you care about their individual performance, that you are available to answer questions, and otherwise help them earn the grade they seek. Let students know your criteria for the various grades they hope to earn. Assure them that, in your view, each of them is capable of successfully completing the course.

Just as it is paramount for instructors to get and keep students' attention, it is equally important to help them understand how to maximize their learning. Students should not see the instructor as the sole source for all their learning. Neither is it possible to cover everything in the text the teacher believes is important for students to learn. Instructors should make it clear that students are expected to learn a significant amount on their own, but that the instructor will always be available to coach and advise, always willing to help the students over the rough spots.

Be Seen, Be Heard, Organize

Ensure that the student in the last row of the class can clearly hear what is said. Speak slowly and clearly so that those students who are unfamiliar with your dialect or accent will not misunderstand you. Stop often, asking students if they hear and understand what you are saying. Maintain eye contact with students. Pick out students in different sections of the classroom to focus on, giving students the impression that you are talking directly to them. To ensure that what you think you said is what students heard, ask students to paraphrase what you have said.

Take care that whatever you write on the board or overhead is large enough and legible enough for the student in the last row to read. Fight the temptation to squeeze in one last line or one more word.

Plan and organize your blackboards so that the students are able to discern a coherent picture from their notes. Give some thought to what you want the students to see when they look at their notes two weeks after the class. It helps to put boxes around or to underline important concepts and to use different color chalk to make diagrams and figures stand out. These techniques help students focus on key concepts during subsequent study periods. As you walk about the class, glance at students' notes to determine if they make sense. If they don't, use the opportunity to clarify the point for the entire class. You will be surprised how often students miscopy something that you think you have explained clearly. Your own organizational structure helps students organize their thoughts, and hence aids their understanding of the subject. Some instructors (Beichner, in press) collect and grade selected students' notes to emphasize the importance of good notes for understanding.

Enjoy Your Work

It is also important for faculty to be enthusiastic. I am amazed at the number of students who tell me about instructors who act as if they are not interested in the subjects they teach. It is much easier for students to learn and appreciate the material if instructors give the impression they love the subject. It is much easier for a student to see the material as important for the overall learning process if the instructor gives the impression that it is important. Additionally, be careful not to give the impression that the subject matter is so difficult that only the very best can understand and comprehend it. The impression that I always try to project is that the material may be difficult, but understanding it is within the capability of every student in the classroom.

Listen to Your Students

Teachers should also know when to stop talking. Learn to read your students so that you know when enough is enough. Don't talk down to the students. When you ask a question, give students time to think and compose an answer (practice waiting). Be careful not to give the student you think knows the answer more time to respond than the student you think does not. Listen carefully to the answers. Too often, instructors respond to the answer they think the student is going to give rather than the one given.

Try to call on students by name. There are various useful techniques to help you remember names. For example, I look at my class roster prior to each class and select names of a set of students I am going to call on. Early in the semester, I also ask students to state their name when asking a question. While the above are important practices for all classes, they are critical for keeping students involved and focused in large classes.

Use Variety

Don't conduct every class in exactly the same manner. Vary your technique, using demonstrations and other aids. When using demonstrations, understand the impact they will have on students. Simply watching you perform the demonstration will not necessarily lead to better student understanding of the concept you are trying to get across. The apparatus should be large enough so that the student in the last row can clearly see what is happening. Sometimes, a camera and projection device is helpful in allowing all students a full view. If the students can't see it, then don't do it! Whenever possible, use students to assist in performing demonstrations. This not only helps the selected students understand the concepts more fully, but also makes the outcome more believable. Using students helps to show that it does not take the special touch of an expert to make science work. Finally, my rule of thumb is that if the demonstration takes longer than five minutes to complete, it should probably be done as a laboratory exercise.

Evaluation

The most overlooked aspect of effective teaching is the evaluation. A significant fraction (as high as 20–25%) of college instructional time is spent evaluating the impact of instruction. Yet most faculty have little or no experience in constructing examinations, in selecting the best form for the examination, or in determining what the results of the examination mean. Furthermore, bad examinations can undermine all the progress that the instructor may make in the course of the semester by giving a message that, while you focus on the concepts in class, the tests focus on solving traditional problems. Jacobs and Chase (1992) have written an excellent guide for developing and using tests effectively.

Techniques That Work

Microcomputer-Based Laboratory (MBL)

Thornton and Sokoloff (1996) have developed a good interactive lecture demonstration strategy—which has been used effectively in large introductory physics classes—for helping students overcome persistent erroneous beliefs. The strategy begins with the instructor orally describing a demonstration and then performing it without taking any measurements. For example, the instructor may set up a demonstration involving the collision of two air carts on an air track, (one stationary light cart and one moving heavy cart). Students observe the collision of the two carts and are asked to record their individual predictions regarding the respective forces the carts exert on each other.

Once the predictions are recorded, the instructor asks students to discuss the situation with neighbors and to predict whether one of the carts will exert a larger force on the other or whether the carts will exert equal forces on each other. After a small-group discussion, students record their final prediction on a hand-out that is collected by the instructor. Invariably, most of the students predict incorrectly that the heavier cart will exert a larger force on the lighter cart.

The instructor then carries out the demonstration using force probes and other MBL equipment that show the forces on each cart in real time. On the computer screen, the students see that the force probes record forces of equal magnitudes but directed in opposite directions. A few students are asked to describe the result and then to discuss those results in the context of the demonstration. After the discussion, students fill out a result sheet that they keep with their notes. The instructor also leads a discussion of analogous physical situations with different surface features. (Different physical situations that are based on the same concept.)

End-of-course examinations show that students who are exposed to the MBL instructional techniques show significantly better understanding of fundamental physics concepts than those who receive traditional instruction.

Classtalk

To help manage the communication and interaction among students in the lecture hall, Dufresne et al. (1996) use a classroom communications system called *Classtalk. Classtalk*, developed and marketed by Better Education, Inc., consists of both hardware and software that allow up to four students to share an input device. Student palmtop computers are connected to a computer that is attached to dual monitors that allow the instructor to observe individual or group responses and permit students to observe group statistics for a given question. Students are given questions that include both qualitative, multiple-choice, single-answer problems, and multiple-step problems in which the numeric or multiple-choice answers are given as individual steps. Students answer those questions through their input device. Answers can be displayed to the class in the form of a histogram, and a permanent record of the data from each student or group of students can be recorded and used as part of the evaluation. Students are encouraged to discuss their solutions prior to recording their answers. Hence, this approach creates an interactive learning environment in a large-class setting. The technology helps to make the student's thinking visible to the instructor, and in many ways promotes critical listening, evaluation, and argumentation in the large-class atmosphere. Most studies indicate that computers do not make a sizable impact on learning unless they are embedded within a carefully structured curriculum that emphasizes student activity and involvement with the material. *Classtalk* allows this to happen.

Peer Instruction

Mazur's (1997) *Peer Instruction* uses student interaction during the lecture and focuses their attention on the underlying concepts. The lecture consists of a number of short presentations on key points, followed by a concept test. The concept test is a series of short conceptual questions on the subject being discussed. The students are given time to formulate answers and then are asked to discuss those answers with neighboring students. The process is designed to force students to think through the arguments being developed and provides them with a way of assessing their understanding of the concept. Each concept test has the following general format:

1) Question posed   1 minute

2) Students given time to think   1 minute

3) Student record individual answers (optional)

4) Student convince their neighbors (peer instruction)   1-2 minutes

5) Students record revised answers (optional)

6) Feedback to the teacher: Tally of answers

7) Explanation of correct answer 2^+ minutes

If most students give the correct answer, the instructor moves on to the next topic. If the percentage of correct responses is less than 90%, the instructor gives more detail, and students take another concept test.

Mazur's *Peer Instruction* gives a step-by-step guide to preparing for a peer instruction lecture as well as a number of concept tests that may be used in the introductory physics course.

Tutorials

McDermott and Shaffer (1998) have developed a set of instructional materials intended to supplement the lectures and textbook of the standard introductory physics course. The emphasis of the tutorials is not to solve the problems found in the back of the textbook, but to help students develop scientific reasoning skills and understand important physical concepts. The tutorials address the growing evidence that after traditional classroom instruction, many students are unable to apply the concepts they have learned to situations they have not previously seen.

The tutorials are intended for use in a laboratory section of the typical lecture course. Students work in groups of three to four. The tutorial questions guide the student through the reasoning necessary to construct concepts and apply those concepts to real-world situations. The tutorials also allow the students to practice interpreting the multiple representations they are likely to encounter in the physics course and helps them move back and forth between those representations.

The tutorials consist of an integrated system of pretests, worksheets, and homework assignments. The pretests are designed to help the student identify what they do and do not understand about the material and what they are expected to understand upon completion of the assignment. Additionally, the pretest informs the instructor about the level of student understanding and provides clues to where additional time and effort should be focused. The worksheets consist of carefully sequenced tasks and questions that students are expected to answer through discussions with peers and with assistance from tutorial instructors. Tutorial instructors do not lecture, but are trained to ask questions designed to help the students find their own answers. Finally, if the tutorials are to be effective, the course examinations must contain qualitative questions that emphasize the material covered in the tutorials sessions.

Tutorials in Introductory Physics, the workbook developed by McDermott's Physics Education Group (McDermott, 1998) at the University of Washington, contains a sufficient number of tutorial questions for a one-year physics course. The questions are suitable for either the calculus- or algebra-based course and is an excellent resource for teachers wanting to introduce tutorials into the course.

Conclusion

There is a growing body of knowledge on how students learn. As Jossem (2000) states, "The body of research on the cognitive and social processes that underlie the learning and performance of individuals and teams has grown to the point that it is a far better guide to training than is intuition or standard practice." Using research results, a number of methods have been developed that maintain an active learning environment in large classes. The results of these methods indicate that collaboration is possible in large classes and has many of the same benefits as small classes. The results show that students respond positively when required to think actively about the subject and are required to stake out a position on the subject. Requiring students to verbally commit to and defend their beliefs in discussions with their peers is a core feature in all of the successful models.

Students bring prior knowledge and conceptions to courses, and often those models are incorrect, but students will continue to use them until forced to concede that they do not work. Even in large classes, carefully constructed instructional models can be used to force students to examine their conceptions, and discard incorrect ones. The large classroom is comforting to the unprepared students who believe they are largely inaccessible to the instructor. Instructors walking about the lecture hall, identifying pockets within the room on which to focus attention, and bringing students to the front of the classroom to assist in demonstrations are all techniques that serve to reduce the perceived inaccessibility of students and lead to increased student preparation.

Finally, technology offers more opportunities for one-on-one attention to the student. Used properly, technology allows students to focus on the concepts and allows them to interact with both the instructor and other students.

References

Beichner, R. (in press). Student-centered activities for large enrollment university physics (SCALE-UP). *Reshaping undergraduate science and engineering education: Tools for better learning.* Proceeding of the Sigma Xi Forum, Minneapolis, MN. [Online]. Available FTP ftp://ftp.ncsu.edu/pub/ncsu/beichner/RB/SigmaXi.pdf.

Bransford, J. D., Brown, A. L., & Cocking, R. R. (Eds.). (1999). *How people learn: Brain, mind, experience, and school.* Washington, DC: National Academy Press.

Dufresne, R. J., Gerace, W. J., Leonard, W. J., Mestre, J. P., & Wenk, L. (1996). Classtalk: A classroom communication system for active learning. *Journal of Computing in Higher Education, 7,* 3-47.

Jacobs, L. C., & Chase, C. I. (1992). *Developing and using tests effectively.* San Francisco, CA: Jossey-Bass.

Jossem, E. L. (2000). The teaching of physics. *American Journal of Physics, 68,* 6.

Mazur, E. (1997). *Peer instruction: A user's manual.* Upper Saddle River, NJ: Prentice Hall.

McDermott, L. C., & Shaffer, P. S. (1998). *Tutorials in introductory physics.* Upper Saddle River, NJ: Prentice Hall.

McKeachie, W. J. (1994). *Teaching tips* (11th ed.). Lexington, MA: D. C. Heath.

National Research Council (1997). *Science teaching reconsidered: A handbook.* Washington, DC: National Academy Press.

Thornton, R. K., & Sokoloff, D. R. (1996). Assessing student learning of Newton's Laws: The force and motion conceptual evaluation and the evaluation of active learning laboratory and lecture curricula. *American Journal of Physics, 64*, 338-352.

Example 15 _____

Personalizing the Large Class in Psychology

Richard P. Halgin and Christopher E. Overtree
University of Massachusetts, Amherst

Large class size (several hundred students) is common in many psychology departments. Instructors face many challenges in their efforts to teach hundreds of students at a time, and most are eager to learn strategies to make the large class work well. In this chapter, we discuss some efforts that we have incorporated into our teaching to make the large lecture class more personal and more effective for students. We hope to add to the excellent ideas provided by educators such as McKeachie (1994) and others who have shared strategies for teaching large classes (Aronson, 1987; Benjamin, 1991; Brooks, 1987; Gleason, 1990; Jenkins, 1991; Knapper, 1987).

One of us (Halgin) has taught large classes for more than 20 years; however, most of the techniques presented in this article are innovations that have been introduced during the past four years with classes ranging from 300 to 525 students. The other (Overtree) has played a central role in the development and refinement of these techniques and has prepared a 26-page manual of policies and procedures (1997) for teaching large classes that has been distributed at campus-wide teaching seminars. Many of the ideas we present in this chapter are elaborated in the manual and represent efforts that we have made to enhance the learning experience for our students.

Establishing a Relationship

Central to our philosophy of personalized education is our belief that in the teacher/student relationship, each has responsibilities. We approach the first class meeting with the mindset that we are about to meet people who are very important, students with whom we want to develop meaningful relationships. We look for ways to convey this concept to them from the outset. For example, on the first day of class we stand at the door and personally welcome and shake the hand of each entering student. The faces of entering students reflect surprise and a bit of amusement, but the message is clear to them from the outset; the relationship with the instructor and the graduate teaching assistant will be different from what they might expect in a large class.

In the first lecture, we emphasize the efforts we will make to establish a climate of mutual respect. We suggest that students can express their respect by being punctual, avoiding disruptive behavior in the auditorium, and treating the teaching staff with courtesy and maturity. In return, we promise that we will do everything possible to make them feel welcomed and valued in this large group.

We urge students to introduce themselves when we meet on campus or in town. In any interaction with a student, we ask for the student's name, which we use in that conversation and try to remember. We arrive at the auditorium a half-hour before each lecture and stay afterwards to talk with students. To create a feeling of community, we invite students to let us know about special events in which they are participating so that we can announce these to the class and make an effort to attend their athletic competitions, gallery openings, plays, and musical performances.

In an attempt to get to know our students better, on the first day we distribute a personal information form on which we ask students the standard information (address, phone, major, etc.) and also inquire about them more personally (hometown, local jobs, personal hobbies and interests, special talents, and experiences). At the bottom of the form, we ask if there is anything more that they would like to say about themselves; to this question, students offer a range of responses from humorous to quite personal. Immediately following the first lecture, we set aside a few hours to read all these forms, so that we can summarize the data at the start of the second class meeting. In this summary, we comment on the many places from which the students hail and mention a few dozen hometowns, especially the more exotic. We speak of the fact that they represent just about every major at the university, ranging from forestry to animal science. We enumerate 20 or 30 workplaces and urge students to look for their classmates in these places. We make a special point of sharing humorous quotations, which at least a dozen students write on their forms. After telling the class about themselves, we tell them about ourselves. In addition to the customary professional data, we offer personal information and answer all the questions that we have asked of them. From our first encounter with our students, we are working to cement an alliance that can thrive throughout the semester.

The Teaching Team

For a large class to work well, we have found that we must rely on the efforts of a staff. At some universities, generous staffing of large lectures with six or seven graduate teaching assistants is possible. That is not the case at our university, where the most that instructors can hope for is one 20-hour-per-week and one ten-hour-per-week graduate teaching assistant to attend to the needs of 500 students. Although lacking in financial resources, we are blessed with ingenuity. In the 1970s, the Department of Psychology established an undergraduate teaching assistant program, in which students can earn three pass/fail practicum credits for contributing ten hours per week assisting a professor with teaching responsibilities. (In departments where this kind of formal opportunity is not available, a similar structure can be established in which work-study students or volunteers function in similar ways.)

Undergraduate Teaching Assistants

For a class of 300 or more students, we rely on the efforts of approximately 20 undergraduate teaching assistants, upper-level psychology majors who have completed the course with a superior grade. The screening process for this position consistently yields a group of aspiring professionals whose contributions are invaluable. Every student in the class is connected to the instructor through one of these teaching assistants.

We regard teaching assistants as members of the staff who are expected to act and dress professionally. We repeatedly emphasize the importance of confidentiality, and we maintain procedures in which only the instructor and graduate teaching assistant have access to student records.

The involvement of undergraduates in the grading process is a sensitive issue. On the syllabus we make it clear that ultimate grading responsibility rests with the instructor who relies on recommendations from the graduate teaching assistant. In turn, the graduate teaching assistant relies on data provided by the undergraduate teaching assistants (e.g., discussion, group attendance, and participation).

Although we give students the option not to have undergraduate teaching assistants in any way involved in their evaluations, few choose this option.

Graduate Teaching Assistants

Critical to the success of managing a large class is the graduate teaching assistant. Those graduate students who apply for this teaching assistantship know that the position is time-consuming, intense, and laden with responsibility. Usually these individuals are interested in an apprenticeship in which they will be centrally involved in teaching. We define the role of the graduate teaching assistant as course manager, with authority to oversee the administration of the course. As course manager, the graduate teaching assistant coordinates the staff of undergraduate teaching assistants and is the person whom students are instructed to contact with all administrative concerns, conflicts, or questions.

Because the class is so large, there are countless contacts between teaching assistants and individual students. Each staff member keeps a log book to document every substantive contact with a student, thereby maintaining a history that is often valuable in resolving misunderstandings about matters such as deadline extensions or assignment modifications.

Communications

When working with a large staff of assistants, good communication is essential. Our work together as a group begins at the start of the semester with a half-day workshop during which we review all course procedures and the responsibilities and duties of each person. During the semester we have a weekly staff meeting during which we continue this discussion. In addition to addressing pragmatic issues, we use the staff meeting for didactic purposes by discussing issues that warrant consideration by those in teaching roles. For example, we address concerns about discrimination, harassment, the potential misuse of power, and other matters that emerge in diverse groups. These meetings serve an important educative role, and also imbue a sense of active participation and responsibility in the teaching enterprise. Many undergraduate teaching assistants state that these meetings provide invaluable contexts in which they derive support, obtain supervision, and discuss their experiences in this challenging role.

Maximizing the Learning Experience

When managing large groups of people, some instructors may find it easier to take a do-it-my-way attitude. While such an approach simplifies the task of administration, it may not address the individualized needs of students. We have tried to develop and implement a service philosophy similar to that used by successful business professionals who solicit and analyze constructive feedback. We distribute course evaluations at the midpoint and end of the semester, carefully scrutinize every comment, and make administrative revisions that we consider pedagogically sound. By studying the feedback of students to determine what helps them learn, we have structured the course in such a way that each student has choices in terms of testing, project options, and special assistance.

Evaluation and Mastery of the Material

For most students the prospect of testing is an anxiety-provoking part of their educational experience. We try to diminish the negativity associated with the testing experience and strive to find ways to help students enjoy learning the material. We use a tutorial assistance system in which study help is provided by undergraduate teaching assistants to any students requesting special attention.

We also actively reach out to all students who self-designate as learning disabled or physically challenged. A teaching assistant is assigned as a liaison for each of these students to provide special assistance if the student is interested. For example, a visually impaired student benefited from having the items in the student study guide read aloud. A learning disabled student developed a greater sense of mastery and self-esteem through interactive study sessions with a tutor. For special needs students, a teaching assistant can take class notes and meet after class to review the material. Teaching assistants also conduct study sessions that are small and flexibly scheduled.

When it comes to testing, we explain to our students that testing and grading are motivational tools rather than ends in themselves, and we offer students options designed to maximize their learning of the material. Although the multiple choice examination is the standard testing format, students may request an essay exam instead. Only a handful of students make this choice, yet most appreciate having the option.

Testing Options

In addition to examinations, students must be involved in a project for the class, which they select from three options: 1) term paper, 2) a weekly discussion group, or 3) a class presentation. For the term paper, we lay out a structured assignment that is specific to this course. Within the assignment, students have considerable flexibility to explore topics of interest. Each student who chooses to write a term paper must meet at least two times with a teaching assistant to present an outline and a rough draft. For those needing special attention, the teaching assistant may arrange additional sessions to work on writing skills or use of library resources.

Each student who chooses to participate in a discussion group makes a 12-week commitment and takes responsibility for facilitating the discussion in one of the meetings. Working with the undergraduate teaching assistant, every student develops a brief presentation designed to engender an interesting and valuable discussion. Approximately 80% of the students in the class choose this option and rate this experience very highly. They speak about the cohesion that develops among the group as they tackle difficult and complex discussion topics each week.

The third option affords students the opportunity of presenting their experiences or ideas to the entire class. In a class of 300, approximately 15 students are usually willing to do this. Several students have personal experiences pertinent to the content of the course and are interested in speaking to their classmates. For example, in abnormal psychology we cover various disorders for which some students in the class have been successfully treated (e.g., substance abuse, panic disorder, eating disorder, etc.). Some are willing to be a resource to others by sharing their experiences in a presentation that explains the disorder, as well as the current scientific understanding regarding etiology and treatment of the condition. For this option, students must present a well-articulated proposal and be interviewed to ensure that the choice of doing a presentation is judicious for the student and of potential value to the class. Each accepted presenter is assigned to an undergraduate teaching assistant who meets regularly with the presenter to prepare an outline, to develop the presentation, and to rehearse in front of a small group for final feedback and refinement. Over the course of several years, these presentations have typically been rated by students in the class as the most effective of all the pedagogical components of the course.

Maintaining Excitement and Flow

We strive to keep the course lively and we are constantly on the lookout for techniques with which we can energize lectures. As part of this effort, we assess the effectiveness of each lecture by soliciting feedback from teaching assistants following class and making appropriate modifications for subsequent lectures during the current or subsequent semester.

We find that it is important to establish a climate in the auditorium that is conducive to learning. By arriving a half-hour early, we have time to assemble lecture materials, settle in a bit before the crowd arrives, and make ourselves available to speak with students. We project an outline for the day's lecture on the screen to help students organize their note taking. The audiovisual assistant sets up the microphone, arranges the videotapes that will be shown, and places reserved seating signs in the first row to save seats for students who need close-up seating.

Students know that the class will begin and end on time. We strive to minimize tardiness by making the initial moments of class especially interesting and compelling. To deal with the problem of students departing before the end of class, we position a teaching assistant at each door to ask anyone departing the room if he or she is ill or needs some kind of assistance. With this procedure we are able to help those who need it and reduce the distractions of unnecessary exits during the lecture.

Capturing and retaining the attention of students involves finding an effective style of speaking to them, as opposed to lecturing at them. Using examples that are salient to the listeners and tapping information that we know about our students strengthens the connection. The pronouns *you* and *I* recur in every lecture, as we ask students to conjure up pertinent images and as we share with them personal experiences, views, and dilemmas.

In preparing each lecture, we ask ourselves several questions. How do we want to be heard by students? What do we want them to remember from the lecture—tomorrow, next week, or ten years from now? How important are the facts we want to convey, and to what extent might the readings or the textbook do the job more efficiently?

In tackling these questions, we remind ourselves that we need not feel responsible for conveying all that there is to know about a topic. In lecture we have the opportunity to give students what the written word cannot. We can bring life to the issues they are studying by engaging them in ways that leave a mark after the lecture is finished.

For each lecture we rely on a rule of thumb that there should be some kind of energy shift about every 20 minutes. In other words, within a 75-minute lecture, we try to refocus the attention of the students approximately three times. Sometimes we invite comments or questions, possibly encouraging the sharing of divergent points of view on a topic under consideration. In other instances, a guest speaker or fellow student addresses the class. Or we might project a brief video. As for video selections, we may show a segment from the evening news, an educational television program, or a TV news magazine such as 20/20 (which can be purchased quite inexpensively from television networks).

Conclusion

We regularly assess our techniques and strategies and have been gratified by the quantitative and qualitative evaluations of our students. Many students comment that the personalized approach of the teaching staff causes them to become oblivious to the large enrollment in the course. In fact, in a review of quantitative student evaluations of the dozens of courses offered in the department, this course received higher ratings than any small class or seminar, lending further support to the notion that the large lecture class can be evaluated by students just as positively as the more intimate learning context.

The efforts that we describe in this article take a great amount of time, energy, and patience. Laborious planning is important, and attention to details is essential, but the emotional pay-off for all involved is tremendous. We hope that the discussion of the philosophy, techniques, and procedures in this chapter will inspire others to share the methods they use to enhance the experience of students in large classes.

References

Aronson, J. R. (1987). Six keys to effective instruction in large classes: Advice from a practitioner. In M. G. Weimer (Ed.), *Teaching large classes well.* New Directions for Teaching and Learning, No. 32. San Francisco, CA: Jossey-Bass.

Benjamin, L. T., Jr. (1991). Personalization and active learning in the large introductory psychology class. *Teaching of Psychology, 18,* 68-74.

Brooks, R. P. (1987). Dealing with details in a large class. In M. G. Weimer (Ed.), *Teaching large classes well.* New Directions for Teaching and Learning, No. 32. San Francisco, CA: Jossey-Bass.

Gleason, M. (1990). An instructor survival kit: For use with large classes. In E. Neff & M. Weimer (Eds.), *Teaching college: Collected readings for the new instructor.* Madison, WI: Magna.

Jenkins, J. J. (1991). Teaching psychology in large classes: Research and personal experience. *Teaching of Psychology, 18,* 74-80.

Knapper, C. (1987). Large classes and learning. In M. G. Weimer (Ed.), *Teaching large classes well.* New Directions for Teaching and Learning, No. 32. San Francisco, CA: Jossey-Bass.

McKeachie, W. J. (1994). *Teaching tips: Strategies, research, and theory for college and university teachers.* (10th ed.). Lexington, MA: Heath.

Overtree, C. E., & Halgin, R. P. (1997). *Procedures and teaching manual for abnormal psychology.* Unpublished manuscript. Amherst, MA: University of Massachusetts, Amherst.

Example 16 ─────────────────

Teaching Social Science to a Small Society

Linda B. Nilson
Clemson University

The Challenge

Large classes aren't just large; they have some of the more insidious characteristics that early social scientists identified in a political mass: apathy, alienation, indifference, and ignorance (Mills, 1956); and a crowd: suggestibility, anonymity, spontaneity, and invulnerability (Le Bon, 1960). Most of our students in large classes are there to fulfill one curricular requirement or another. They come in with low motivation, low interest in the material, and little personal or educational investment. Collectively, the class is extremely heterogeneous in learning styles, attitudes and values, academic and intellectual ability, and levels of readiness to learn, varying from ill-prepared freshmen to cynical seniors. For the instructors, the sheer numbers present daunting grading duties.

Our disciplines add difficulties to the mix. Many students think that the social sciences lack legitimacy, that their knowledge bases constitute no more than common sense and/or relativistic opinion. They don't seem very practical either, as they do not open any well-paying, structured career paths. To make matters worse, some of our material is highly controversial and politically charged. Neither adult nor traditional students of socially or politically conservative leanings receive it graciously and unquestioningly. In addition, our courses often dictate student learning objectives that go beyond the cognitive. To be meaningful and life-changing, they call for high-order cognitive, affective, social, and ethical objectives as well. If this is the case, traditional large-class lecturing, no matter how eye-catching our PowerPoint slides, simply won't do the job.

The Strategies

When we have to teach a large class, we social scientists have an advantage over our colleagues in other disciplines: We have a sense of social engineering. We may even fantasize about how we'd set up a government, an economy, a culture, or a whole society to bring out the best in people. I think it is helpful to take a social engineering approach when planning a course for a multitude.

Social Engineering

Stripped to the basics, social engineering is simply 1) deciding which attitudes, cognitive abilities, and behaviors we want to bring out in people; and 2) setting up a system of incentives, rewards, and sanctions that encourage what we want to bring out and discourage the attitudes, cognitive processes, and behaviors we don't, especially those that mitigate against the desired ones.

We already have a pretty good idea of what most people want and don't want in life, so we can deduce many incentives, rewards, and sanctions. Students specifically desire extrinsic positives like good grades, additions to their resumes, and career opportunities, and intrinsic ones such as the following: a sense of achievement, the respect and recognition of peers and authority figures who matter to them, positive social interaction, interesting and fun experiences, and new knowledge and skills that they see as useful in improving their lives. By contrast, they strive to avoid negatives like summative criticism and failure, shame, guilt, social rejection, meaningless effort, and boredom.

Returning to people in general, most also try to avoid change, uncertainty, and risky, novel experiences, but learning can't take place without them. So we don't aim to set up a utopia—just an orderly, efficient, productive classroom society with minimal waste and redundancy.

To Meet Student Learning Objectives beyond Factual Memorization and Comprehension

Just because a class is large is not a reason to abandon lofty student learning objectives. We just have to ensure that our students are doing more than reading books and listening to us. It's true that lecture serves us well when we need to distill, structure, summarize, or evaluate material and can't find a printed source that does it as well. It is also an effective way to convey our passion for the subject, thereby motivating and inspiring our students. Lectures can be an especially powerful motivational tool for those who have a dynamic, penetrating platform persona. But lectures are not as successful as other teaching methods when our student learning objectives include the following (McKeachie et al., 1990; McKeachie et al., 1994; Bonwell & Eison, 1991):

- Higher-order cognitive abilities: application of knowledge to new situations, problem solving, research skills, analysis, synthesis, and evaluation

- Affective change: examining and possibly changing attitudes; exploring controversial or ambiguous material with an open mind; tolerating uncertainty and ambiguity; acquiring empathy, compassion, and a sense of humanity

- Social abilities: working cooperatively in a group, developing leadership skills, communicating and interacting with diverse people, participating in civil discourse and debate

- Ethical change: incorporating the interests of parties beyond the self in decision-making, evaluating the trade-offs of various courses of action, increasing tolerance and reducing prejudice

For these student outcomes, there is no substitute for the following types of experience: conducting research; applying knowledge to problems; practicing new ways of thinking and systematic cognitive operations; collaborating on a project with others; seeing one's world view fail in light of new evidence (Nelson, 1991); and the experience of feeling how someone in very different circumstances feels, either through social interaction or simulation exercises. Besides, most people don't retain much of what they read, hear, or even see. All they remember for long is their life experience. So our task as instructors is to make our courses a series of significant life experiences for our students.

Here are some methods that do the job. They appeal to many learning styles, including the predominant ones in today's college classrooms. But they only work if 1) they flow naturally out of our student learning objectives, 2) they are integrated into our course readings and other assignments, and 3) we have our students reflect on and communicate their impact. McKeachie et al. (1994) and I (Nilson, 1998) offer guidance on implementing and managing these methods.

Experiential learning. This is the more general term for out-of-the-classroom learning experiences, which include field work (e.g., collecting and/or analyzing real-world data), service learning (working with community agencies), internships, and cooperative education. These link theory and practice as no other teaching formats do. For purposes of large classes, we will focus on the first two.

Field work develops students' research and analytical skills, of course, and often their tolerance for uncertainty and ambiguity. We can have our students collect and analyze data by conducting surveys, analyzing content messages on various media, observing cultural norms, examining government documents, or investigating local archeological remains. Or we can focus on quantitative analysis by giving them web access to large data sets (e.g., national elections, census, opinion polls, criminal justice, substance abuse, mental health, aging, education, etc.) through the Social Science Research and Instructional Council / Teaching Resources Depository of the California State University System (www.csubak.edu/ssric). Typically, students write up and/or orally present their findings, and may even publish them.

Service learning is famous for developing students' application and problem-solving skills and in promoting affective and ethical maturity (Eyler & Giles, 1999; Stanton, Giles, & Cruz, 1999; Zlotkowski, 1998). It works by bringing students into unfamiliar, real life situations that make them question their preconceptions, and it has a much stronger impact than anything we can say in class or assign as reading. Lest it be just a volunteer experience, students must be required to reflect and write on their experiences, first integrating them with the course concepts and theories, then analyzing how they have changed students' assumptions about people, organizations, society, politics, culture, etc. Internships and cooperative education also calls for reflective writing.

Service learning in particular can present management problems in a large class, even if students work in teams. Public agencies are not generally prepared to absorb so much help at once, so we have to pave good relations with several agencies in advance. If your campus has a campus service learning or volunteer work center, you may able to send your students there for suitable assignments. Another challenge is the reflective essays. We must lay out very precise, rigorous expectations to avoid getting meaningless personal ramblings, and we face a great deal of grading since each student must write his or her own essay.

One challenge can be avoided, however. Service learning need not involve students' working for or in a public agency. Clemson University psychology professor Patricia Connor-Greene (2000a) has her abnormal psychology students serving the community at large, and she integrates service learning with problem-based learning (discussed below). Her students work in teams to collect in-depth information about a specific psychological disorder and its treatment and to assess the availability and appropriateness of local treatment options. They conduct their research as if one of their own family members had the disorder. Each team's written report appears on the web and in flyer form for actual community use.

Experiential learning activities usually merit an entry on a student's resume, so we should announce this added reward to our classes.

Simulations. These are simplified enactments of social situations that model key aspects of reality. Some are available in whole or part on disk or CD-ROM. Some of the human ones can be played in part outside of class. While most are specific to a discipline or specialty (urban planning, formal organizations, international relations, economic markets, cultural conflict, specific historical events, aspects of business and management), a few apply across the social sciences—classics like SIMSOC, Star Power, Prisoner's Dilemma, and Bafa Bafa. Several also are adjustable to different topics. Karraker (1993) developed a mock trial simulation with a range of cases on which to base it: industrial safety, religious practices, community development, affirmative action, individual rights, securities markets, environmental protection, and more. You will find hundreds of simulation options in the applicable journals and Internet resources at the end of this chapter. They may even inspire you to devise your own.

Gibler (2000), a political science professor at the University of Kentucky, has developed his own simulations and runs them in his large classes. In one he calls *Realism,* he divides his students into states, where large groups represent democracies and small groups dictatorships, and allocates power points according to different actions the groups may take (forming alliances, getting into arms races, etc.). He has also created an arms race game (using paper airplanes) that eventually reveals the wisdom of strategic arms reduction.

Running simulations in large classes is not easy, but students become very involved. With a sufficient debriefing opportunity (such as a class discussion), they usually undergo attitudinal and ethical change (Dekkers & Donatti, 1981). But to reap the cognitive outcomes as well as the complete attitudinal and ethical benefits, we should have our students write the same kind of reflective essay that we'd require after a service learning experience.

Case method. Presented with a problematic, real-world or realistic situation, students apply course material to analyze the issues and formulate workable solutions and/or prevention strategies. A case may be a few sentences or many pages long, already published or created by the instructor, and presented in print or dramatized on videotape or interactive CD-ROM. It may be a one-time story or a series of unfolding segments. It may even be sequential interactive if the instructor gives students additional information as they request it to narrow down their decisions and solutions (Nilson, 1998). What is essential is that a case contain uncertainty and risk, offer more than one justifiable approach or solution, and require students to synthesize their accumulated knowledge of the subject matter.

Cases engage students in otherwise boring material. I found that students zoned out when I brought up the topic of poverty, starting with the statistics and structural causes. But when I presented realistic cases of local families and individuals who were thrown into poverty after the loss of a job, a divorce, health problems, or the birth of a mentally or physically challenged child, the students perked up. Because they could relate to the protagonists, they opened their minds to the realities of poverty and discovered some of the structural causes on their own in the course of the debriefing.

The case method fosters all the higher-level cognitive skills (application, analysis, synthesis, and evaluation) and, with the right case, can induce attitudinal and ethical change (Fitch & Kirby, 2000). Cases make challenging small-group activities, homework assignments, paper topics, and test questions (both essay and multiple-choice). They also serve well as springboards for discussion and review.

Problem-based learning (PBL) A PBL problem is much like a case for which students must conduct outside research (records, legal, survey, library, observational, etc.) to formulate and justify a good solution. The course material alone does not supply the answers. So one of the first tasks students face is identifying the relevant knowledge and data they do have and the additional knowledge and data they need to acquire. Typically students work on one complex problem in small groups over a period of weeks. Their product may be a report, a poster, a multimedia presentation, a web page, a budget, a proposal, a plan of action—whatever suits the problem. If it has community use or impact, as in Connor-Greene's (2000a) abnormal psychology classes, the project also constitutes service learning.

PBL promotes the same favorable student outcomes as the case method with the added benefit of teaching research skills and encouraging students to assume responsibility for their own learning (Edens, 2000). Sometimes PBL projects are worth a line on students' resumes.

Cooperative learning. All the methods above can and usually should be implemented using cooperative learning. I say *should* because we know from the research that it increases higher-order learning, generates higher-quality student products, develops students' social skills, and reduces the number of major assignments to grade by a factor of three, four, or five, depending on the size of your groups (Millis & Cottrell, 1998; Nilson, 1998). In large classes in particular, cooperative learning reduces the anonymity, impersonality, and negative aspects of heterogeneity. It is important to follow certain guidelines for distributing students into long-term groups, building in positive interdependence and individual accountability, structuring the assignments, keeping groups on task, ensuring equitable divisions of labor, etc., and these are readily available in sources such as Michaelson, Fink, and Black (1996), and/or Michaelson (1992), Millis and Cottrell (1998), and Nilson (1998).

Large classes demand adjusting a few of these guidelines. When we ask students to form ad hoc groups—that is, to work with those sitting near them—we can't possibly hear every group's decision or solution. So we need to move around the room and just take a random sample. Then we can ask if there are any different responses. When we get a range, we can take a poll and solicit justifications for the varying answers. Such ad hoc group activities double as classroom assessment techniques.

When we assign major projects to long-term groups, it's best if we allow some class time for members to meet face-to-face. Students often have trouble coordinating busy schedules to meet outside of class, so we should try to facilitate online communication options. In addition to ensuring that all team members have each other's email addresses, we can set up team listservs, chat rooms, or bulletin boards on our course web site, assuming our campus IT system allows it. We can also acquaint students with Microsoft Word's Track Changes feature (under Tools), which allows us to ensure that group papers are collaboratively written. We can monitor students' editorial comments and suggested changes on one another's work (Connor-Greene, 2000b).

Interactive lecturing. Bonwell and Eison (1991) cite several studies showing that students learn much more from a lecture and take better notes when an instructor delivers it in 10-20-minute chunks interspersed with brief activities in which the students review or use the material just presented. Here are some possible student-active breaks that students can do individually, in pairs, or in ad hoc small groups (Nilson, 1998) :

• Summarize, rebut, or react to the material

• Review and fill in lecture notes

• Answer a multiple-choice question

• Solve a problem or quick case study

• Outline an answer to an essay or discussion question

We should follow the guidelines for ad hoc group assignments that were previously discussed in the cooperative learning section. These activities not only enhance learning but also give us invaluable classroom assessment information.

Old-fashioned discussion is still an option in large classes for those of us who don't mind acting the role of a talk-show host. Playing this role requires a cordless microphone (or two or three of them) and the energy to walk quickly up and down the aisles (or TAs to do it for us). Kain (1986) uses this technique when he brings up current events that illustrate the relevance of sociological principles, data, or methods. He invites students to voice their opinions on the events and ties their answers back to sociology. A good discussion question need not ask for opinions, but it should have more than one respectable answer and be followed up by a request to justify your response. Kain also recommends taking class surveys of attitudes, behavior, or demographics, an activity that lends itself to the social sciences.

To Develop a Close Rapport with Our Students

There are downright practical reasons for fostering a close rapport with our students in large classes—for example, our own student evaluations of our teaching. The fact that most of our students are taking our course to satisfy a requirement will tend to depress their evaluations (Cashin, 1988; Centra, 1979). Developing a good rapport with them (being seen by students as friendly, caring, approachable, helpful, and open-minded) positively affects evaluations (Murray, 1985) and may help compensate for the requirement effect. In a large class, students sometimes give us extra credit for going that extra mile for them. While there is no research to back up this statement, it makes sense that the better our rapport with students, the greater their personal loyalty to us and the higher their motivation to learn, to do the coursework, and to behave considerately in class.

First, we can learn the students' names, at least their first names, so we can address each of them as a human being. Our effort to do so will dissolve much of their sense of anonymity, which probably will in turn reduce disruptive classroom behavior. We should learn as many of their names as we can and not worry that our memory will fail us on occasion—students appreciate our attempt. I personally know faculty who master 200 to 250 names in one class each semester. The Teaching and Learning Center at the University of Nebraska, Lincoln lists about two dozen name-learning techniques on its web site (www.unl.edu/teaching/Names.html). These include name tents and tags, a seating chart, and student-prepared passports. Obtaining or taking a photograph of each student is also helpful.

Second, we should require that our students come to talk with us for ten to 15 minutes during our office hours, if not individually then in small groups (perhaps the cooperative learning groups we set up). Either way, we will go far in learning their names this way. We can send around an appointment sheet in class to sign them up.

Finally, we can reinforce our face-to-face interaction with our students by communicating personally with each one of them by email at least once. If we use cooperative learning, we should communicate at least once with each team as well.

To Get Our Students to Keep Up with the Readings

This is a real challenge for us because most of today's undergraduates will not do readings, certainly not by the day they are due, unless we hold them accountable. This unfortunate fact holds especially true in large courses on non-cumulative subjects, such as most social science courses. In fact, we will actually discourage students from doing the readings if we re-lecture them in class. (Why should students bother to read the material if we're going to give it to them in simpler form the next day, then post our notes on the web?) To hold students accountable for the readings, we have to set up incentives, rewards, and sanctions.

Small-group activities. Regular, daily small-group activities that require having done the readings will motivate some students to prepare for class out of a sense of social pressure and personal pride. But this incentive is not nearly as reliable and powerful as one's individual grade. If we rely heavily on small-group work, then we should set up long-term groups in which members evaluate and grade each other on their contributions, social skills, preparation, etc. These peer performance evaluations should count at least 10% of the final course grade.

Quizzes. Our simplest incentive is frequent (daily or weekly) in-class individual quizzes or exercises that demand a decent mastery of the readings. Immediately after collecting the quiz or exercise, we can have students retake it in their small groups to enrich its learning value (Michaelson, 1992; Michaelson, Fink, & Black, 1996). Or we can simply review the test or exercise, getting all the answers from the students. We shouldn't be the ones to say whether an answer is right or wrong. We can generate discussion by allowing the students to evaluate, support, debate, and even vote on different answers.

Class size is no barrier to frequent quizzes. We can dictate the questions or problems or display them on slides or overhead transparencies. We can make all the questions closed-ended and use an optical scanning machine to grade them. We can tell our students to copy down their answers before turning them in so we won't have to hand anything back. We can test at a high cognitive level with a few well-constructed multiple-choice items that require conceptual understanding, application, analysis, synthesis, and/or evaluation. We can base the items on a brief case, data set, problem, table, chart, or diagram. We can even use some of the same items on a later test.

Writing assignments. Another option is to require our students to hand in a brief writing assignment on the readings at the beginning of class. It may be a summary of the readings, an answer to a question or two on the readings, a reflection/reaction piece, or two-to-four quality questions on the reading, possibly for us to use later on a test. (This last option requires our teaching levels/types of questions.) These exercises can be graded quickly on a plus-check-minus scale. Coggeshall (2000), a Clemson University anthropologist, says it takes him an hour or less to grade 75 short essays on the readings on a six-point scale.

The more frequent and less predictably scheduled our quizzes or exercises, the higher our attendance will be and the fewer other tests we'll have to give. Grading on attendance, if we choose to do so, will also be easy. In addition, our students will appreciate the many grading and feedback opportunities that frequent quizzes and exercises afford.

To Manage Controversial Topics

Can we avoid controversy in a social science, what with deep social cleavages over affirmative action, speech codes, evolution, abortion, gay rights, race relations, welfare, sexual morality, political candidates, and so many other topics we visit? Disagreement can't be suppressed; all views must be aired before any can change. What is important is that students learn to examine, justify, and civilly discuss their positions.

At the first meeting, it's wise to warn the class about the specific controversial subjects that the course will cover, then explain the rules of civil discourse. If we and our students develop a classroom-behavior contract, we should ensure these rules are included. If an exchange gets out of hand, we can calmly refer back to these rules.

Controversy management can be built into our course design and teaching methods. In the cooperative learning format, structured (or academic) controversy, students are randomly assigned to groups of four, and pairs take turns arguing one side of an issue, then the other, as persuasively and accurately as they can. (Groups are long-term if students conduct outside research.) Then the group examines all the evidence to synthesize a single, best possible position on which members all can agree. Finally, each group presents its position and the evidence for it, orally or in writing. No matter how broad and ambitious our student learning objectives, this method fosters them all: higher-order cognitive abilities, attitudinal change, social skills, and ethical change (Johnson & Johnson, 1995; Johnson, Johnson, & Smith, 1996.) Structured controversy should be no more difficult to manage in a large class than any other student-active method coupled with cooperative learning (e.g., PBL). If each group deals with a different controversy that we want the whole class to understand thoroughly, but we don't have the class time for so many student presentations, we can have some or all the groups put their research and positions on the web. Then we can make these required reading for the final exam.

Of course, controversy can erupt spontaneously as well, in which case we may have a teachable moment. Rule one is to stay calm and even-handed. We can and should press the students to state their justifications, evidence, and underlying assumptions, but we must press both sides equally. We should avoid taking sides; our opponents may haunt us in student evaluations. We can dissipate tension by broadening participation in the debate. For instance, we can ask for reactions to a student's comments, solicit other views on the issue, and pose critical thinking questions to the class, such as, "What do you think is the most basic assumption that determines which side people take?" We don't have to reach resolution before moving on.

A Final Word on Managing Our Time

Grading still looms as the major challenge, but there are shortcuts. A large class calls for grade management software (e.g., MicroGrade, EasyGradePro, Blackboard's CourseInfo, WebCT, or Mallard, or we can turn an Excel spreadsheet into a gradebook), especially if we give daily or weekly quizzes. In the social sciences, we'll have to grade essays, group projects, or the like, for which Gibler (2000) recommends developing a grading rubric form. He marks the dimensions on which a work falls short (e.g., grammar, punctuation, spelling, organization, lack of supporting evidence, logical inconsistency, etc.), then writes one brief paragraph on the most egregious errors and the most praiseworthy strengths. We can use a similar form to assign points or grades on each dimension. If we have TAs, such a form helps ensure uniform grading standards.

Teaching a large social science course is not easy under any circumstances, and teaching it effectively with student-active methods takes time. Still, we should think of the time we'll save not preparing lectures that rehash the readings, not telling students what they missed last class, and not getting sidetracked by classroom disruptions. Besides, we'll have better prepared, more motivated students.

References

Bonwell, C. C., & Eison, J. A. (1991). *Active learning: Creating excitement in the classroom*. ASHE-ERIC Higher Education Report No. 1. Washington, DC: George Washington University, School of Education and Human Development.

Cashin, W. E. (1988). Student ratings of teaching: A summary of the research. *IDEA Paper* No. 20. Manhattan, KS: Center for Faculty Evaluation and Development, Kansas State University.

Centra, J. A. (1979). *Determining faculty effectiveness*. San Francisco, CA: Jossey-Bass.

Coggeshall, M. (2000, 3 May). Writing for discussion in introductory anthropology classes. Lecture presented at the Communication across the Curriculum Symposium. Clemson, SC: Clemson University.

Connor-Greene, P. (2000a). Using problem-based service learning in an abnormal psychology class. In S. Madden (Ed.), *Service learning across the curriculum.* Lanham, MD: University Press of America.

Connor-Greene, P. (2000b, 3 March). Using CLE team space to facilitate group projects. Workshop sponsored by the Office of Teaching Effectiveness and Innovation. Clemson, SC: Clemson University.

Dekkers, J., & Donatti, S. (1981, July/August). The integration of research studies on the use of simulation as an instructional strategy. *Journal of Educational Research, 74* (6), 424-427.

Edens, K. M. (2000, Spring). Preparing problem-solvers for the 21st century through problem-based learning. *College Teaching, 48* (2), 55-60.

Eyler, J., & Giles, D. E., Jr. (1999). *Where's the learning in service learning?* San Francisco, CA: Jossey-Bass.

Fitch, B., & Kirby, A. (2000, Spring). Students' assumptions and professors' presumptions: Creating a learning community for the whole student. *College Teaching, 48* (2), 47-54.

Gibler, D. M. (2000, 9 May). Personal correspondence.

Johnson, D. W., & Johnson, R. T. (1995). *Creative conflict: Intellectual challenges in the classroom.* Edina, MN: Interaction Book Company.

Johnson, D. W., Johnson, R. T., & Smith, K. A. (1996). *Academic controversy: Enriching college instruction through intellectual conflict.* Washington, DC: George Washington University, Graduate School of Education and Human Development. (ASHE-ERIC Higher Education Report Vol. 25, No. 3)

Kain, E. (1986). The mass class as theatre: Suggestions for improving the chances of a hit production. In R. McGee (Ed.), *Teaching the mass class.* Washington, DC: ASA Teaching Resources Center, American Sociological Association.

Karraker, M. W. (1993). Mock trials and critical thinking. *College Teaching, 41* (4), 134-137.

Le Bon, G. (1960). *The mind of the crowd.* New York, NY: Viking.

McKeachie, W. J., Pintrich, P. R., Lin, Y. G., Smith, D. A. F., & Sharma, R. (1990). *Teaching and learning in the college classroom: A review of the research literature* (2nd ed.). Ann Arbor, MI: NCRIPTAL, University of Michigan.

McKeachie, W. J., Chism, N., Menges, R., Svinicki, M., & Weinstein, C. E. (1994). *Teaching tips: Strategies, research, and theory for college and university teachers* (9th ed.). Lexington, MA: D. C. Heath.

Michaelsen, L. K. (1992). Team learning: A comprehensive approach for harnessing the power of small groups in higher education. In D. L. Wulff & J. D. Nyquist (Eds.), *To improve the academy: Vol. 11. Resources for faculty, instructional, and organizational development.* Stillwater, OK: New Forums Press.

Michaelsen, L. K., Fink, L. D., & Black, R. H. (1996). What every faculty developer needs to know about learning groups. In L. Richlin (Ed.), *To improve the academy: Vol. 15. Resources for faculty, instructional, and organizational development.* Stillwater, OK: New Forums Press.

Millis, B. J. & Cottrell, P. G., Jr. (1998). *Cooperative learning for higher education faculty.* Phoenix, AZ: Oryx.

Mills, C. W. (1956). *The power elite.* New York, NY: Oxford University Press.

Murray, H. G. (1985). Classroom teaching behaviors related to college teaching effectiveness. In J. G. McDonald & A. M. Sullivan (Eds.), *Using research to improve teaching.* New Directions in Teaching and Learning No. 23. San Francisco, CA: Jossey-Bass.

Nelson, C. (1991, 6 February). Fostering critical thinking. Lecture presented in the Chancellor's Lecture Series. Nashville, TN: Vanderbilt University.

Nilson, L. B. (1998). *Teaching at its best: A research-based resource for college instructors.* Bolton, MA: Anker.

Stanton, T. K., Giles, D. E., Jr., & Cruz, N. I. (1999). *Service-learning: A movement's pioneers reflect on its origins, practice, and future.* San Francisco, CA: Jossey-Bass.

Zlotkowski, E. (Ed.). (1998). *Successful service-learning programs: New models of excellence in higher education.* Bolton, MA: Anker.

Additional Resources

Books

Goldsmid, C. A., & Wilson, E. K. (1985). *Passing on sociology: The teaching of a discipline.* Washington, DC: American Sociological Association Teaching Resources Center.

Madden, S. (Ed.). (2000). *Service learning across the curriculum.* Lanham, MD: University Press of America.

McGee, R. (Ed.). (1986). *Teaching the mass class.* Washington, DC: American Sociological Association Teaching Resources Center.

VanGundy, A. (Ed.). (1998). *101 great games and activities.* San Francisco, CA: Jossey-Bass.

Journals

American Psychologist
Anthropology and Education
ASHE-ERIC Higher Education Report Series
Behavioral Science Teacher
College Teaching
Communication Education
Developments in Business Simulation and Experiential Learning (proceedings of the Meetings of the Association for Business Simulation and Experiential Learning)
Educational Psychologist
Exchange: The Organizational Behavior Teaching Journal
Feminist Teacher
Journal of Economics Education
Journal of Education for Business
Journal of Educational Psychology
Journal of Educational Research
Journal of Experiential Learning and Simulation
Journal of Experimental Education
Journal of General Education
Journal of Higher Education
Journal of Management Education
Journal of Marketing Education
Journal of Moral Education
Journal of Planning Education and Research
Journal of Teaching in International Business
Organizational Behavior Teaching Review
Political Science Teacher
PS: Political Science and Politics
Religious Education
Research in Higher Education
Sociology of Education
Teaching College
Teaching Excellence
Teaching History: A Journal of Methods
Teaching of Psychology
Simages (contains reviews)
Simulations and Games: An International Journal of Theory, Design, and Research
Simulations/Games for Learning: The Journal of the Society for Academic Gaming and Simulation in Education and Training (contains reviews)
Simgames: The Canadian Journal of Simulation and Gaming
Teaching Sociology

Internet Resources

Simulations and games
www.geneva.edu/centersandoutreach/ecc/bussim.html
www.microbuspub.com
simulations@worldnet.att.net

Teaching large classes
www.id,ucsb.edu/IC/indexFrames.html
www.psu.edu/celt/largeclass/lcfaqs.html
wolf.its.ilstu.edu/CAT/online/tips/largec.html
www.inform.umd.edu/CTE/lcn/index.html
ase.tufts.edu/cte (with numerous links)

Example 17 _____

Transforming the Horde

Robin Nagle
New York University

Remembering

No matter how many times I teach a large class, the first session is a shock. There might be 80 or 100 or 120 students registered, but it inevitably feels like there are many more in the room than on the roster. As they settle into their seats, they resemble a quiet horde, some casting director's idea of what urban undergraduates might look like when clumped together. I feel a little overwhelmed. How, I wonder, will I reach even half of them? How will I transform the horde into a collection of individuals? Most importantly, how can their education be personal and relevant, when they are so many and I am only one?

To ease my anxiety, I recall two things. First, I remember that teaching can only be a one-to-one experience. If each student believes I am talking to her as an individual, she will be more likely to pay attention to what I am saying. In other words, if I find a way to my students, then perhaps they will find a way to the subject. Second, I draw on my discipline—anthropology—to remind myself that the class is no horde but merely a group drawn together for a specific social function, grounded in larger cultural expectations, patterns, and quirks. Anthropology is not unique in its usefulness here. A scholar of English or comparative literature can surely imagine the rich collection of drama and narrative represented by his students' stories, and as the semester unfolds can even see variations on the themes of classic texts echoed in their lives. To make the subject relevant to students' lives, we as professors must make clear those echoes and resonances.

It is the dual challenge of touching students as individual thinkers and bringing them a few steps closer to the discipline I love, while using that discipline to meet these goals, that makes teaching large undergraduate classes one of my favorite assignments.

Listening

The single most important key to effective teaching is effective listening. If I don't hear what my students are saying, I can't know how to talk to them or with them. I use some simple strategies to help me listen better. To start, I need to know my students a little and to understand what they expect of the class. In turn, they need to understand my assumptions and methods, and what I expect of them.

When the class meets for the second time (not the first, because registration will still shift by about a third), I ask my students to write the answers to a few questions. I want to know how old they are, what year they are in, their major, their reasons for taking the class, and most importantly, the goals they have for the class. They answer anonymously so that they will feel free to be blunt. The first three questions give me a shorthand demographic profile, a key step in transforming them from a horde into a group of students. The fourth question lets me know how many are in the class because it's convenient for their schedule or fulfills a requirement, versus how many are there because they are curious about anthropology. This knowledge helps me shape the tone of the early classes. Those registered because of schedule conveniences need a different kind of pitch than those whose curiosity about the discipline has already been sparked.

The fifth question usually brings mixed responses. Students are not used to being asked about their specific goals for a class. Common replies are, "My goal is to learn more about anthropology," or the occasional "To do as little work as possible for a B." It is rare to find a student who says, "I want my assumptions exploded," or "I want to become really excited by a subject that's new to me," but those answers crop up, too.

To keep communications balanced, I tell students about my training, my research, what other courses I teach, and especially why I love anthropology. I also tell them that I hope they will all become anthropology majors. Some groan in disbelief that I would actually voice such a dumb idea; they are already committed to demanding pre-med courses, or they are headed straight to business school when they graduate. Their groans are my cue to explain that even for those students who will never be anthropology majors, the insights of the field are helpful in any walk of life, and perhaps by the end of the semester every student will have enough knowledge to use key anthropological concepts in a variety of settings. In fact, if I do my job right, by the end of the term they will fold anthropological perspectives into their daily thinking without even being aware of it.

Again, this is not a unique strength of anthropology. Anyone teaching a large class in a college or university should be involved with a subject that he or she loves and that is relevant beyond the classroom. Students might not readily see connections between French literature or medieval history, for instance, and their struggles with a nagging roommate or sagging finances. But insights from history, literature, languages—indeed, from any subject in the humanities—can illuminate unexpected connections between immediate, even seemingly mundane problems and older, more universal expressions of human struggle and pathos. Helping students see those links brings the subject off the page and into the blood.

Cracking the Wall

This second class meeting is also the time to warn students about my teaching style. I call on them even when they don't volunteer (if I call on a student who has nothing to say, I offer her the chance to pass, in which case I call on another student). I refer to this as cold calling. It always elicits groans.

To call on students, one must learn their names. This is the biggest but most important chore at the start of the semester. It cracks the wall of anonymity that separates me from them. I'm not suggesting that a professor remember all the names of all the students in a class of, say, 120 (though I have colleagues who do just that). And I can't claim to remember my students' names a year after the class is over. On the other hand, it's not so difficult to learn and regularly use the names of a quarter to a half of the students during the semester. In evaluations of my large classes, I am consistently praised for making an effort to learn names. "It makes a big class less intimidating," noted one student. "In this big class, unlike other big classes, I am not anonymous," wrote another. (A small but consistent number of students also chide me for cold calling, so this technique is not universally popular).

I don't have magical tricks for remembering names. One semester I asked students to write their names in big, dark letters on a piece of paper large enough for me to see from across the room, and to put it on top or in front of the desks attached to their seats. While I could then call on students very easily, I never actually learned anyone's name, and so it was a technique I decided not to use again. A professor who is sincere in trying to learn students' names will be forgiven a week or two of stumbling.

One of my colleagues uses his course roster as his guide. In each class session, he writes the name of six or seven students in the upper right hand corner of the blackboard. When he has a question during class, he will ask for volunteers, but he will also call on those specific students whose names are on the blackboard. If one of those students is absent, he puts her name on the board at the following meeting. Students singled out this way have the right to pass, and some do. My colleague reports, however, that some quiet students who might never talk in class contribute insightful comments when their name comes up on the list, and after learning that it was not so painful to speak up, become enthusiastic contributors.

Early one semester I called on a student whose name I remembered but whom I didn't actually see when I spoke. In scanning the room, I noticed a small commotion in the farthest corner. The student was dozing, slumped back in his seat with his baseball cap pulled over his eyes. His buddies were jabbing him with their elbows, trying to wake him. I considered him for a moment and remarked to the class that since he wasn't actually with us just then, I would call on someone else. When the student came to, his friends explained in hushed voices what had just happened. To my surprise and delight, he never again sat in the back, nor did he ever again nap during class. Instead he took a seat in the front row for the rest of the semester and became an ardent and knowledgeable participant in class discussions.

When calling on students, I know that their comments or answers will not always pertain to the point I am trying to make. Using class discussion as a teaching tool is rather like conducting an orchestra without knowing for sure what instruments are present or will be played. Only the professor has the score, but she must elicit its intellectual melody from the students clearly enough for them to hum it once they leave. It's easy to let the focus of the class wander when students make remarks that, while not on the subject, are interesting. Or the focus wanders as the professor tries to make an off-the-wall contribution seem relevant. I always struggle to maintain a balance between encouraging my students to speak in class and finding something useful in their sometimes oddball remarks.

When a student is off-base, I'll acknowledge the comment but ask that we "hover" it. It may be relevant to a prior point, or it may pertain to a set of readings we'll do a few weeks later, which I'll note. Occasionally I'll be completely stumped and will simply admit it: "Thanks for your comment, but I'm unsure how it fits here. Can you explain more fully?" If a student sees that he is respected as an individual, even if his comment is loopy, he will be more attentive and, one hopes, become more attuned to the class.

For this reason, I try to avoid the phrase, "That's a good question." If I can't say it to every student who asks a question, it sets up a quiet hierarchy between normal questions and good questions. Besides, it's usually what a teacher says when she doesn't know the answer.

Space

The classic image of a large class is a room full of seated students facing a single lecturer, who stands in front and drones for an hour or more while some students take notes, some gaze into space, and some doze.

Besides using students' names to acknowledge them as individuals, not just as a collective, it makes sense to use the classroom space as much as possible. Staying trapped behind a desk or lectern or at the blackboard guarantees that the class dynamic will fade, no matter how evocative the lecturer. Even in crowded rooms, aisles are clear (or are supposed to be) and allow the professor to wander. Students who like to sit in the back so that they can balance their checkbooks or write letters (or doze) soon learn that they are no longer invisible. It is also easier to call on students in the far corners when the teacher is physically closer to them.

If the space is big enough to hold fifty or more students, it's big enough to swallow voices, so vocal energy must be strong. Professors, for the most part, are used to filling large rooms vocally, or they have microphones that make the effort less taxing, but students often speak quietly. When a student speaks, unless he has spoken loudly and clearly, he will have to repeat the comment or question to the class. If paraphrasing, it's polite to confirm with the student that her contribution was conveyed accurately. To encourage a student sitting nearby to speak loudly enough for everyone to hear, back away as she speaks (the first few times I do this I explain why I'm doing it).

Class Dynamics

Group Work

Small-group work is one of my favorite strategies for making a big class more personal and for really bringing students into a text. It works best when focused on assigned readings. I ask the class to count off in groups of six or eight or ten, depending on how many students there are and what size I want for the small groups. As small as five is ideal, but as big as ten can also work.

Many students dislike small-group work, in part because it disrupts their rhythms and requires them to get intimate with difficult reading. I used to ask if they wanted to break into groups, but after the first time, they always said no, so I stopped giving them the choice. I have found no method as successful for getting students to do close analysis of readings, and without fail they bring back more and deeper insights into the material than I could give them or elicit from them through a lecture.

The groups meet according to number and gather in corners of the room, or occasionally also in the hall. They must have with them the text assigned for that day (I bring extra copies). One student in each group is chosen as the facilitator and another as the recorder. Each group is given a question or two that focuses on a detailed aspect of the reading. The facilitator is responsible for eliciting a comment about the question from every member of the group. The recorder is responsible for writing down that comment. Groups are given 15 or 20 minutes to work, depending on their size and on the difficulty of the text. The professor must move from group to group, animating and guiding those that are unfocused or low in energy.

The class is then reconvened and the questions answered sequentially. The recorder of each group relays the answers (make sure she knows about this part of the job before she agrees to take it on), but before moving on to the next group, the teacher must make sure that members of the first group feel that their contributions were accurately reflected by the recorder. When doing this double-check, I've often found quiet students speaking up for the first time, clarifying or elaborating their comments. Hearing from each group usually takes the rest of the class session and a good part of the next. The questions around which each group focuses must be diverse enough to give a breadth of perspectives on the text but also integrated enough to bring those perspectives into a coherent whole.

Guest Speakers

Another way to break up the monotony of mere lecturing is to bring in guest speakers. When teaching a class about non-Western religious traditions, for instance, I invited a voudou priest and drumming master to join us. The class had read about voudou in Haiti and in New York City, but it was the speaker's account of his faith practices that made the tradition vivid to them, and that moved it from the exotic to the recognizable. He brought several of his drums, and to my amazement had a dozen students, including some of the shyest, dancing and drumming together in the front of the room before he was done.

Storytelling

An additional technique on which I continually rely is probably one of the most ancient teaching tools known to humankind, but it is still among the most effective. I tell stories. I sketch the biographies of authors we study, especially details about how they came to their subject, what the politics were behind a particular text, how their personal lives influenced their work. I tell stories from the news media about events near or far when those illustrate a point. I tell stories about friends or acquaintances (always anonymously, of course, and always with their permission) when the tale is relevant to a lesson. And I tell stories about myself. I don't dwell on myself as some font of endlessly useful narrative, but when it makes a lesson clearer, I find that an occasional personal example helps students understand how their own lives also reflect some of the key themes of the class.

Some professors will never be comfortable with personal revelations. Some even feel that such examples are indulgent and inappropriate. Personal stories are only one possible category of narrative to use as a pedagogical tool. The point is not that the stories are personal, but that they are memorable. Anyone can enliven a class with tales relevant to the material in such a way that students remember class themes much more vividly.

End-of-Class Feedback

A final tool I use regularly is end-of-class feedback that can help me identify problems and correct them quickly. If students have had trouble with a set of ideas, or if I just feel like I wasn't reaching them well, I'll take seven to ten minutes at the end of class and ask them to tell me what they've learned from that class session and what confusion or questions they might have. This, again, is anonymous. It can be an immense help in figuring out where I went wrong in explaining something difficult, or in learning what assumptions I'm using that make my communication less effective than it needs to be.

Regardless of the technique on a particular day—small groups, guest speakers, storytelling, end-of-class feedback, or even just lecturing—I try to remember that teaching is always performance. Many academics take offense at this idea, but when I'm in front of a classroom, it helps me to keep in mind that I am there in the role of teacher, and if I can remember what a good teacher looks and sounds like, I'm more likely to be better at my job. At the same time, when I recall what the role of student looks and sounds like, I'm more likely to be patient with my students, even with the dozers.

A word about dozers. Students' schedules have probably never been as intense as they are today, and in making choices about how to spend their time, students often cheat themselves of sleep. When they find themselves sitting still for more than 20 minutes, regardless of the time of day, fatigue can prevail. I used to think that if I were really a good teacher, everyone would be so engaged in the class that no one would even be sleepy, much less actually nodding off. I became angry at the students who occasionally napped, and angry at myself for failing them. But then I began to appreciate that their lives are full, their commitments many, and their energies finite. At the beginning of each semester, and periodically throughout, I tell students that I empathize with grogginess once in a while, but that I don't want to see anyone actually dozing. A student who feels that she's losing the battle with sleepiness is welcome to stand up, go to the back of the room, and stretch.

One day a fellow in the middle of the room fell into a deep sleep, his head bobbing forward. The seats next to him were empty to the aisle. I was wandering the room while I lectured and noticed his state, so as I spoke I moved down the row of empty seats and sat next to him, still speaking to the class as a whole. The sleeper slowly awoke, startled to see the professor lecturing from the seat next to him. The class, of course, was focused on him. He looked at me in alarm. I asked him quietly if he was okay, then asked him to stay awake for the rest of class, reminding him that he was welcome to use the space in the back of the room to move around if he grew sleepy again. The student stayed awake, and he didn't fall asleep in class again.

In hindsight, I see that I embarrassed him, and it was a moment I would not repeat. Since then, I try to catch dozers before they are actually asleep and invite them to stretch in the back of class. Most don't take me up on the offer, but once they know that I've noticed their drooping eyes, they become more alert. Other students realize that I'll notice them fading and are less likely to let it happen.

Good Listeners, Good Learners

My fundamental goal in any classroom is to excite my students to the richness of anthropology while simultaneously teaching them that they are smart, respected individual thinkers and learners. I want them to understand that even a seemingly obscure topic—say, for instance, inheritance rules among the Trobriand Islanders of Papua New Guinea—is not only a valuable piece of knowledge in its own right but can also teach them insights about their own lives and cultures.

By the end of a semester, the horde has long since been transformed into a fascinating, eclectic collection of individuals. As at the start of the term, I have questions for them at the end, but now I know a little about them and so their answers have more weight. I ask them to recall the goal they set for themselves at the beginning of the semester, if that goal was met, and if so, how, or if not, why not. I ask what they know and like or dislike about anthropology, if they want to take another anthropology class, and whether or not the discipline has helped them better understand the cultural dynamics that shape their lives.

Much more than class evaluations, these questions give me a measure of the semester. Students are always surprising me with their answers. The most rewarding are those who tell me that they've decided to become majors, but the most memorable are those who tell me, sometimes gently and sometimes bluntly, what I missed in trying to teach them. Difficult as those are to read, they are the replies that teach me how to teach better next time. Though I'll never completely master the art of teaching, working on it will always be a thoroughly satisfying challenge.

Summary of Key Concepts for Teaching Large Classes

M. Erin Porter
University of Texas, Austin

Christine A. Stanley
Texas A&M University

This book offers a broad range of cross-disciplinary strategies for teaching large classes in higher education. The chapters range from identifying key concepts cited in the research literature and supported by practice in teaching large classes to sharing strategies from award-winning faculty from a variety of disciplinary backgrounds and institutional settings. The teaching strategies and recommendations in each chapter illustrate how faculty, faculty development professionals, and administrators can improve the quality of teaching large classes in higher education.

A review of the contributing authors and their respective universities illustrates that large classes are a fact of life in today's academic setting. The authors' experiences, examples, and illustrations for effective teaching in large classes clearly demonstrate that it is hard work, if done well. The authors in this text are strongly committed to providing a challenging environment for their students. Ultimately, the development of collegiality across disciplines with faculty peers who teach large classes is one of the most rewarding aspects for members of this "elite club."

Engaging Large Classes supports the basic concepts of the importance of effective, creative, and interactive teaching in large classrooms for all academic disciplines. As you review the key concepts and disciplinary chapters, there are far more areas of commonality in effective teaching and learning in large classes than there are differences. This negates the concept that a particular approach or methodology is applicable to only one discipline or one size class. Good teaching in large classes is challenging and rewarding for both the student and the instructor. A summary of the similarities, strategies, and key issues raised in each chapter are highlighted in this chapter, though the full meaning of this summary can be best understood and appreciated by reading the individual chapters themselves.

Start Planning Early

The assignment to teach a large class is, to some extent, dependent on structural issues imposed by the institution, scheduling, physical location, classroom amenities, legal requirements, and technology availability. Departments and colleges also establish additional expectations about the course content, course objectives, and learning outcomes for each course. These issues are to be taken into account when planning to teach a large class. The amount and level of detail required for large classes are numerous and demand careful, early attention.

Manage Your Time Well

More students mean more demands on the instructor's time, TAs' time, tutors, and support staff time. Pre-planning becomes even more important in order to keep the many details under control from the first day of a large class and to ensure that the administration of the class is handled smoothly. The authors suggest you start the process early by developing appropriate course goals, outcomes, and instructional strategies to teach a large class. The end result is a learning-centered syllabus that becomes a contract between the instructor and the students.

Seek Advice from Experienced Large-Class Teachers

New faculty or faculty new to teaching a large class have access to many excellent resources on and off campus. The contributing authors in this text believe that experienced large-class teachers can be a rich resource of information. They suggest a review of their course syllabi and a visit to their classes. Faculty developers can also play an important role in enhancing an instructor's repertoire of instructional strategies. Many teaching and learning centers and experienced teachers have suggestions for low- and high-risk active teaching and learning strategies that have been tested in large classes.

Get to Know Your Students

The size of some large classes is daunting for both the instructor and some students. Moreover, many students see the large class as an opportunity for anonymity and passivity. Reducing student anonymity involves developing creative strategies to capture and hold their attention and increasing motivation by getting to know the students as individuals. Develop a method for learning students' names that works for you. Some suggestions from our authors include the following:

• Use index cards with basic information about each student along with a picture to help you recognize faces.

• Ask students to remind you of their names when they see you.

• Encourage students to greet you on campus and talk for a minute or two.

• Make plans to see students before and after class as possible.

• Encourage students to come to office hours with you and the graduate teaching assistants.

A small amount of attention goes a long way toward improved student rapport in large classes.

Attend to Classroom Management

Getting to know students and their reasons for taking the course helps you manage large classes and creates an atmosphere that encourages civility. Other strategies include the following:

• Let students know what to expect and when.

• Clarify course expectations in the syllabus.

• Establish guidelines for appropriate behavior during class.

• Review the attendance policy.

• Share your philosophy of teaching.

• Seek feedback from students and colleagues.

- Devise efficient ways of distributing information and exams to the students so that chaos and lost class time don't ensue.

- Work closely with TAs.

- Communicate, communicate, communicate.

The authors agree that promoting classroom civility begins with the instructor modeling these behaviors at all times.

Use Active Teaching and Learning Strategies

Although the lecture format has been the traditional approach to teaching large classes, the overwhelming and consistent response from the authors in this text is that active learning is essential to improved learning in large classes. Among the many suggestions for active learning and engagement that authors describe and suggest using are:

- Creative learning scenarios from business fairs

- Real world assignments

- Assignments requiring teamwork

- Free writing

- Think-pair-share

- Role plays

- Debates

- Hypo teams

- Academic controversies

- Undergraduate peer tutors

- Interactive technology

Active learning works well in large classes, but the activities must be thoughtfully preplanned, consistently and fairly monitored, and continuously assessed.

Use Technology Appropriately

Instructors are the key to student learning and technology is a valuable, creative, and powerful tool. The authors in this book suggest that technology be used in accordance with course and learning goals to organize the course and provide timely feedback for instructor and students. Technology is used most efficiently for short intervals in the classroom and remains a means to vary the presentation of information for students. Planning for glitches in the use of technology and having an alternative plan when they occur are part of a large-class instructor's organizational game plan.

Develop Effective Testing Mechanisms and Grading Procedures

Testing in large classes is still generally accomplished via multiple-choice tests; however, other activities that provide additional ways to assess student learning can be effectively woven into the fabric of the course. Providing these other means of evaluating student learning is essential as, for the most part, multiple-choice tests measure mere intake of information rather than meaningful understanding. Although multiple-choice tests reduce administrative problems for the large-class instructor, they do not take into consideration the magnitude of diverse student learners. Assigning grades to active learning activities provides an avenue to enhance student feedback on learning and retention of course content. Create a structured procedure for review of course grades and share it with the students, TAs, and support staff.

Select and Train Teaching Assistants and Support Staff

Select graduate students who have an interest in teaching and work with them to develop their teaching skills. Meet with your support staff several times before the class begins so that the individuals have a clear understanding of your teaching philosophy and can work in concert with you and your goals. Even with training, TAs and undergraduate staff require support, coaching, observation, feedback, and positive reinforcement as they work with the instructor to make the course the best possible learning environment for all concerned.

Teach for Inclusion

A class of 100, 300, or 500 students naturally presents a rich diversity in students' age, gender, race, ethnicity, culture, nationality, religion, physical and learning abilities, and sexual identity: The class is reflective of society and the university as a whole. Not only do students have different learning styles and abilities; they also represent differences in their orientation towards time, communication style, view of the subject matter, and view of the world.

Instructors set the tone for balancing emotional and intellectual growth and for valuing student differences by knowing their students, mentoring, broadening their repertoire of instructional strategies, establishing classroom norms that emphasize respect and fairness, and using examples or illustrations drawn from diverse life experiences.

Remember that Large Classes Provide Teaching and Learning Challenges

The general consensus in higher education is that teaching small classes is the premier assignment for faculty members. It may be, but large classes are a fact of life on college and university campuses today. At very large institutions, their numbers are expanding quickly as funding wanes and enrollments increase. In many academic areas—such as those represented by authors in this book (including law, hard sciences, business, engineering, computer sciences, social sciences, humanities, and pharmacy)—large classes are the norm and have been for decades. Most faculty members can excel and become better teachers with large-class experience.

Bibliography

Achilles, C. (1993). If all I needed were facts, I'd just buy your book. *People in Education, 1* (4), 424-435.

Adler, P. A. (2000). Employing a team approach in teaching introductory sociology. Personalizing mass education: The assistant teaching assistant (ATA) program. In G. S. Bridges & S. Desmond (Eds.), *Teaching and learning in large classes* (pp. 209-213). Washington, DC: American Sociological Association.

Alimi, M. M., Kassal, B., & Azeez, T. (1998, March). Managing large classes: Team teaching approach. *Forum, 36* (1), 50-53.

Allen, R. R. (1991). Encouraging reflection in teaching assistants. In J. D. Nyquist, R. D. Abbott, D. H. Wulff, & J. Sprague (Eds.), *Preparing the professoriate of tomorrow to teach* (pp. 313-317). Dubuque, IA: Kendall/Hunt.

Amada, G. (1999). *Coping with misconduct in the college classroom: A practical model.* Asheville, NC: College Administration Publications.

Amores, M. J. (1999). Preparing the graduate TA: An investment in excellence. *Foreign Language Annals, 32* (4), 441-468.

Angelo, T. A., & Cross, K. P. (1993). *Classroom assessment techniques: A handbook for college teachers* (2nd ed.). San Francisco, CA: Jossey-Bass.

Appleby, D. C. (1990). Faculty and student perceptions of irritating behaviors in the college classroom. *Journal of Staff, Program and Organizational Development, 8* (2), 41-46.

Aronson, J. R. (1987). Six keys to effective instruction in large classes: Advice from a practitioner. (pp. 31-38). In M. G. Weimer (Ed.), *Teaching large classes well.* New Directions for Teaching and Learning, No. 32. San Francisco, CA: Jossey-Bass.

Arreola, R. A. (2000). *Developing a comprehensive faculty evaluation system* (2nd ed.). Bolton, MA: Anker.

Baldwin, R. G. (1997-98). Academic civility begins in the classroom. *Essays on teaching excellence: Toward the best in the academy, 9* (8). Athens, GA: The Professional and Organizational Development Network in Higher Education.

Bargh, J. A., & Schul, Y. (1980). On the cognitive benefits of teaching. *Journal of Educational Psychology, 74* (5), 593-604.

Baska-Vantassel, J. (1998). Problem-based learning in teaching educational administration courses. In R. Muth & M. Martin (Eds.), *Toward the year 2000: Leadership for quality schools.* The sixth yearbook of the National Council of Professors of Educational Administration. Lancaster, PA: Technomic.

Bean, J. C. (1996). *Engaging ideas: The professor's guide to integrating writing, critical thinking, and active learning in the classroom.* San Francisco, CA: Jossey-Bass.

Bednar, A. K., Cunningham, D., Duffy, T. M., & Perry, J. D. (1995). Theory into practice: How do we link? In G. J. Anglin (Ed.), *Instructional technology: Past, present, and future* (2nd ed.), (pp. 100-112). Englewood, CA: Libraries Unlimited.

Beichner, R. (in press). Student-centered activities for large enrollment university physics (SCALE-UP). *Reshaping undergraduate science and engineering education: Tools for better learning.* Proceeding of the Sigma Xi Forum, Minneapolis, MN. [On-line]. Available FTP ftp://ftp.ncsu.edu/pub/ncsu/beichner/RB/ SigmaXi.pdf.

Belenky, M. F., Clinchy, B. M., Goldberger, N. R., & Tarule, J. M. (1986). *Women's ways of knowing: The development of self, voice, and mind.* New York, NY: Basic Books.

Bell, D. (1997). *Constitutional conflicts.* Cincinnati, OH: Anderson.

Benjamin, L. T., Jr. (1991). Personalization and active learning in the large introductory psychology class. *Teaching of Psychology, 18,* 68-74.

Bereiter, C., & Scardamalia, M. (1989). Intentional learning as a goal of instruction. In L. B. Resnick (Ed.), *Knowing, learning, and instruction: Essays in honor of Robert Glaser* (pp. 361-392). Hillsdale, NJ: Lawrence Erlbaum Associates.

Berquist, G., Tiefel, V., & Waggenspack, B. (1986). Coping with the critical essay in a large lecture course. *Communication Education, 35* (4), 396-399.

Bligh, D. A. (2000). *What's the use of lectures?* San Francisco, CA: Jossey-Bass.

Bloom, B. S. (1956). *Taxonomy of educational objectives: The classification of educational goals.* New York, NY: David McKay.

Boehrer, J., & Chevrier, M. (1991). Professor and teaching assistant: Making the most of a working relationship. In J. D. Nyquist, R. D. Abbott, D. H. Wulff, & J. Sprague (Eds.), *Preparing the professoriate of tomorrow to teach* (pp. 326-330). Dubuque, IA: Kendall/Hunt.

Boice, B. (1996). Classroom incivilities. *Research in Higher Education, 37* (4), 453-487.

Bonwell, C. C., & Eison, J. A. (1991). *Active learning: Creating excitement in the classroom.* ASHE-ERIC Higher Education Report No. 1. Washington, DC: George Washington University, School of Education and Human Development.

Bonwell, C. C. (1996). Enhancing the lecture: Revitalizing a traditional format. In T. E. Sutherland & C. C. Bonwell (Eds.), *Using active learning in large classes: A range of options for faculty.* New Directions for Teaching and Learning, No. 67. San Francisco, CA: Jossey-Bass.

Bostian, L. R. (1983). Even in classes of 100 to 150, personalization is possible. *Journalism Educator, 38* (2), 8-10.

Boyer, E. L. (1990). *Scholarship reconsidered: Priorities of the professoriate.* Princeton, NJ: Carnegie Foundation for the Advancement of Teaching.

Bransford, J. D., Brown, A. L., & Cocking, R. R. (Eds.). (1999). *How people learn: Brain, mind, experience, and school.* Washington, DC: National Academy Press.

Brinko, K. T., & Menges, R. J. (1997). *Practically speaking: A source book for instructional consultants in higher education.* Stillwater, OK: New Forums.

Brookfield, S. D.(1988). *Understanding and facilitating adult learning.* San Francisco, CA: Jossey-Bass.

Brooks, R. P. (1987). Dealing with details in a large class. In M. G. Weimer (Ed.), *Teaching large classes well.* New Directions for Teaching and Learning, No. 32. San Francisco, CA: Jossey-Bass.

Brophy, J. (1987). Synthesis of research on strategies for motivating students to learn. *Educational Leadership, 45* (2), 40-48.

Brown, A. L., Ash, D., Rutherford, M., Nakagawa, K., Gordon, A., & Campione, J. C. (1993). Distributed expertise in the classroom. In G. Salomon (Ed.), *Distributed cognitions: Psychological and educational considerations* (pp. 188-228). Cambridge, EN: Cambridge University Press.

Brown, J. S., Collins, A., & Duguid, P. (1989). Situated cognition and the culture of learning. *Educational Researcher, 18,* 32-42.

Brown-Wright, D. A., Dubick, R. A., & Newman, I. (1997). Graduate assistant expectation and faculty perception: Implications for mentoring and training. *Journal of College Students Development, 38* (4), 410-415.

Buskist, W., & Wylie, D. (1998). A method for enhancing student interest in large introductory classes. *Teaching of Psychology, 25* (3), 203-205.

Carbone, E. (1998). *Teaching large classes: Tools and strategies.* Thousand Oaks, CA: Sage.

Carbone, E. (1999). Students behaving badly in large classes. In Richardson, S. (Ed.), *Promoting civility: A teaching challenge.* New Directions for Teaching and Learning, No. 77. San Francisco, CA: Jossey-Bass.

Carbone E., & Greenberg, J. (1998). Teaching large classes: Unpacking the problem and responding creatively. In M. Kaplan & D. Lieberman (Eds.), *To Improve the Academy: Vol. 17. Resources for faculty, instructional, and organizational development* (pp. 311-326). Stillwater, OK: New Forums Press.

Cashin, W. E., & Perrin, B. M. (1978). *IDEA technical report # 4: Description of IDEA standard form database.* Manhattan, KS: Center for Faculty Evaluation and Development.

Cashin, W. E. (1988). Student ratings of teaching: A summary of the research. *IDEA Paper* No. 20. Manhattan, KS: Center for Faculty Evaluation and Development, Kansas State University.

Centra, J. A. (1979). *Determining faculty effectiveness.* San Francisco, CA: Jossey-Bass.

Centra, J. A., & Creech, F. R. (1976). *The relationship between student, teachers, and course characteristics and student ratings of teaching effectiveness.* Project Report 76-1. Princeton, NJ: Educational Testing Service.

Chan, C. S., & Treacy, M. J. (1996). Resistance in multicultural courses. *American Behavioral Scientist, 40* (2), 212-221.

Cheydleur, F. D. (1945, August). Criteria of effective teaching in basic French courses. *Bulletin of the University of Wisconsin* (Monograph No. 2783). Madison, WI: University of Wisconsin.

Chirol, M. (1999). A touch of class! Creating a handbook on logistics and administrative duties: Advantage for TAs and language program coordinators. *The Canadian Modern Language Review, 56* (2), 355-362.

Chism, N. V. N. (1989, June). Large enrollment classes: Necessary evil or not necessarily evil? *Notes on Teaching, 5,* (pp.1-8). Occasional papers published by The Center for Teaching Excellence at The Ohio State University: Columbus, OH: The Ohio State University. (ERIC Document Reproduction Service ED 334 875)

Christensen, C. R., Garvin, D. A., & Sweet, A. (Eds.). (1991). *Education for judgment: The artistry of discussion leadership.* Boston, MA: Harvard Business School Press.

Christensen, T. (1994). Large classes and their influence on language teaching. *Journal of Hokusei Junior College, 30,* 121-129.

Chronicle of Higher Education. (1998). *Is rudeness on the rise?* Online discussion, 3/23/98. www.chronicle.com/colloquy/98/rude/01.html

Civikly, J. M., & Hidalgo, R. (1992). TA training as professional mentoring. In J. D. Nyquist & D. H. Wulff (Eds.), *Preparing teaching assistants for instructional roles: Supervising TAs in Communication.* Annandale, VA: Speech Communication Association.

Clark, D. J., & Bekey, J. (1979). Use of small groups in instructional evaluation. *Insight into Teaching Excellence, 7* (1), 2-5.

Coggeshall, M. (2000, 3 May). Writing for discussion in introductory anthropology classes. Lecture presented at the Communication across the Curriculum Symposium. Clemson, SC: Clemson University.

Connor-Greene, P. (2000a). Using problem-based service learning in an abnormal psychology class. In S. Madden (Ed.), *Service learning across the curriculum.* Lanham, MD: University Press of America.

Connor-Greene, P. (2000b, 3 March). Using CLE team space to facilitate group projects. Workshop sponsored by the Office of Teaching Effectiveness and Innovation. Clemson, SC: Clemson University.

Cook, R., Tessier, A., & Klein, D. (1996). *Adapting early childhood curriculum for children in inclusive settings* (4th ed.). Englewood Cliffs, NJ: Merrill-Prentice Hall.

Coppola, B. P. (1995). Progress in practice: Using concepts from motivational and self-regulated learning research to improve chemistry instruction (pp. 87-96). In P. R. Pintrich (Ed.), *Understanding self-regulated learning.* New Directions for Teaching and Learning, No. 63. San Francisco, CA: Jossey-Bass.

Coppola, B. P. (2001a). Literature-based examinations and grading them: Well worth the effort (pp. 84-86). In E. D. Siebert & W. J. McIntosh (Eds.), *College pathways to the science education standards.* Arlington, VA: NSTA Press.

Coppola, B. P. (2001b). Full human presence. In A. G. Reinarz, & E. R. White (Eds.), *Beyond teaching to mentoring.* (pp. 57-73). New Directions for Teaching and Learning, No. 83. San Francisco, CA: Jossey-Bass.

Coppola, B. P., Daniels, D. S., & Pontrello, J. K. (2001). Using structured study groups to create chemistry honors sections. In J. Miller, J. E. Groccia, & M. Miller (Eds.), *Student assisted teaching and learning* (pp. 116-122). Bolton, MA: Anker.

Coppola, B. P., Ege, S. N., & Lawton, R. G. (1997). The University of Michigan undergraduate chemistry curriculum. 2. Instructional strategies and assessment, *Journal of Chemical Education, 74,* 84-94.

Corwin, P. (1996, July). Using the community as a classroom for large introductory sociology classes. *Teaching Sociology, 24,* 310-315.

Cox, M. D. (2001). Faculty learning communities: Change agents for transforming institutions into learning organizations. In D. Lieberman & C. Wehlburg (Eds.), *To improve the academy: Vol. 19. Resources for faculty, instructional, and organizational development* (pp. 69-93). Bolton, MA: Anker.

Cuban, L. (1990). Reforming again, again, and again. *Educational Researcher, 19,* 3-13.

Dannells, M. (1997). *From discipline to development: Rethinking student conduct in higher education.* Washington DC: Office of Educational Research and Improvement. (ASHE–ERIC Higher Education Report, Vol. 25, No. 2).

Davis, B. G. (1993). *Tools for teaching.* San Francisco, CA: Jossey-Bass.

Day, S. (1994). Learning in large sociology classes: Journals and attendance. *Teaching Sociology, 22,* 151-165.

Dekkers, J., & Donatti, S. (1981, July/August). The integration of research studies on the use of simulation as an instructional strategy. *Journal of Educational Research, 74* (6), 424-427.

Downs, J. R. (1992). Dealing with hostile and oppositional students. *College Teaching, 40* (3), 106-08.

Drummond, T. (2000). *A brief summary of the best practices in college teaching: Intended to challenge the professional development of all teachers.* http://nsccux.sccd.ctc.edu/~eceprog/bstprac.html

Duba-Biedermann, L. (1994). Graduate assistant development: Problems of role ambiguity and faculty supervision. *The Journal of Graduate Teaching Assistant Development, 1* (3), 119-125.

Dufresne, R. J., Gerace, W. J., Leonard, W. J., Mestre, J. P., & Wenk, L. (1996). Classtalk: A classroom communication system for active learning. *Journal of Computing in Higher Education, 7,* 3-47.

Edens, K. M. (2000, Spring). Preparing problem-solvers for the 21st century through problem-based learning. *College Teaching,48* (2), 55-60.

Edmondson, J. B., & Mulder, F. J. (1924). Size of class as a factor in university instruction. *Journal of Educational Research, 9,* 1-12.

Ege, S. N., Coppola, B. P., & Lawton, R. G. (1997). The University of Michigan undergraduate chemistry curriculum 1. Philosophy, curriculum, and the nature of change. *Journal of Chemical Education, 74,* 74-83.

Elbow, P. (1973). *Writing without teachers.* New York, NY: Oxford University Press.

Eyler, J., & Giles, D. E., Jr. (1999). *Where's the learning in service learning?* San Francisco, CA: Jossey-Bass.

Feldhusen, J. R. (1963). The effects of small and large-group instruction on learning of subject matter, attitudes, and interests. *Journal of Psychology, 55,* 357-362.

Feldman, K. A. (1984). Class size and college students' evaluations of teachers and courses: A closer look. *Research in Higher Education, 21* (1), 45-116.

Feldman, K.A. (1991, April 7). *Grade inflation and student ratings: A closer look.* Paper presented at the 72nd annual meeting of the American Educational Research Association. Chicago, IL.

Fisch, L. (1996). *The chalk dust collection.* Stillwater, OK: New Forums Press.

Fitch, B., & Kirby, A. (2000, Spring). Students' assumptions and professors' presumptions: Creating a learning community for the whole student. *College Teaching, 48* (2), 47-54.

Fowler, B. (1996). Increasing the teaching skills of teaching assistants through feedback from observation of classroom performance. *Journal of Graduate Teaching Assistant Development, 3* (3), 95-103.

Frederick, P. (1986, Spring). The lively lecture: Eight variations. *College Teaching,* 43-50.

Frederick, P. (1987, Winter). Student involvement: Active learning in large classes. In M. G. Weimer (Ed.), *Teaching large classes well.* New Directions for Teaching and Learning, No. 32, pp. 45-56.

Freeman, M. (1998). Video conferencing: A solution to the multi-campus large classes problem? *British Journal of Educational Technology, 29* (3), 197-210.

Gaff, J. G., Pruitt-Logan, A. S., Weibl, R. A., & participants in the Preparing Future Faculty Program. (2000). *Building the faculty we need: Colleges and universities working together.* Washington, DC: Association of American Colleges and Universities.

Galton, M. (1998a). Class size: A critical moment on the research. *International Journal of Educational Research, 29,* 809-818.

Galton, M. (1998b). Guest editor's introduction: Class size and pupil achievement. *International Journal of Educational Research, 29,* 689-690.

Gess-Newsome, J., & Lederman, N. G. (Eds.). (1999). *Examining pedagogical content knowledge.* Dordrecht, The Netherlands: Kluwer.

Ghosh, R. (1999). The challenge of teaching large numbers of students in general education laboratory classes involving many graduate student assistants. *Bioscience, 25* (1), 7-11.

Gibler, D. M. (2000, 9 May). Personal correspondence.

Gilbert, S. (1995, Winter). *Quality education: Does class size matter?* CSSHE Professional Profile, 14, pp. 1-6. Association of Universities and Colleges of Canada.

Glassick, C. E., Huber, M T., & Maeroff, G. I. (1997). *Scholarship assessed: Evaluation of the professoriate.* San Francisco, CA: Jossey-Bass.

Gleason, M. (1990). An instructor survival kit: For use with large classes. In E. Neff & M. Weimer (Eds.), *Teaching college: Collected readings for the new instructor.* Madison, WI: Magna.

Gray, T., & Halbert, S. (1998). Team teach with a student: New approach to collaborative teaching. *College Teaching, 46* (4), 150-153.

Grunert, J. (1997). *The course syllabus: A learning-centered approach.* Bolton, MA: Anker.

Hamlin, J. & Janssen, S. (1987, January). Active learning in large introductory sociology courses. *Teaching Sociology, 15,* 45-54.

Hammons, J. O., & Barnsley J. R. (1992). Everything you need to know about developing a grading plan for your course (well, almost). *Journal on Excellence in College Teaching, 3,* 51-68.

Harcharick, K. (1993, October). *Problems and opportunities in teaching a large class.* Presented at the meeting of the CSU Institute for Teaching and Learning Exchange, San Jose, CA.

Hardiman, R., & Jackson, B. (1997). Conceptual foundations for social justice courses. In M. Adams, L. Bell, & P. Griffin (Eds.), *Teaching for diversity and social justice: A source book* (pp. 16-29). New York, NY: Routledge.

Hargrove, R. (1995). *Masterful coaching: Extraordinary results by impacting people and the way they think and work together.* San Francisco, CA: Jossey-Bass/Pfeiffer.

Hargrove, R. (2000). *Masterful coaching deluxe trainer's package .* San Francisco, CA: Jossey-Bass.

Harwood, W. S. (1996, March). The one-minute paper. *Journal of Chemical Education, 73* (3), 229-230.

Hastie, P. A., Sanders, S. W., & Rowland, R. S. (1999). Where good intentions meet hard realities: Teaching large classes in physical education. *Journal of Teaching in Physical Education, 18,* 277-289.

Heady, J. E., Coppola, B. P., & Titterington, L. C. (2001). Assessment standards. In E. D. Siebert & W. J. McIntosh (Eds.), *College pathways to the science education standards.* (pp. 57-63). Arlington, VA: NSTA Press.

Hensley, T. R., & Oakley, M. (1998). The challenge of the large lecture class: Making it more like a small seminar. *Political Science & Politics, 31* (1), 47-51.

Hepler, C. D., & Strand, L. M. (1990 March). Opportunities and responsibilities in pharmaceutical care. *American Journal of Hospital Pharmacy, 47* (3), 533-43.

Hoffmann, R., & Coppola, B. P. (1996). Some heretical thoughts on what our students are telling us. *Journal of College Science Teaching, 25,* 390-394.

Howes, R., & Watson, J. (1982, January). Demonstrations to wake up large classes. *The Physics Teacher,* 40-41.

Hoyle, J. (1991). *Good bull: Thirty years of Aggie escapades.* Bryan, TX: Insite Press.

Hoyle, J. (1995). *Leadership and futuring: Making visions happen.* Thousand Oaks, CA: Corwin Press.

Hurd, P. D. (2000). Active learning. *Journal of Pharmacy Teaching, 7* (3/4), 29-47.

International Data Corporation. (1999). Online Distance Learning in Higher Education, 1998-2002. (Online). http://www.idc.com/

Jacobs, L. C., & Chase, C. I. (1992). *Developing and using tests effectively.* San Francisco, CA: Jossey-Bass.

Jenkins, J. J. (1991). Teaching psychology in large classes: Research and personal experience. *Teaching of Psychology, 18,* 74-80.

Johnson, D. W., & Johnson, R. T. (1995). *Creative conflict: Intellectual challenges in the classroom.* Edina, MN: Interaction Book Company.

Johnson, D. W., Johnson, R. T., & Smith, K. A. (1991). *Active learning: Cooperation in the college classroom.* Edina, MN: Interactive Book Company.

Johnson, D. W., Johnson, R. T., & Smith, K. A. (1991). *Cooperative learning: Increasing college faculty instructional productivity.* Washington, DC: The George Washington University, School of Education and Human Development. (ASHE-ERIC Higher Education Report No. 4).

Johnson, D. W., Johnson, R. T., & Smith, K. A. (1996). *Academic controversy: Enriching college instruction through intellectual conflict.* Washington, DC: George Washington University, Graduate School of Education and Human Development. (ASHE-ERIC Higher Education Report Vol. 25, No. 3).

Jossem, E. L. (2000). The teaching of physics. *American Journal of Physics, 68,* 6.

Kain, E. (1986). The mass class as theatre: Suggestions for improving the chances of a hit production. In R. McGee (Ed.), *Teaching the mass class*. Washington, DC: ASA Teaching Resources Center, American Sociological Association.

Karayan, S. S., & Crowe, J. A. (1997). Student perceptions of electronic discussion groups. *T.H.E. Journal, 24* (9), 69-71.

Karraker, M. W. (1993). Mock trials and critical thinking. *College Teaching, 41* (4), 134-137.

Keller, J. M. (1983). Motivational design of instruction. In C. M. Riegeluth (Ed.), *Instructional design theories and models: An overview of their current status.* Hillsdale, NJ: Lawrence Erlbaum.

Kilmer, P. (1998). When a few disruptive students challenge an instructor's plan. *Journalism & Mass Communication Educator, 53* (2), 81-84.

Knapper, C. (1987). Large classes and learning (pp. 5-16). In M. G. Weimer (Ed.), *Teaching large classes well.* New Directions for Teaching and Learning, No. 32. San Francisco, CA: Jossey-Bass.

Kracht, J., & Nolan, S. (1999). *Texas social studies framework.* Austin, TX: Texas Education Agency.

Kurfiss, J. G. (1988) *Critical thinking: Theory, research, practice and possibilities.* Washington, DC: Association for the Study of Higher Education. (ASHE-ERIC Higher Education Report No. 2).

Le Bon, G. (1960). *The mind of the crowd.* New York, NY: Viking.

Lester, F. K. (1985). Methodological considerations in research on mathematical problem-solving instruction. In E. A. Silver (Ed.), *Teaching and learning mathematical problem solving: Multiple research perspectives* (pp. 41 –70). Hillsdale, NJ: Erlbaum.

Lewis, D. C., Treves, J. A., & Shaindlin, A. B. (1997). Making sense of academic cyberspace: Case study of an electronic classroom. *College Teaching , 45* (3), 96-100.

Litke, R. A. (1995, Feb.). *Learning lessons from large classes: Student attitudes toward effective and ineffective methods in large classes.* Paper presented at the Western States Communication Association, Communication and Instruction Interest Group. Portland, Oregon. (ERIC Documents Reproduction Service. ED 384 088)

Lowman, J. (1987). Giving students feedback. In M. G. Weimer (Ed.), *Teaching large classes well* (pp. 71-83). New Directions for Teaching and Learning, No. 32. San Francisco, CA: Jossey-Bass.

Lowman, J. (1995). *Mastering the techniques of teaching* (2nd ed.). San Francisco, CA: Jossey-Bass.

Lowman, J., & Mathie, V. A. (1993). What should graduate TAs know about teaching? *Teaching of Psychology, 20* (2), 84-88.

Macomber, F. G., & Siegel, L. (1957). A study of large-group teaching procedures. *Educational Research, 38,* 220-229.

Macomber, F. G., & Siegel, L. (1960). *Experimental study in instructional procedures.* Final report. Oxford, OH: Miami University Press.

Maier, N. R. F., Solem, A. R., & Maier, A. A. (1975). *The role-play technique: A handbook for management and leadership practice.* Lajolla, CA: University Associates.

Marchesani, L., & Adams, M. (1992). Dynamics of diversity in the teaching-learning process: A faculty development model for analysis and action. In M. Adams (Ed.), *Promoting diversity in the college classroom: Innovative responses for the curriculum, faculty, and institutions.* New Directions for Teaching and Learning, No. 52. San Francisco, CA: Jossey-Bass.

Marchetti, E. (2000). Peer assisted study sessions (PASS). In G. S. Bridges & S. Desmond (Eds.), *Teaching and learning in large classes* (pp. 221-226). Washington, DC: American Sociological Association.

Marsh, H. W. (1983). Multi-dimensional ratings of teaching effectiveness by students from different academic settings and their relation to student/course/instructor characteristics. *Journal of Educational Psychology, 75,* 150-166.

Marsh, H. W. (1987). Student evaluations of university teaching: Research findings, methodological issues, and directions for future research. *International Journal of Educational Research, 11,* 253-388.

Marsh, H. W., Overall, J. U., & Kesler, S. P. (1979). Class size, students' evaluations, and instructional effectiveness. *American Educational Research Journal, 16* (1), 57-69.

Martin, M., Murphy, M., & Muth, R. (1993). Problem-based learning: A new approach to preparing school leaders. In J. Hoyle & D. Estes (Eds.), *NCPEA: In a new voice.* The first yearbook of the National Council of Professors of Educational Administration. Lancaster, PA: Technomics.

Martino, G., & Sala, F. (1996). *Engaging students in large classes.* A paper presented at the Tenth Annual Conference on Undergraduate Teaching of Psychology. Ellenville, NY. (ERIC Document Reproduction Service. ED 405 033)

Mazur, E. (1997). *Peer instruction: A user's manual.* Upper Saddle River, NJ: Prentice Hall.

McCroskey, J. C., & Andersen, J. F. (2000). The relationship between communication apprehension and academic achievement among college students. Retrieved September 12, 2000 from the World Wide Web: http://www.as.wvu.edu/~jmccrosk/67.htm

McDermott, L. C., & Shaffer, P. S. (1998). *Tutorials in introductory physics.* Upper Saddle River, NJ: Prentice Hall.

McKeachie, W. J. (1980, Feb.). Class size, large classes, and multiple sections. *Academe,* 24-27.

McKeachie, W. J. (Ed.). (1994). *Teaching tips: A guide for the beginning college teacher* (9th Ed.) Lexington, MA: D. C. Heath.

McKeachie, W. J. (1999). *Teaching tips: A guide for the beginning college teacher* (10th ed.). Lexington, MA: D.C. Heath.

McKeachie, W. J. (1999). *Teaching tips: Strategies, research, and theory for college and university teachers* (10th ed.) Boston, New York: Houghton Mifflin.

McKeachie, W. J., Pintrich, P. R., Lin, Y. G., Smith, D. A. F., & Sharma, R. (1990). *Teaching and learning in the college classroom: A review of the research literature* (2nd ed.). Ann Arbor, MI: NCRIPTAL, University of Michigan.

McKeachie, W. J., Chism, N., Menges, R., Svinicki, M., & Weinstein, C. E. (1994). *Teaching tips: Strategies, research, and theory for college and university teachers* (9th ed.). Lexington, MA: D. C. Heath.

McCleod, D. (1985). Affective issues in research on teaching mathematical problem solving. In E.A. Silver (Ed.), *Teaching and learning mathematical problem solving: Multiple research perspectives* (pp. 266–280). Hillsdale, NJ: Erlbaum.

Merriam, S. B., & Caffarella, R. S. (1991). *Learning in adulthood.* San Francisco, CA: Jossey-Bass.

Meyers, S. A. (1995). Enhancing relationships between instructors and teaching assistants. *Journal of Graduate Teaching Assistant Development, 2* (3), 107-112.

Michaelsen, L. K. (1992). Team learning: A comprehensive approach for harnessing the power of small groups in higher education. In D. L. Wulff & J. D. Nyquist (Eds.), *To improve the academy: Vol. 11. Resources for faculty, instructional, and organizational development.* Stillwater, OK: New Forums Press.

Michaelsen, L. K., & Black, R. H. (1994). Building learning teams: The key to harnessing the power of small groups in higher education. In L. K. Michaelsen & R. H. Black (Eds.), *Collaborative learning: A sourcebook for higher education, Vol. 2.* State College, PA: National Center for Teaching, Learning, and Assessment.

Michaelsen, L. K., Fink, L. D., & Black, R. H. (1996). What every faculty developer needs to know about learning groups. In L. Richlin (Ed.), *To improve the academy: Vol. 15 . Resources for faculty, instructional, and organizational development* (pp. 31-58). Stillwater, OK : New Forums Press.

Michaelsen, L. K., Fink, L. D., & Knight, A. (1997). Designing effective group activities: Lessons for classroom teaching and faculty development. In D. DeZure (Ed.), *To improve the academy: Vol. 16. Resources for faculty, instructional, and organizational development* (pp. 373-397). Stillwater, OK: New Forums Press.

Miller, J. E., Groccia, J. E., & Miller, M. S. (Eds.). (2001). *Student-assisted teaching: A guide to faculty-student teamwork.* Bolton, MA: Anker.

Millis, B. J. & Cottrell, P. G., Jr. (1998). *Cooperative learning for higher education faculty.* Phoenix, AZ: Oryx.

Mills, C. W. (1956). *The power elite.* New York, NY: Oxford University Press.

Milton, O., Pollio, H., & Eison, J. (1986). *Making sense of college grades.* San Francisco, CA: Jossey-Bass.

Moore, M. G., & Thompson, M. M., with Quigley, A. B., Clark, G. C., & Goff, G. G. (1990). The effects of distance learning: A summary of the literature. *Research Monograph No. 2.* University Park, PA: The Pennsylvania State University, American Center for the Study of Distance Education. (ED 330-321).

Moore, R. L. (1982). Teaching the big class. *Journalism Educator,* 10-11, 78.

Moss, G. D., & McMillen, D. (1980). A strategy for developing problem solving skills in large undergraduate classes. *Studies in Higher Education, 5* (2), 161-171.

Mueller, A. D. (1924). Class size as a factor in normal school instruction. *Education, 45,* 203-277.

Mueller, A., Perlman, B., McCann, L. I., & McFadden, S. H. (1997). A faculty perspective on teaching assistant training. *Teaching of Psychology, 24* (3), 167-171.

Murray, H. G. (1985). Classroom teaching behaviors related to college teaching effectiveness. In J. G. McDonald & A. M. Sullivan (Eds.), *Using research to improve teaching.* New Directions in Teaching and Learning No. 23. San Francisco, CA: Jossey-Bass.

Nachman, M., & Opochinsky, S. (1958). The effects of different teaching methods: A methodological study. *Journal of Educational Psychology, 49,* 245-249.

National Research Council (1997). *Science teaching reconsidered: A handbook.* Washington, DC: National Academy Press.

Nelson, C. (1991, 6 February). Fostering critical thinking. Lecture presented in the Chancellor's Lecture Series. Nashville, TN: Vanderbilt University.

Nilson, L. B. (1998). *Teaching at its best: A research-based resource for college instructors.* Bolton, MA: Anker.

Notarianni-Girard, D. (1999). Transfer of training in teaching assistant programs. *Journal of Graduate Teaching Assistant Development, 6* (3), 119-147.

Nova (1988). *Can we make a better doctor?* (video). Boston, MA: WGBH.

Nungester, R. J., & Duchastel, P. C. (1982). Testing versus review: Effects on retention. *Journal of Applied Psychology, 74* (1), 18-22.

Nyquist, J. D., Manning, L., Wulff, D. H., Austin, A. E., Sprague, J., Fraser, P., Calcagno, C., & Woodford, B. (1999). On the road to becoming a professor: The graduate student experience. *Change, 31* (3), 18-27.

Nyquist, J. D., & Wulff, D. H. (1992). TA training as professional mentoring. In J. D. Nyquist & D. H. Wulff (Eds.), *Preparing teaching assistants for instructional roles: Supervising TAs in Communication.* Annandale, VA: Speech Communication Association.

Nyquist, J, D., & Sprague, J. (1998). Thinking developmentally about TAs. In M. Marincovich, J. Prostko, & F. Stout (Eds.), *The professional development of graduate teaching assistants* (pp. 61-88). Bolton, MA: Anker.

Oblinger, D. G. (1995). Educational alternatives based on communication, collaboration and computers. IBM Corporation. (Online). http://www.iat.unc.edu/publications/oblinger/oblinger.html

Ore, T. E. (2000). Employing a team approach in teaching introductory sociology. In G. S. Bridges, & S. Desmond (Eds.), *Teaching and learning in large classes* (pp. 241-248). Washington, DC: American Sociological Association.

Ormand, J. (1995). *Education psychology: Principles and applications.* Englewood Cliffs, NJ: Merrill-Prentice Hall.

Ouellett, M. L., & Sorcinelli, M. D. (1995). Teaching and learning in the diverse classroom: A faculty and TA partnership program. In E. Neal & L. Richlin (Eds.), *To improve the academy: Volume 14. Resources for faculty, instructional, and organizational development* (205-217). Stillwater, OK: New Forums Press.

Ouellett, M. L., & Sorcinelli, M. D. (1998). TA training: Strategies for responding to diversity in the classroom. In M. Marincovich, J. Prostko, & F. Stout (Eds.), *The professional development of graduate teaching assistants* (pp. 105-120). Bolton, MA: Anker.

Overtree, C. E., & Halgin, R. P. (1997). *Procedures and teaching manual for abnormal psychology.* Unpublished manuscript. Amherst, MA: University of Massachusetts, Amherst.

Palmer, P. J. (1998). *The courage to teach: Exploring the inner landscape of a teacher's life.* San Francisco, CA: Jossey Bass.

Paris, S. G. (1997). Private communication to the author.

Paris, S. G., & Cross, D. R. (1983). Ordinary learning: Pragmatic connections among children's beliefs, motives and actions. In J. Bisanz, G. Bisanz, & R. Kail (Eds.), *Learning in children,* (pp. 137-169). New York, NY: Springer-Verlag.

Paris, S. G., Lipson, M. Y., & Wixson, K. (1983). Becoming a strategic reader. *Contemporary Educational Psychology, 8,* 293-316.

Pea, R. (1993). Practices of distributed intelligence and designs for education. In G. Salomon (Ed.), *Distributed cognitions: Psychological and educational considerations* (pp. 47-87). Cambridge, EN: Cambridge University Press.

Perlman, B., & McCann, L. I. (1998). Students' pet peeves about teaching. *Teaching of Psychology, 25,* 201-02.

Perry, R. P. (1991). Perceived control in the college classroom. In J. C. Smart (Ed.), *Higher education: Handbook of theory and research (Vol. 7)*. New York, NY: Agathon.

Perry, W. (1970). *Forms of intellectual and ethical development in the college years: A scheme*. New York, NY: Holt, Rinehart, and Winston.

Pescosolido, B. & Aminzade, R. (1999). *The social worlds of higher education: Handbook for teaching in a new century*. Thousand Oaks, CA: Pine Forge Press.

Pintrich, P. R. (1987, April). *Motivated learning strategies in the college classroom*. Paper presented at the annual meeting of the American Educational Research Association Convention, Washington, DC.

Pintrich, P. R. (2001). University of Michigan, private communication.

Pregent, R. (1994). *Charting your course: How to prepare to teach more effectively*. Madison, WI: Magna.

Prieto, L. R. (1999). Teaching assistants' preferences for supervisory style: Testing a developmental model of GTA supervision. *Journal of Graduate Teaching Assistant Development, 6* (3), 111-118.

Resnick, L. (1987, December). Learning in school and out. *Educational Researcher, 16,* 13-20.

Resnick, L. B. (1989). *Knowing, learning, and instruction: Essays in honor of Robert Glaser*. Hillsdale, NJ: Lawrence Erlbaum.

Richardson, S. (Ed.). (1999). *Promoting civility: A teaching challenge*. New Directions for Teaching and Learning, No. 77. San Francisco, CA: Jossey-Bass.

Roberts, G. A., & Dunn, P. M. (1996). *Electronic classrooms and lecture theatres: Design and use factors in the age of the mass lecture*. Washington, DC: United States Department of Education, Office of Educational Research and Improvement. (ERIC Document Reproduction Service ED 396 743)

Rosenkoetter, J. S. (1984, April). Teaching psychology to large classes: Videotapes, PSI, and lecturing. *Teaching of Psychology, 11* (2), 85-87.

Russell, T. L. (1999). Web Based Training. (Online). http://cuda.teleeducation.nb.ca/nosignificantdifference/

Sadker, M., & Sadker, D. (1991). *Teachers, schools, and society* (2nd ed.). New York, NY: McGraw-Hill.

Sarason, S. (1998). Some features of a flawed educational system. *Daedalus, 127* (4), 1-12.

Schmitz, B., Paul, S. P., & Greenberg, J. D. (1992). Creating multicultural classrooms: An experience-derived faculty development program. In L. L. Border & N. Chism (Eds.), *Teaching for diversity*, (49, 75-87). San Francisco, CA: Jossey-Bass.

Schneider, A. (1998, March 27). Insubordination and intimidation signal the end of decorum in many classrooms. *Chronicle of Higher Education*, pp. A12-A14.

Schoenfeld, A. H. (Ed). (1987a). Cognitive science and mathematics education: an overview. In *Cognitive science and mathematics education* (pp. 189–216). Hillsdale, NJ: Erlbaum.

Schoenfeld, A. H. (Ed). (1987b). What's all the fuss about metacognition? In *Cognitive science and mathematics education* (pp.1–32). Hillsdale, NJ: Erlbaum.

Seymour, E., & Hewitt, N. M. (1997). *Talking about leaving: Why undergraduates leave the sciences.* Boulder, CO: Westview Press.

Shulman, L. (1999, July/August). Taking learning seriously. *Change*, 11-17.

Silver, E. A. (1987). Foundations of cognitive theory and research for mathematical problem-solving. In A. H. Schoenfeld (Ed.), *Cognitive science and mathematics education* (pp.33-60). Hillsdale, NJ: Erlbaum.

Silver, P., Bourke, A., & Strehorm, K. C. (1998). Universal instructional design in higher education: An approach for inclusion. *Equity and Excellence, 31* (2), 47-51.

Slavin, R. E., & Karweit, N. L. (1981). Cognitive and affective outcomes of an intensive student team learning experience. *Journal of Experimental Education, 50* (1), 29-35.

Smith, K. A., & MacGregor, J. (2000). Making small group learning and learning communities a widespread reality. In J. MacGregor, J. L. Cooper, K. A. Smith, & P. Robinson (Eds.), *Strategies for energizing large classes: From small groups to learning communities.* New Directions for Teaching and Learning, No. 81. San Francisco, CA: Jossey-Bass.

Sorcinelli, M. D. (1994). Dealing with troublesome behaviors in the classroom. In K. W. Prichard and R. M. Sawyer (Eds.), *Handbook of college teaching: Theory and applications.* Westport, CT: Greenwood Press.

Sprague, J., & Nyquist, J. D. (1991). A developmental perspective on the TA role. In J. D. Nyquist, R. D. Abbott, D. H. Wulff, and J. Sprague (Eds.), *Preparing the professoriate of tomorrow to teach* (pp. 295-312). Dubuque, IA: Kendall/Hunt.

Sprague, J., & Nyquist, J. D. (1989). TA supervision. In J. D. Nyquist, R. D. Abbott, & D. H. Wulff (Eds.), *Teaching assistant training in the 1990s* (pp. 37-53). New Directions for Teaching and Learning, No. 39. San Francisco, CA: Jossey-Bass.

Stanley, C. A. (2000-2001). Teaching excellence: Toward the best in the academy. *Professional and Organizational Development Network in Higher Education, 12* (2).

Stanton, T. K., Giles, D. E., Jr., & Cruz, N. I. (1999). *Service-learning: A movement's pioneers reflect on its origins, practice, and future.* San Francisco, CA: Jossey-Bass.

Steffens, H. (1991, May/June). Using informal writing in large history classes: Helping students to find interest and meaning in history. *The Social Studies*, 107-109.

Strauss, M., & Fulwiler, T. (1989, December/1990, January). Writing to learn in large lecture classes. *Journal of College Science Teaching, 19*, (3), 158-163.

Streibel, M. J. (1995). Instructional plans and situated learning: The challenge of Suchman's theory of situated action for instructional designers and instructional systems (pp. 145-160). In G. J. Anglin (Ed.), *Instructional technology: Past, present, and future* (2nd ed.). Englewood, CA: Libraries Unlimited.

Svinicki, M. (1991). Practical implications of cognitive theories. In R. J. Menges & M. D. Svinicki (Eds.), *College teaching: From theory to practice* (pp. 27-37). San Francisco, CA: Jossey-Bass.

Svinicki, M. (1995). A dozen reasons why we should prepare graduate students to teach. *Journal of Graduate Teaching Assistant Development, 3* (1), 5-7.

Theall, M., & Franklin, J. (Eds.). (1990). *Student ratings of instruction: Issues for improving practice.* New Directions for Teaching and Learning, No. 43. San Francisco, CA: Jossey-Bass.

Theall, M., & Franklin, J. (Eds.). (1991). *Effective practices for improving teaching.* New Directions for Teaching and Learning, No. 48. San Francisco, CA: Jossey-Bass.

Thornton, R. K., & Sokoloff, D. R. (1996). Assessing student learning of Newton's Laws: The force and motion conceptual evaluation and the evaluation of active learning laboratory and lecture curricula. *American Journal of Physics, 64,* 338-352.

Trout, P. (1998, July 24). Incivility in the classroom breeds 'education lite'. *Chronicle of Higher Education,* p. A40.

Vance, M., & Deacon, D. (1995). *Think out of the box.* Franklin Lake, NJ: Career Press.

Walvoord, B. E., & Anderson, V. J. (1998). *Effective Grading: A tool for learning and assessment.* San Francisco, CA: Jossey-Bass.

Weimer, M. (Ed.). (1987). *Teaching large classes well.* New Directions for Teaching and Learning, No. 32. San Francisco, CA: Jossey-Bass.

White, J. B. (1974). How to handle large classes. *Improving College and University Teaching, 22* (4), 262-266.

Willemsen, E. W. (1995) So what is the problem? Difficulties at the gate. In R. J. Menges (Ed.), *Fostering student success in quantitative gateway courses* (pp. 15–22). San Francisco, CA: Jossey-Bass.

Williams, D. D., Cook, P. F., Quinn, B., & Jensen, R. P. (1985). University class size: Is smaller better? *Research in Higher Education, 23* (3), 307-317.

Willoughby, S. (1990). *Mathematics education for a changing world.* Alexandria, VA: Association for Supervision and Curriculum Development.

Wilson, K., & Barsky, C. (1998). Applied research and development: Support for continuing improvement in education. *Daedalus, 127* (4), 233-258.

Wilson, R. C. (1986). Improving faculty teaching: Effective use of student evaluations and consultants. *Journal of Higher Education, 57* (2), 196-211.

Wilson, R. C., & Tauxe, C. (1986). *Faculty views of factors that affect teaching excellence in large lecture classes.* Research on Teaching Improvement and Evaluation, Teaching and Evaluation Services (TIES). Berkeley, CA: University of California, Berkeley. (ERIC Document Reproduction Service. ED 323 902)

Wittrock, M. C. (Ed.). (1986). Students' thought processes. In *Handbook of research on teaching* (pp. 297–314). New York, NY: Macmillan.

Wlodkowski, R. J., & Ginsberg, M. B. (1995). *Diversity and motivation: Culturally responsive teaching.* San Francisco, CA: Jossey-Bass.

Woolfolk, A. (2001). *Education psychology.* Boston, MA: Allyn & Bacon.

World Future Society (2000-2001). *The Futurist Journal.* Bethesda, MD.

Wulff, D. H., Nyquist, J. D., & Abbott, R. D. (1987). Students' perceptions of large classes. In M. G. Weimer (Ed.), *Teaching large classes well* (pp. 17-30). New Directions for Teaching and Learning, No. 32. San Francisco, CA: Jossey-Bass.

Zietz, J., & Cochran, H. H. (1997, Fall). Containing costs without sacrificing achievement: Some evidence from college-level economics classes. *Journal of Education Finance, 23,* 177-192.

Zlotkowski, E. (Ed.). (1998). *Successful service-learning programs: New models of excellence in higher education.* Bolton, MA: Anker.

Index